MEDIA
Matters

John Fiske

MEDIA Matters

Everyday Culture and Political Change

University of Minnesota Press
Minneapolis
London

Published by the University of Minnesota Press
111 Third Avenue South, Suite 290, Minneapolis, MN 55401-2520
Printed in the United States of America on acid-free paper

Library of Congress Cataloging-in-Publication Data

Fiske, John.
  Media matters : everyday culture and political change / John
Fiske.
    p.   cm.
  Includes bibliographical references and index.
  ISBN 0-8166-2462-3
  1. Popular culture—United States.   2. Mass media—Political
aspects—United States.   3. Politics and culture—United States.
4. United States—Politics and government—1989-1993.   5. United
States—Politics and government—1993-   I. Title.
E169.04.F574   1994
306'.0973—dc20   94-8991

This book is dedicated to some people who really matter:
For fine and intimate love—
    Lisa, Lucy, and Matthew
For refusing to submit—
    The Kantako family, Anita Hill, Rodney King
For a death that will not be the end—
    Latasha Harlins

Contents

Contents

Sidebars

Sidebars

Acknowledgments

I am grateful to all my colleagues in the Department of Communication Arts for contributing to an environment that makes ideas and scholarship easier and more pleasurable to produce, but some have had a direct, rather than general, influence, and I wish to thank them personally. They are Julie D'Acci, David Bordwell, and Michele Hilmes. Our graduate students have been every bit as influential as my colleagues, and I thank them all collectively while acknowledging some individually who have given me identifiable ideas, criticisms, and references; they are Steve Classen, Kevin Glynn, Dan Marcus, Matthew Murray, Darrell Newton, Lisa Parks, Pam Wilson, and Yong-Jin Won. Students outside the department to whom I am equally indebted are Vernon Andrews, Rose Byrd, Gyu Chen Jeon, Jason Loviglio, Mike Willard, and Elizabeth McLemore. Herman Gray and Howie Pinderhughes gave me insightful suggestions and warnings, as has Alan Cantwell, for which I thank them. I want to record my gratitude also to Mbanna Kantako for keeping me informed of his work at Black Liberation Radio, for taking the time out of his nonstop schedule to comment on my account of it, and for encouraging me to take it to a different audience, despite the risks involved. Mike Townsend, a dedicated supporter of Kantako, has also helped me. Photographer Ken Burnette of Springfield, Illinois, provided the photo of Kantako that appears in chapter 5. Some of the material on Anita Hill, Rodney King, and Black Liberation Radio is drawn from my previous book *Power Plays Power Works*.

I wish to thank, too, Janaki Bakhle, my editor, for providing me with well-chosen readers at early and late stages of the manuscript and, more directly, for her own productive comments, sharp criticism, and unfailing support. Paddy Rourke, in our media center, has given me unstinting and vital technological support, and Linda Henzl, as ever, has been consistently enthusiastic and energetic in helping me get the manuscript into shape. But I owe most of all to Lisa, my wife, for comments at all stages of writing, for encouragement in the low stretches and deflation in the high, but mainly for her unreserved belief in the project and in me. Thank you, Lisa.

Prologue: "The Juice Is Loose"

On a sultry June night in 1994 the consciousness of the United States was, once again, absorbed by the media. As with the Gulf War, the Anita Hill-Clarence Thomas hearings, and the Rodney King beating, the electronic image was the reality that America experienced. In this case, the media event that was relayed live into the homes, motels, and bars of America from seven news helicopters was the police chase and arrest of O.J. (the Juice) Simpson, a football hero, sportscaster, and media celebrity, accused of the murder of his ex-wife, Nicole Brown Simpson, and Ronald Goldman, a friend of Nicole. This was no conventional television car chase—no tires squealed, no cars scattered piles of boxes on the sidewalk, and not a fender was dented. It was a chase that kept within the speed limits and obeyed all the rules of the road. The man driving O.J., his lifelong friend Al Cowlings, was eventually charged with harboring a fugitive, but not with reckless driving. Indeed, the event became more like a parade, even a victory parade, than the chase and arrest of a suspected murderer. Twelve police cruisers followed O.J.'s white Ford Bronco at a safe distance, making no attempt to intercept, as Cowlings drove carefully along the Southern California freeways while O.J. used his cellular phone to talk to his mother and the police used it to talk to him. Other motorists, listening to news about the event on their radios, pulled over to allow the cavalcade to pass, and, as it did, many waved encouragement and support to O.J. Still others who had been watching at home on television drove to the freeway with hastily lettered banners proclaiming their support for their hero. They packed the freeway overpasses, shouting, "We love you, O.J." and, recalling an ironically appropriate chant from his days as a record-setting running back, "The Juice is loose." Interviewed on television afterward, some who had lined the freeway to watch the procession explained that this was their first chance, or, for others, their last, to see their media hero in the flesh, or, we might think, to add a material dimension to their experience of his electronic reality. The procession eventually came to halt in O.J.'s driveway, where the star sat for an hour in the Bronco, still apparently threatening suicide, until the negotiations produced a safe, tame, and anticlimactic final curtain.

A week earlier, Nicole Simpson and Ron Goldman had been found dead of multiple stab wounds outside her townhouse. In the days between the killings and the arrest, the media carried many stories and much discussion of the frequent beatings and verbal abuse that Nicole had suffered during her marriage to O.J. O.J. Simpson is a Black man, Nicole Simpson was a white woman, and the nation was as fascinated with their drama as it had been with the equally compelling one involving Anita Hill and Clarence Thomas. These events, together with the Rodney King beating and the uprising that followed, and the lesser but politically significant fuss over Murphy Brown's fatherless baby, provide compelling evidence that the cultural crises of the United States in the 1990s all ignite that explosive mix of race, gender, and sexuality. With the collapse of communism and the loss of a clear role in international relations, the political energy of America has turned inward, and now it is these domestic and personal politics that engage people most urgently, most anxiously, and most intimately.

This book traces the racial, sexual, and economic conflicts of the contemporary United States as they played out in key media events of the early 1990s — the "family values" debate between Dan Quayle and Murphy Brown, the Anita Hill-Clarence Thomas Senate hearings, and the Los Angeles uprisings that followed the acquittal of the police officers who were videoed beating Rodney King into submission. As I, along with 93 million others, watched the white Bronco carrying a Black man into the living rooms of America, I began to get the eerie feeling that what I was watching was a rerun, or at least a new episode in a familiar series. There were uncanny echoes of Anita Hill's sexual harassment in Nicole Simpson's abusive marriage, and O.J.'s drama seemed the final scene in a story line in which Bill Cosby turned into Rodney King. It seemed that all the cultural currents that I had traced in the media events I had already analyzed were transfixing America's attention once again. And this prologue is the result.

All these events were as significant as they were, first, because they were *media* events; that is, they were events that were mediated around the nation and the world, and events whose reality lay, in part, in their mediation. They were events characteristic of a postmodern world, for in them there was no clear and obvious distinction between electronic mediation and physical happenings, or between media figures and real people. This is not to say that there is no nonmediated reality — Nicole Simpson *was* murdered, Rodney King *was* beaten — but that the mediation of the murder and the beating modified or magnified what they really were. The reality of Anita Hill and of Rodney King was a product of their mediation: O.J. Simpson's chase was not just shown on television, it was a product of television, just as O.J. himself is. There is no "authentic," nonmediated O.J. that we can use to measure the accuracy or truth of his representations, for O.J. is the accumulation of an individual personal history and a set of public mediations, and each is so tangled up with the other that the two are literally inseparable. We can no longer think of the media as providing secondary representations of reality; they affect and produce the reality that they mediate. We live in a world of media events and media realities.

The second reason for the high importance of these media events lies in the way that they give a visible and material presence to deep and persistent currents of meaning by which American society and American consciousness shape themselves. The figures who play the key roles in these events literally embody the politicocultural meanings and the struggles over them about which America is most uncertain, most anxious, and therefore most divided. If they did not, they would not have become the resonant cultural figures that they have. It is fashionable but fruitless to bemoan the personalization of politics, for politics that are not embodied in a figure and played out by that figure in a media event will never be fully realized or widely engaged within a media-saturated world. The struggles to produce the "real" O.J. Simpson (the all-American hero, or the wife abuser, or the Black male embodying the racial-sexual threat to white America) echo the struggles over Anita Hill (harassed woman, obsessed woman, pawn of white feminists, a Black Delilah or a new Sojourner Truth) and over Rodney King (a victim of police brutality or a new Willie Horton, a victim of white society or a threat to it). These events become media events only because they give a specific form to these deeply flowing and deeply conflictual cultural currents. O.J. Simpson, Rodney King, Clarence Thomas, Willie Horton, Mike Tyson, Marion Barry are all different people, but they are all resonant media figures of the 1990s because they are all Black men whose mediated racial identity was sexualized, whose masculinity was racialized, and who were all, whether found guilty or not, criminalized: race, sex, and (white) law and order were mixed differently in the way that each was made into a media figure, and the significance of each figure lies in his particular embodiment of this explosive mix. These men do not figure as unique individuals, but only as products of the white imagination; they figure as embodiments of the white fascination with and terror of the Black male and his embodiment of a racial-sexual threat to white law and order. What we have to understand in these figures and the events in which they were involved is not their uniqueness, but their cultural typicality: the same cultural currents and conflicts will resurface in different figures and different events, but they will reoccur. The more America becomes divided along its multiple axes of social difference, of which race, ethnicity, gender, class, and age are only some of the most salient, the more frequently we can expect these media events and figures to occur, the more intensely they will grab the American imagination, and the more bitter will be the struggles to inflect them in one direction or another. A media event is significant because of the inevitability of its reoccurrence and the clarity it gives to murky anxieties and political differences; it is significant because it serves as a public arena wherein the American people engage in urgent political debate and effective political action. Media events are the shaping events of a postmodern world.

Until the murders, O.J. Simpson had sat alongside Bill Cosby in the white American imagination, a much-loved African American who typified the successful, nonthreatening, tamed Black male, a living figure who proved not only that Blacks could make it in a white society, but that whites could love them and welcome them into their homes, electronically at least, as family friends. O.J. was the first Black man whose image was nonthreatening enough for him to become a major promoter of goods and services to a white market. He was as loved as the rushed executive weaving through the crowds at the airport on his way to his Hertz rental car as he was dodging the tacklers on the football field. O.J. preceded Bill Cosby as the figure of the Black male that enabled white America to prove to its own satisfaction both that it was not racist and that those nonwhites who failed to prosper did so because of their own deficiencies and not because of white racism. O.J. had been a hugely popular football star, a Heisman Trophy winner, and a multiple record breaker. His ready smile and engaging personality enabled him to shift easily from football field to Hollywood, where he played smallish, but popular, roles in a number of movies. But television was the medium that made him, for there he could appear as "himself," and people could love him for who he "was," the friendly, successful, engaging Black man.

But in the racial climate of the contemporary United States, the figure of the tamed Black male can never shake itself free of its sinister obverse—the racial-sexual threat to white law and order that the 1988 Bush campaign figured so successfully in Willie Horton. It was easy, then, for the media to Hortonize O.J., as the LAPD lawyers Hortonized Rodney King. The police mug shot of O.J. was used for the covers of both *Time* and *Newsweek*, and it led the *New York Times*'s front-page story. The tabloids reproduced blurred telephoto images of O.J. being led away in handcuffs by the cops. In all these images, the familiar O.J. was hardly recognizable, but that was not their point: what was perfectly recognizable was the even more familiar image of the Black-male-criminal. Not content with the ability of the mug shot alone to tap into the criminalized meanings of Blackness, *Time* "blackened" him even more—its cover picture darkened O.J.'s skin by several shades, a move that provoked angry discussion on an African American electronic bulletin board. Contributors to the debate accused *Time* of "niggerizing" O.J., of "tapping into deep-seated racism and capitalizing on it," and of taking America through the Willie Horton incident once again. This none-too-subtle intensification of the signs of the Black threat and therefore of white fear worked to increase the distance between the races, and the uproar that it caused led the magazine to devote a page of its next issue to an apology cum justification.

Time's intensifying of the image was, in the sphere of race relations, unnecessary, though in that of economics it was probably effective in increasing impulse buys by whites. The unintensified images on the cover of *Newsweek* and the front page of the *New York Times* tapped the same cultural currents and performed the same political function. This photograph, however, was only one among many, and, hardworking though it was in its own right, it can be understood properly only in relation to all the others. O.J. and Nicole Simpson were so photogenic that the press and television, from the serious news to the tabloids, were awash with photographs of them. Numerous though these images were, they fit neatly into four preexisting categories mainstream America uses to make sense of its social experience.

Alongside the photographs of the "Black-male-criminal" were the "family values" ones that showed a happy, conventional family of Mom, Dad, and two beautiful children that even the religious right would be proud to endorse. The only unconventional note was sounded by the racial identities of the parents. When originally published, the photos may well have signified that "family values" can overcome racial difference, but the divorce, the wife beating, and the murders reversed the racial meanings and consequently moved the "family values" to the right and whitened them. Now the family photos could perform the same job as Dan Quayle when he blamed the Los Angeles "riots" on the lack of family values in Black America and charged Murphy Brown with eroding them even further (see chapter 1). In this ultraconservative but loudly voiced imagination, the traditional family upon which U.S. society apparently depends for its stability is implicitly white, and the threat to it, therefore, is colored. Unsurprisingly, this imagination has made the single Black young mother on welfare stand for everything that the all-American family is not. The knowledge that this interracial family was broken by divorce, was, of course, never photographed, but was, nonetheless, present in every picture. Viewers could trace under the smiling face of the father the scowling expression of the mug-shot criminal.

Another category of pictures was sensational, exploitable, and widely exploited. These were pictures that showed the blood of the white woman. The murders were excessively bloody, and images of the huge red stains on the sidewalk paving were widely reproduced in the media. Again, the photographs could not show that the blood was that of a white woman killed by a nonwhite man, but they did not need to. As I point out later in this book, America has a long tradition of using the beauty and vulnerability of the white woman as a metaphor for its social order. The nonwhite male out of sexual and social control, then, individualizes and sexualizes the threat of the other race, now primarily the Black race, though in the nineteenth century the figure of the male American Indian threatening the white female captive functioned identically. Sergeant Stacey Koon offered as justification for beating Rodney King the fear that King posed a "Mandingo" threat to a white policewoman. Willie Horton had raped a white woman.

The pictures in these three categories were accompanied by stories in which two themes consistently recurred. One narrated O.J.'s constant womanizing throughout, and after, his marriage, and painted him as a man unable to control his own sexuality. In handling the other, the media went to great pains to stress that Nicole Simpson's relationship with Ron Goldman was nonsexual, that he was with her late at night only because he had returned a pair of glasses that her mother had left at the restaurant where he worked, and that there was evidence to show that he died trying to defend her. Everything fit all too conveniently into the stereotypical mold of the good white man protecting the pure white woman against the racial-sexual threat of the Black man out of control.

The fourth category of pictures consisted of photos of O.J. as the football hero, the TV personality, the movie actor, the "celeb." There were no contradictory notes in them, for white America has no problems in celebrating, loving, and identifying with powerful Black men whose power is confined to the domains of sport and entertainment. When this photographic category is related to those of the criminal Black male, of the broken interracial marriage, and of the white woman's blood, it can all-too-easily serve to promote the racialized common sense that, sport and entertainment are cultural ghettos in which to confine Black success, and that, outside them, the powerful Black man is always a potential danger. When the Juice is loose on the football field and heading for the end zone, we can cheer him on, but when that same Juice is loose in our suburbs, it becomes a different matter entirely.

The figure of the Black male out of control is a cultural nightmare for whites that played a central role in all the racial media events of the 1990s. Its resonance and its terror are so deep because of the symbolic and social connections between the individual body of the Black male and the social body of Black America. If the individual body of Rodney King escaped the control of the LAPD officers, there was the danger, realized twelve months later, of the body of Black Los Angeles escaping the same white control. It is this fear that provides the clearest links between O.J. and Rodney King. In the media coverage of the first forty-eight hours of the uprisings, the media constantly voiced the white fear that they would spread from Black L.A. to white L.A., and from L.A. to the nation at large. The few instances of looting in Beverly Hills occasioned as much media coverage as, and more media panic than, the widespread destruction in South-Central Los Angeles, and every broadcast of the events in L.A. linked them to lesser, but still whitely terrifying, uprisings in Atlanta, Las Vegas, and San Francisco, and even to the absence of an uprising in New York. In this context the images of the blood of the white woman in the white suburb showed the nightmare become reality.

In the culture and politics of contemporary white America, the problem of the Black male/Black America is conventionally viewed through the lens of "the drug problem" to the extent that "the drug problem" has become code for "the

Black problem," and the war on drugs of the Reagan-Bush administrations was widely decoded by African Americans, at least, as a war on Blacks. Narcoticizing the Black body serves to magnify the threat of its uncontrollability. The bodies of both O.J. and Rodney King were discursively filled with drugs: in the white imagination of Sergeant Stacey Koon, Rodney King appeared to be high on PCP, a drug that produces a superhuman (read "animal") strength; similarly, the media were full of O.J.'s cocaine problem and widely attributed the brutality (read "animality") of the murders to the effects of drugs. White America doubly magnifies the threat that terrifies it by simultaneously sexualizing and narcoticizing racial difference.

This racialization of the sexual danger to women might lead us to wonder how one widely reproduced "family" photograph may have been read, for it showed O.J., Nicole, and their first child naked, with O.J.'s arms encircling the two lighter-skinned people. The *Star* (July 12, 1994) used this photo on its cover, with the caption "How this dream family portrait turned into a murderous nightmare," and surrounded it with teasers for the stories inside: "Sex secrets that drove O.J. crazy"; "Shocking truth about Nicole's 911 call, O.J. caught her making love while kids slept in next room"; and "Revealed at last, he beat his first wife too." The fact that the white horror of sex between a Black man and a white woman cannot be spoken aloud in post-civil rights America, at least by the mainstream, does not mean that it has disappeared. What it does mean, however, is that either it must be allowed to work silently (as when photos of the interracial marriage that failed were printed alongside ones of the blood of the white woman) or, when spoken, the voice that speaks it must be discredited or marginalized. The *Globe* (July 5, 1994) headlined the view that "O.J. was framed" by the Mafia and explained the motive for the framing as retribution for his habit of dating white women. Putting such deep racial-sexual anxieties into the mouths of criminal or the discredited (such as the Klan) serves white America well, for it allows it simultaneously to speak them and disavow them. For Black America, however, the same voice rings not with disavowal but with truth. The *Globe* attributes beliefs about the Mafia frame to unidentified "friends" of O.J., and those friends can readily be seen as Black. In this case, the voice that is marginalized by whites speaks from a more central position in Black America, for although it may not be true, or provable, that O.J. actually *was* framed by white extremists (the suspicion was voiced repeatedly on an African American computer bulletin board), the motive for the alleged framing is very much part of a broader truth that is explicit in Black knowledge of contemporary race relations and repressed, though still active, in the way that whites know them.

As the prosecution piled up the official evidence against O.J. and then leaked it to the media, the popular support for him also gained ground. Outside the courthouse during the preliminary hearing, ten different T-shirts were on sale, all of them supporting him, and the *New York Times* story on the onxx   lookers quoted only those who still loved him and believed in his innocence. This popular knowledge of O.J. relied sometimes on personal, deeply felt experience—one woman said that by looking into his gentle eyes she was able to tell that he could not have done it—and sometimes on the social experience of being a member of a subordinated social group, whether by race, gender, or class, whose life experience had taught the wisdom of never believing what "the power structure" says or trusting what it does. The O.J. affair became an event that African Americans could use to remind themselves of the importance of maintaining their own racial identity and solidarity against the white power structure's constant attempts to undermine them. Perris Clark, for instance, was selling a T-shirt urging, "Turn the Juice Loose," and was careful to explain to a *New York Times* reporter the difference between him and two other vendors (whose shirt read, "Say it ain't so, O.J."): "They're just here for the money, I'm trying to uplift my community" (*New York Times*, July 2, 1994, p. 20).

White America could use simple but powerful stereotypes to make its sense of the interracial marriage, but in Black America the issue was fraught with many more contradictions. Black nationalists used the racial difference between O.J.'s wives (his first marriage was to an African American) to point to the danger of "sleeping with the enemy" and to teach the value of separatism, but also made the more moderate point that successful Black men were always cut down by whites, whether justifiably or not, and that this case must be understood as typical, not unique. Some Black women argued that, in light of the shortage of "good" Black men, those who marry white women deprive their race of a much-needed resource and contribute to the intraracial negation of Black women. And one Black woman cried on the computer bulletin board, "The media has another Black man to show the world as being a REPRESENTATION of ALL BLACK MEN. I HATE THAT !!!!" There was widespread, angry, and sad recognition among African Americans that white America's obsession with the murder is a direct result of its racial dimension, and that if O.J.'s first wife, a Black woman, had been the victim, the media coverage would have been much more restrained. The racism perceived by these African Americans lay not so much in the manner of the media coverage as in the excessiveness of it and in America's fascination with it. But if, as in the Clarence Thomas-Anita Hill hearings, Black America was much more conflicted than white America in its response, there was still a general agreement that, whatever the outcome of the trial, whites would win and Blacks would be set back.

The reality was that a white woman and a white man were murdered, that her Black ex-husband, who was a sports and entertainment celebrity, was charged with the crime, and that the events of his arrest did happen. But reality does not contain its own meanings or its own politics, its events do not instruct us to see them in the light of others, nor do those involved tell us how to make sense of them. We do not merely make sense of a raw, neutral reality, but our ability to perceive that reality, to get access to it at all, is part of the sense-making process in which the media play a number of roles, roles that are significant but not necessarily as all-determining as their critics often allege. TV stations did decide to send seven news helicopters to cover O.J.'s chase and arrest, and the networks did decide to interrupt their schedules to cover the events live. Similarly, the preliminary hearing to determine if the prosecution had a *prima facie* case were covered live by the networks (and in some markets, as many as 42 channels carried them). At their peak, the ratings surpassed those of Super Bowl games, and even approached those for the Gulf War, perhaps the supreme media event ever—so far. These decisions were instrumental in changing the nature of the events into media events, but they were not arbitrary. Indeed, it is possible to argue that the decisions were made not in the executive offices of media corporations, but in the living rooms and bars of America. In this scenario, the executives could claim to be merely mediating, that is, making themselves and their technology into a two-way channel by which events could be made known to the people and by which the people could influence the selection of events that mattered, events that gave material form to the concerns, interests, and anxieties that were already in social circulation. The meanings generated in the multiple associations among the photos of the Black-male-criminal, of interracial sex, and of the white woman's blood are all the more powerful for being unspoken, and their cultural power lies not in any of the photos themselves, or in their aggregation in the media, but in the way that they make visible conflictual currents that normally run deep under the surface of everyday life but that, in crises, erupt into high visibility to remind us that any smoothness of that surface is both misleading and unstable. An event becomes a media event not at the whim of the media alone but also to the extent that it gives presence to abstract cultural currents that long precede it and will long outlast it.

For instance, of the ten most recent previous occasions on which the networks suspended schedules to carry live events, nine were presidential—either addresses by President Clinton or the death and funeral of former President Nixon—and the tenth was a natural disaster, an earthquake in Los Angeles. None of the presidential events became media events. It is not the media coverage alone that produces media events, but a coalition of interests between the media and the public. It is important to make this point because, although we must always maintain a critical eye, sometimes a sharply critical one, upon the media, we must not shut the other one that should be turned upon ourselves. What the media do is intimately bound up with who we are, both individually and socially. *Time*'s blackening of O.J.'s mug shot deserves fierce criticism, but our criticism of the social conditions out of which that decision came and within which its results had their effect must be fiercer still. *Time*'s decision was not the product of a white supremacist conspiracy, but of a market economy in a covertly racist society. The members of that society who are well served by its covert racism are as responsible as *Time*'s managing editor for that decision. The cultural forces that made the O.J. affair, the Hill-Thomas hearings, the Rodney King beating, and the L.A. uprisings into media events are not confined to the media corporations, but are socially pervasive.

Although the media may not be solely responsible for turning events into media events, all events that matter in a postmodern society must be multimediated, and the way we know them will always depend upon media technology. Knowledge is a production of mediatech, and those who are media illiterate and technophobic will be cut off from producing it, from circulating it, and from engaging in the struggles over it: in a mass-mediated culture they are sidelined, and their voices bemoaning the loss of literacy grow fainter by the year. As the police cruisers and helicopters "chased" O.J. along the freeways, TV commentators and cameras in helicopters relayed the events over the airwaves and cut to reporters on the ground who were monitoring police radio to learn what was being said on cellular phones. People phoned friends and family to tell them to watch the events on TV and to discuss what they were watching. Those with access to electronic bulletin boards swung into instant communication; talk radio received and broadcast calls by the thousands. Local people watching the chase on TV went to O.J.'s house to be there at the showdown, but took their portable TVs with them in the knowledge that the live event was not a substitute for the mediated one but a complement to it. On seeing themselves on their own TVs, they waved to themselves, for postmodern people have no problem in being simultaneously and indistinguishably livepeople and mediapeople.

Like popular culture, the law, too, has lost any sense of a clear boundary between the representation and the real, between the public opinion of a mediated society and the rational opinion of a courtroom. The trials of Anita Hill and of Rodney King showed that truths established in the committee room or the courtroom may not be accepted in this broader arena, and when they are not it is hard to say which is the more powerful truth. Whose knowledge of Rodney King was truer—South-Central's or Simi Valley's? Who knew Anita Hill more accurately—the Senate Judiciary Committee, the white women of America, or the African American community? As the lawyers for O.J.'s defense and prosecution prepared first for the preliminary hearings and then for the trial, they put into practice lessons learned from these previous trials and hearings. They realized that the mediated court of public opinion could not be kept cleanly separated from the "real" court of legal opinion, and that they had to make their cases on the media as well as in the courtroom. In a postmodern world, the jury no longer provides the objective, transcendent truth of the "reasonable man"; now, a jury is representative not of human rationality, but of its immediate society, and its truth cannot be separated from the ways in which that society struggles to understand its own experience. The lawyers in this case were savvier than their colleagues in the Anita Hill and Rodney King cases in recognizing that "jurytruth" cannot be separated from, or granted hierarchical precedence over, "mediatruth."

The media do not just report and circulate knowledge, they are involved in its production. *Time* and *Newsweek* were actively involved in producing a particular truth of O.J. by using his mug shot for their covers, and *Time*'s blackening italicized it: the computer enhancement inclined the truth in the direction of white racism. In the same way, the computer enhancement of the video of Rodney King's beating was used by the defense to tilt its "truth" in the same direction. The *National Enquirer* published a computer-produced "photograph" of O.J. in the Bronco pointing a gun at his head and speaking into his car phone, an image that only a computer could produce, for no camera could have been present to take it. Yet this was not a "lie," but a mediatruth, whose effect was not to italicize another mediatruth, such as the police mug shot, but to extend mediatruth beyond the scope of the camera alone. Of the two computer-produced photographs, the *Enquirer*'s was the more skillfully postmodern, for it clearly labeled itself a "computer artist's dramatization" and an "artist's dramatic re-creation" (July 5, 1994, p. 27) and thus offered readers the pleasure of seeing how mediatruth can be produced in a way that *Time* did not. Tabloid readers are probably more mediatech savvy than *Time*'s for they are used to "composigraphs," or computer-manipulated photographs of, for instance, what Elvis looks like today, or of a space alien offering advice to Bill Clinton, and consequently they have become adept at controlling their own movement between belief and disbelief in a way that *Time*'s have not, for that journal would never provoke its readers to disbelieve what it prints. The furor over *Time*'s cover was justified, and its managing editor was less than convincing in his claim that the "photo-illustration" (his term for a composigraph) was free of racism and that it "lifted a common police mug shot to the level of art, with no sacrifice to truth" (July 4, 1994, p. 4). Part of this statement, at least, is accurate, if only unwittingly—truth was not sacrificed, it was produced. To participate fully in a postmodern culture, one has to be savvy to mediatech, and *Time* does not appear to wish to help its readers to become so.

The women's movement, however, needed no lessons: its representatives were as successful in using Nicole Simpson's murder to focus the nation's attention upon wife battering as they had been in using Anita Hill's testimony to turn it to sexual harassment. They appeared to meet remarkably little opposition: it was as though the media and the nation experienced a form of confessional relief at being able to bring the "hidden crime" into the bright light of public inspection. So paper after paper linked Nicole Simpson's death with those of the 1,400 women murdered annually by their male partners, and took pains not only to link her history of marital abuse to the half a million cases brought before the authorities each year, but also, in an unusually confessional mode, to cast their own role in covering up O.J.'s abusive relationship as symptomatic of the more general cover-up by which America refuses to recognize one of its most common crimes. Representatives of the men's movement also seized the opportunity and publicized studies showing that domestic violence is more often initiated by women than by men but that men do not report husband battering, which consequently becomes a doubly hidden crime. The eagerness with which the media covered reports of spouse abuse played as a nation's therapeutic confession, and the coverage often echoed the backlash against the Republican "family values" campaign in the 1992 election, for it consistently stressed that the most dangerous place for women is the home and that the most threatening relations are marital.

For two days, the nation listened obsessively to a tape of a 911 call made by Nicole Simpson nine months before she was killed, in which she pleads for police protection as O.J. can be heard beating her door down and yelling unintelligibly. In a smart move in the public opinion war, the prosecution had released the tape to the media. TV and radio replayed it endlessly, the press reprinted transcripts, and some papers made it available to their readers, who could dial a local number to listen to it whenever and as often as they liked. The tape provided a graphic and rarely experienced insight into the terror that battered women experience. It also provided an insight into the legality of terrorizing, for police explained that they could not arrest O.J. because he was simply beating down his ex-wife's door and threatening her verbally, neither of which are crimes (a point that Rush Limbaugh repeated frequently on his right-wing radio talk show). Computer enhancement of the tapes clarified O.J.'s shouts and enabled Rush Limbaugh, and the *Globe* (July 12, 1994), to hear that he had been provoked by her extramarital sex, which, for Limbaugh at least, was enough to justify his behavior.

The serious media discussed the statistics of spouse abuse and the failure of courts and police to respond adequately, and interviewed representatives of women's organizations and women's shelters. The tabloids took a different tack, and surrounded their O.J. coverage with other stories of wife beating. They made no explicit connections among the stories, but allowed their readers to turn the pages and learn of spouse abuse involving celebrities such as Queen Elizabeth, Mike Tyson, Elizabeth Taylor, Dolly Parton's sister, Whitney Houston, and Halle Berry. These revelations of the hidden lives of celebs were interspersed with those of ordinary people, of truck drivers who admitted to wife beating, and of women who had suffered it. It is hard to know which of the different ways of establishing that spouse abuse is both widespread and widely repressed is the more effective. Another difference between the high- and the low-brow news was that the high was self-critical of its failure to pay adequate attention to earlier reports of O.J.'s wife battering, and saw this as symptomatic of society's more general repression of the crime. The tabloids, on the other hand, congratulated themselves in screaming headlines for telling their readers about the abuse that the rest of the media covered up. The *National Enquirer*, for example, reprinted the headlines of its stories of O.J.'s wife battering from

1989, 1991, and 1992, together with the words of Dr. Joyce Brothers: "If others in the news business had done what the ENQUIRER did—digging hard five years ago and exposing the awful truth about this football hero—maybe Nicole would be alive today."

Women fought not only to get spouse abuse into the nation's consciousness, but also to prevent Nicole Simpson from becoming the nonperson, whose identity was confined to that of the woman-victim, in a replay of the way that spouse abuse had become the noncrime. *Who* Nicole Simpson was received very little attention in comparison with the excessively detailed accounts of O.J.'s family and personal histories. Women were right to recognize the political danger of this information vacuum, for there are early signs that it may be filled with antiwomen information and that, like Anita Hill, Nicole Simpson will be subject to attempts to turn her into someone who was responsible for her own victimhood. There are reports that she took pleasure in provoking O.J.—"She knew how to rile him up, how to press the buttons," as one of his friends put it—and stories that she enjoyed dating young, brain-dead men, and that O.J. had caught her having sex while the children were asleep in the next room, but perhaps the most insistent was that she stayed with him because of his money and, by implication, voluntarily put up with his abuse in exchange for the lifestyle he offered. The woman victim who thus consents to her victimhood by putting and keeping herself in situations that maintain it figures centrally in the defense of men in gender trials—whether for rape, spouse abuse, or sexual harassment.

Both the Anita Hill-Clarence Thomas hearings and the first Rodney King trial justified women's fears that this knowledge vacuum around Nicole Simpson might be turned against her. The Republicans supporting Clarence Thomas were successful in turning the focus of the hearings away from what he did and onto who Anita Hill was. Similarly, the equally successful strategy of the defense in the trial of the police officers charged with excessive force in the beating of Rodney King was to redirect the court's attention away from their actions and onto his. If O.J.'s defense does not adopt a similar strategy, or fails in its attempt, it will be difficult to avoid concluding that the explanation lies in the different races of the victims, and that the figure of the white woman as target of the racial threat is so deeply engraved in the white imagination that not even the nation's most expensive lawyers or its widespread blame-the-victim syndrome could dislodge it.

There is a possible downside to the nation's readiness to confess its failure to deal with spouse abuse, for it may be evidence of a national relief at having found a way of talking about the O.J. affair in a way that was socially responsible but that excluded race. Mainstream America is much better equipped conceptually and thus better prepared psychologically to address the shortcomings in its gender politics than those in its racial politics. The gender relations of the marriage could, therefore, be subject to explicit, careful, and thorough analysis that faced America squarely with its problem and offered some hope that it would be addressed. The racial dimension, however, was rarely subject, by whites at least, to the same explicit analysis, and thus its dominant politics were kept off the agenda for change and allowed to continue their insidious and unseen work.

In focusing attention upon the gender rather than the racial politics of the O.J. affair, the media and most of white America were repeating the pattern of their initial responses to the Clarence Thomas-Anita Hill hearings. Mark Kaufman, for instance, wrote a column for Hearst Newspapers in which he incisively analyzed a letter O.J. had written for public consumption as typical of the ways in which wife abusers explain their behavior. Calling Simpson "a textbook wife batterer," Kaufman showed how the letter was "jam-packed with many of the standard excuses and denials cherished by men who beat their spouses," as a result of which he was able to delude himself that at times he felt like a battered husband or boyfriend. The article is an excellent analysis of how America persuades itself that wife abuse is not really a problem—the only pity is that no equivalent article asked the same questions about race. Similarly, the week after they used O.J.'s police mug shot for their covers, both *Time* and *Newsweek* devoted their covers and their lead stories to battered women and argued, quite properly, that the Simpson case had focused America's attention upon this problem as the Anita Hill case had focused it upon sexual harassment. Neither, however, devoted its lead story and cover of the subsequent week to the racial issues involved, either at the personal level of interracial marriage or at the social level of race relations in general. The *New York Times* featured an article by Michiko Kakutani analyzing "why we still can't stop watching O.J. on TV" (July 7, 1994, p. 10) that never once mentioned the racial dimension but confined itself to the myth of the renegade on the run. Kakutani's repression of race, however, was momentarily revealed by the way that her reference to Norman Mailer's essay "The White Negro" mentioned only his belief that violence is often equated with virility and creativity and ignored the racial issue that is apparent in the essay's title. In the same way, the *New York Times* article (cited above) on the onlookers outside the courtroom specified the genders of those it quoted, but never their races. *Time*'s managing editor did the same thing when he justified the computer manipulation of O.J.'s mug shot by calling it art that "subtly smoothed and shaped [it] into an icon of tragedy. The expression on his face was not merely blank now; it was bottomless. This cover, with the simple, non-judgmental headline, 'An American Tragedy,' seemed the obvious, right choice." His erasure of racial considerations from his editorial decision-making process is typical of both the media and white society. The "race neutrality" that is claimed implicitly by his use of the term "non-judgmental" serves as an alibi for the white refusal to discuss race in ways that might prevent covert racism continuing its work under the cover of this silence. The media's failure to use the O.J. case as an opportunity to encourage white

America to analyze and interrogate the forms that contemporary racism can take is both instrumental in maintaining what I refer to later in this book as "nonracist racism" and symptomatic of our self-delusion that racism was a historical problem that has been largely solved by the civil rights movement.

The media coverage of the O.J. Simpson case was rarely overtly racist, but, in a society as deeply if covertly racist as this one, it did not need to be for the whole affair to widen the divide between the races. It is difficult to distinguish between the "race neutrality" of not harping on O.J.'s Blackness and his wife's whiteness from the "race blindness" that works to keep racism comfortably out of sight by strategically not noticing it; racial blindness is a luxury of liberal whites. The difficulties faced by the media can be illustrated by the way the case seemed inevitably to associate Black masculinity with criminality. The press and TV showed the mug shots and photos of O.J. under arrest or in handcuffs. They would have been derelict not to. In their background stories on O.J., the media told of his childhood in the ghetto, of his gang membership and trouble with the law. Again, we should not criticize them for this, for they showed how by talent and hard work he was able to rise above his beginnings and live out the American dream. These are all events that should be reported, yet, when the reports reverberate with the submerged currents of covert racism, they can have a racist effect for which the media are only partially, if at all, responsible. The media did not, for example, explicitly rewrite the final pages of O.J.'s story of the American dream to make it end in a form of essentialist racism. Yet they also did nothing to counter such an ending's being supplied by their readers; they allowed at least the right wing of white America to make O.J. stand for all Black men and to read his downfall as the story of a racial reversion to type. They expressed no regret at the neatness with which O.J. fit the stereotype of the Black male, and thus allowed his case to reinforce it. More seriously, perhaps, they ignored the existence of this stereotype in white America, and thus lost the opportunity to explore its origin and effects. This is a form of racism by omission rather than commission, for ignoring the stereotype is a white privilege in which African Americans cannot share.

Coincidentally, as the events of the O.J. affair were unfolding, the *New York Times* featured an article in its color magazine by Leonce Gaiter in which he did subject this stereotype to critical scrutiny. Writing as a member of the Black bourgeoisie, he gave a number of instances of the stereotype's shaping painful but ordinary incidents in his everyday life and concluded by begging the reader to "imagine being told by virtually everyone that in order to be your true self you must be ignorant and poor, or at least seem so" (*New York Times*, July 26, sec. 6, p. 43). The article shows how the stereotype leads white America to overlook and devalue the Black bourgeoisie, how it splits the Black community by dividing the successful from the underclass, and how it perpetuates the liberal racism that believes that Black America can be saved only by white help

xxviii   and that therefore interprets Black success as a sign not of Black ability but of the effectiveness and benignity of white help.

This sort of analysis was never used in the media coverage of the O.J. affair in an attempt to control any damage to race relations. We can, then, criticize the media for race blindness, for their failure to address the issues that the O.J. story inevitably raised in a racist society, and we can criticize them for their failure to recognize that in such a society race-neutral reporting can trigger racially divisive meanings: they know that racism is active in the contemporary United States, and the absence of any attempt to reduce or to prevent its activation in this case may, in its effects, have been as racist as *Time*'s cover. But, and this may be the most important point of all, we must not allow our criticism of the media to turn into scapegoating, by which we can displace the sins of ourselves onto our media and absolve ourselves of the criticisms that we all-too-readily direct upon them. Our critical analysis must be directed at least as intensely upon our own fascination with the O.J. media event as on its media provocation.

Introduction

Events and a Metaphor

In its review of 1992, *Life* called it "a year dominated by a presidential race, a firestorm in L.A. and a single mom named Murphy."[1] The election of the president of the United States and the costliest urban uprisings in this nation's stormy history would conventionally be considered historic events, but the birth of a baby to the unmarried heroine of a sitcom hardly appears, at first sight, to be of the same order of significance. Yet, four months earlier, *Time* had made the same editorial judgment.[2] In May 1992, Murphy Brown's single motherhood was thrust into political prominence when Vice President Dan Quayle identified it as symptomatic of the causes of the L.A. "riots" (see *Sidebar: Dan Quayle*, p. 68). In August, the actress Candice Bergen won an Emmy for her portrayal of Murphy Brown, and in her acceptance speech thanked the vice president for helping her win it. *Time* used Murphy as the peg for a story on the Republican attack on "Hollywood's liberal elite," and strained a simile to bring the Los Angeles "riots" into the discussion: "The gang-stomping of Dan Quayle at the Emmy Awards ceremony two weeks ago resembled a Rodney King beating by the Hollywood elite."[3]

While viewing the unanimity of *Time* and *Life* with the skepticism appropriate to the knowledge that *Time*, *Life*, and *Murphy Brown* are all owned by the same company, I, like they, view those events as key indices of a crisis in the structure of feeling in the United States. Unlike periodicals, however, a book does not need to confine itself to arbitrary periods such as a calendar year, so I look back a little further than they, to the fall of 1991 and the Clarence Thomas-Anita Hill hearings, as a result of which Clarence Thomas won a seat on the U.S. Supreme Court and Anita Hill became a rallying point in the struggles of women and African Americans toward equality.

This book charts some of the cultural currents as they swirled and eddied around these "media events." That last phrase raises one of the questions that runs throughout: Can we separate media events from nonmedia events, or are all events today, or at least the ones that matter, necessarily media events? The   1

2   editors of *Life* and *Time* made no editorial distinctions among the heroine of a sitcom, major urban uprisings, and the election of the first Democrat president in twelve years. Indeed, it could be argued that Murphy Brown's baby was more directly influential in the social and political currents that put Bill Clinton in the White House than were the L.A. uprisings, for the Democrats were almost as silent as the Republicans on the racial and economic problems of the inner cities. As a media event, Murphy Brown's baby was as real as Anita Hill's humiliation or Rodney King's beating.

Events do happen, but ones that are not mediated do not count, or, at least, count only in their immediate locales. Rodney King's beating was a media event. A few months after it, a Black motorist in Detroit, Malice Green, was similarly beaten by cops until he died.[4] His beating was not videoed, and though it mattered intensely in its own immediate conditions, in the final analysis it counted for less than Rodney King's—and the difference lay in the mediation.

Anita Hill's (officially unproven but widely believed) sexual harassment by her boss, Clarence Thomas, consisted of a few dirty remarks and pressure to date; objectively, it was far less oppressive than that suffered by millions of working women. Yet mediation made those remarks into the political volcano of 1991 while far worse cases went ignored, except, of course, by their victims. Murphy Brown may have been a fictional single mother, but her debate with Vice President Dan Quayle over "family values" in the 1990s was mediated by press and TV across the nation, and the absence of any "real" (i.e., nonfictional) event behind the mediated one did nothing to reduce the reality of the media event that the debate became.

The term *media event* is an indication that in a postmodern world we can no longer rely on a stable relationship or clear distinction between a "real" event and its mediated representation. Consequently, we can no longer work with the idea that the "real" is more important, significant, or even "true" than the representation. A media event, then, is not a mere representation of what happened, but it has its own reality, which gathers up into itself the reality of the event that may or may not have preceded it.

This use of the term brings it close to Baudrillard's ideas of hyperreality and the simulacrum, both of which are "implosive" concepts. *Implosion* refers to the collapse of the organizing differences that were characteristic of a stably structured world. So "hyperreality" implodes the binary concepts of reality and representation into a single concept, and the simulacrum similarly merges the "copy" with the "original," the "image" with its "referent." Baudrillardians could argue with some conviction that the Clarence Thomas-Anita Hill hearings were hyperreal: there were no "real" Senate hearings that television then represented; the way that people behaved in them and the conduct of the hearings themselves was televisual. Had there been no television, the hearings would have been different. Their reality included their televisuality.

Baudrillard's theory of hyperreality and the simulacrum lacks a dimension that I consider crucial, that of struggle, and I turn to a theory of discourse to supply it. *Discourse* is an elusive term, for it refers both to a general theoretical notion and to specific practices within it. At the theoretical level, "discourse" challenges the structuralist concept of "language" as an abstract system (Saussure's *langue*) and relocates the whole process of making and using meanings from an abstracted structural system into particular historical, social, and political conditions. Discourse, then, is language in social use; language accented with its history of domination, subordination, and resistance; language marked by the social conditions of its use and its users: it is politicized, power-bearing language employed to extend or defend the interests of its discursive community.

Discourse analysis differs from linguistic analysis in focusing on *what* statements are made rather than *how* they are. The discursive analyses of this book, then, are not concerned with tracing the regularities and conventions of discourse as a signifying system, but with analyzing what statements were made and therefore what were not, who made them and who did not, and with studying the role of the technological media by which they were circulated. Discourse can never be abstracted from the conditions of its production and circulation in the way that language can. The most significant relations of any piece of discourse are to the social conditions of its use, not to the signifying system in general, and its analysis exemplifies not an instance of that system in practice, but its function in deploying power within those conditions. At this level, then, discourse is the means by which those conditions are made to make sense within the social relations that structure them. It is structured and structuring, for it is both determined by its social conditions and affects them. The discourse of capitalism, for instance, is a product of capitalist societies, but the form that the discourse is given shapes the present and future development of them.

Discourse also operates at a lower level on which a number of discourses put discourse-in-general into practice, and this is the level where it can be most particularly analyzed. Here discourse has three dimensions: a topic or area of social experience to which its sense making is applied; a social position from which this sense is made and whose interests it promotes; and a repertoire of words, images, and practices by which meanings are circulated and power applied. To make sense of the world is to exert power over it, and to circulate that sense socially is to exert power over those who use that sense as a way of coping with their daily lives.

My account of discourse so far is deeply indebted to Foucault, but the material complexities of the events in this book require me to go beyond his theorizing. He was concerned with the dominant discourses by which power was applied in post-Renaissance Europe, but the contemporary United States is a far more highly elaborated and socially diversified society than any that he

4   studied, so its discursive circulation is more complicated, more contradictory, and, in particular, more contestatory than the discourses that he analyzes. His work describes discourse as a technique of power in a monodiscursive society. The contemporary United States, however, like most late capitalist nations, is a multidiscursive society, as it is a multicultural one, and any analysis of its culture must be as concerned with discursive relations as with discursive practices. It must uncover the processes of discursive contestation by which discourses work to repress, marginalize, and invalidate others; by which they struggle for audibility and for access to the technologies of social circulation; and by which they fight to promote and defend the interests of their respective social formations.[5]

Here, and throughout this book, I use the prefix *multi* in opposition to forms of the word *plural* in order to distinguish my perspective from that of liberal pluralism (though I do use the word *liberal*, albeit with some reluctance, to refer to the more progressive positions within mainstream society). Multidiscursivity and multiculturalism do not exist within the permissive and ultimately consensual structure of differences that is envisioned by liberal pluralism. Dominant social formations and their discourses are constantly trying to control, restrain, minimize, and even destroy social, and therefore discursive, differences. The social diversity that is both the outcome and the origin of multidiscursivity has to be fought for, sometimes viciously. Multidiscursivity can occur only in a structure of inequality, and its interdiscursive relations are typically, therefore, ones of hostility. For Foucault, also, discourse was a technique of inequality, but it was not a terrain of struggle, whereas for me it can be nothing else: because discourse is a social product with political effects in a society of inequalities, it always has the potential to be turned into a site of struggle.

The way that experience, and the events that constitute it, is put into discourse—that is, the way it is made to make sense—is never determined by the nature of experience itself, but always by the social power to give it one set of meanings rather than another. There is a nondiscursive reality, but it has no terms of its own through which we can access it; it has no essential identity or meaning in itself: we can access this reality only through discourse, and the discourse that we use determines our sense of the real. Although discourse may not produce reality, it does produce the instrumental sense of the real that a society or social formation uses in its daily life. But though this nondiscursive reality may never be accessible in its own terms and never has an essential identity of its own, it nonetheless remains a necessary concept, for it reminds us that any event can always be put into discourse differently. We can know an event only by putting it into discourse, so an event is always continuous with its discursive construction, but it still always contains the potential to be differently constructed. This continuity between event and discourse produces a "discourse event" or "media event," not a discourse *about* an event. No discourse event is ever complete in itself but always carries traces of the other, competing, discourse events that it is not. No piece of reality contains its own essential existence; equally, it cannot dictate the discourse into which it will be put.

Racial difference is, for example, part of reality, but at the same time, its "reality" is a product of the discourse into which it is put. There is a discourse of racism that advances the interests of whites and that has an identifiable repertoire of words, images, and practices through which racial power is applied. But we must remember that this is not the only way in which racial difference can be put into discourse, though it is the dominant way in white supremacist societies. At a lower level still, one that we might call a "subdiscourse" that works through a subset of the discursive repertoire, we can trace its particular application through, for instance, the animalization of Black men. Officers of the Los Angeles Police Department described Rodney King as "bearlike," and they referred to other African Americans as "gorillas." The blows of their truncheons were the same discursive repertoire put into behavior instead of words (in the official discourse of the LAPD, however, these were not "blows" of "truncheons," but "strokes" of "batons"). Discourse does not represent the world; it acts in and upon the world.

Discourse, then, is always a terrain of struggle, but the struggle is never conducted on a level field. The dominant discourses, those that occupy the mainstream, serve dominant social interests, for they are products of the history that has secured their domination. Discursive struggles are an inevitable part of life in societies whose power and resources are inequitably distributed. They can take as many forms as the ingenuity of the people can devise, but we can catalog the main ones:

The struggle to "accent" a word or sign, that is, to turn the way it is spoken or used to particular social interests: The image of Murphy Brown holding her baby awkwardly may, when "spoken" in a liberal accent, mean that mothering involves social skills that have to be learned, but, when "spoken" in the conservative accent of Rush Limbaugh, it means that single mothers are unnatural.

The struggle over the choice of word, image, and therefore discursive repertoire: The events in Los Angeles could be put into discourse as "riots" or "insurrection" ("uprising," "rebellion," "revolution"). Each word has a set of appropriate images to go with it in a discursive repertoire that makes a particular sense of the events that serves particular social interests and that has particular material effects. The "riot repertoire," for instance, is easily articulated with the discourse of criminality, with the effect of using trials and punishment of individual rioters/criminals as the way of resolving the crisis.

The struggle to recover the repressed or center the marginalized: A discourse produces its own meanings and represses others. The "family values" discourse in which the argument between Murphy Brown and Dan Quayle was conducted repressed or marginalized issues of race and of sexual orientation, and the discourse of "senseless rioting" repressed the organization and political purpose behind the attacks on businesses.

The struggle to disarticulate and rearticulate: Discourse not only puts events into words or images, it also links, or articulates, them with other events. By calling the hearings a "lynching," Clarence Thomas disarticulated them from gender behavior in the workplace and rearticulated them to racist behavior in history and thus changed their meanings. The mainstream media articulated accounts of firefighters being attacked by "rioters" with words and meanings of them as public servants; Black Liberation Radio, however, articulated these accounts with instances of the tardiness of white firefighters in responding to fires in Black neighborhoods that resulted in unnecessary deaths.

The struggle to gain access to public discourse in general or the media in particular—the struggle to make one's voice heard: Some Black women saw that Anita Hill was breaking their silence, and they fought to use the opportunity to "speak" that she had opened up. African Americans in Los Angeles used the uprisings as a form of loud public speech, and exploited as far as they could the access to the media they provided.

Discourse is the continuous process of making sense and of circulating it socially. Unlike a simulacrum, discourse is both a noun and a verb, it is ever on the move. At times it becomes visible or audible, in a text, or a speech, or a conversation. These public moments are all that the discourse analyst has to work on, but their availability does not necessarily equate with their importance: discourse continues its work silently inside our heads as we make our own sense of our everyday lives. Though discourse is used privately and individually, it remains inescapably social, so those who share discourse are likely to form social and political alliances, for they will share broadly an understanding of the world and the way that their interests can best be secured within it.

We use discourse, then, both to form our sense of the social world and to form the relations by which we engage in it. In the realm of social relations, discourse works through a constant series of invitations and rejections by which it attempts to include certain social formations in its process and exclude others. Discourse offers continuous but unequal opportunities for intervention, and discursive guerrillas are key troops in any political or cultural campaign.

Discourse is socially rooted. It provides a social formation, or alliance of formations, with ways of thinking and talking about areas of social experience that are central in its life. The struggle over whose discourse events should be put into is part of the reality of the politics of everyday life. The discursive patterns of domination, subordination, and contestation are where the weaving of the social fabric is politicized.

An informing metaphor of this book likens culture to a river of discourses. At times the flow is comparatively calm; at others, the undercurrents, which always disturb the depths under even the calmest surface, erupt into turbulence. Rocks and promontories can turn its currents into eddies and countercurrents, can change its direction or even reverse its flow. Currents that had been flowing together can be separated, and one turned on the other, producing conflict out of calmness. There are deep, powerful currents carrying meanings of race, of gender and sexuality, of class and age: these intermix in different proportions and bubble up to the surface as discursive "topics," such as "family values" or "abortion" or "Black masculinity," and these discursive "topics" swirl into each other—each is muddied with the silt of the others, none can flow in unsullied purity or isolation. Media events are sites of maximum visibility and maximum turbulence. The hearings, the uprisings, and the debate were such sites. They are useful to the cultural analyst because their turbulence brings so much to the surface, even if it can be glimpsed only momentarily. The discursive currents and countercurrents swirling around these sites are accessible material for the analyst to work upon: from them s/he must theorize the flows of the inaccessible and invisible currents of meaning that lie deep below the surface, and that will never be available for empirical study. Their invisible movements and workings must be theorized from the visible, because this inaccessible level typically carries the most significant connections between the points of visibility.

Like any metaphor, this one has limits. Within them it may be useful in representing culture as the constant circulation and recirculation of discursive currents, in emphasizing their intermingling and the muddiness caused by silt from one floating inevitably into the others. In describing the emergence and submergence of discursive topics it recognizes that invisibility does not mean absence. Finally, it invites us to think of fluidity, of constantly changing conformations that are not random, not free of topographical determinations— rivers do flow in certain directions and not others, they are confined within limits, and certain social formations have privileged access to their banks and their waters.

Here we begin to run up against the limits of the metaphor. The naturalness of a river can imply an inevitability in flow and counterflows, can reduce media events to tourist spectacles that people watch from the safe distance of specially constructed viewing platforms (or media representations)—risking only a dousing with spray if the wind blows from the wrong direction. In other

8   words, the river metaphor can reduce or even eliminate political intervention, social agency, and discursive struggle. The topography of a river may be the metaphoric equivalent of the structuring or determining social conditions within which the processes of culture have to operate, but, unlike rivers in nature, cultural countercurrents and eddies are produced as much by motivated, intentional, and interested interventions as by natural conditions such as rocky outcrops or fallen trees. People build dams, sluice gates, and irrigation channels in attempts to turn the flow of water to the advantage of their own social formations, and away from the advantage of others.

Although the river metaphor may be useful in representing culture as the constant process of discursive circulation, recirculation, and countercirculation, it is less effective in representing the struggles and contestations that are the driving forces behind this process and that make it not natural but political, not inevitable but directable, if only within limits.

A media event, then, as a point of maximum discursive visibility, is also a point of maximum turbulence (in calm waters currents are mostly submerged). It also invites intervention and motivates people to struggle to redirect at least some of the currents flowing through it to serve their interests; it is therefore a site of popular engagement and involvement, not just a scenic view to be photographed and left behind. Its period of maximum visibility is limited, often to a few days, though the discursive struggles it occasions will typically continue for much longer.

As I write this in the spring of 1993, Anita Hill and Clarence Thomas are still figures of contestation (this week's *Newsweek* has an article by George Will claiming to unravel "Anita Hill's Tangled Web," and in doing so to reclaim some of the ground that she and her supporters "won" from the right); the repercussions of the L.A. uprisings show no signs of lessening their intensity (last night I watched a PBS documentary on Los Angeles after the riots, the second Rodney King verdict was handed down only a couple weeks ago and is still the subject of wide discussion, and the trial at which Damian Williams and the L.A. Four + were found not guilty of the main charges in the beating of Reginald Denny is still a few months ahead); and with the loss of the election, Dan Quayle has become less visibile, and the ripples of his debate with Murphy Brown are subsiding, but they have not died (the March issue of the *Atlantic* screamed in huge headlines on its cover, "Dan Quayle Was Right," and the religious right is working hard to recover ground that it lost when Murphy "won" the debate).

There are similarities between the metaphor of culture as a river of discursive currents and Raymond Williams's concept of a "structure of feeling," particularly when set in his theory of dominant, residual, and emergent cultural currents.[6] He coined the phrase to refer to what it feels like to be a member of a particular culture, or to live in a particular society at a particular time. It is a necessarily diffuse concept, because it stretches seamlessly from the realm of

Introduction

the subject to that of the social order. It encompasses the formal political processes and institutions of a society, its law courts, its workplaces, its military,
its schools and churches, its health care system, as well as its more informal
ones, such as the family and everyday social relations in its streets, stores, and
workplaces. It includes the arts and cultural industries, sports and entertainment, and, at the micro level, the ordinary ways of talking, thinking, doing,
and believing. It is, then, a large and amorphous concept that fits well with
other concepts in his thought that appear so generalized as to be almost plati-
tudinous: "Culture is ordinary"; "Culture is a whole way of life."

There is both value and danger in thinking at this level of generality as well
as at the more detailed level on which most of this book operates. It is useful to
be able to turn to a concept that enables us to ask whether living in the United
States under Clinton "feels" different from the experience of living here under
Reagan or Bush. The notion of a structure of feeling asks us to trace ways in
which, for instance, the facts that the new surgeon general is a Black woman
who promotes condom distribution in schools and that the attorney general is
a white woman who believes that the roots of crime are to be found in people's
social conditions rather than in their morality might affect, if only indirectly,
the "feeling" of "being American." It points to one possible dimension of the
difference between the verdict of the first Rodney King trial (the police found
not guilty) and the verdicts of three similar ones — the second Rodney King trial
(two policemen found guilty), the Malice Green trial (police found guilty), and
the Damian Williams trial (defendants found not guilty of the main charges).
These differences can be explained in part by differences in the legal strategies
and skills of the lawyers, in part by local social conditions (the authorities in
Detroit immediately condemned and suspended the officers involved in beating Malice Green, as their counterparts in L.A. did not), and in part by the social composition of the juries; but we might also wish to ask, at the highest level
of generality, where links do not exist in empirically traceable form, whether
what went on in the jurors' heads and what went on in the national electorate
were not in some way connected. If they were, the concept of a changing structure of feeling allows us to theorize the connections. The change in administration occupying the White House may be one indication of such a change, but
is neither the cause nor the effect of it. Changes in something as complex and
diffuse as a structure of feeling do not occur along simple lines of cause and
effect. Similarly, we must not take Clinton's electoral victory as a sign that the
change has occurred — it has not, though I believe one is in progress.

Change is not experienced or felt equally at all points in the structure, nor is
any change that is felt necessarily in the same direction. The danger of the notion of a "structure of feeling" is that of homogenizing and universalizing, and
of smoothing over the struggles that go on within it. We may need to concep-
tualize it as an unstable aggregation of smaller-scale structures of feeling by
which different social formations relate differently to the larger one. Rush Lim-

10   baugh's conservative men "feel," for example, differently about their social identities and positions than do Murphy Brown's "today's women" (see chapter 1). ("Today's woman" was used by the vice president [see *Sidebar: Dan Quayle*, p. 69] to identify and denigrate a particular formation of women — those white professional ones whose liberalism he considered to be undermining "family values.") But though each social formation may experience the general structure of feeling differently through their own differently structured ways of "feeling American," each is still part of the same more general structure, and neither Rush Limbaugh's nor Murphy Brown's can be understood from outside or experienced from within except in relation to the other.

Change also occurs at different speeds at different parts of the social structure, and meets differently solid reactionary forces. It is, thus, a messy ongoing business, not a rapid revolutionary one. At any point, to return to our river metaphor, certain currents may dominate the flow; others that once dominated still carry residual traces of what they once were; and yet others that were weakly confined to the margins or depths are gaining strength, and preparing to emerge and challenge the dominant ones. The religious right and Rush Limbaugh are examples of strong residual currents, "today's woman" is a strong emerging one, perhaps by now a dominant one, and each struggles with the other to dominate the cultural flow. The Bush campaign overestimated the strength of residual currents and, late in the day, tried unsuccessfully to swim out of them: Clinton's campaign harnessed emergent currents such as those of youth, or sexual orientation, and swam on them to the White House.

The media are crucial in the social circulation of discourse and thus play a formative role in social and political change. But in general, our public discussions of this role tend to be critical: at times they criticize the low level of political involvement of the average U.S. citizen and blame the media for it; at others they charge the media with increasingly inadequate and superficial coverage of political concerns, of excluding many issues of high political import and of repressing minority or oppositional voices. All of these charges are well based, particularly when they are directed at the mainstream media's coverage of foreign affairs, of economic policy, and, to a lesser extent, of activity in Washington.

But these political arenas, important though they are, do not constitute the whole of political life. There are other arenas (sometimes not recognized as political by media commentators and political scientists) that span the continuum from subjectivity (the politics of identity) to social relations. These arenas include the intensely domestic politics of gender, race, class, and age that are central in the politics of everyday life, and in them the mainstream media cannot be charged with inactivity. Dan Quayle knew this when he attacked Murphy Brown, and the Republicans knew this as they campaigned against "Hollywood's liberal elite," which, in their eyes, was leading the nation away from its traditional (i.e., Republican) values. They were correct in identifying the centrality of the media in these "internal" politics, and correct in recognizing the connections between them and the official politics of Washington and the campaign trail. They were wrong, however, in modeling these connections as ones of cause and effect: Hollywood's alleged liberalism did not cause the Republicans' electoral defeat. But if Hollywood was more liberal than the Republican party, and if its representations of liberal values had increased during the Reagan and Bush presidencies (an unproven assertion), and if the film and TV industries had continued to prosper (an unarguable assertion, despite their numerous flops), then these conditions may be symptomatic of the fact that Hollywood was better able to swim with emergent currents in a changing structure of feeling than was the Republican party.

In making this point, I do not wish to imply that the media are passive—far from it. The sitcom *Murphy Brown* was active in promoting and circulating the discourse of "today's woman" and active in the choice of that discourse and the rejection of others. But it did not originate that discourse: "today's woman" would be part of today's social reality had *Murphy Brown* never existed, for the sitcom's heroine "figured" a social and political identity that long preceded her and will long outlast her. *Murphy Brown* strengthened the public presence of that identity, inflected it in certain ways, and, in embodying it, made it more powerful in people's imagination. Murphy Brown's popularity was not just the result of the creative skills of her creator, Diane English, and her performer, Candice Bergen, but of their ability to give form and presence to a discursive current and the social identity it produced.

This same current also produced Anita Hill and Hillary Rodham Clinton as different figures of the same social identity, and the connections between figures such as these are some of the ways by which the internal politics of entertainment can flow into the external politics of voting. The political domains of international affairs, the economy, and the internal politics of everyday life swirl into each other in the general politics of a nation's structure of feeling. This is why the media matter, for their alleged inadequacies in the first two are more than compensated for by their incessant activity in the third.

There are conjunctural links among *Murphy Brown*'s victory over Dan Quayle in the "family values" debate (see chapter 1); Anita Hill's victory in the public arena, despite Clarence Thomas's one in the Senate (see chapter 2); and the fact that the majority of women voted for Clinton and men for Bush. I do not wish to imply that there is a perfect match between program preferences in the media and political preferences in the polling booth, but I do believe there are significant overlaps. Political programs and media programs are both produced within the same historical conditions, and similar currents can be traced in the popularity, or unpopularity, of each. Politicians are like advertisers (and therefore media producers) in that both need to get their messages to an audience, at times the largest possible, at others, and increasingly, the most accurately targeted possible. So voting demographics do show patterned similari-

12   ties to audience demographics. The same discourse will serve both political and media personalities to push similar buttons in similar audiences, for discourse is a feature of a social formation, not the invention of an individual, however public or prestigious.

   CNN described people's behavior during the L.A. uprisings: "At stores that are looted, it's almost like a feeding frenzy, they pour in, grab what they want, and run out. . . . it seems as each hour passes, the strength of the masses grows—people realize that they can get away with something, so they do" (see *Sidebar: LaMotte on the Spot*, p. 179). Pat Buchanan, opening the Republican convention, said, "The mob had burned and looted every building on the block but one, a convalescent home for the aged. And the mob was headed in to ransack and loot the apartments of the terrified old men and women inside" (see *Sidebar: Buchanan*, p. 56). The politician and the news reporter were using the same discourse ("mobs" and "masses" out of control) to press the same panic buttons in audiences with significant overlaps. Rush Limbaugh (see *Sidebar: Limbaugh on King*, p. 131) and the defense lawyers defending the LAPD officers used a similar discourse to prove that Rodney King's behavior caused the police behavior, and that he directed his own beating. These are all examples of "top-down" discourse: it was top-down discourse, too, that Dan Quayle used in his "family values" debate with Murphy Brown. But Murphy's response put "family values" into a discourse that spoke for and with those in the "nontraditional" families that Quayle was attacking (see *Sidebar: Murphy Brown's Response*, p. 72). Similarly, Oprah Winfrey allowed members of Buchanan's "mob" to talk on her show (see *Sidebar: Race and Class*, p. 172) and thus contested the top-down discourse of Buchanan and CNN. Both Murphy and Oprah, of course, advance women's interests in a way that Buchanan and CNN do not.

   We might say, using Raymond Williams's terms, that the discourse of "today's women" is carried by an emerging current pushing its way to the center of the mainstream, whereas that of "yesterday's men" is being sidestreamed into a residual one, and Rush Limbaugh speaks their dissatifaction. The voting patterns in the 1992 election give some support to this idea. Clinton was sent to the White House by women, by Blacks and Latino/as (with an exceptionally strong endorsement from Black women), by first-time voters and young people, by gays and lesbians, and by lower-income families. All of these groups were, and still are, trying to emerge from the margins and the depths into which Reaganism had pushed them, to claim places for themselves nearer the center of the mainstream. The two major demographic groups that voted for Bush, on the other hand, were white men and families from the two highest income brackets. Smaller groups who supported him were white born-again Christians (who gave him his strongest endorsement of all) and Asian Americans. Only one-sixth of the voters considered that "family values" were important, and only one-tenth thought abortion was. One-third, however, remembered Clarence Thomas and said that presidential nominations to the Supreme Court were "very important" in determining their vote—of these, half went for Clinton, and only a third for Bush.[7]

Anyone who analyzes change while it is in progress and is foolish enough to predict its direction must be prepared for history to prove him or her wrong. I accept the risk, for I do believe that these four media events—the hearings, the debate, the uprisings, and the election—were sites where Americans struggled to come to terms with, and to exert some influence on, the slow and messy social changes that are inevitable as the United States transforms itself from a society organized around a relatively homogeneous, Eurocentric consensus to a more diverse, multicultural social order. These changes take place at all levels, from the inexorable change in the demographics of our society, through far more contested changes in the regime of power, to incomplete and uneven changes in the structure of feeling. The process is painful but profound, and the United States that emerges will feel very different to its citizens from the United States of the nineteenth and twentieth centuries.

Underlying this book is the argument that, in the cultural struggles that went on around these four media events, we can trace processes of change by which older dominant currents were transformed into residual ones, and emergent ones pushed up from the depths and in from the margins to challenge for a place in the dominant. The events marked the right-wing extremity of the electoral pendulum, and thus provoked a variety of social alliances to speak up against, and eventually vote against, those who had swung it so far.

A change in a structure of feeling involves a change in the proportion of the ingredients that constitute the cultural mix, a change in which of the currents come to the surface and which are submerged. But not all currents change. In the politics of age, gender, and sexuality we can trace visible changes: the election put more women into Washington than ever before, Bill Clinton has put a slew of women and non-Caucasians into powerful positions, and the White House staff is younger and more ethnically diverse than previously. The chapters in this book will trace some of the struggles, the gains and losses, that have been part of these changes and the variety of fronts on which they have been fought for and resisted. The White House and Washington, however, are not the only sites of cultural and political activity, and in many ways are unlike others. A change in administration is abrupt, complete, and visible. No other change is. Most cultural currents are much muddier and any change in them harder to discern. We must not allow the clarity of the change in administration to misrepresent the muddiness of any changes that underlie it, nor its high visibility to magnify their extent. Changes in the structure of feeling are less clear, more gradual, and more partial than changes in party government.

Not all currents change: there is, in these early days of the new administration at least, less perceptible change in the currents of race. The strength of the Black and Latino vote for Clinton appears to be more of a reaction against the overt rac-

14 ism of the Republicans than a response to a more positive plank in the Democrats' platform. But less change does not mean less turbulence—far from it. What it means is that the insecurely dominant current of white supremacy has not yet been changed into a residual one by the strongly emerging currents of multiethnicity, and that the turbulence as these currents contest each other's position will be a constant and dangerous feature of our immediate future. Such mainstream turbulence can erupt into violent uprisings such as those that took place in Los Angeles. Other emerging currents seek different channels, such as Black Liberation Radio, an illegal, micro-radio station serving a ghettoized African American community in Springfield, Illinois (see chapters 4 and 5). This book is concerned primarily with the mainstream, but what the mainstream carries depends in part on what other, smaller side streams bear away on their own waters, so I will pay considerable attention to what is said on Black Liberation Radio in order to illustrate what is not said in the mainstream media, and thus to highlight the limits of what is. The currents in these side streams may well gain enough volume and momentum to disrupt the mainstream seriously at some point further down the river. And that point may not lie too far ahead.

A Chronology

Chronology, too, is based upon a metaphor of history as a river, though a far calmer one than the river I have described. It simplifies by taking a topographical view of the general direction of flow and ignoring the eddies and countercurrents. As I believe that contemporary culture is characterized as much by contestations and countercurrents as by a general flow, I have not organized this book chronologically. Nonetheless, chronologies are helpful in mapping the terrain: whatever the countercurrents between the events, Bush's nomination of Clarence Thomas did lie upstream of his electoral defeat, and Rodney King was beaten by cops before Dan Quayle blamed Murphy Brown for the L.A. uprisings. Events did happen in temporal sequence, and here, in brief, it is.

1991

March

3 Rodney G. King, a Black motorist, is beaten by white Los Angeles police officers. George Holliday, a resident of a nearby apartment, videotapes the incident; his tape becomes the most widely replayed video of the year.

15 A Los Angeles County grand jury indicts Sergeant Stacey C. Koon and Officers Laurence M. Powell, Theodore J. Briseno, and Timothy E. Wind on charges of excessive force in the beating of Rodney King.

16 Korean grocery store owner Soon Ja Du kills a fifteen-year-old African American, Latasha Harlins, on suspicion of attempting to steal a bottle of

orange juice. The incident is videotaped by the store's security camera and   15
shown on television throughout L.A.

April

1 In response to the beating of Rodney King, L.A. mayor Tom Bradley appoints a commission, headed by former deputy secretary of state Warren Christopher, to investigate the Police Department. (Christopher will later become Clinton's secretary of state.)

June

27 Thurgood Marshall announces his retirement. He was the first African American ever to serve on the Supreme Court and a leading civil rights justice.

July

1 President Bush nominates Clarence Thomas, forty-three, a Black conservative federal appeals court judge, to replace Marshall. Thomas is soon opposed by many civil rights and women's groups.

23 The State Second District Court of Appeal allows the trial of the police officers accused of beating Rodney King to be conducted outside Los Angeles County.

September

3-9 Discussions are held between Anita Hill and Democrat senators on whether she will testify before the Senate Judiciary Committee about her sexual harassment by Clarence Thomas ten years previously, when he was head of the Equal Employment Opportunities Commission.

10-20 The Senate Judiciary Committee holds eight days of public hearings on Thomas. He testifies for five days, followed by three days of outside witnesses. By the end of these hearings, his confirmation is likely.

12-23 Hill and committee staff discuss making allegations about sexual misconduct by Thomas. On September 23, Hill sends a "personal statement" to the committee making the allegations.

27 Shortly before the committee is to vote on confirming Thomas's nomination, several copies of Hill's statement are made available to committee members. Two copies of the FBI report on their interview with Hill are left with Biden and Thurmond, but none is distributed to the other members. To help ensure confidentiality, the staff retrieves Hill's statement after the vote. It appears that not all members read all the materials, and some Republicans were not even briefed. Chairman Biden and other committee members dismiss the charges and decide not to make them public.

The Judiciary Committee splits, seven to seven, on whether to confirm Thomas. Six Republicans and one Democrat vote for Thomas. No mention

16   is made of Hill's charges at the public meeting; opponents say Thomas is too
conservative and not qualified enough to get a life term on the high court. The
Thomas nomination goes to the Senate without recommendation.

October

1 Senate Majority Leader George Mitchell (Dem.-Maine), who has
been told by Biden about Hill's allegations, gets unanimous agreement to begin
debate on the confirmation on October 3 and to vote on the nomination at 6 P.M.
on October 8.

3-4 Senate debate begins, with both supporters and opponents agree-
ing Thomas will be confirmed.

6 National Public Radio and *New York Newsday* break the story of Hill's
allegations.

7 Hill gives a televised news conference in Oklahoma about her
charges; some senators and women's groups call for a delay in the vote, but
Mitchell says it will be held and Biden defends his handling of the allegations.

8 Thomas requests a delay in the Senate vote. His denial of the allegations is made public. Pressure mounts throughout the day for a delay as several
Democrats say they will withhold their votes unless the charges are investi-
gated. Thomas releases an affidavit denying the charges. At 6 P.M., the vote is
put on hold, and at 8:15 P.M., Mitchell gets agreement to postpone the vote one
week so that the committee can investigate Hill's charges.

11 The hearings reopen, carried live on ABC, CBS, NBC, and C-SPAN.
Thomas appears first, denies the charges, and says his reputation has been ruined
by unfair proceedings; Hill then gives graphic testimony about sexual comments
that she says Thomas made to her about pornographic films starring Long Dong
Silver, his own sexual prowess, and a pubic hair on his can of Coke. Thomas re-
turns in the evening to call the hearings "a high-tech lynching for uppity Blacks."

14 The committee finishes its hearing without reaching a conclusion
about whether Hill's charges are true. Biden says Thomas should get the benefit of the doubt.

16 The Senate votes, 52-48, to confirm Clarence Thomas as associate
justice of the Supreme Court.

November

15 Judge Joyce Karlin sentences Soon Ja Du to pay a $500 fine and per-
form four hundred hours of community service for the voluntary manslaughter
of Latasha Harlins, and puts her on probation but not in prison.

26 Judge Stanley M. Weisberg chooses neighboring Ventura County as
the new venue for the trial of the officers charged with the beating of Rodney
King. The specific location will be Simi Valley.

1992

March

4 Opening arguments are given before the jury in the trial of the officers charged in the Rodney King beating. Ten jurors are white, one is Latina, and one is Asian.

April

23 The case goes to the jury.

29 The jury is hung on one count against Mr. Powell and announces verdicts of not guilty on all other charges. The L.A. uprisings begin. Reginald Denny, a white truck driver, is pulled from his truck and beaten by Black youths. The beating is videoed live by television cameras in a helicopter and by a bystander on the ground.

30 The final episode of *The Cosby Show* is broadcast.

May

2 The uprisings die down.

19 Dan Quayle delivers a speech, "Restoring Basic Values," in which he blames the L.A. "riots" upon the poverty of values exemplified by *Murphy Brown*.

20-21 The media escalate Quayle's criticism of Murphy Brown.

July

16 Bill Clinton accepts the Democratic nomination for president at the party's national convention in New York.

August

5 A federal grand jury indicts the four officers who beat Rodney King on civil rights charges.

17-20 The Republican party holds its annual convention in Houston. Its "backlash" politics stirs national interest and concern.

September

21 In the season premier of *Murphy Brown*, the character replies to Dan Quayle and charges him with defining the family too narrowly.

November

3 Bill Clinton is elected president of the United States of America.

1993

January

20 Bill Clinton is sworn in as president of the United States of America.

18   **22** Zoë Baird, Clinton's nominee for attorney general, withdraws because she had employed an illegal alien as a child-care worker. Clinton lifts Reagan-Bush restrictions on abortion.

26-28 Clinton's attempt to lift the ban on gays and lesbians serving in the military runs into a firestorm of opposition.

February

22 A federal jury made up of nine whites, two Blacks, and one Latino is sworn in for the federal trial of the officers charged with violating Rodney King's civil rights. The trial is held in Los Angeles County.

March

9 Rodney King testifies, offering his first courtroom account of the beating.

April

17 The jury finds Officers Koon and Powell guilty. The other officers are acquitted. There are no uprisings. Damian Williams and the "L.A. Four +" are still in custody awaiting trial for the beating of Reginald Denny and assaults on others.

May

5 I write this chronology.[8]

Postscript: On October 20, Damian Williams was found not guilty of major charges in the Denny beating, including attempted murder, but guilty of aggravated mayhem and four misdemeanors, for which he was sentenced to ten years in prison.

Before moving to the substance of the book, I wish to comment on the obvious. I have written it from a position of privilege, for I am white, male, middle-class, and middle-aged. The issue of racial and gender identities is currently a hot one, and its temperature makes it difficult for someone positioned as I to contribute to the debate without appearing to exploit his privileged social identity. I do not think that there is any generally agreed-upon "proper" way by which one of the privileged can understand or write of the experiences of those who are oppressed by the social axes that privilege him. Yet not attempting to do so seems to me to be worse than doing so improperly, because it would continue their erasure from the analytic as well as the political world. I accept the inevitablity that I will blunder at times and offend some whom I would dearly wish not to. To them I offer my apologies in advance, and ask them to point out to me, hopefully not too antagonistically, where I went wrong.

There are many Caucasian Americans who are keen to do whatever they can to reduce racism, to mitigate its effects, and to learn how to avoid practicing it.

We are perplexed and angered to realize that, despite the civil rights movement, despite antidiscrimination laws and affirmative action programs, the United States has not reduced its racism, but has merely changed the forms by which it is exerted. In this book I have tried to analyze some of the forms of what I have called "nonracist racism" in the belief that understanding the problem is a necessary first step toward attacking it. But it is a step that we liberal whites cannot take alone: those who daily experience the effects of racism can see it more clearly than we, and any analysis of it must be informed by their perceptions. The parts of this book that mean the most to me personally are those that record my attempts to listen to and learn from subaltern voices, particularly African American ones: in writing it I am trying to relay those voices further into white society. I hope that in citing and summarizing the voices of the subaltern I have not given the impression that they cannot speak for themselves and need someone else to speak for them: that is manifestly and emphatically untrue. What is true, however, is that many who are situated comfortably within the power structure of this society are unwilling or unable to listen to them. If I can use my position of privilege to open their ears and minds to subaltern voices, I believe I will have used it responsibly. Similarly, my interpretations of Black voices are for whites: I am not trying to tell African Americans about their own experiences, though they may find it interesting to see what a white man makes of them and how he passes them onward. Any success this book may have in increasing the social audibility and credibility of their voices will be a comment on the powerful's inability to listen, not the subaltern's inability to speak.

Chapter 1

Murphy Brown, Dan Quayle, and the Family Row of the Year

On May 19, 1992, shortly after the Los Angeles uprisings, Dan Quayle, the vice president of the United States, delivered a speech to the Commonwealth Club of California in San Francisco. In it he argued that the root cause of the uprisings was the collapse of traditional family values, particularly among African Americans. Toward the end of the speech he turned to a prime-time sitcom, *Murphy Brown*, and suggested that the situation had been made worse by the decision of its eponymous heroine to become a single mother (see *Sidebar: Dan Quayle*, p. 68).

Next day, the press went ballistic: across the nation, papers headlined the vice president's attack on a sitcom (see *Sidebar: Press Headlines on* Murphy Brown, p. 22). The day after, the *New York Times* devoted its front-page photograph and lead story to the issue. The photograph, or rather photographic layout, was far removed from the objective style appropriate to the nation's "paper of record," and was closer to that of a tabloid. At its center was a soft-focus photograph of Murphy and her baby in a fuzzy-edged oval, and the top corners of the layout were occupied by small head shots of Dan Quayle and Marlin Fitzwater, "the White House spokesman" (*sic*).[1] Under each was a pair of quotations. Dan Quayle's read:

TUESDAY AFTERNOON

It doesn't help matters when prime-time TV has Murphy Brown . . . mocking the importance of fathers by bearing a child alone and calling it "just another lifestyle choice."

WEDNESDAY MORNING

I have the greatest respect for single mothers. They are true heroes [*sic*]. Marlin Fitzwater's were as follows:

WEDNESDAY MORNING

The glorification of the life of an unwed mother does not do good   21

Press Headlines on *Murphy Brown* (as shown on *Murphy Brown*)

USA Today	Quayle: Murphy No Role Model
Chicago Sun Times	Quayle Reads Riot Act to Murphy Brown
New York Times	Views on Single Motherhood Are Multiple at White House

New York Post	Dan Rips Murphy Brown
Daily News	Quayle to Murphy Brown: You Tramp
La Journal de France	Murphy A Donne Naissence en Scandale
The News	Quayle Has a Cow

service to most unwed mothers who are not highly paid, glamorous anchorwomen.

WEDNESDAY MIDMORNING

The Murphy Brown Show [exhibits] pro-life values, which we think are good.

At the bottom of the layout was a remark by President Bush to the Canadian prime minister during a televised news conference in which U.S.-Canadian relations had received less attention than Murphy Brown: "I told you what the issue was. You thought I was kidding." (The telecast of this remark was replayed on the episode of the show in which Murphy replied to Quayle.)

Immediately below the photographic layout was the headline "Views on Single Motherhood Are Multiple at White House" (see *Sidebar: The* New York Times, p. 23) and the story began with a slightly uneasy comparison between the seriousness of "real" politics and the triviality of this issue.[2] This playful skepticism, quite untypical of a *New York Times* lead story, is symptomatic of the paper's own uncertainty about how to handle a seemingly trivial issue that had become so important, an uncertainty mirrored in that of the White House. Throughout the election campaign, the "official" media showed signs of concern that much of the public debate was taking place in arenas beyond their control. The Democrats were using TV and radio talk shows, MTV and telephone call-ins; Ross Perot was using talk shows, thirty-minute "infomercials," and grassroots organizing; and the second TV debate among the presidential

WASHINGTON, May 20—Thailand is in turmoil, the Federal deficit is ballooning and hot embers of racial resentment still smolder in the ruins of inner-city Los Angeles. But today the high councils of government were preoccupied with a truly vexing question: Is Murphy Brown really a tramp? A day after Vice President Dan Quayle suggested that the television show has served to hasten the erosion of family values by glorifying unwed motherhood, the White House first applauded, then dithered, then beat a befuddled retreat. . . .

The show's creator and longtime producer, Diane English, issued a statement in Hollywood on Tuesday saying: "If the Vice President thinks it's disgraceful for an unmarried woman to bear a child, and if he believes that a woman cannot adequately raise a child without a father, then he'd better make sure abortion remains safe and legal." . . .

In fact, the most serious politics were at work here. The President's political advisers have advertised for months that Mr. Bush would try to make the decline of American morals and family values a major campaign issue, and the disintegration of the two-parent family was the theme of the President's most recent speech, on Sunday at the University of Notre Dame. Advisers to Mr. Bush's re-election campaign were described as delighted by the attention given to Mr. Quayle's message on family values, which appeared in some major newspapers near articles on an appearance by Gov. Bill Clinton of Arkansas, the likely Democratic Presidential nominee, before an enthusiastic crowd of gay and lesbian supporters. . . .

CBS executives declined to comment on Mr. Quayle's remarks. But a senior executive at the network who spoke on the condition of anonymity said that at a shareholders' meeting last week the issue of the unwed pregnancy on "Murphy Brown" was criticized by a representative of the conservative media watchdog group Accuracy in Media. . . .

Asked early today about Mr. Quayle's speech, Mr. Fitzwater said that Mr. Bush shared "society's concern" about "television networks' production and writers and their glorification of social situations."

"We are certainly concerned about family values and the breakup of the American family and again our concern is with the television networks and the production people who need to be aware of the ramifications of their programming," he said. Minutes later, however, Mr. Fitzwater pre-empted his attack, saying he was "not comfortable getting involved in criticism" of the "Murphy Brown" show. Indeed, he said, the program exemplifies "pro-life values, which we think are good," he said. "She is having the baby."

"In many ways, it does dramatize the difficulty of the social questions involved, questions it's good for the American people to see and grapple with," he added. "It demonstrates strong family values." . . .

The Vice President warmed to his subject later today, telling reporters, "Probably the only reason they chose to have a child rather than an abortion is because they knew the ratings would go up higher having the child."

Bathed in the glow of national publicity, he dismissed the comments of the President's spokesman about the positive attributes of the "Murphy Brown" program with a smile.

"I think it's important what I say and what the President says," Mr. Quayle said. "Marlin Fitzwater supports whatever I say."

24   candidates even dispensed with the traditional panel of journalists, with their power to ask balanced, informed, and probing questions, in favor of allowing members of the public in the audience to set their own agenda and ask questions for themselves. And here was a TV sitcom, way off the beat of a serious journalist, raising some of the most passionate interest in the campaign so far. What style should the "paper of record" adopt to cope with the paradox that under the triviality of a sitcom "the most serious politics were at work here"?

Obviously, *Murphy Brown* did not win the election for Clinton, but the show was a point of high visibility in the election campaign: it served as an important site where the discourse of "family values" could be fought over, where the meanings of each of the phrase's two heavily laden words could be contested, and where people could relate those meanings to the conditions of their everyday lives. The show was a discursive "relay station": it drew in the already circulating discourse of "family values," boosted its strength, directed it slightly leftward, and sent it back into circulation again.

Television often acts like a relay station: it rarely originates topics of public interest (though it may repress them); rather, what it does is give them high visibility, energize them, and direct or redirect their general orientation before relaying them out again into public circulation. But although television may be very effective in giving a topic high public visibility, its power to affect the direction in which that topic continues its circulation is more open to question, and therefore to contestation. If, in this instance, television was more powerful than the White House, and Murphy Brown more influential than Dan Quayle, we must not understand this in terms of a cause-and-effect model of television, or as a sign of TV's essential powerfulness; it can be understood only in terms of its particular historical context, the structure of feeling that characterized the end of Bush-Reaganism. Murphy Brown "won" because she was more closely aligned with the emerging currents than was Dan Quayle. When Dan Quayle claimed, in his speech to the Republican convention, that "on behalf of family values, we've taken on Hollywood and the media elite, and we will not back down," he was following an established Republican tradition of misunderstanding the role of the media by blaming Republicans' electoral setbacks on the liberalism of "the Hollywood elite" (of whom Murphy Brown was obviously a leading member). In the social circulation of meanings a relay station is, with its ability to redirect signals, immensely important, but it is neither the primary origin of those meanings nor the primary cause of any sociopolitical effects they might have.

Four months later, on September 21, in the opening episode of the new season, Murphy Brown replied to Dan Quayle. The episode replayed CBS News's sound bite of the vice president's speech attacking Murphy and allowed its heroine to reply on air to his accusation. Murphy Brown is a television journalist who works on a current affairs show called *FYI*. She delivered her reply in character to *FYI*'s fictional and unseen audience, but as she spoke all signs of

her fictionality were erased from our screens and she appeared to be speaking   25
directly to us, the real, not fictional, audience, answering a real, not fictional,
Dan Quayle (see *Sidebar: Murphy Brown's Response*, p. 72). As she finished, she
left her desk on the *FYI* set and moved to the floor of the studio (now simultaneously the fictional *FYI* one and the real *Murphy Brown* one), where she had
gathered a group of real, not fictional, single parents and their children. She
invited a number of them to introduce themselves and their children by their
real names, and they did so.

"Today's Woman" and Family Values

Murphy Brown delivered her response to Dan Quayle at a politically charged
moment. One month earlier, the Republican party had held its annual convention in Houston, and speaker after speaker had returned to the theme of "family values." Two months after Murphy's response, the Republican presidential
candidate, George Bush, with Dan Quayle at his side, lost the election to Bill
Clinton, and a Democrat entered the White House for the first time in twelve
years.

At the time of Murphy's response, the Republican campaign was in trouble,
Bush was trailing Clinton by a full ten points in the polls, and, in particular, its
conservative attack on any lifestyle that did not conform to its traditional "family values" had provoked a backlash. Two copies of the episode's script had
been leaked in advance, one to Dan Quayle's office and the other to Rush Limbaugh, an ultraconservative radio and TV talk-show host. Both were prepared
for the show and poised to recover any gains that it might have made for the
Democrats.

One hour after the episode ended, I watched my local CBS affiliate news in
Minneapolis-St. Paul. It told how both Republicans and Democrats attempted
to recycle Murphy's and Quayle's accounts of single motherhood and turn
them to their own political advantage (see *Sidebar: Local News*, p. 26). Next day,
CNN gave a longer account that explicitly linked Murphy Brown with the Republican convention and the failure of the "family values" campaign to resonate with enough of the electorate (see *Sidebar: CNN News*, p. 27). Next day
also, Rush Limbaugh, in his syndicated TV talk show, made Republican meanings out of Murphy Brown's single motherhood (see *Sidebar: Rush Limbaugh on
Murphy Brown*, p. 28).[3] The episode recounted Murphy's not very successful
attempts to cope with her new baby. One scene showed her not knowing how
to hold him or how to soothe him to sleep. Later in the episode, she learned
both techniques from her friend and colleague Frank. This offered up the nontraditional meanings that motherhood is not an instinctual element of women's
nature, but a set of skills and techniques that can be learned by, or from, either
gender. Toward the end of his monologue, Rush Limbaugh replayed the image
of Murphy holding the baby awkwardly, replaced her voice with his, and

Local News

FEMALE ANCHOR: Presidential politics and TV entertainment blended together in the season's opener of *Murphy Brown.* Last summer, the pregnancy of the show's unmarried title character became a rallying point in the issue of "family values." Tonight, the man who led the charge against the show watched it in the company of single

mothers in Washington, D.C. Quayle said earlier that he had respect and understanding for single mothers; he also said he sent Murphy's baby a card and a toy elephant, hoping to make him a Republican.

Here in the Twin Cities, supporters of Democrat Bill Clinton used tonight's *Murphy Brown* as an excuse for a fund-raiser, charging $15 for the chance to watch the show in the proper political company. The evening raised $2,000. . . .

MALE ANCHOR: Earlier today, someone asked a member of Dan Quayle's staff why did the vice president send a real toy to a fictional baby. He answered, "You tell me where fiction begins and reality ends in this whole business."

turned it into evidence supporting Dan Quayle's accusation. He used the term "serial murderer," whereas Dan Quayle used "rioters" and "killers," but all three terms are from the same discursive construction of the collapse of "family values."

Howard Stern, another talk-show host, joined the conservative chorus when he wrote in *TV Guide*: "This is parenthood as designed by people with zero love for children. . . . Say what you will about the much-mocked Ozzie and Harriet, in their world the kids came first. In Murphy's, as in ours, they far too often come last."[4]

Stern believes the TV sitcom is one of the key sites where family values are contested, for not only is the sitcom conventionally about the family, it is designed to be watched by the family. It has often, therefore, served as a central site of struggle over family values (see chapter 2). He also makes clear that Murphy, as a figure of, to use Dan Quayle's phrase, "today's woman," is part of, and partly responsible for, the collapse of these values. From the Republican viewpoint, she embodies antifamily values—she puts her career ahead of family, women ahead of men, independence ahead of housewifery, and being single ahead of being married.

And she brings a baby into this perverted world she has created. As the figure of "today's woman," Murphy Brown stands in for Hillary Rodham Clinton. Their visual representations underscore their figurative equivalence: both are

CNN News

ANCHOR: The vice president tried to get some mileage out of the show, too. He watched it with single mothers, trying to make the point that he was not attacking them when he attacked Murphy Brown.

DAN QUAYLE: I'm honored that Hollywood would donate an hour of prime-time TV to answer one sentence of a speech that I made a number of months ago, but unfortunately Hollywood still doesn't get it, because I was never criticizing single mothers.

BLACK WOMAN (at demonstration): We knew that the press would come out and maybe that some of the issues we in the Black community are trying to have addressed would be addressed for a change, and most of these people came to talk about issues other than just Murphy Brown.

ANCHOR: Quayle's Murphy Brown bashing

was the opening volley in the GOP's family values campaign that reached a crescendo in the Republican convention in Houston.

PAT ROBERTSON: When Bill Clinton's talking about family values he's talking about a radical plan to destroy the traditional family.

PAT BUCHANAN: There is a religious war going on in this country for the soul of

America. It is a cultural war as critical to the kind of nation we shall be as the Cold War itself, for this war is for the soul of America.

ANCHOR: The Bush campaign has been pulling back from that sort of harsh rhetoric. When Mr. Bush dropped

by for dinner with some of Pat Robertson's flock, the president talked about the economy, not hot-button social issues. Mr. Bush has long supported an amendment to ban abortion, but what the Bush camp is emphasizing these days is that the White House wants to change attitudes about abortion, not change the legal right to it.

DAN QUAYLE: We're working to change attitudes in this country. I want more reflection on the issue of abortion.

Rush Limbaugh on Murphy Brown

You've heard a lot of people say a lot of things about this show, but I'll tell you the most important thing is that they got very defensive about what a family is, they trot

out all these various examples of what a family is, and that's not what the vice president or any of the family values people have been talking about, the key word in all this is "values," not "family," nobody criticizes families except those that are dysfunctional, that's why I like to call it "functional values," anyway. The family is just the first place you learn the difference between right and wrong, if it's a good family, the family is just the first place you learn the differences between right and wrong, and how to respect people and, er, how to take life seriously and all that, that's why the family aspect of this is important, but it's just adults teaching kids, it doesn't matter what the composition of the family is, and nobody has been critical of that.

When Quayle said that they glorified single mothers what he was trying to point out, my friends, was, and I think this show last night proved it, and this is another thing, this show's got an agenda and they say all day long they don't have an agenda and last night's show proved it—it's okay that they have an agenda, just say so, like this show, we're perfectly up front and honest about what I am, and what I believe on this show, and we'll let that float out in the marketplace and let you accept it as it is, there's no attempt here to fool you, there's no attempt here to deny what I am,

but that's what they're all about. This show, ladies and gentlemen, was strictly about trying to prove the irrelevance in the modern era of fathers. It wasn't just me who said this, I talked to people at CBS, I have high-placed friends, and I also talked to some people who are liberals, and I read the newspapers today, Tom Shales in the *Washington Post*, Matt Roush of *USA Today*—none of these people thought this show was funny, and that's another point, it wasn't funny. These are entertainment shows, people don't watch these shows for messages, and they got very defensive and took it very seriously.

Now there's another aspect to this, though, that I haven't heard anybody mention, and I would like to illustrate it for you and show you now, we've got some footage from the show last night, I would like you to watch the way Murphy Brown handles a baby, she supposedly loves this baby, this baby is supposedly one of the highlights in her life, you watch how she—roll the tape, Turner—and watch, folks, how she handles baby Brown, look at her, acting like it's a bomb, look at her, where's the nearest trash can, what can I do with this thing? Would you hold your baby that way? Look at the poor baby's arms, that baby can't possibly be loved and be happy. I mean that kid, Murphy, if you don't, you don't start handling that kid right you're going to end up with a serial murderer on your hands, that kid is not going to be loved.

tall, blonde women, physically fit and active, in the prime of life, with confident facial expressions and assertive body language. Early in their campaign, the Republicans attacked Hillary Clinton as the new woman who would destroy the traditional one (figured as Barbara Bush) and her "natural" role in the family. Hillary Clinton's off-the-cuff remark that she had chosen a professional career over staying at home and baking cookies became one of the most controversial and politically charged remarks in the early stages of the campaign! Even the Democratic campaign managers wondered if such a comment might not be too extreme for the American electorate and attempted to pull Hillary Clinton closer to the center by staging a cookie bake-off between her and Barbara Bush. They also "softened" her hairstyle and manner of dressing, quietly dropped the public use of her family name Rodham, and made sure she held hands with Bill whenever the cameras were on them.

Perhaps fortunately for the Democrats, earlier problems in the Clintons' marriage had been so thoroughly exploited and explored by the other Democratic candidates in the primaries that any explosive charge still left in them was too weak to be of use to the Republicans. Be that as it may, the Republicans' attack on Hillary Clinton was recycled in Quayle's and Limbaugh's on Murphy Brown and resurfaced again in Buchanan's speech at the convention (see *Sidebar: Buchanan*, p. 56). Both Rush Limbaugh and Phyllis Schlafly (another ultraconservative public voice) saw the connections between Hillary Rodham Clinton and Anita Hill, not just that both were professional career women (coincidentally both lawyers), but that both served as means for covertly advancing the feminist agenda (see *Sidebar: Today's Legal Women*, p. 30). Dan Quayle and Rush Limbaugh gave the same gender spin to the debate with their insistence on the importance of fathers. Murphy Brown's "nonhusband" was turned by them into the signifier of the "nonman" that would result from this new woman with a "nonfamily" identity. The concern of both that her single motherhood demonstrates the "irrelevance of fathers" carries the masculinist fear that the new woman's independence demonstrates the irrelevance of men. In this context, when Quayle called single mothers "heroes" (as reported in the *New York Times*), the sexism of his discourse implicitly reinserted the father whose absence was causing such anxiety in the conservative imagination.

Class and Family Values

When this frightened masculinism is given a blue-collar accent, it becomes a potent political force. Although Rush Limbaugh and Dan Quayle use similar words and similar arguments, Limbaugh speaks for and with the blue-collar in a way that Quayle cannot.

Rush Limbaugh is a red, white, and blue conservative (red necked, white skinned, and blue collared). The oralcy of his language compared with the literacy of Quayle's (and of Murphy Brown's) hints at its class position and brings

Today's Legal Women

Historically, the American Bar Association has been a conservative group led by men in pinstripes and wingtips. But at this year's annual convention in San Francisco, the lawyer's group took a distinctly liberal turn.

On Sunday, Hillary Clinton, who until 1991 chaired the A.B.A.'s commission on women, paid tribute to one of the profession's most recent female celebrities, Anita Hill. "All women who care about the equality of opportunity, about integrity and morality in the workplace, are in Professor Anita Hill's debt," said Clinton, a corporate lawyer. Hill received an award from the A.B.A. and a standing ovation from the crowd. Later in the week, the A.B.A. voted to fight laws that restrict a woman's right to an abortion; the group also allowed the National Lesbian and Gay Law Association to join.

The A.B.A.'s tilt to the left on these issues is attributable partly to the increasing political clout of women. In the past 12 years, women have gone from 8% of the legal profession to 21%. Said the A.B.A.'s outgoing president, Talbot D'Alemberte: "The future of this profession lies largely with women, and women care passionately about abortion. Predictably, the A.B.A.'s action displeased fellow lawyer Dan Quayle. . . . "The American Bar leadership," said the Vice President last week, "is just one more special interest group of the Democratic Party. We now know why Bill Clinton can never support legal reform."

(Accompanying this story was a picture of Anita Hill captioned "HILL ASCENDANT: Anita Hill received an award from the A.B.A. for speaking 'eloquently and persuasively on behalf of millions of women.' ")

(*Time*, August 24, 1992, 11)

to the surface the role of class in the family values debates (compare *Sidebars: Rush Limbaugh*, p. 28 and p. 131, *Dan Quayle*, p. 68, and *Murphy Brown's Response*, p. 72). In transcription, the rawness of Limbaugh's language contrasts sharply with the grammatically correct language of Murphy Brown and Dan Quayle. When spoken live, however, its strengths lie precisely in what transcription makes into deficiencies—from the viewpoint of the educated middle classes, at least. It is an embodied language, rooted in the slightly overweight body and the sincere yet humorous voice of Rush Limbaugh himself. It is a language that passes easily from him to his listeners, not only because of the directness of its address ("my friends," "you," "I," "we," "watch, folks," "Would you hold your baby that way?"), but because it recognizes who they are and where they are socially positioned. The language of both Murphy Brown and Dan Quayle is more generalized and abstracted from the immediate conditions of its speaking.

Limbaugh's unfinished sentences and the redirection of his argument before he has arrived where he appeared to be going are evidence of an immediacy, a thinking with his tongue that, in its rawness, gives a sense of authenticity. This embodiedness that ties his speech to the immediate conditions of its speaking is a characteristic of oralcy, and thus of deprived social formations whose com-

parative lack of resources and social power (economic, political, and legal as   31
well as discursive) binds their daily lives and their speech into their immediate
material conditions. I shall argue in chapter 3 that the original video of the Rodney King beating shared characteristics with Limbaugh's speech—its unedited
rawness, loss of focus, and swings of the camera gave it an authenticity that
enabled it to speak with the accent of the disempowered.

Although Murphy Brown and Dan Quayle may be making opposite arguments, the ways in which they make them are similar. Rush Limbaugh and
Quayle, on the other hand, are saying the same thing, but saying it very differently. It is a hallmark of Limbaugh's commentary to provide blue-collar
translations of white-collar conservatism, and in doing so to inflect them with
tones of anger and outrage that articulate the resentment of a newly disenfran-
chised social formation, one that had its wallets emptied by Reaganomics while
Reaganism massaged its egos.

The blue-collar end of this formation was, a generation ago, in the engine
room of the U.S. manufacturing economy, but now feels threatened with job
insecurity and, as a result, gender insecurity. The polls of the Yankelovich
Monitor Survey have shown that for at least the past twenty years Americans
have considered the prime definer of masculinity to be a man's ability to be a
"good provider for his family." When the blue-collar worker experiences his
economic decline through his sense of masculinity it is not surprising that his
resentment is directed along gender rather than class lines.[5] In 1982, Ronald
Reagan joined him in this misdirection of resentment when he argued, "Part of
the unemployment is not as much recession as it is the great increase of the
people going into the job market and—ladies, I'm not picking on anyone but—
because of the increase in women who are working today."[6] In his eyes, gender complicates his economic wounding still further, not only by reducing the
number of jobs open to him, but also by reducing the pay of many of those that
remain, for the jobs in the information and service economies that have replaced the manufacturing ones are lower paying and feminized (these two
characteristics always go together in a patriarchal society). This economic deprivation results in racist, as well as sexist, attitudes: the Limbaughian sees that
his blue-collar jobs have gone to the "third" world, and "third" world immi-
gants, as well as Blacks and women, compete for the ones remaining in the
"first" world that should be rightfully "his."

Susan Faludi shows that this 1980s phenomenon of the downwardly mobile
male extended from the blue- into the white-collar classes. The middle of the decade produced a new social formation of young single men at the tail end of the
baby boom who had just missed the yuppie gravy train. They were slipping down
the income ladder as the train left them behind, and they were furious about it.[7]
We shall meet members of this social formation again as they perform a particularly vicious politics of resentment around the doors of abortion clinics.

32   This social formation of men on the lower levels of "respectable" society feels little of the security (economic and physical) enjoyed by those on its higher rungs. They are the most vulnerable—many lack job security, health insurance, and pension plans, and are likely to live in less safe areas of town. They feel vulnerable because they are closest to what they see as the threatening underclass—of the unemployed, the drug addict, the criminal, the Black, the illegal immigrant—and they fear that any social change will affect them most and will affect them worst because they have the fewest resources upon which to draw to see them through it. The undermining of organized labor and the alternative source of security it offered is another factor in the insecurity of the blue-collar end of this formation.

Such blue-collar conservatism is not a new phenomenon: in both the civil rights and the anti-Vietnam War movements there was strong blue-collar or "hard hat" opposition to middle-class student and, in the first case at least, Black activists. But, as the trickle-down economics of Reaganism didn't, the hats have become harder, the collars bluer. Such conservatism digs deep trenches, for it is caught between the two positions where the motivation for the social change it fears is strongest. Ranged against it on one front are the forces of liberalism, which in the United States are found almost exclusively in the middle to upper-middle classes—those among whom Murphy Brown moves so freely. And on the other front lies the deprived underclass, who have nothing to gain by maintaining the status quo. The paradox of blue-collar conservatives is that Reaganomics destroyed their economic security by exporting their jobs and dismantling their unions while Reaganism, especially through its "family values," offered them a compensatory illusion of gender and racial power.

Pat Buchanan recognized both this class resentment and that the Republicans were, not surprisingly, in danger of losing the votes of those who felt it. Calling them "the conservatives of the heart," he told the Republican convention, "We need to reconnect with them. We need to let them know we know how bad they're hurting." His fear was justified. The lower-middle classes (those with family incomes of $15,000 to $29,000) voted strongly for Reagan in 1984 (57 percent to 42 percent), just stayed with Bush in 1988, but swung solidly to Clinton in 1992 (45 percent to 35 percent, with 22 percent going to Ross Perot).[8] Against the damage that Reaganomics did to their wallets, the rhetoric of Reaganism could keep most of them loyal for only so long.

Republican campaign strategists were quick to spot Limbaugh's ability to connect with those they so wistfully called "conservatives of the heart." They urged Marvin Fitzwater to persuade Bush to listen to a tape of Limbaughisms, and when they picked up signs early in the campaign that all was not going well, Rush Limbaugh was invited to spend the night of June 3 at the White House, where the president of the United States personally carried the radio jock's overnight bag to the Lincoln bedroom.[9] Some months later, when the picture was even bleaker, William Buckley's conservative journal, the *National Review*, invited Limbaugh to join a forum giving last-ditch advice to the president. His proved to be particularly inept: "Mr. Bush must unmask Bill Clinton and Al Gore as the liberals they really are. . . . The liberal 'outing' of Clinton can be achieved in part by simply identifying Clinton's support base. Just look at the Emmy awards show and all the daffy leftist groups supporting him."[10] He went on to claim that Clinton's support came also from "militant feminists, the ACLU, NAACP, NEA, and Big Labor, the AIDS, animal-rights and environmental activists, and the Democratic Congressional leaders," thus identifying in one off-the-cuff list most of the social formations whose open and well-publicized support for Clinton put him in the White House. Like Quayle and Buchanan, Limbaugh understands his own constituency well, but that of others not at all: he is, therefore, good at speaking for it, but not at expanding it.

The Limbaughian conservatism of the insecure is also tapped into by "tabloid television" and the "reality-based" shows that grew as rapidly in the latter half of the Reagan years as did the social formation that constitutes their core audience. Shows such as *Cops* and *Rescue 911* offer the reassurance that "the system" can protect its vulnerable. The appeal of this reassurance is class specific, for the protection is provided by the blue-collar members of the system, not by its executive class, who are rarely seen on screen. It is the stout-hearted heroism of the paramedic, the ordinary cop, or the firefighter that protects members of their own class. So, too, programs such as *America's Most Wanted* show the fallibility of the official system of law and order until "ordinary people" come to its aid, and do for themselves what "the system" could not do for them.

There are stylistic similarities between these shows and Rush Limbaugh's language. Their shaky hand-held cameras, their breathlessness and sensationalism, their embodiedness and direct address are all, in a way, "Limbaughesque," and serve to distinguish their style sharply from that of "official" news. This difference is, like that between Limbaugh and Murphy Brown, one of social position as well as of televisual style.

In Murphy Brown's social position, as in her discursive style, we can see traces of her conditions of production. Diane English, her producer and creator, is often considered to be the model for her own character. Barnet Kellman, the director of the series, considers that "Diane was writing from her gut about a woman wanting to achieve the things that she wanted and the obstacles that were in her way,"[11] and in their book-length study of the series, Alley and Brown emphasize the similarities among the three "today's women" who constitute the figure of Murphy Brown—Diane English, Candice Bergen, and Murphy Brown herself.[12] Indeed, they say unequivocally, "Diane English is Murphy Brown," and, a few chapters later, "Candice Bergen is Murphy Brown." (The two statements, of course, are complementary, not contradictory.) Diane English is explicit about Murphy Brown's privilege, describing the

34   show as one in which "people had whatever they wanted—it was a sort of cautionary tale about getting what you wished for." She identifies it as a 1980s show, in contrast to the next one she produced, *Love & War*, which she calls "a requiem for the 80s" and "a recession-era comedy." The class politics of *Murphy Brown* are also evident in English's production policies, particularly her anti-union stance. She fired the union crew hired to shoot the pilot of *Love & War* and replaced them with nonunion labor because it was cheaper not to pay union benefits, particularly health insurance, and not to meet their camera staffing levels. "I'm not anti-union," English commented, "but I'm also not a socialist."[13]

Despite her position of privilege, Murphy Brown did have to struggle to balance the demands of job and motherhood; she did have to cope with feelings of inadequacy and guilt. These struggles resonated with women in different classes and allowed the formation of interclass alliances between her and the nine million single, and the twenty-two million working, mothers in the United States whose collective presence made family values such a hot political issue, and is thus directly, if only partly, responsible for *Murphy Brown's* popularity and economic success. And successful it is. It has won fifteen Emmys, is consistently among the top twenty shows, commands one of the highest advertising rates of any network program ($310,000 per thirty seconds in 1992) and sells in reruns for $1 million per episode. Its advertising rates are so high because its core audience is one that advertisers are desperate to reach—the upper middle classes with a consumerist lifestyle. "Today's woman" is not only a progressive social formation, it is also a valuable market segment.

Prime-time TV needs a prime audience. Talk radio, with its lower production costs, can speak to and for less affluent audiences than *Murphy Brown's*. It thus can give their red, white, and blue conservatism a national forum. The radio is readily available in the workplace, and the telephone (particularly if the boss pays for it) allows those who are normally silenced access to the public through its airwaves. Talk radio gives the private talk of the workshop and the neighborhood bar a public airing and builds a sense of community with those who are geographically distant but politically close. As soon as he (was) retired from his position as chief of the L.A. Police Department, Daryl Gates acquired a radio show, from where he could talk to Limbaugh's insecure conservatives and promote verbally the same social interests (of keeping the underclass under) that he had protected so physically in his previous position.

The class and gender politics of talk radio and the issues it discusses can take many forms. One hotly contested issue on talk radio handed the new Clinton administration its first public defeat on an issue that was swirling around in the Murphy Brown affair: this was "the child-care issue," to focus on its gender politics, or the "illegal alien issue," to foreground its class and racial ones. Zoë Baird, a lawyer reputedly earning $500,000 a year, was Clinton's first nominee for the post of attorney general. During her confirmation hearings it emerged

that she had employed a Peruvian couple who were illegal immigrants, the   35
woman to care for her child and the man for her yard. Because they were undocumented, she could pay below the minimum wage and avoid paying social
security taxes. The populist use of the low-tech media of talk radio and the telephone (calls not only to radio and TV talk shows, but also to the White House
and to senators) eroded the Democratic support for Baird so rapidly that she
had to withdraw. Clinton's second choice, Kimba Wood, refused the nomination because she too had employed an "illegal alien" to look after her children
(though before it was illegal to do so): "trial by talk radio" was the main reason
she gave for refusing the nomination. Clinton's third, and ultimately successful
nominee, Janet Reno, was an unmarried, childless woman.

Provision of child care for working women of all classes was an important
plank in the Democratic platform. But for the less-privileged women whose anger burned along the telephone lines and the airwaves, the key issue was the
social privilege that allowed wealthy women to solve the problem by employing immigrant labor, whereas they had to struggle to cope with the demands of
job and family with far fewer economic resources to draw upon. The sight of a
woman earning half a million dollars a year saving a few by employing "illegal
aliens" not surprisingly stuck in their collective throat. As Rush Limbaugh
knows, the "illegal alien" poses as great a threat from below as does the "lim-
ousine liberal" from above. Those in minimum-wage jobs are as poor as they
are partly because nonunion, illegal, and therefore exploitable, immigrant labor, often "undocumented" (an employers' euphemism for "illegal"), has been
used to depress wages so far that it now takes more than one and a half minimum-wage jobs to lift a family of four up to the poverty line.

Race is intertwined with economics here, for not only is today's wage-de-
pressing immigrant likely to be *from* the "third" world, but the shortage of
blue-collar jobs results from the transfer of much U.S. manufacturing *to* the
"third" world. In addition, the need to maintain U.S. competitiveness against
the cheap labor of the "third" world is a standard conservative argument
against raising the minimum wage in the United States. Both employed and
unemployed blue-collar workers thus feel a three-pronged assault from the
"third" world. And there is a fourth prong to the spear. As we shall see in
chapter 3, one component of the Los Angeles uprisings was the displacement
throughout the 1980s of Black unionized labor by nonunion, cheaper, often illegal, immigrant labor.

Because those displaced from the lowest rungs of the labor market by the
immigrant (illegal or not) are disproportionately Black, racial politics complicates the mixture of class and gender in the Zoë Baird affair. Patricia King, a
Black lawyer, argued that "her confirmation as attorney general would be an
insult to all of us. Moreover, descended from people who once did domestic
work, I know that payment of Social Security taxes is essential for people with
that kind of meager income to ward off destitution."[14] In this light, it is hardly

36   surprising that one of the first senators to call for Zoë Baird's withdrawal was
      Carol Moseley Braun, the Black Democrat from Chicago whose electoral victory
      was widely understood as one positive effect of Anita Hill's "defeat" (see chap-
      ter 2). The Zoë Baird affair prefigures in miniature one of the complex currents
      underlying the L.A. uprisings—that most white employers (industrial or do-
      mestic) prefer to hire Latino/a rather than Black workers, for Latino/as appear
      less threatening and more deferential, and, crucially, cost less (see chapter 3).[15]
      And here Murphy Brown circles back into sight. Like the "illegal alien," she,
      too, was one of the perceived causes of the L.A. uprisings. Like Zoë Baird, she,
      too, had to employ child care, but, unlike Baird, Murphy Brown used her eco-
      nomic privilege to employ a legal alien (and a very upper-class one), an English
      nanny, and when that did not work out, she used the privilege of a high-level
      professional job (excess work space in her office and a flexible work schedule)
      to take the baby to work with her: legal, but very privileged.
          Women's groups worked hard to overcome class differences in the child-care
      issue, and claimed that making it a "women's issue" was sexist. Mr. Baird and
      Mr. Wood, they pointed out, were never held responsible for employing the
      illegal aliens to look after children that were unarguably theirs. Women argued
      that male nominees for public office are never questioned about their arrange-
      ments for child care, and that confining the problem of balancing the demands
      of work and family to women is deeply sexist. To support their arguments,
      they pointed to Ron Brown, chair of the Democratic party and Clinton's nom-
      inee for secretary of commerce, who admitted that he had once hired an illegal
      alien as a maid: his admission raised scarcely an eyebrow, never became an is-
      sue on the talk shows, and in no way hindered his confirmation.
          The backlash politics by which Rush Limbaugh misdirects class resentment
      onto gender does have some solid achievement against which to lash back.
      Though equality with men is still far out of sight over the horizon, the Western
      professional woman has fought for and achieved a position of relative power,
      freedom, and independence that has made her arguably the most liberated
      woman in the world. Indeed, this professional women's movement offers one
      of the few examples of successful progressive politics in the 1980s. "Today's
      woman," by whom Dan Quayle felt so threatened, is a way of putting the ma-
      terial effects of women's struggles throughout the 1980s into conservative dis-
      course and thus making it available for Republican politics. This fearful conser-
      vative imagination used the concept explicitly against Murphy Brown and
      Hillary Rodham Clinton and implicitly against Anita Hill. But, like all discur-
      sive categories, it is open to contestation, and its emancipatory meanings can
      never be entirely swamped by the Republican ones.
          Backlash is inevitable in the highly elaborated societies of late capitalism, for
      in them, power is always exerted along multiple lines of force, and those lines
      can be intertwined or separated out according to the political objectives of the
      alliances formed around them. Backlash politics works by isolating progressive

social formations, particularly ones showing some success, and thus preventing them from forming alliances with others. They can be opposed only
through an active attempt to extend alliances and thus to counter the inevitable
conservative strategy of isolating any progressive movement.

Race and Family Values

A consistent program of racism lurks just below the surface of the family values
campaign. The elaborated nature of our society means that racism is never exerted or experienced autonomously, but is always interwoven with other axes
of power. This affords whites strategic opportunities to divert racial power
along its interwoven axes, so hiding it from mainstream visibility and providing those exerting it with an alibi if it should happen to be noticed. If racism can
be recoded into discourses that are not explicitly concerned with race, it can be
spoken silently, its power can be exerted invisibly, and it can guard itself
against that contradiction noted by Foucault—that although power is exerted
through discourse, discourse makes power visible and visibility makes resistance possible.

Stuart Hall distinguishes between overt and inferential racism and implies
that inferential racism is ultimately the more dangerous, not only because it is
harder to identify, but because it is often exerted by liberals with an explicitly
antiracist intent.[16] Intentionality, which refers to the strategic promotion of social interests, is not the same as individual intent, nor is it dependent upon it.
Indeed, intentionality may run counter to intent, because intentionality is
coded into the dominant discourse and its discursive frames, and even discursive practices that oppose racism may not avoid continuing to an extent that
which they contradict. Inferential racism would be at work, for example, in an
analysis of "the race problem" that has the overt intent to find ways to mitigate
it, but that derives from and never questions the assumption that "the problem" is, at heart, *within* and *for* the Black community, not the white one, and
that liberal white social formations need to help Black America, but not to
change themselves. On the micro level, inferential racism works even in the
liberal or progressive use of the word *minority*, with its implications of the state
of being a minor, not yet fully adult, and thus one who can properly be spoken
for and looked after by members of the majority (*majority* refers to social maturity or adulthood as well as quantity).

Inferential racism is the necessary form of racism in a society of white supremacy that proclaims itself "nonracist." The United States was until comparatively recently legally racially segregated, and the suffering and deaths involved in changing that overt racism have left mainstream white America with
the belief that desegregation has produced a nonracist society, and thus with
the problem of continuing its racism in nonovert ways. It has elaborated inferential racism into many forms within what we might call a "nonracist racism."

38   Although there can be no comprehensive list of the forms that nonracist racism can take, for new forms are constantly being developed to meet new circumstances, we can identify some of its strategies. One is that of recoding. Here racial meanings are not spoken directly but are recoded into another discourse; racial power is not exerted nakedly but is redirected along other axes. Dan Quayle's speech on Los Angeles (see *Sidebar: Dan Quayle*, p. 68) provides good examples. He recodes the racial problems of L.A. into the discourse of "family values" and thus locates them not in white racism but in the "poverty of values" that he sees in African America. Similarly, by calling the nonwhites who rose up on the streets of South-Central Los Angeles "rioters" and "killers," he is recoding racial politics into the discourse of law and order, so that the difference between lawbreakers and law abiders is used to make sense of the difference between nonwhites and whites, and the "riots" can then be understood not as racial protest but as criminality in which race plays no part. Racial power can thus be exerted along the axis of legal power and the Black and Brown "rioters" tried as colorless individuals. This erases racial difference from official discourse while ensuring that it remains in the racially disproportionate makeup of the prison population and in the white "commonsense" linking of color with criminality.

The phrase "poverty of values" is richly recoded when it is applied to the problems of Black urban America. One meaning of "values" allows racism to be recoded into the discourse of morality and individual responsibility: its other allows economics to be the recoding vehicle. "The poor you always have with you, the Scripture tells us": in reminding his audience of that convenient certainty, Dan Quayle silently recodes nonwhiteness into poverty, and by making both of them inevitable, natural, and scripturally legitimate, excludes them from the agenda of social change. In the word "poor" race is recoded into class, a common and convenient strategy in a meritocracy, for it implies that those who are at the bottom of the economic pyramid are there because they deserve to be, and therefore those poor Blacks who are un-American enough not to treat their poverty as a transitional stage to prosperity remain poor because of their "poverty of values," not because of their Blackness in a white society.

Another form of nonracist racism is denial. Explaining the most racially explosive verdict of the decade, a white juror on the Rodney King trial said, "They kept trying to bring race into it, but race had nothing to do with it." George Bush, on introducing Clarence Thomas as his nominee for the U.S. Supreme Court, announced on TV, in an unintended parody of the style he had made his own, "He is the best person for this position, and the fact that he is black and a minority, has nothing to do with this, in the sense that he is the best qualified at this time." Anthony, the Black character on *Designing Women* (see chapter 2), was not taken in (like most Blacks, he saw racism more clearly than do most whites—though few of us could have missed it on this occasion!):

"They keep saying that race has nothing to do with it, whereas it's perfectly obvious the only thing they like about him is that he's Black."

Denied racism is a strategy particularly favored by conservatives; liberals, who profess vehemently their antiracism, are more likely to exert a form of nonracist racism unintentionally by marginalizing or silencing any explicit reference to the topic. The white liberals who marginalized Anita Hill's Blackness in their support for her gender provide one example. This episode of *Murphy Brown* provides another in the way that it, too, foregrounds gender and marginalizes or silences race. It clarifies the contradictions between Murphy and Dan into those between women and men, particularly single mothers and absent fathers, or vice versa. For Dan Quayle, the problem is that Murphy Brown, as a woman-mother, does not have a man. Murphy Brown does at least define what she means by family values in a way that Dan Quayle does not: verbally she emphasizes the diversity of family structures in today's society and explicitly criticizes the narrowness of his unspoken definition, without once mentioning race as a component of this diversity. The camera, however, does, for it shows racial difference, albeit marginalized, in that there are Black and white single-parent families in her exemplary group. (Incidentally, her extended definition of the family does not reach far enough to include homosexual parents, a point to which we shall return below.)

Race and class were both recoded in Dan Quayle's speech, but were marginalized to varying degrees by the media as they recirculated it. But for recoding to be effective, it cannot erase entirely that which is recoded; traces of racism must remain, and it is these traces that enable the recoded to be recovered and the politics of its marginalization to be opposed. So, Murphy Brown's response to Dan Quayle could marginalize racial differences but not erase them: her group of exemplary single parents did contain both races, though her verbal discourse did not. An hour later, on the late evening news, many local TV stations showed Dan Quayle watching the program in the company of single mothers (not fathers), all of whom were Black. My local news in Minneapolis-St. Paul also showed a group of Democrats watching the program as a campaign fund-raiser; none of them was Black (see *Sidebar: Local News*, p. 26).

Only the camera showed racial difference explicitly. No one who spoke referred to it, neither Murphy Brown nor Dan Quayle, neither news anchors nor reporters. But perhaps they did not need to. The white conservative imagination already has a clear figure of "the welfare mother," whose race is inferred and need not be spoken (see chapter 2). Murphy Brown, single mother though she is, is upper-class and white; submerged beneath her high visibility is the much more threatening figure of the poor, Black, unwed mother who not only undermines Republican family values but squanders Republicans' tax dollars. She, not Murphy Brown, was Dan Quayle's true target.

The next day, CNN again showed Dan Quayle with his group of single mothers, and followed this with a quick shot of a Black woman at a local dem-

40   onstration who was allowed to say, "We knew that the press would come out and maybe some of the issues that we in the Black community are trying to have addressed would be addressed for a change, and most of these people have come to talk about issues other than just Murphy Brown" (see *Sidebar: CNN News*, p. 27). CNN simultaneously allowed her to speak and silenced her, for it never mentioned what those issues were, never defined the demonstration, but just left the sound bite dangling for its viewers to make of it what they would or could. The Black single mothers who formed the backdrop to Dan Quayle were never allowed to speak for themselves (neither, we might recall, was Rodney King): they were triply "minored" — as women, as single mothers, and as Blacks. Instead, insultingly, they were recruited to speak for Dan Quayle; their presence was a crude (and probably ineffective) attempt to authenticate his assertion that "Hollywood still doesn't get it, because I was never criticizing single mothers," a comment that *still* avoids mentioning their race.

    The marginalization of race by Murphy Brown, Dan Quayle, and CNN's editor is a form of "inferential racism." Herman Gray notes other liberal discursive practices that are racialized without appearing to be so in some recent television criticism.[17] One, which is particularly regrettable when it occurs, as it often does, in liberal validations of "difference" as a vital political principle, is the relegation of the specifics of contemporary racism to the "border spaces of footnotes, endnotes, asides and parenthetical statements." Another, exemplified by Mimi White's otherwise exemplary analysis of *Frank's Place*,[18] occurs when white liberal critics treat their own reading as the only one, and ignore what may be very different Black ones: "Missing [from White's analysis] is an appreciation of the different meanings which the very appearance of the show activated for African Americans."[19] White's analysis is intentionally antiracist; in it, she deplores what she sees as the show's domestication and incorporation of racial difference. The intentionality of her analysis, however, is inferentially racist, for it ignores the fact that, for African Americans, *Frank's Place* served to validate racial difference rather than domesticate it. The critic silenced African Americans in the sphere of reception as effectively as the networks did in that of production. This liberal form of inferential racism may well be the most insidious and hardest to counter, because its recoding enables those who exert it to believe sincerely in their own antiracism.

    The CNN news broadcast that similarly showed and silenced the African American woman continued the repression of race by linking the declining fortunes of the Bush campaign with a public backlash against the "family values" campaign, particularly as it had been articulated at the Republican convention by Pat Robertson and Pat Buchanan (see *Sidebar: Buchanan*, p. 56). Pat Robertson's "accusation" that Clinton planned to destroy the traditional family restated Quayle's criticism of Murphy Brown, as CNN recognized in putting the two together in this story: discursively, the voices of Pat Robertson and Dan Quayle were one voice.

CNN's choice of Buchanan's sound bite as the one to recirculate necessarily involved rejecting others. One that was not chosen was, "And Hillary has compared marriage and the family as institutions to slavery and life on an Indian reservation." This explicit linking of racial and gender politics within the meanings of the family makes overt what is strategically more effective when inferential. Buchanan's overt use of the most shameful results of racism to defend sexism could have been effective only among the most rabid Republicans: mainstream America likes its racism and sexism more modestly hidden, so CNN hid it.

Racism is always a difficult problem for whites to address, and probably there is no safe, and certainly no correct, way to do so. But I agree with Herman Gray that avoiding the issue or relegating it to a footnote helps nobody. I agree with him, too, that a critical exposure of the ways in which racism is exerted, valuable though that is, can, if that is *all* the critic provides, infer that subordinate races have no presence other than that of victim. Such an inference is one against which we white liberals have to be constantly on guard, for we are prone to it: in this chapter, for instance, I have analyzed some strategies of racism, but have paid no attention to the tactical ways that subordinated races have devised of dealing with those strategies, an omission I shall rectify later. It is whites who originated and who practice racism, but the analysis of its operations and the attempts to find ways of mitigating it must be multiracial. Liberal whites who address the problem from their point of view alone, however antiracist their intention, inferentially repress and devalue what it is that the oppressed bring to the struggles against it.

Whiteness

Whiteness is where racism originates, and the three events around which this book is organized not only revealed racist strategies, but also, in varying degrees, put whiteness into crisis. They were sites where whiteness rushed to reconstitute itself and rebuild its defenses. My analysis of this process will at times appear speculative, because it begins from the observation that there is (almost) nothing to analyze, for a key strategy of whiteness is to avoid definition and explicit presence. As George Lipsitz points out, "Whiteness is everywhere in American culture, but it is very hard to see."[20] So what we have to analyze is why, for the likes of Dan Quayle, whiteness was never one of the constituent elements of the events in South-Central, whereas the Blackness of the "broken family" was. And we have to understand its strategic absence from the issues that Murphy Brown and Rush Limbaugh chose to recirculate as they struggled over the meanings of Quayle's speech. The way that the white media kept whiteness out the mainstream debates around and public understanding of these events parallels the way in which, in the first "Rodney King trial," the white defense turned the focus of the investigation away from the behavior of the police (white) and onto the behavior of Rodney King (Black).

42   When Clarence Thomas likened the hearings to a lynching, he brought whiteness perilously close to visibility, and consequently, many whites rushed to
disqualify the term by arguing that no Black man had ever been lynched for
abusing a Black woman. Some African Americans agreed with this, but others,
including many who were opposed to Thomas's nomination, understood, as
did he, that the hearings did indeed constitute a lynching, in which the perpe-
trators were the white Senate and the white media, and the victims were all
African Americans.

The understanding of whiteness that informs this book is that it is not an essential racial category that contains a set of fixed meanings, but a strategic deployment of power. It comprises the construction and occupation of a centralized
space from which to view the world, and from which to operate in the world. This
space of whiteness contains a limited but varied set of normalizing positions from
which that which is not white can be made into the abnormal; by such means
whiteness constitutes itself as a universal set of norms by which to make sense of
the world. When faced with a crisis—that is, a situation that demands solution—
whiteness can withdraw into its self-constructed normality and never question its
assumption that the abnormal—that is, that which threatens whiteness—is what
must change in order to resolve the crisis. Constructing and occupying the space
of whiteness, then, is simultaneously constitutive of the viewer-occupier, the process of viewing, and that which is viewed.

Whiteness is not an essence but a power whose techniques differ according
to the conditions of its application. The most common can be cataloged, though
not exhaustively, for new techniques will always be developed to meet new
conditions. Currently, however, the catalog must include the techniques of exnomination, normalization, and universalization, which in practice are never
separate, but are put to work in various combinations.

Exnomination is the means by which whiteness avoids being named and
thus keeps itself out of the field of interrogation and therefore off the agenda
for change. Using the term *whiteness* is in itself a move to counter this strategy,
and is thus, in my judgment, worth doing, despite the risk that the word itself
may tend to essentialize and homogenize the phenomenon in a way that runs
counter to my argument. One practice of exnomination is the avoidance of self-
recognition and self-definition. Defining, for whites, is a process that is always
directed outward upon multiple "others," but never inward upon the definer.
Drawing definitional lines around the identities of "others" constructs for
whiteness the powerful and naturalized status of being, simply, not the other.
If whiteness can maintain itself as a space delineated only by its differences
from that which it is not, then the social interests that can be exerted from
within this space can avoid the interrogation that definition makes possible.

This refusal of definition is crucial to the process of "othering" that has long
been recognized as a key white strategy of colonialization. Edward Said, for example, shows how "European culture gained in strength and identity by setting

itself off against the Orient as a sort of surrogate and even underground self."[21]   43
He argues that European "othering" of the Orient worked through a "strategic
formation" of texts and representations to construct the "strategic location" of
Westernness from which to view it.[22] Said's account of the Westernness deployed
through and constructed by Orientalism might also describe whiteness in general:
"[It] depends for its strategy upon this flexible *positional* superiority, which puts
the Westerner in a whole series of possible relationships with the Orient without
ever losing him the relative upper hand."[23] An "undergound self" with the "upper hand" is a particularly evocative definition of whiteness.

In *Playing in the Dark: Whiteness and the Literary Imagination*, Toni Morrison
gives a generally similar account of whiteness to Said's, but argues that it takes
a particular form in the United States. What she calls "American Africanism"
played a key role in the "self-conscious but highly problematic construction of
the American as a new white man."[24] Africanism did for the white American
what Orientalism did for the Westerner—it constructed the "other" from
which whiteness could understand itself as different. Africanism is "a fabri-
cated brew of darkness, otherness, alarm and desire that is uniquely American"[25] and that serves as "the vehicle by which the American self knows itself
as not enslaved, but free; not repulsive, but desirable; not helpless but licensed
and powerful; not history-less, but historical; not damned but innocent; not a
blind accident of evolution, but a progressive fulfillment of destiny."[26]

Dan Quayle's speech on Los Angeles provides a plethora of examples of
whiteness universalizing its norms (see *Sidebar: Dan Quayle*, p. 68). He begins
his account of black poverty with statistics on the comparative absence of Black
fathers and of the illegitimacy rate among Black mothers, and concludes, "Nature abhors a vacuum. Where there are no mature, responsible men around to
teach boys how to be good men, gangs serve in their place." By "othering"
Blackness into immaturity, irresponsibility, and gang membership, he exnom-
inates whiteness as the space from which to make sense of it and then mobilizes Nature (and the laws of physics) to universalize the process of othering
(that is, of normalization and abnormalization) by which whiteness constitutes
itself. Whiteness is the space from which words like "no mature responsible
men" can be made to make sense of both the nonwhite "riots" and the whiteness that is making that sense.

Similar processes are at work as Buchanan concludes his account of L.A.
(see *Sidebar: Buchanan*, p. 56):

> Greater love than this hath no man than that he lay down his life for
> his friend. Here were nineteen-year-old boys ready to lay down their
> lives to stop a mob from molesting old people they did not even
> know. And as those boys took back the streets of Los Angeles, block
> by block, my friends, we must take back our cities, and take back

our culture, and take back our country. God bless you, and God bless America.

Whiteness constitutes itself as the universal *"man* who hath no greater love," and encompasses within itself everything that the "mob" of others is not. In different contexts whiteness can universalize itself into Americanness or into humanity in general (the "you" and the "America" that God will bless). This undefined, amorphous whiteness is momentarily stabilized in Buchanan's speech as the point whence Black behavior can be understood as simultaneously non-American and nonhuman, but it can achieve this only by evacuating itself both from the formative conditions within which the behavior occurs and from the process of constructing that behavior as Black. Whiteness cannot be part of the problem, or part of the solution, because it is not even "there," and its absence allows the "problem" to be defined as monochromatically "Black."

Similarly, in the currents of meaning swirling around "today's woman," marriage, and single mothers, whiteness is the signifying absence. Traces of it, however, remain. They can be seen, for example, in Quayle's articulating together Murphy Brown "bearing a child alone" and the two-thirds of Black children "born to never-married mothers"; they can be glimpsed, too, in Buchanan's charges that "Hillary has compared marriage and the family as institutions to slavery and life on an Indian reservation." Here his implicit definition of "normal" marriage as "white" comes close to becoming explicit and thus making its whiteness fully visible. Buchanan and Quayle abnormalize Murphy Brown and Hillary Rodham Clinton into faintly but adequately racialized others, in opposition to whom "family values" can be made both universal and white. The fact that both of them have white skins underscores the strategic nature of Buchanan's "whiteness" that casts white-skinned women who cross the boundary into the abnormalized other as contaminators of the white purity that the boundary protects.

Omi and Winant suggest that essentialist racism, in which whites see themselves as inherently superior to Blacks, was an early form of U.S. racism that has now been superseded by others.[27] But our history is never left behind us, and on the right wing of our society at least, traces of racial essentialism can be seen in conservative deployments of whiteness. When Quayle locates the causes of the high incidence of single Black motherhood in the absence of "family values/morality" in Black America, he denies any white role in the structuring conditions that produce the phenomenon. This evacuation of whiteness and its social conditions implies that the lack of values among African Americans can be explained only in terms of the essential inferiority of Blacks to whites. The exnomination of whiteness always allows the "abnormality/inferiority" of its racialized others to be essentialized: if whiteness does not "exist" it cannot be responsible for the differences produced by the boundary it draws around its space, and these differences must therefore be essential to those others in which they are located and whose 45 otherness they define.

One of the reasons whiteness can be so effectively kept invisible and off the agenda for interrogation is the ease with which it can be deployed along other axes of power and through other discourses. The three most active of these are sexuality, economics, and maturity. Whiteness is particularly adept at sexualizing racial difference, and thus constructing its others as sites of savage sexuality; the Black man and the Black woman are victims of this hypersexualization of the other, and, as the next two chapters will trace, both Anita Hill and Rodney King were subject to it. The Black racial theorist Cress Welsing argues that the white sexualization of racial difference derives from the fact that whiteness is carried by a recessive gene, and if whites allowed interracial breeding, the white race would become extinct (see chapter 4). The Black male, with his threat to the race's genetic survival, thus becomes magnified into a figure of immense sexual prowess, whose lynching/castration is therefore a defense of the white race rather than an assault on the Black. Similarly, but obversely, the hypersexualization of the Black female is mobilized as an alibi for the long history of her sexual abuse by the white male. The white female, in her purity and vulnerability, is thus made to symbolize the white social order under a racial threat. Deeply inscribed in the white imagination is the figure of this white female captured by the male "other," whose savage masculinity symbolizes the intensity of the threat, and whose race is determined by the central antagonism of the time. Thus, when the West was being conquered the figure of the white woman captured by the Indian appeared frequently in journalism, fiction, and painting, and then World War II brought us propaganda images of the same white woman being carried off naked by a grinning Japanese soldier.[28] This hypersexualization of race is strategic, for it permits whites to view their racial assault upon the other as no more than a defense of their own position. White racism, then, is cast not as imperialist, but defensive. The jury agreed that the white police were not assaulting Rodney King, but were defending themselves and white society against the threat that he posed.

Economic, or class, differences are also racialized. In the United States members of other races are kept in low-paying jobs and thus in the lower classes, and many are yet more comprehensively othered by being confined to an "underclass," whose very name identifies them as under, rather than part of, the white social order. The racial othering of the body of labor, upon which slavery depended, has continued under global capitalism as the "third" world has been made into the working class of the "first." Economic racism is rampant in Los Angeles, and here, as elsewhere, is a particularly effective deployment of whiteness, for it mobilizes the workings of a "free" labor market in a meritocracy to provide whites with economic "proof" of the inferiority of the other.

Less explicitly, but still extensively, whites recode racial difference into comparative maturity, so that their societies can be understood as mature and fully

46 developed and the "third" world as "developing," or immature. The most widely used word to describe other races—*minority*—is also used to mean juvenility, and its opposite—*majority*—means both numerical superiority and maturity. The infantilization of the other results from a form of racial Darwinism that constructs whiteness as the evolutionary goal to which others will "naturally" develop, and thus decisively implies that whiteness is properly unchanging, whereas otherness will and must change to more closely approximate it. Racial Darwinism can also result, in its more extreme forms, in the animalization of the other, to which Rodney King was constantly subjected. In its more benign forms, infantilizing the other can produce a liberal, paternalist form of racism.

At different times, then, American Indians, Japanese, and African Americans have all been put into white discourse as savage, infantile, and hypersexual, and thus as "the primitive." The absence of any racial specificity from this construction of an other that exists only as not-white works as a strategy of discursive domination to hinder, if not prevent, any other from forming an identity that is a product of its own history and under its own control, but allows it only to identify itself in relation to the dominant whiteness. One of the aims of identity politics is to disarticulate the identity of a subaltern racial formation from its long history of white domination and othering, and to rearticulate it with its nonwhite history and thus to establish its relations with other subaltern racial formations in ways that are not controlled by and do not serve the interests of dominating whiteness.

But the process of othering by which whiteness defines and deploys itself involves more than distancing and inscribing lines of difference, for the fascination of whiteness with its others points to a desire for that which it has forbidden, an anxiety that it may have purified itself into sterility. The paradox that whiteness deploys its power so relentlessly and extensively and yet remains so terrified of its others may be explained in part by this fascination for the other, the fear and the hope that traces of otherness have not been expunged completely from the space of whiteness.

Despite its long history of fortifying its base, whiteness is still driven by fear: whiteness is terrified, and underneath its multiaxial deployments we can trace the fear of the other, the fear of retribution for its history of domination. The nature of this fear is changing in the post-civil rights United States and in postcolonial European nations, whose increasing multiethnicity means that the other is now next door, the other is within.[29] Under these conditions, the problem of identifying and monitoring the other causes greater anxiety than when the other was down in the plantation or away in the colony. To cope with this proximity, whites have been eager to develop a technologized means of othering—that of surveillance. Surveillance is the power to know without being known, to see without being seen, and is ideally suited to deployment from the undefined position of superiority from which whiteness operates. Foucault might as well be describing whiteness when he writes, "The perfect disciplinary apparatus would make it possible for a single gaze to see everything constantly. A central point would be both the source of light illuminating everything and a locus of convergence for everything that must be known."[30]

Because racial difference is so readily visible, the video camera has become a strategic weapon in the white arsenal, although, like any weapon, it can be captured and turned against its inventors. Racial struggles now, and, I believe, increasingly, must involve the struggle over surveillance. The surveillance camera played a central role in the events in Los Angeles, the television camera showed the racial dimension of the Clarence Thomas hearings, and it prevented racial difference from being totally erased from the Murphy Brown-Dan Quayle debate. The video camera, whether used openly in the mass media or more covertly in nonmediated surveillance, is proving supremely efficient in ensuring the visibility of the other. But technology does not determine the uses to which it is put, and video guerrillas are devising ways of turning it upon whiteness and making that visible. In the mass media, too, its all-seeingness can be expropriated by the subaltern to make racial difference overt when whiteness would prefer to keep it covert; its use in surveillance, on the other hand, makes such resistant reversals of the politics of seeing harder, if not impossible, to achieve, and in the final chapter I trace some instances and implications of the racialization of surveillance.

The race relations upon which this book focuses are primarily those between white and Black, though my account of the events in L.A. does refer to the intersubaltern race relations among African Americans, Korean Americans, and Latino/as. I justify this focus both because the public discourse of race around the hearings, the L.A. uprisings, and the "family values" debate was dominated by signs of Blackness and also because, to whites, Blackness distills and concentrates the fear of otherness, the fear of what the African American educator Joyce King calls "nigger chaos."[31] This sociosexual disorder that looms so darkly in the white imaginary is embodied in the Black American. My argument is becoming speculative here, but in this white imaginary the machismo of the Latino male does not appear to threaten the white female and thus white society to the extent that Black potency does; in it, also, the threat of the American Indian male to the white woman captive has lost much of the resonance that it once had, and the Asian American male has been so feminized as to offer no threat at all. Similarly, although both the Latina and the Asian woman are sexualized by whiteness, their sexualization is less threatening and less "hyper" than that of the Black female, and the American Indian woman signifies only by her absence. While in this riskily speculative mode, we might also wonder if the hearings would have caught the white imagination so intensely if Anita Hill and Clarence Thomas had been Latino/a, Asian, or American Indian.

Whiteness survives only because of its ability to define, monitor, and police the boundary between itself and its others and to control any movement across

48   it. Because its space is strategic and not essential, there is movement into and
out of whiteness: "today's women," for example, however white skinned, can,
on occasion, be excluded, and those with pigmented skins, such as Korean
store owners in South-Central L.A., can be included—as Buchanan did—if
only temporarily. Its space is accessible by invitation only, and the occasions
when others can be invited in are carefully selected, and limited in both extent
and time. Both Clarence Thomas and Korean store owners could be invited in,
on a temporary and limited basis, but only insofar as the invitation could secure the boundary that they were apparently crossing. Some, at least, of the
Koreans in South-Central regret having accepted the invitation, because white
behavior in the uprising showed how easily they could be pushed out the door
back among the others, where they were unwelcome because they had been
tinted white (see chapter 3).

Whiteness is a space of positions, not a fixed point, and there can be conflict
among them: whiteness is not homogeneous. Its deployments discussed above
are conservative ones; they are the most overt and thus the easiest to analyze.
Liberal deployments are much subtler, harder to analyze, and harder to evaluate, for they may contain potentialities, however faint, for change. In her
analysis of ways in which white women talk about race, Ruth Frankenberg
identifies color evasion and power evasion as among the more common.[32] She
sees this as a performance of the liberal humanist cliché that "we are all sisters
under the skin." The problems with this color blindness, or rather evasion of
racial difference, are, first, that it allows whites to ignore the history of power
that has constructed racial difference to their advantage, and second, that it allows whites to accept pigmented people as "normal" only by ignoring the color
difference and thus bracketing off whiteness. Murphy Brown's group of single
parents is visibly composed of two races, but her "color blindness," her implicit assumption that they are all the same under the skin, makes it all too easy
for white liberals to deny the existence of white power and privilege in their
perception of a common humanity, and thus implicitly to accept the normativ-
ity of that humanity as white. The same power-evasive color blindness can be
seen behind white liberal responses to the Huxtable family in *The Cosby Show*
such as those that Lewis records: "When quizzed about the Huxtables' race,
. . . one person put it 'you can't notice it at all.' . . . 'You lose track of it,' said
[another] woman, 'because they're so average.' "[33] Lewis traces this color
blindness back to a universalization process that we have identified as a practice of whiteness.

Michael Eric Dyson tells of the danger signals he sees whenever he hears a
discussion of race turn to universal "human beings"; when he hears a Black
sports star such as Michael Jordan ask to be seen not as Black and not as white
but just as "a person," he knows that in a culture structured by dominant
whiteness such a desire can only disconnect that person from Black interests
and ally him or her with white ones. Such erasures of racial difference and

power difference stem from a failure to understand "the differences between enabling versions of human experience that transcend the exclusive gaze of race and disenabling visions of human community that seek race neutrality."[34] Mbanna Kantako also recognizes the danger of allowing the power differences between Blacks and whites to be submerged into a notion of their common humanity: on Black Liberation Radio he consistently foregrounds the difference but inverts the norms by which it works—for him, whites are minority, less than 7 percent of the world's population; the normative humanity is Black, and whites, by their history of unrelenting cruelty to Black people, have defined themselves out of it so that whiteness is antihuman. When Sister Adwba gives listeners her account of the L.A. uprisings (see chapter 3), she reminds them that the original humans were Black and that therefore they should teach their children to spell the word "hueman." These Black refusals to allow color-power difference to be evaded recognize the whiteness of evading it, and support Frankenberg's claim that "color blindness, despite the best intentions of its [white] adherents, in this sense preserves the power structure inherent in essentialist racism."[35] While concluding that color evasion and power evasion finally produce a "white self innocent of racism,"[36] Frankenberg does recognize the ambivalence of these evasions, albeit an asymmetrical one—while averting white gaze from the harsh realities of power difference, they still assert a common cross-racial humanity that may, when eyes are fully open, serve as the basis for interracial alliances.

The eagerness with which whites avoid naming their whiteness is matched by the eagerness of African Americans to name it. bell hooks calls it "the terrible, the terrifying" and whites "terrorists,"[37] and Cress Welsing explains it as a constant overcompensation for whites' genetic and numerical inferiority (see below). Mbanna Kantako reverses both animalization and primitivism: for him whiteness is the "beast" that his people have to confront every day of their lives, and those whites who deploy it are "cavemen" or "cavewomen" in recognition of the fact that because the original civilizations of this planet were Black the whiteness that differs from their norms must therefore be of the Stone Age. Following Malcolm X, he also calls whiteness "the Devil," reversing the connotative link of black with evil and white with good. He is clear, however, that both whiteness and Blackness are strategic and not essential: "I have no white friends," he says, "but many of my friends have white skins," and he refers to African Americans who do not behave Black as "Afro-Saxons," a term that neatly encapsulates the whitening of Blackness. These Black nominations of whiteness abnormalize and deuniversalize it in ways that counter directly its key deployment by whites.

While arguing that whiteness is better identified by what it *does* than by what it *is*, and by defining it as a flexible positionality from which power operates, we must not forget that people with white skins have massively disproportionate access to that power base. While not essentializing whiteness into

50 white skins, or Blackness into Black ones, we must recognize that whiteness uses skin color as an identity card by which to see where its interests may best be promoted and its rewards distributed. Whiteness may not be precisely co-terminous with white skin, but white skins embody it best, and, indeed, whites would not have constructed the invisible and exclusive space of white-ness if most people with their skin color could not benefit from occupying it.

Liberal deployments of whiteness often treat its boundaries as permeable, so that liberal whites may cross them at will and enter the space of the other, where they will often expect their crossing and weakening of the boundary to earn them a welcome. Movement that crosses boundaries and enables one to enter the space of others and to form alliances with them is clearly crucial, but the politics of such movement depends upon its motivation and the control of its direction: if the movement *into* is the result of an invitation and not an in-trusion, however friendly, and if a reciprocal movement is equally invited, then interracial alliances may be formed. Alliances will not be formed, how-ever, if the entry is that of the missionary, whose sincerity and desire to help the other may not be in question, but who assumes the right of uninvited en-try, and who reserves to him- or herself the right to define what constitutes "help" and who is the proper provider of it. Hall's "inferential racism" is often exerted by liberals who genuinely want to mitigate the problem and who feel a sincere guilt both at the unearned benefits that a racist society has granted them and denied others and at their own responsibility, not as individuals but as whites, for the historical development of racism. The white liberal assump-tion that, as "we" are the cause of the problem "we" must provide the solu-tion, can result in a form of inferential racism driven by "white guilt" that can, at its worst, exclude the victims of oppression from the processes of analyzing it and of devising ways to combat it.

One of the informing assumptions of this book is that culture always has material dimensions, and that, consequently, power is put to work in both do-mains. In an important paper, George Lipsitz traces ways in which "possessive investment in whiteness" has worked throughout the history of the white oc-cupation of North America to secure the material dimension of white suprem-acy.[38] This materiality consisted of both the power to control place and eco-nomic power, and its historical effects were often most marked when the two came together in the same operation. A key example of this is provided by the Federal Housing Administration, which, in the years after World War II, sys-tematically channeled housing loans away from inner-city areas to white sub-urbs. But the FHA is not alone: Lipsitz lists example after distressing example of economic and property development policies and decisions that effectively ensured that African Americans were granted severely limited opportunities to own property and acquire capital—conditions that exist fundamentally un-changed today. As a result, African Americans have been, and to a large extent still are, reduced to wage dependency, and the deregulation of Reaganomics intensified the lack of security inherent in the condition. Even within such an insecure position in the labor market, a form of economic racism depressed their opportunities even further, for, as Lipsitz puts it,

> In the post-World War II era, trade unions refused to fight for full employment, universal medical care and old age pensions, or for an end to discriminatory hiring practices. Instead, they negotiated contract provisions giving private medical coverage, pensions and job security largely to the mostly white organized workers in mass production industries.[39]

We shall see in chapter 3 how the residents of the ghettos of South-Central Los Angeles did not experience them as communities because they were denied property ownership and any control over their economies, and that the uprisings were in part an expression of this sense of material deprivation and of the desire to change it. The blindingly white light of the mainstream media, however, showed none of this, for to recognize it explicitly would bring the whiteness that produced it into the visibility that whiteness shuns. But whiteness cannot ignore totally the material differences between its position and that of its others, for the difference is crucial to its identity: it must, however, make the difference operate at the level of naturalized, unnoticed common sense and not in the white light of a "social problem." CNN, then, in discussing the fear that the unrest might spread, could use a discourse that "naturally" called the (Black) places where it originated "areas," and those (white ones) to which it might spread "communities." The racialized difference between "community" and "area" provides an example of what Toni Morrison calls "race talk, the explicit insertion into everyday life of racial signs and symbols that have no meaning other than pressing African Americans to the lowest level of the racial hierarchy."[40]

In their quite different ways, the three media events whose stories I tell in this book all put whiteness into crisis. In the family quarrel that Dan Quayle picked with Murphy Brown whiteness was largely successful in keeping itself unnoticed; it tried hard to achieve the same invisibility in the Clarence Thomas–Anita Hill hearings, but African Americans brought it to the surface and refused to allow the hearings to remain a deracialized story of gender conflict. Similarly, in the L.A. uprisings, the mainstream media, most of the politicians, and all of the police and National Guard strove mightily to confine the causes, the effects, and the manifestations of the crisis to Black America and to confine white America to the roles of baffled victim and benevolent helper. But all of their discursive and material power could not quell the white fear that is symptomatic of the white crisis. This crisis has many causes, symptoms, and effects, some of which will be analyzed below, but the one to which I wish to draw attention here is the very material and inescapable one of demographic change.

Demography can never live up to its claims of being scientific; rather, it is the art of guesstimation, and demographers will always differ in their scenarios

52 for the future, and, in particular, their projections of the speed at which demographic changes will occur. But all agree that the demographic balance of this country is changing radically and rapidly. One study suggests that in the lifetimes of most of my students, European Americans will cease to form the majority of the population and that the United States will consist of three roughly equally numerous groups of European Americans, African Americans, and Latino/as, with a fourth, slightly smaller, mixed group of Asian Americans, Native Americans, and others.[41] Other studies suggest that this is an exaggeration, and that it will be the second half of the next century before whites will become a minority, but they agree with the direction and inevitability of the change.[42] Currently, European Americans constitute close to 80 percent of the population, so the change, from our point of view, will be dramatic. It is also well under way: in Los Angeles, for example, European Americans are no longer the majority, and by the year 2000 the same will be true for California as a whole.[43] Demographic changes, however, are always faster by far than changes in the regime of power; the gap between the two is where racial antagonism will increase and the crisis of whiteness will intensify.

　　If we wish to defuse one, we shall have to defuse both together, for they are mutually inextricable. The process will be fraught with difficulty, for it will involve whiteness making itself as visible as any other color; it will involve whiteness seeing itself as part of the problem and not as the position from which the problem must be solved; and it will involve whiteness changing its relation to Americans of other ethnic origins, and thus both its own identity and its sense of what being American involves. Martha Farnsworth Riche, director of policy studies at the Population Reference Bureau, makes the point simply when she writes, "Without fully realizing it, we have left the time when the nonwhite, non-Western part of our population could be expected to assimilate to the dominant majority. In the future, the white, Western majority will have to do some assimilation of its own."[44] The change may be easily described, but it will be difficult and painful to achieve, for we whites have no history of assimilating or adapting to those we have designed as inferior others; indeed, our whole global history has been of inducing them to assimilate to us. And the task is made harder by powerful conservative voices arguing against it in all social domains; it is made harder by the rapid construction of white enclaves, both material and discursive/mental, by which to confine the inevitable changes to the "other" America; and it is made harder by white fear that is based partly upon white guilt and partly upon reluctance or inability to understand those whom whiteness has othered. Reactionary whiteness is making changes harder and is unnecessarily magnifying its own crisis.

　　There are also more liberal positions within whiteness that are occupied by those who wish to make changes but are uncertain how to go about it. It is from such a position that I have written this book. We know now that the liberal "missionary" role that preached the equality of all while refusing to listen is not the one to adopt, for the changes it promoted were always of "them" to "us." In the hope that correcting the refusal to listen may help us devise means of white assimilation, I have tried to discover a little of what we can learn from listening to some voices of the racially oppressed, particularly those of African Americans, in order to learn something of what it feels like to live in those conditions. This book is, in part, an attempt to extend whatever it is I have heard a little further into white society. If we white liberals are to contribute usefully to mitigating the worst of the savagery of racism, I believe that our attempts must be based upon whatever we can learn of what racism feels like to those who suffer it. We can never contribute usefully by looking only at our own white guilt; the experience of those who benefit from and exert racism, even without wanting to, can never provide an adequate basis for solutions to it— the best it can do is provide the motivation to search for them. The oppressed know far better than even the most reluctant and self-critical of the oppressors what needs to be done to oppose oppression in the immediate conditions and specific forms by which it bears upon them. Those conditions and forms lie outside our experience, yet some understanding of them, however incomplete, is the essential prerequisite of any contribution toward modifying them. White liberals must continue to "help" the racially oppressed in whatever ways we can, but we must neither define the nature of that "help" nor control the terms upon which it is "offered." We must wait to be invited into interracial alliances and behave in them as guests.

But we must not wait at all in opposing the conservative and more overt forms of racism that are deployed from different positions within the whiteness that is ours as well. The effects of white guilt can be positive when they are directed against strategies that increase it: we may not be able to avoid sharing whiteness with the likes of Pat Buchanan, but we must do everything in our power to obstruct and oppose their deployment of it to increase racial inequality and thus our guilt.

Abortion and Family Values

Currents of gender constantly swirl around those of race in the "family values" campaign, and inevitably bring to the surface the topic of abortion. CNN's account of the Dan-Murphy debate and the Republican convention slides effortlessly from family values into abortion, bringing to the surface something that both Dan and Murphy wished to keep unspoken.

Like race, abortion is a socially difficult topic, but the difficulty is of a different type: rather than avoiding confronting people with their own racism, what has to be avoided is taking a position in a way that would allow those on the other side to transfer their opposition to the holder of that position. When Murphy Brown decided to have a baby, abortion was ruled out as an option for her (and for some women this exclusion detracted from the progressiveness of the

54   way in which she discussed the pros and cons of single mothering). Abortion is generally a taboo topic on prime-time TV (on daytime, of course, TV taboos exist only to be broken), because advertisers and sponsors dare not offend either side of the debate and risk this offense being transferred to their products (*Cagney & Lacey* is the one well-known exception).[45]

Pro-choice and pro-life are positions that do not coincide precisely with political party lines, and the 1992 presidential campaign was in its late stages before either party unequivocally positioned itself on one side or the other. The problem was particularly acute for the Republicans, for although their religious right was the political home base of the pro-lifers, there were many pro-choice Republican women. Like Murphy Brown, the leading players preferred to keep quiet about the issue, and, when that proved impossible, to handle it circumspectly. But the issue could not be avoided altogether, for some of the bitterest social confrontations of the Bush-Reagan period occurred on the steps of abortion clinics. It was a problem for politicians because political analysts could give only conflicting advice: for those involved it was the most important issue facing the nation, but their alignments over abortion did not coincide with political party alignments; many of the noninvolved, however, were fed up with the attention the issue was getting and wished to turn their thoughts elsewhere. Exit polls confirmed this: Catholics divided their votes among Clinton, Bush, and Perot in almost the same proportions as the electorate as a whole, and only 10 percent of voters considered abortion to be important at all.[46]

The highly charged, highly conflicted nature of this topic meant that its social circulation was full of contradictions: here I wish to trace some of the movement of the abortion current as it swirls and eddies around Clarence Thomas and Anita Hill, Murphy Brown and Dan Quayle, Bill Clinton and George Bush. In the Dan-Murphy debate, abortion was for the most part kept below the surface, although the *New York Times* did carry comments from Diane English, Dan Quayle, and Marlin Fitzwater that made the topic explicit (see *Sidebar: The* New York Times, p. 23). One must also wonder about the frequent and at times italicized use of the word "choice" by both the protagonists, particularly in the phrase used by both, though accented quite differently, "lifestyle choice." In the articulation of "family values" with L.A., abortion was not a foregrounded issue, but when "family values" are articulated with Republican social policy in general, it necessarily pokes its head above the surface. Like the *New York Times* story, CNN's report (see *Sidebar: CNN News*, p. 27) also brings together Murphy Brown, Dan Quayle, Pat Buchanan, and the Republican convention and campaign, as sites where the abortion and family values currents intermingle. Less explicitly, Rush Limbaugh also articulated Murphy Brown's single motherhood with abortion: as he replaced Murphy's words with his own he used a common symbol in the antiabortion rhetoric—the trash can where abortionists are said to dump their murdered fetuses was rhetorically similar to the one in which Murphy was supposedly about to dump her baby. What "they" do in abortion

clinics is the same as what "they" do when "they" have their babies out of   55
wedlock (the gender repressiveness in the roots of the word encourages conservatives to use it freely).

Dan Quayle's speech to the Republican convention is linked to his speech on
L.A. not only by the fact that *he* spoke both, but by their titles: "Restoring Basic
Values: Strengthening the Family" (on L.A.) and "The Family Comes First: We
Cannot Take Orders from Special Interests" (to the convention). In the conven-
tion speech, he reiterated his respect for single parents in a discursive conjunc-
ture of God, family, and adoption that silently encoded an anti-choice position:

> Marilyn and I have tried to teach our children these values, like faith
> in God, love of family, and appreciation of freedom. We have also
> taught them about family issues like adoption. My parents adopted
> twins when I was ten years old. We've taught our children to respect
> single parents and their challenges—challenges that faced my
> grandmother many years ago, and my own sister today.

As a leading player in this drama, Dan Quayle could be no more overt in his
abortion stance than Murphy Brown in hers. As an extra, however, Pat Buchanan
was under no such restraint. Although he failed in his challenge to George Bush
for the Republican presidential nomination, he did win three million Republican
votes, so the scriptwriters had to treat him as a major minor character, and they
gave him the convention's opening speech (see *Sidebar: Buchanan*, p. 56). In it he
explicitly aligned himself and the Republican party with the right to life position
on four separate occasions. Pro-life, family values, and the L.A. riots are all associated together in his speech, and set in opposition to Bill and Hillary Clinton and,
through her, to Murphy Brown. He also brings Clarence Thomas into the picture
through his references to the Supreme Court, *Roe v. Wade*, and Clinton's so-called
litmus test for Supreme Court justices. Clarence Thomas's position on the validity
of the *Roe v. Wade* decision that granted the right to abortion was a central issue in
his original confirmation hearings. It was the point around which much of the
most vehement opposition to his confirmation was organized, and Republican
supporters were able to call it the "litmus test" that Democrats used to measure
the eligibility of a Supreme Court nominee.

This discursive conjuncture resurfaced four months later, when, on his first
day as president, Clinton signed executive orders repealing restrictions placed
on abortion rights by Presidents Bush and Reagan. This day was also the twentieth anniversary of the Supreme Court's *Roe v. Wade* decision, and he signed
the orders to the sounds of 75,000 pro-life marchers outside the White House,
some of whom carried banners that read, "Buchanan for 1996." (These banners
were nowhere mentioned in press accounts, but they were clearly visible in
ABC's telecast—another occasion when the camera carried discursive traces
that the word processor did not.)

Buchanan

The Election Is About Who We Are: Taking Back Our Country

by Pat Buchanan, Presidential Candidate and Columnist

Delivered at the Republican National Convention, Houston, Texas, August 17, 1992

... George Bush is a defender of right to life, and a champion of the Judeo-Christian values upon which this America was founded. Mr. Clinton, however, has a different agenda. At its top is unregulated, unrestricted abortion on demand.

... A militant leader of the homosexual rights movement could rise at [the Democratic] convention and say, "Bill Clinton and Al Gore represent the most pro-lesbian and pro-gay ticket in history." And so they do.

... And Hillary has compared marriage and the family as institutions to slavery and life on an Indian reservation.

Well, speak for yourself, Hillary.

Friends, my friends, this is radical feminism. The agenda that Clinton and Clinton would impose on America — abortion on demand, a litmus test for the Supreme Court, homosexual rights, discrimination against religious schools, women in combat units — that's change, all right. That's not the kind of change America needs. It's not the kind of change America wants. And it is not the kind of change we can abide in a nation that we still call God's country. ...

... And there were the brave people of Koreatown who took the worst of those L.A. riots, but still live the family values we treasure, and who still believe deeply in the American dream.

Friends, in those wonderful twenty-five weeks of our campaign, the saddest days were the days of that riot in L.A., the worst riot in American history. But out of that awful tragedy can come a message of hope.

Hours after that awful tragedy can come a message of hope.

Hours after that riot ended I went down to the Army compound in south Los Angeles, where I met the troopers of the 18th Cavalry who had come to save the city of Los Angeles. An officer of the 18th Cav said, "Mr. Buchanan, I want you to talk to a couple of our troopers." And I went over and met these young fellas. They couldn't have been twenty years old, and they recounted their story.

They had come into Los Angeles late in the evening of the second day, when the rioting was still going on, and two of them walked up a dark street, where the mob had burned and looted every building on the block but one, a convalescent home for the aged. And the mob was headed in to ransack and loot the apartments of the terrified old men and women inside. The troopers came up the street, M-16s at the ready, and the mob threatened and cursed, but the mob retreated because it had met the one thing that could stop it: force, rooted in justice, and backed by moral courage.

Greater love than this hath no man than that he lay down his life for his friend. Here were nineteen-year-old boys ready to lay down their lives to stop a mob from molesting old people they did not even know. And as those boys took back the streets of Los Angeles, block by block, my friends, we must take back our cities, and take back our culture, and take back our country.

God bless you, and God bless America.

The eddies and swirls repeat themselves. Abortion rights, women's rights, 57 Anita Hill, Quayle, and the Clintons came together yet again at the American Bar Association's 1992 Convention (see *Sidebar: Today's Legal Women,* p. 30), where, significantly, they joined homosexual rights (the topic of the next section). The Republican convention moved to the right and the ABA convention to the left, so each articulation of these issues and their protagonists "spoke" differently—eddies may reverse direction while carrying the same debris.

These constant if uneven discursive currents swirled around a limited cast of public figures and a limited set of locations; in them, meanings of family values and abortion were so intermingled that it was impossible to cleanse one of the silt of the other. Similarly, the discourses of gender, class, and race could not be separated out from one another, though at times the swirls of one could be made more apparent than the eddies of the others.

Gay and Lesbian Issues

The *New York Times* may have taken a day longer than other papers to realize that Dan Quayle's attack on Murphy Brown was the hottest issue in his speech, but the extra twenty-four hours allowed it to recognize that the clash stirred up many of the key issues in the election campaign and brought them, if not to high visibility, at least close to the surface. Abortion was one, gay and lesbian rights was another (see *Sidebar: The* New York Times, p. 23).

One of Clinton's campaign promises was to repeal the law discriminating against gays and lesbians in the military. To show support for them, and to win their votes, the Democrats invited gays and lesbians onto their convention platform. The Republicans, on the other hand, applauded as Pat Buchanan inveighed against "the amoral idea that gay and lesbian couples should have the same standing in law as married couples." Calling the Clinton-Gore ticket the most pro-lesbian and pro-gay one in history, he trumpeted the homophobia of the right as he defended his version of family values against all the missiles the Democrats were launching against them (see *Sidebar: Buchanan,* p. 56).

Homosexuality and homophobia cause mainstream Americans immense anxiety, with the result that overt references to either are typically repressed from public or popular discourse, except, of course, when they are the subject of a news report. In entertainment they are repressed as efficiently as references to abortion, and for similar reasons. Murphy Brown was no exception: the exemplary group she introduced to the viewers did include single parents of two races, but same-sex couples were not represented, despite the increasing number of cases, faced by almost every state in the union, of lesbian and gay couples demanding rights equal to those of heterosexuals, rights including marriage, pensions, adoption, health benefits, taxation, and hospital and prison visitation. Legally, gays and lesbians are excluded from not only the military but also the family. Most of middle America prefers neither to think nor to

58 talk about the fact that up to 10 percent of U.S. society is still legally discrimi-
nated against, so the *New York Times* was unusual both in recognizing that homosexual rights were swirling around in the Dan Quayle-Murphy Brown clash
and in bringing them to the surface, however briefly.

Media coverage of the L.A. uprisings was more typical. The mainstream media
virtually ignored the gay and lesbian protests against the Rodney King verdict.
Readers had to turn to the alternative press, such as the *LA Weekly*, to read that
lesbians and gays organized themselves by fax, phone, and word of mouth to
hold a protest march within hours of the verdict. Signs such as "Queers of All Colors Unite" and "Stop LAPD Racism" linked homosexual with racial discrimination, and although homophobia is at least as prevalent in Black America as in
white, it is not universal, and some African Americans appreciated the solidarity
of gays and lesbians in protesting the injustice of the verdict—the rapper Ice-T did,
for one: "When I was up here in Hollywood cooling out," he told Terry Gross on
National Public Radio, "the gay people were rolling through Hollywood, Queer
Nation, about three thousand of them, and they were, like, 'get with us,' and
they're up here mad."[47] Four days later, the Reverend Carl Bean told the lesbian
and gay congregation at South Central's Unity Fellowship Church:

> It's become too comfortable to hate a Jew, a gay, a Latino, a woman,
> a black person. As gays of color, we know the way the "isms"—and
> the denial America has about them—are tearing our country apart.
> The violence on the streets is about state violence that was not
> prosecuted for many years. I say "See the links, America," that
> means Gay America, too.[48]

The words used by Steven Corbin, cochair of the people-of-color caucus at
ACT-UP LA, as he helped in the cleanup, return us to the family values debate,
even if obliquely: "Shunned by straight blacks and rejected by white gays I
have felt like the child of a mixed marriage."[49]

Though gay and lesbian issues were generally submerged in the cultural
currents eddying around the presidential campaign, they erupted like a geyser
immediately afterward. Besides tackling abortion rights in the early days of his
presidency, Clinton also moved quickly on his promise to end homosexual discrimination in the military. The opposition from the Pentagon, the Armed Services Committee, and Colin Powell, the head of the Joint Chiefs of Staff, who
had become a national hero as a result of the Gulf War, was explosive. The public joined the debate with similar intensity. The 513,325 calls to the congressional switchboard on January 27 outnumbered the 472,641 generated six days
earlier by the Zoë Baird issue and broke all records.[50] In this case, however,
unlike that of Baird, the calls appeared to be organized, for they came in waves,
the first against and the second for the Clinton plan. The result of the furor was
that Clinton had to modify his reform while remaining committed to ending
discrimination against homosexuals with an unprecedented outspokenness.

Many gays and lesbians felt that in him they had a friend in the White House for the first time ever, and that their votes had not been wasted. Indeed, President Clinton has admitted that without the gay vote he would not have won the election. In April, lesbians and gays were granted a meeting in the White House in order to discuss, among other issues, their request that Clinton address a march organized to support his policies. CBS News opened its report of the historic meeting—the first official one ever between the president of the United States and homosexuals—by highlighting White House staffers' uncertainty about protocol, which resulted in the delegation being led to a side door, an act whose presumably unintended symbolism, was, to say the least, ironic. Protesting that such second-class treatment continued the discrimination the president was pledged to end, the delegation was granted front-door entry, and the TV camera, with no hint of irony, showed the Marine guard, in full dress uniform, standing in respectful salute as the group passed through.[51]

The "gays in the military" issue joined the Zoë Baird affair in handing the new administration an early and highly visible public setback. Telephone call-ins played an important role in each, but the similarities did not stop there. I have suggested that professional women were one of the few nondominant social groups to advance their cause during Reaganism. Arguably, gays and lesbians were another. Devastating though AIDS has been to the gay community, the debate around it has given them a public forum, and the deaths of prominent and popular gays, particularly in the worlds of entertainment and fashion, have aroused public sympathy and concern. AIDS also, of course, has aroused homophobia elsewhere in society, and although sympathy and concern may have increased, so too have moral condemnation and physical assaults. The argument about whether AIDS is or is not a gay disease has given gay issues a public prominence that has been rare and, in the eyes of some African Americans at least, works to disguise the racism in the origin and treatment of the disease. Other African Americans, however, have more sympathetically understood that gays are their covictims in genocide (see chapter 4). Despite Clinton's widespread support among gays and lesbians, he came under increasingly fierce criticism from them for his long delay in appointing an AIDS czar, and for his apparent reluctance to divert more funds to research. Black Liberation Radio (see chapter 4) would not be surprised. For its "war correspondents," the Clinton administration is as white as the Bush one.

Class enters into the perception of gays and lesbians as it does into that of "today's woman." If these groups did advance their interests at all during the 1980s, class privilege may have been a factor. One 1993 survey showed that gays and lesbians had higher education and income levels than the national average: the average household income of gays was $51,624, of lesbians, $42,755, whereas the national average was $37,992. The precision of these figures must be suspect, for they are presumably based upon self-reported or "out" homosexuals, who are likely to be disproportionately from the higher

60   social classes. The general trend, however, seems accurate, even down to the gendered economic difference within the gay community![52] The virulent homophobia may well be fueled in part by class resentment, much like the anti-feminism backlash. Both intertwine gender and class politics in similar ways. For instance, according to a recent poll, women supported gay rights more than men, the educated more than the uneducated, the under fifties more than the over fifties, and those on the coasts more than those in the South or the Midwest.[53] This pattern of support is embodied in the figure of Murphy Brown (an educated woman, younger than fifty, living on the East Coast); the opposition, on the other hand, is embodied in the older, less-educated male who lives in the center of the social formations spoken for by Rush Limbaugh, Pat Buchanan, and Dan Quayle.

    It was predictable, then, that Clinton's support for gay and lesbian rights in the military should run into the same opposition as his support for abortion rights. Randall Terry, the leader of Operation Rescue, the most virulent of the religious right's antiabortion groups, is also a leader of Resistance, an equally activist homophobic group. He welcomed Clinton's early moves to extend both abortion and homosexual rights as a "godsend" behind which to rally his forces.[54] And these forces are recruited, according to Susan Faludi, from those social formations who listen so fervently to Rush Limbaugh: virtually all of Operation Rescue leaders and about 50 percent of its members are low-paid, resentful men in their mid-twenties to early thirties.[55] It is worth noting here that the demographic group that voted most strongly for Bush was the "white born-again Christian."[56] Randall Terry implicitly brings Murphy Brown into the same frame as homosexuals and abortion rights supporters when he blames working women for "the destruction of the traditional family unit."[57] This mobilization of class and gender resentment can be directed at will against single mothers, working women, homosexuals, or abortion rights. Indeed, the *New York Times* reports that the religious right is turning away from the abortion issue and tapping into homophobia as a more effective way to raise funds and advance its agenda.[58]

    The gay and lesbian Washington march that the delegation to the White House had urged Clinton to address took place on April 26, and although estimates of the numbers involved varied from 300,000 by the U.S. Park Police to 1.1 million by the organizers, accounts were unanimous that it was one of the largest ever. The numbers exceeded those who heard Martin Luther King's "I have a dream" speech in the historic 1963 civil rights march (to which it was frequently compared) but were fewer than in the 1992 march for abortion rights. It is significant that the press brings these three topics together once again. "Family values" do not remain submerged for long either; one marcher, a doctor, said that

      she had come to Washington to march for legal and social rights that

aren't extended to gays, lesbians and bisexuals—such as the rights to adopt, marry or be recognized as family. "That's a big issue for me—to say we're a family," said Ross.[59]

The Republicans used "family values" to endorse social attitudes upon which racist, classist, sexist, and homophobic policies could be based. This involved not only a narrow definition of the family, but also a narrow sense of values that included only those ethicoreligious ones that could be internalized into the individual family as an autonomous, self-sufficient unit. To keep social values off the agenda, they had to cast the relationship between the family and society as one-way, so that the manifest social problems of the contemporary United States could be understood in the blinding simplicity that moral certainty needs as the result of the "collapse of the family," and not as a conjunctural contributor to it. This also involved seeing these values as unchanging ones that could, and should, refuse to respond to changing social conditions. In this the Republicans were not only simple, but shortsighted. The Democratic campaign's emphasis on health care, educational reform, and secure employment was also, though unrecognized as such by the Republicans, a campaign about family values. It was, however, one that posited a two-way relationship between family and society—a family can maintain itself and its values only if society can play its part in keeping its members healthy, educated, and employed. The left must challenge the Republican insistence, over at least the last three presidential campaigns, that it alone is the party of "family values" and that the Democrats and liberals are antifamily. Quite the opposite is in fact the case; the Democrats want to strengthen and extend the family, and to find ways of ensuring its continued health in changing times. This is true even among those whom the leaders of the right claim are trying to destroy it: far from wanting to weaken the family, gays and lesbians want to become families, as do single mothers and fathers. What is wrong with "family values" is both the authoritarian, racist, and sexist inflection of the values involved and their political use to oppose social policies in the realms of health, education, and employment. If family values do underlie the L.A. uprisings, they do so only in their extension into the social order, not as an ethical proscription—if the problems of the United States were solvable from its pulpits, America would now be Utopia.

Hyperreality

Three instances, out of many, can serve to raise the question of this section. The fictional Murphy Brown watches the news report of the "real" Dan Quayle criticizing her single motherhood. One hour later, TV news shows Dan Quayle, in the company of real single mothers, watching Murphy Brown watching him. The report ends with the information that he has sent her fictional baby a real toy.

In the hearings, Orrin Hatch raises a copy of William Peter Blatty's novel *The*

Exorcist and claims that Anita Hill's memory of Thomas's remark on the pubic hair on his Coke can comes from the novel and not her "real" experience (see *Sidebar: Hyperreality Hypersexuality*, p. 77). No one knows (or appears to care) whether or not she has read the novel.

On CNN news, the lawyer who has successfully defended Stacey Koon replays the Rodney King video in slow motion, freezes it at a key moment, talks over it, and proves that Rodney King was "really" in control of his own beating.

Baudrillard's theory of hyperreality is an attempt to come to grips with the fact that we live in an image-saturated culture. Any evening's television will present each one of us with more images than a member of a non- or preindustrial culture would see in a lifetime. And the typical image is a realistic one, that is, an image with claims to a truth that is grounded in a reality that exists in its own right, and is then represented and communicated by the image. Realism is a characteristic of both factual and fictional representations and has been the dominant style of European modernity from the Renaissance onward. It is also, according to Baudrillard, the style of early capitalism because, being a reproduction of reality, it is particularly well suited to mass production and reproduction, which is that era's defining mode of production.

Hyperreality is a postmodern sense of the real that accounts for our loss of certainty in being able to distinguish clearly and hierarchically between reality and its representation, and in being able to distinguish clearly and hierarchically between the modes of its representation. Postmodernism undercuts any belief that it is possible to experience reality directly, without mediation, and that this direct experience of the real can serve as a touchstone by which to measure the truth or accuracy of its representation. Similarly, it refutes any hierarchization of the different truths produced by the different modes of representation that descends from the indicative mode of what *is* (the factual documentary, the science textbook) through the mode of what *could be* (realistic fiction) to what *might be* (more "imaginative" or cartoonlike or futuristic fiction) and even to what *could not be* (the surreal, the anti-real). These organizing distinctions were set in a hierarchy of believability, and could function effectively only when images could be controlled. The postmodern promiscuity of images swamps any attempt to control them; it overwhelms any neat distinction between representation and reality, between fact and fiction. It refuses to allow "truth" a place in reality alone, for it cannot see that reality still has its own place for truth to make a home in. An image-saturated culture differs from a culture of controlled and organized representations not just in degree, but in kind. And this, postmodernism tells us, is what characterizes its world as generically different from the modern. But we don't live in a completely postmodern world, we live in a world where the modern and the postmodern (and the premodern) coexist uneasily.

Although there is plenty of evidence of hyperreality around us, there is also evidence of modernism's dogged survival. The hyperreal may destroy the cat-

egories that once organized the differences between representation and reality or between different modes of representation, but our sense of those differences is not killed off as easily as postmodernism assumes.

When Orrin Hatch acted as though there were no difference between the pubic hair in the gin in *The Exorcist* and that on Thomas's Coke can in the EEOC office he was not being postmodern, though he was exploiting the conditions of postmodernity. He was not claiming equivalence among the three hyperreal pubic hairs—the one in the novel, the one in Anita Hill's memory, and the one on Clarence Thomas's Coke can—but he was using the fictionality of the first to discredit the second and thus to erase any reality of the third. It was a very modern use, because it depended upon hierarchically structured categories within the postmodern destabilization of reality and of truth. Equally, the confirmation of Clarence Thomas's seat on the Supreme Court was no postmodern moment, though Bush's statement that his confirmation demonstrated that "all men are created equal" was utterly postmodern in its denial of any real truth that could serve to authenticate or, in this case, to disqualify its representation.

On September 21, 1992, *Time* put Murphy Brown/Candice Bergen on its cover and gave her a prominent lapel button that read "Murphy Brown for President." *Time* is a newsmagazine, the lapel button is a fiction that did not occur even in the fictional TV series, and there is no way of telling if the woman wearing it is Candice Bergen or Murphy Brown (the caption on the photo, "Murphy Brown's Candice Bergen," is no help at all). This postmodern fluidity, however, overlaps a modern certainty: Warner Bros. owns both *Time* and *Murphy Brown*, this issue preceded Murphy's reply to Dan Quayle by a week, it carried teasers from the script, and, in a hoped-for self-fulfilling prophecy, called the episode "a surefire ratings blockbuster." Corporate capitalism, perhaps the crowning achievement of modernity, can exploit the conditions of the postmodern just as readily as can Orrin Hatch.

On *Murphy Brown*, some characters are shown reading real newspapers' accounts of Dan Quayle's attack, and others are reading fictional ones (see *Sidebar: Press Headlines on* Murphy Brown, p. 22): the only point of mixing real and fictional papers together seems to be to deny that the difference between them matters, and to offer viewers the postmodern pleasure of recognizing that it does not "really" exist. The two local news anchors who smilingly agreed with Quayle in not knowing where fiction ended and fact began were experiencing (and passing on) the pleasure of this denial of difference (see *Sidebar: Local News*, p. 26).

The structural difference, for instance, between information and entertainment television (roughly, between fact and fiction) is a residue of modernity that contains the hierarchical evaluation that the former is superior to the latter. This structured difference continues into the domains of gender and class by associating the former with masculinity and higher social position, and the latter with femininity and lower social formations. When Rush Limbaugh casti-

64 gates Murphy Brown for having "an agenda," he is chastising what he considers ought to be a "feminine" show (entertainment) for taking on "masculine" characteristics (information) and thus trespassing where it has no business — the masculine world of "real" politics (an agenda).

Many commentators have noted that much of the 1992 campaigns were conducted through the "entertainment" genres of television and radio, particularly talk shows, but also MTV and, as in this case, a sitcom. Most of those who deplored this were the old white men of journalism, for their function as mediators (read "controllers") was bypassed by the politicians' refusal to conform to the structuring discipline of where politics "ought" to be located in the media. History does not allow us the comfort of explaining its processes as coincidences, so we must trace some connections, however tenuous, between the dispersal of political debate across the media spectrum and the facts that this election was marked, in comparison to the previous three, by greater public interest and involvement, a higher voter turnout, and a Democratic victory. Lower-brow television is low only because its taste patterns appeal to disempowered and subordinated social formations (particularly by gender, class, and age), and so dissolving the structured relationship between politics and serious, informational media encouraged more social formations to participate in the political process. Extending the political arena to include a sitcom such as *Murphy Brown* did not necessarily include more women in political debate (for women have long been active in official politics), but it did give them a feminine terrain on which to fight, unlike the (still) masculine terrains of the party conventions, party organizations, and mainstream news. On this more feminine terrain Murphy Brown "beat" Dan Quayle, and his feeble attempt to fight back by surrounding himself with single mothers on the TV news regained little, if any, of the ground she had taken from him. When the terrain of a sitcom is as politically real as that of TV news or of a party convention, and its effectivity in an election campaign is indistinguishable from theirs, then the postmodern can be seen in process, and that process can be seen to contain significant emancipatory elements. We must be clear, however, that any emancipation lies both in the meanings or political effects that are achieved and in the control over the process. Murphy Brown's "victory" over Dan Quayle in this one battle for position may well have contradicted its emancipatory progress in gender politics by continuing repressive politics of class and race if only in its failure to extend any emancipatory gains into either domain. Rush Limbaugh, equally freed from the constraints of meanings anchored in reality, can "turn" the image of Murphy awkwardly holding her baby to regain ground that some men think they have lost to the women's movement. And Orrin Hatch can exploit the implosion of fact and fiction into each other for equally conservative ends. As with any other cultural phenomenon, the politics of postmodernism must be evaluated by how it is used, not by what it is or what it promises.

Multiaxiality

The metaphor of culture as multiple currents is an attempt to depict the multiple axes of power that crisscross our daily lives and the identities and relations that we form and re-form as we move through them. As hyperreality dissolves stable categories of modes of representation, so multiaxiality transforms any stability of categories into the fluidities of power. The core axes in this messy business may be the classic trio of class, race, and gender, but they are far from the only ones. For analytic purposes we may, on occasion, highlight one over the others, but in lived experience they intermingle in innumerable configurations, and, indeed, the effectiveness of any one can never be traced singly but only in its interminglings with the others.

In using the term *class*, I need to divest it of some of its old assets: no longer can we think of it as a social category to which we can ascribe individuals or groups with an accuracy that they would themselves accept; no longer can we identify clear boundaries between the classes, or a describable class consciousness, identity, or solidarity within any one of them. Class is better conceived as a scale of privilege that is primarily, but not exclusively, economic, and that has objective and subjective dimensions that may coincide more or less closely. Objectively, it is possible to rank social groups by their income and to correlate their economic positions fairly accurately with access to political power, to the media, and to the best table in a restaurant. One can also correlate, to a degree, economic position (which includes both the amount of money and how it was acquired) with cultural taste; that is, with people's preferences in reading, listening, viewing, eating, housing, clothing, vacationing, and so on. The prime functions of class are first to establish social distinctions and then to hierarchize them.

As the distinctions become finer and their grouping into solid "classes" becomes harder, so the subjective or perceptual dimension becomes more important. One common way of making useful sense of class difference is through the categories of the "haves" and the "have-nots." These are fluid and multiaxial categories; they have no objective position in the social order, but exist only in their use. Korean store owners in L.A., for instance, may be placed in the "haves" by local African Americans and Latinos, but may see themselves as "have-nots" in comparison to whites in Orange County. Similarly, a blue-collar white man may fall into either category, depending on the point from which the categorization is made, or the social relations he enters at the point at which the category is used. Related to Murphy Brown in one direction or to a homeless man in the other, he changes category appropriately.

Other terms in common usage are "upper and lower echelons," or, to refer to alliances among the upper, "the power structure." All these share a sense of gradation and of multiaxiality that are less marked in the word *class*. Their imprecision allows a flexibility in usage, so that at times the "haves" may be de-

66 fined more by their whiteness and masculinity than by their economics: at others, the priorities among the axes of power and definition will be changed. Although the axial mix will vary according to tactics and strategies judged best for its conditions of use, the powers that are exerted along those axes are still systematically related, though not structurally determined, and thus not always predictable in their configuration. There is, for instance, a systematic tendency for class privilege, whiteness, and masculinity to pull in the same direction, though they will not always do so. Even an account such as this runs the risk of ascribing to each axis of power a degree of autonomy that in practice it lacks. It is not enough to say, for instance, that race and class mix differently in different conditions: we must recognize that racial difference is strategically constructed, in part, by economic power, and, equally, that class privilege is colored. Race and class are not separate power axes that can be applied together or separately, but racial power can be exerted along class lines and class power along racial ones. Class directs social relations differently among European Americans than among African Americans, and differently again in interracial relations. For many white critics of *The Cosby Show*, for example (see chapter 2), the Huxtables' class privilege signified yuppie conservatism, and for others it meant that they had been whitewashed or made into honorary whites and thus disarticulated from the category used by these whites to make sense of "normal" Blacks. For some African Americans, however, their signs of class privilege were reasons for hope and pride: they contradicted the prevalent white strategy of representing African Americans as criminals, failures, or threats. Interracially, the Huxtables' class privilege may have whitened them for whites; for Blacks, however, it did not overpower their Blackness but rather inflected it into a representation of African American life that Blacks were pleased to show to whites. The dominant system of representation makes Blacks into the mysterious or threatening other, and the Huxtables' class privilege countered this strategy by normalizing them.

Gender enters the picture to complicate it further, but not to change it. Class and racial powers are exerted along the axis of gender, just as gender power flows along theirs. Gender difference is experienced and operationalized differently within different racial and class formations, and the differences are magnified when applied in interracial and interclass relations.

Age, too, is an axis of power, a current of meaning with political effects. There is a multiaxiality of powers within which, for instance, a / young / Black / unemployed / male / in South-Central Los Angeles has to negotiate his daily life, his sense of social identity, and his multiple relations to the dominant social order. Clinton's electoral campaign, to give a quite different example, used age politics, among others, to distinguish itself from Bush's. And age is not the only axis we need to add to the big three: because power is everywhere, it flows along all the axes of social difference.

Multiaxiality means that the configuration of power in any specific set of social   67
conditions cannot be predicted in advance. It thus requires a degree of socially interested agency through which people form alliances and identities by which to
advance or defend their interests and devise tactics and strategies appropriate to
their aims. Here I follow de Certeau in using the term *strategy* to identify the deployment of power to promote or maintain the interests of the power structure
and *tactics* to refer to the operations by which the less powerful defend or promote
their interests.[60] Class, race, and gender, then, are not so much stable social categories as axes of power along which strategies are deployed and tactics practiced:
they are terrains of struggle. They are, of course, social categories as well, but their
stability is disrupted by their strategic or tactical uses, and the power that flows
through them can be diverted by struggles against it.

The stability of categories is disrupted, too, by the necessity of negotiating our
lives through forming social alliances according to the exigencies of our situation.
These alliances may coincide relatively closely with categorical boundaries, or they
may transect them; they may be relatively stable and long-term, or fluidly formed,
dissolved, and reformed. Multiaxiality means that the social order needs to be
conceptualized as in constant process, as a constant interplay of power, not as a
stable categorical structure. Indeed, we need to drop the concept of *social category*
and replace it with *social formation*. The latter is a term of process that points to the
fact that race, class, and gender, for instance, may have categorical dimensions,
but that understands categorical differences as terrains upon which alliances are
formed and strategies deployed, not as fixed determinants.

This brings me to one, final, vexed term—the *underclass*. There is a danger
that the mere use of the term will reify it, and will fix or even naturalize people
of color, poverty, and the inner city into a fact of life. We must not understand
it in this way. It too is a strategic construction by which racial, economic, and
spatial power excludes certain social formations from any meaningful participation in the social order. It is a construct of dominant social formations that
serves their interests by excluding the pauperized groups, for whose existence
they are largely responsible, from being considered as valid members of society, and Dan Quayle used it in this way to describe the residents of South-Central (see *Sidebar: Dan Quayle*, p. 68). It is not a term of any use to those to whom
it is applied. We must be careful, therefore, to use it only in ways that expose
its strategy and not in ways that reify it.

Figuring People

The loss of "reality" as a self-contained and authentic concept and the dis-
solution of stable social categories extends into our understanding of people.
Who is Anita Hill? Who is Rodney King? Is Murphy Brown really Candice
Bergen (the actress who plays her) or is she really Diane English (the
writer/producer who created her), and isn't who Candice Bergen is at least as

Dan Quayle

Restoring Basic Values: Strengthening the Family

by Dan Quayle, Vice President of the United States of America, Delivered at the Commonwealth Club of California, San Francisco, California, May 19, 1992

... When I have been asked during these last weeks who caused the riots and the killing in L.A., my answer has been direct and simple: Who is to blame for the riots? The rioters are to blame. Who is to blame for the killings? The killers are to blame....

In a nutshell: I believe the lawless social anarchy which we saw is directly related to the breakdown of family structure, personal responsibility and social order in too many areas of our society. For the poor the situation is compounded by a welfare ethos that impedes individual efforts to move ahead in society, and hampers their ability to take advantage of the opportunities America offers....

There is no question that this country has had a terrible problem with race and racism. The evil of slavery has left a long legacy. But we have faced racism squarely, and we have made progress in the past quarter century. The landmark civil rights bills of the 1960s removed legal barriers to allow full participation by

blacks in the economic, social and political life of the nation. ...

The poor you always have with you, Scripture tells us. And in America we have always had poor people. But in this dynamic, prosperous nation, poverty has traditionally been a stage through which people pass on their way to joining the great middle class. And if one generation didn't get very far up the ladder—their ambitious, better-educated children would.

But the underclass seems to be a new phenomenon. It is a group whose members are dependent on welfare for very long stretches, and whose men are often drawn into lives of crime. There is far too little upward mobility, because the underclass is disconnected from the rules of American society. And these problems have, unfortunately, been particularly acute for Black Americans.

Let me share with you a few statistics on the difference between black poverty in particular in the 1960's and now.

—In 1967 68 percent of black families were headed by married couples. In 1991, only 48 percent of black families were headed by both a husband and wife.

much a product of Murphy Brown as vice versa? The figure of Murphy Brown-Candice Bergen-Diane English is a hyperreal figure in which none of the components can be said to produce or reproduce any of the others, but in which all exist equivalently in producing what Baudrillard calls a "simulacrum," an image that is its own reality and is not a representation of another one. A figure, as I use the term here, is a human simulacrum, one that simulates a person, and its simulation is what a person has become in hyperreality. Murphy Brown includes the reality of Diane English, a professional career woman dedicated to advancing women's interests as she sees them through

— In 1965 the illegitimacy rate among black families was 28 percent. In 1989, 65 percent—two thirds—of all black children were born to never-married mothers.

— In 1951 9.2 percent of black youth between 16-19 were unemployed. In 1965, it was 23 percent. In 1980 it was 35 percent. By 1989, the number had declined slightly, but was still 32 percent.

— The leading cause of death of young black males today is homicide. . . .

The intergenerational poverty that troubles us so much today is predominantly a poverty of values. Our inner cities are filled with children having children; with people who have not been able to take advantage of educational opportunities; with people who are dependent on drugs or the narcotic of welfare. To be sure, many people in the ghettos struggle very hard against these tides—and sometimes win. But too many feel they have no hope and nothing to lose. This poverty is, again, fundamentally a poverty of values. . . .

And right now, the failure of our families is hurting America deeply. When families fail, society fails. The anarchy and lack of structure in our inner cities are testament to how quickly civilization falls apart when the family foundation cracks. Children need love and discipline.

They need mothers and fathers. A welfare check is not a husband. The state is not a father. It is from parents that children learn how to behave in society; it is from parents above all that children come to understand values and themselves as men and women, mothers and fathers.

And for those concerned about children growing up in poverty, we should know this: marriage is probably the best anti-poverty program of all. Among families headed by married couples today, there is a poverty rate of 5.7 percent. But 33.4 percent of families headed by a single mother are in poverty today.

Nature abhors a vacuum. Where there are no mature, responsible men around to teach boys how to be good men, gangs serve in their place. In fact, gangs have become a surrogate family for much of a generation of inner-city boys. . . .

Ultimately, however, marriage is a moral issue that requires cultural consensus, and the use of social sanctions. Bearing babies irresponsibly is, simply, wrong. Failing to support children one has fathered is wrong. We must be unequivocal about this.

It doesn't help matters when prime time TV has Murphy Brown—a character who supposedly epitomizes today's intelligent, highly paid, professional woman—mocking the importance of fathers, by bearing a child alone, and calling it just another "lifestyle choice."

her conservatively worn liberal spectacles: it includes the reality of Candice Bergen, a professional career woman who puts her career before her "family values" by continuing to work on the show instead of moving to France to live with her husband (as he has reportedly asked her to), and it includes the reality of Murphy Brown, a professional career woman whom prime time TV distributes across the nation, and who has decided to have a baby and not a husband or an abortion. A figure is a hyperreal person whose reality includes both a body (or more than one) composed of flesh, bone, and blood and a body of infinitely reproducible signifiers or electronic dots on a TV screen. Anita Hill,

70   Rodney King, Murphy Brown, and even Dan Quayle are all figures in this sense.

Dan Quayle watching himself on Murphy Brown in the company of single mothers in a real apartment is as much a figure as is Murphy Brown addressing him in the company of single-parent families on a TV sitcom. Neither event is any more or less real, any less or more scripted, than the other; both are made-for-TV moments whose reality is equally electronic and physical, and whose reality effects are thus precisely comparable. The discursive contestations among the meanings of single motherhood, fathers, and family values, and the party political contests among the social coalitions formed in the election campaign around those meanings are not affected by the supposed realness of one figure and the supposed fictionality of the other. Figures serve as social terrains whereby others engage in the figuring process. Murphy Brown is a means whereby to figure out single motherhood in the 1990s, and to calculate whether or not to figure in abortions, father figures, or racial differences.

Anita Hill was a figure of much political calculation. Some subtracted her previous support for Judge Bork and multiplied her harassment into that of women everywhere. Others divided her Blackness from her femininity, calculating that they could add more to their cause by doing so, and yet others insisted that her total must include both, though in different proportions. These calculations were performed upon her only because she was equally a body of flesh and blood and one of electronic dots, one who could occupy simultaneously the physical place of the witness table in the Senate and the electronic place of everywhere: she could occupy each place only by the virtual reality of occupying the other. The figure of Anita Hill that, two years after the hearings, still lectures to packed halls carries her electronic body within her flesh-and-blood one, and occupies the podium only because both bodies are present, both there and in the imagination of her audiences. She is still a figure, but, presumably, as the urgency of the calculations she embodies so precisely begins to diminish and the inflection of those calculations starts to change, she will ease out of hyperreality, and, no doubt, be replaced by an equivalent whose historical moment is more pertinent.

Figures are simulacra that speak and take up positions, and thus social interests can speak through them, occupy positions within them. Their degree of agency in the figuring process is open to question: the extent to which their personal history before their figurehood prefigures it or merely precedes it can be analyzed only in each configuration. Rodney King was emptied of his individual history, not allowed to speak in the trial that popularly, if not officially, bore his name. His prefiguration seems confined to his being a Black male who, almost incidentally, drank too much beer, drove too fast, and, crucially, refused to submit. From that point, his agency and his own calculation counted for little. Anita Hill, on the other hand, spoke clearly and tenaciously, though Rush Limbaugh, and others, contend that she did not speak but was spoken. To those aligned with her, her agency and calculation were active, and part of the alliance; to those opposed to her, they were minimized, the calculation was that of others and she merely the body in which those calculations could be given public form and political effects. The individual's history is often the least significant component of a figure. Its fluidity and volatility do not allow it to serve as the final truth of the figure, but the still-lingering belief that truth lies in this individual history, whichever truth is being claimed, allows it to function as an authenticator, as a sign of truth (see *Sidebar: Pinpointing Clarence*, p. 102).

The other components, which are more significant, often depend upon this authenticator to secure those effects by which their significance is established. These components are, first, the larger social history of domination and subordination, of the play of power upon bodies, and, second, the contemporary pertinence that makes the figure an appropriate terrain of contestation, that makes it matter. Anita Hill incarnated, or put into bodily form, the multiple histories of the deracialized female victim and of the deracialized female threat; equally she gave presence to the long, very racialized histories of the Black female as both victim and threat. Each figuring and refiguring was of a different social history that used a different individual history to authenticate it. Like any history, hers was the product of who wrote it, and each writing figured her differently, inserted her into different social alliances and thus articulated quite different meanings of her. Her unique body, with its unique history, may have set the limits of the struggle—it prevented her being figured as a white male, to take an extreme example, or as a prostitute, to take another that was only just kept out of sight. But within those limits, it could do comparatively little—it could require neither her Blackness to be figured in nor her conservativeness to be figured out. Her history and her presence provided a bodily shell, but what filled it was determined by the choice of the history written upon her and the power alliance into which she was recruited.

But although the body of the individual is comparatively powerless in determining the way he or she is to be figured, it is extremely powerful in giving the histories and alliances a material presence, in making them live, in making them visible and audible, and in making them matter in, and become the matter of, everyday life. If not figured into a living body, the clash of social alliances and of different histories can seem abstracted and distant, difficult to visualize, hear, and engage with. Unembodied issues are appropriate for books, for an age of literacy and for the literate classes in this age; but for an age of electronic figures and of hypervisibility, embodied histories and politics are the ones that matter, the ones that people are most ready to engage in, because alliances, for or against, are more easily formed with a figure than a political position. This process may be seen, negatively, as the individualizing of politics: it may, however, be understood alternatively as a way of transferring the liveness and inescapability of physical presence into the political arena. Anita Hill was not an individual in an essentialist sense, but a figure of contestation

Murphy Brown's Response

(Extracts from the episode aired on September 21, 1992)

Extract 1: (Murphy and her friend and colleague Frank are watching the news)

TV NEWS ANCHOR: Dan Quayle had some strong comments on what he termed a "poverty of values," citing Murphy Brown as an example. . . .

MURPHY: Was that about me?

FRANK: It sounded like it.

DAN QUAYLE (on TV News): It doesn't help matters when prime time TV has Murphy Brown . . .

MURPHY: He is talking about me.

DAN QUAYLE: . . . today's intelligent, highly paid professional woman, mocking the importance of fathers by having a child alone and calling it just another lifestyle choice.

TV NEWS ANCHOR: Mr. Quayle later expanded on his remarks to say that he believed that examples like Murphy Brown glamorized single motherhood.

Extract 2: (In the *FYI* offices)

MILES (looking at polls): Amazing, not only do people think Murphy would make a better parent than Dan Quayle, they think she'd make a better president too!

CORKY: I was raised to believe that if you had a child out of wedlock you were bad. Of course, I was also raised to believe a woman's place is in the home, segregation was good and that presidents never lied! Oh, this is so confusing!

Extract 3: (Murphy Brown's broadcast on *FYI*)

MURPHY BROWN (to camera): The American family and American values. This reporter has a unique perspective on the topic because in a recent speech Vice President Dan Quayle used me as an example of the poverty of values in this country, and implied that I was a poor role model for our nation's youth. Some might argue that attacking

whose individuality was one of the prizes. Her individuality was a simulacrum, not an essence that could be represented.

As a simulacrum, the individuality of the figure can be infinitely reproduced: Murphy Brown may simulate Hillary Rodham Clinton, Zoë Baird, Diane English, Janet Reno, Candice Bergen, or any of "today's women": no individual is the original of any other, and the reality of any one only figures as the simulacrum of all. As Murphy Brown simulates today's woman and is filled with past and present struggles, so too, in their individual bodies, both Willie Horton and Rodney King figure particular racist histories and politics, as do Clarence Thomas and Bill Cosby. The individual history of each does not individualize those histories and politics but embodies them: it makes them hyperreal figures and prevents them being real individuals with a different and prior existence to that of their representations.

my status as a single mother was nothing more than a cynical bit of election year posturing; I prefer to give the vice president the benefit of the doubt. These are difficult times for our country, and in searching for the causes of our social ills, we could choose to blame the media, or the Congress, or an administration that's been in power for twelve years, or we could blame me.

And while I will admit that my inability to balance a checkbook may have had something to do with the collapse of the savings and loan industry, I doubt that my status as a single mother has contributed all that much to the breakdown of Western civilization.

But tonight's program should not be simply about blame. The vice president said that he felt it was important to open a dialogue about family values, and on that point we agree. Unfortunately, it seems that for him the only acceptable definition of the family is a mother, a father, and children. And in a country where millions of children grow up in nontraditional families, that definition seems painfully unfair. Perhaps it's time for the vice

president to expand his definition, and recognize that whether by choice or circumstance, families come in all shapes and sizes. And ultimately, what really defines a family is commitment, caring, and love.

With that in mind I'd like to introduce you to some people who might not fit into the Vice President's vision of the family, but they consider themselves families, nonetheless. They work, they struggle, they hope for the kind of life for their children that we all want for our children, and these are the kind of people we should be paying attention to.

(She turns to a group of "real-life" single parents and their children.)

Welcome to *FYI*. Would you introduce yourself please . . .

These figures cannot be conjured up merely out of their own or our fevered imaginations. However discursively useful they are to strategists and tacticians, they cannot be a discursive production alone. One component of a figure is a sense of historical fortuitousness, that it happens to have been produced in an unplanned, unforeseen historical conjuncture. Anita Hill, Rodney King, and Murphy Brown were all fortuitous in this way, and their figuring involved grasping the opportunity offered. Willie Horton was, in this sense, a fortuitous event that the Bush campaign seized: Rodney King was equally fortuitous, particularly in his video form. Although Anita Hill and Murphy Brown may both seem to be more intentional products, there is still a sense of the fortuitous and the unplanned in the way they became such highly charged figures.

Of course, history does not deal us a sequence of fortuitous happenstances: the figure of Rodney King was as inevitable as fortuitous. Similarly, the steadily

74   increasing backlash against women's assertion of their rights meant that the
      figure of Anita Hill had to happen, if not around her individuality, then around
      someone else's. It is the inevitability within the fortuitousness that enables the
      figure to be so highly charged, for the inevitability is a product of those clash-
      ing social forces that engage with each other in the struggle to produce a figure
      that counts for them.

      Whatever else a figure is, it is always a body of discourse, a point where
      circulating meanings are made visibly and audibly public, where they are en-
      ergized, their momentum increased. Sometimes a figure has comparatively lit-
      tle effect upon the direction of this circulation; its main function is to increase
      its rate of flow and make it spectacular, so that drops spray out and saturate a
      large area. At others, it may disrupt a relatively smooth current, making it eddy
      and turn back on itself. As nouns, figures are the sites of circulation and con-
      testation; as verbs, they are agents in the process—and they are always both.

      This chapter has focused primarily on the struggles over which statements
      are made and which are not, over the power of mainstream discourse simulta-
      neously to produce and repress meanings. The racial meanings of "family val-
      ues" were generally repressed and the people of color who wished to contrib-
      ute to the debate were generally silenced. Such is not the case in the events
      analyzed in the next two chapters. The Clarence Thomas-Anita Hill hearings
      (the topic of chapter 2) provided opportunities for African Americans, particu-
      larly African American women, to engage publicly in struggles over the mean-
      ings of race and gender, and they grasped them at least as effectively as white
      liberals grasped those provided by the Murphy Brown-Dan Quayle debate.
      The hearings were not explicitly related to "family values," though implicitly
      they were, primarily through the cultural figuring of Black women and Black
      men. The next chapter analyzes the struggles around the hearings, and relates
      them to the family values debate as it was continued around other sitcoms, par-
      ticularly ones such as *The Cosby Show* and *The Simpsons*, which brought racial
      issues into it. In the multiaxial struggles traced in this chapter, racial struggles
      played a comparatively minor role: from this point of the book onward, how-
      ever, they are central, for the hearings and the uprisings foregrounded race in
      a way that the debate did not.

Chapter 2

Hearing Anita Hill
(and Viewing Bill Cosby)

The Senate Judiciary Committee's hearings into Anita Hill's allegations that Clarence Thomas, Bush's nominee to fill the Supreme Court seat vacated by Thurgood Marshall, had sexually harassed her when he was her boss at the Equal Employment Opportunity Commission caused some of the greatest cultural and political turbulence of the early 1990s. They stirred up all the murkiest currents of race, gender, class, and party politics into a maelstrom that involved a multiaxial complex of struggles in which defeats could be turned into victories, ground gained could be lost and regained, and the only certainties were instability, fluidity, and contestation.

The two Black figures at the center of the storm were put into white discourse most vividly and dangerously by racialized and sexualized metonyms. Anita Hill accused Clarence Thomas of, among other things, making two sexually offensive remarks to her: he compared his own penis to that of Long Dong Silver, a Black porn star, and he claimed to have discovered a pubic hair on his can of Coke. Because the Republican strategy was to focus the hearings not upon what Clarence Thomas *did*, but upon who Anita Hill *was*, the politics of the female pubic hair were, in this case, more decisive than those of the male penis. In other cases, such as that of Willie Horton (see *Sidebar: Willie Horton*, p. 144), the Black male is cast as the sexualized racial threat to the white social order and its "family values," and we must note here how eagerly white discourse circulated these metonyms of both male and female versions of the always already sexualized Black body. In one sense this pubic hair was as hyperreal as Murphy Brown's baby, for both existed only in discourse, but that discourse was material in both its presence and its applications. In another sense, however, its hyperreality was intensified because it could sink its taproots into a figure that is deeply engraved and deeply hidden in the white imagination—that of the hypersexualized Black female.

Hypersexuality, like hyperreality, gathers into itself the conceptualization of both "reality" and its representations, both the real and the imaginary, and becomes a concept whose power is greater than the sum of its components. 75

Hyperreality Hypersexuality

The Senate Judiciary Committee

Statement of Anita Hill: One of the oddest episodes I remember was an occasion in which Thomas was drinking a Coke in his office. He got up from the table at which we were working, went over to his desk to get the Coke, looked at the can and asked, "Who has put pubic hair on my Coke?" On other occasions he referred to the size of his own penis as being larger than normal and he also spoke on some occasions of the pleasure he had given to women with oral sex. (October 11, 1991)

Cross Examination 1

ANITA HILL: I recall at least one instance in his office at the EEOC when he discussed, er, some pornographic material, and he brought up the substance, of the content, of the pornographic material.

JOSEPH BIDEN: Again, it's difficult, but for the record, what substance did he bring up in this instance in the EEOC in his office? What was the content of what he said?

ANITA HILL: This was a reference to an individual who, er, had a very large penis, and he used the name that he had been referred to in the pornographic material, er . . .

JOSEPH BIDEN: Do you recall what it was?

ANITA HILL: Yes I do, the name that was referred to was Long Dong Silver.

Cross Examination 2

ORRIN HATCH (referring to Anita Hill's testimony): That's a gross thing to say, isn't it? Whether it's said by you or by someone else, it's a gross thing to say, isn't it?

CLARENCE THOMAS: As far as I am concerned, Senator, it is. And it's something I did not, nor would I, say.

ORRIN HATCH (holding up a copy of *The Exorcist*): Ever read this book?

CLARENCE THOMAS: No.

Hypersexuality condenses into itself both racial-sexual differences and the white imaginations of them: it is hyperreal, not just because it is unreal and surreal (which it is), but because it it is super-real, more than real, for its affective reality is magnified and accelerated, and so its material effects, or

ORRIN HATCH: *The Exorcist?*

CLARENCE THOMAS: No, Senator. . . .

ORRIN HATCH: You said you never did say, "Who has put pubic hair on my Coke?" You never did talk to her about Long Dong Silver. I submit those things were found. On page 70 of this particular version of *The Exorcist*, [he reads] " 'Oh Burke,' sighed Sharon. In a guarded tone she described an encounter between the senator and the director, 'Denny remarked to him in passing,' said Sharon, 'that there appeared to be—quote—an alien pubic hair floating around in my gin—unquote.' " Do you think that was spoken by happenstance? And she would have us believe that you were saying these things because you wanted to date her!

Designing Women: The Strange Case of Clarence and Anita

BERNICE: Well, I don't see what all this fuss is about, anyway, even if these things did happen. I've eaten at Long John Silver's a number of times and I've never gotten a hair in my Coke, but I'll tell you if I did, I wouldn't hesitate to send it back! And it wouldn't be ten years later, either! . . .

JULIA: It shows they've learned their lesson well.

CHARLENE: What lesson is that?

JULIA: The one that says, all men are created equal.

MARY JO: Evidently, they haven't seen Long Dong Silver.

LAWRENCE SHILES, a student of Anita Hill's at Oral Roberts University: "Sitting next to me [in class] were fellow students Jeffrey Landoff and Mark Stewart. Upon opening the assignments and reviewing our grades and comments made by Anita Hill, I found ten to twelve short black pubic hairs in the pages of my assignment. I glanced over at Jeff Landoff's assignment and saw similar pubic hairs in his work. At that time I made the statement to Landoff that either she had a low opinion of our work or she had graded our assignment in the bathroom. Mark Stewart overheard the conversation and said he had similar pubic hairs in his assignment also. This became the standing joke among many students for the remainder of the year in her classes" (quoted in David Brock, "The Real Anita Hill," *American Spectator*, March 1992, 27).

effective materiality, are more intensively condensed and extensively dispersed. It is a powerful concept that should be approached with caution by those who wish to weaken it rather than deploy it. Both bell hooks and Paula Giddings (see below) warn that any reference to the hypersexualized Black

78   woman can be dangerous to Black women, and it is difficult for a critic such
as I to refer to it without increasing that danger. But if we leave the figure
undisturbed we can never dislodge it from its centrality, nor weaken its grasp:
a critical analysis of the way it is used should be able to turn it against its users.
As this figure became the prime weapon in the white Republican battle to
discredit Anita Hill, we must fight back to discredit both it and those who
use it.

The pubic hair became a resonant sign by which this hyperreal figure
was put into public discourse, and therefore became a site of discursive
struggle. Orrin Hatch, the Republican senator, was the first into the fray: a
few short hours after Anita Hill's testimony, he brandished a copy of *The Exorcist* and remade the pubic hair into a sign not of Clarence Thomas's sexuality
but of Anita Hill's fantasy, and thus a symptom of her pathologized hypersexuality (see *Sidebar: Hyperreality Hypersexuality*, p. 76). He then located
this white construction of Black female hypersexuality in William Peter Blatty's
fiction of the horrific threat of the unknown and the uncontrollable. Linda
Bloodworth-Thomason did not let him get away with that for long. In her sitcom *Designing Women* she fought back and attempted to reclaim the gender politics of the pubic hair (as well as of the penis), if not its racial ones, by turning
it away from masculine horror and into a feminized dirty joke (see *Sidebar: Hyperreality Hypersexuality*, p. 77). The dirty joke is normally a male way of controlling women, not only in its content but also in the act of telling it. Thomas's
original remark, "Who put the pubic hair on my Coke can?" was a dirty joke of
this conventional, sexist type. But giving it a feminine accent trivializes not
only the man's pride in his sexuality and performance but also his need to exert
its power in public discourse, and thus attempts to reclaim, momentarily at
least, not just the meaning of the pubic hair but the gender politics of the dirty
joke.

This episode of *Designing Women* charts the movement of gender politics
from the private to the public as it passes through the domains of the body, of
personal conversation, of the workplace, and of the state. The show closes on
the public end of the continuum with a shot of George Bush flanked by the
victorious Clarence Thomas proclaiming to the press assembled in the White
House rose garden that Thomas's confirmation proves that, in the United
States at least, "all men are created equal." This is turned against him twice:
once jokingly by Mary Jo pointing out that the men who believe that "evidently
haven't seen Long Dong Silver," and once seriously by the shot of Anita Hill's
exhausted face as he speaks, which showed all too painfully that, whatever
equality there may be, it was certainly men's.

The meanings of "men" and "equal" become prizes to be vied for, and,
when won, the reclaimed meaning has to be stabilized by being allied with
other meanings, or articulated with them. Articulation involves the process of
forming linkages among meanings by which they are made politically usable.

Three articulations are at work here, making three differently usable meanings
of "men" and "equal": the first articulation of "men" is with Clarence
Thomas's Blackness (in which case men = human beings), the second is with
Anita Hill's femaleness (men = males), and the third is with men's sense of the
phallus (men = the penis). With each rearticulation of "man" there is an equivalent rearticulation of "equal."

Racial-Sexual Articulations

Designing Women's rearticulations of "men" and "equal" were white, and in advancing gender politics they could be seen to put back or at least repress racial
ones. Many whites did not perceive how the racial politics of the hearings
might appear to African Americans, at least not initially. We discussed them
ardently and at length, but, until African Americans pointed it out to us, many
of us failed to realize clearly enough that allegations of Black sexual harassment
made public on white media differed significantly from similar allegations in an
all-white workplace, despite their important similarities. When race did enter
our discussions, the issue that we saw most clearly was Thomas's strategic
turning of the explicit politics of the hearings from gender to race in his now-
famous description of them as "a high-tech lynching of an uppity Black man."
And we dismissed this as a misuse of racial politics, for we saw only half the
issue—we understood well enough that no Black man had ever been lynched
for abuse of a Black woman, but not that the hearings and their televising
might have been, through their treatment of Anita Hill as well as Clarence
Thomas, a symbolic lynching of African Americans in general. Our focus on
gender politics was, to an extent, justified: the official topic of the hearings
was, after all, sexual harassment, and race was rarely mentioned by any of the
protagonists or media commentators. But the television camera showed racial
difference clearly in shot after shot of white questioners, Black respondents,
and white listeners. The white skin of Thomas's wife was as vivid in the visual
discourse as it was silenced in the verbal.

I don't wish to suggest either that all white discussions of the hearings were
color-blind (I'm sure they were not) or that my circle of friends is a representative sample of whites in general. But I do want to point out that our comparative neglect of the racial dimension was widely reproduced in the public discourse of the white media, and that our discussions could be legitimately
described as "white" in that they differed significantly from those that, as we
later learned, were taking place among Black Americans. During and immediately after the hearings, these Black responses were confined largely to the
Black community and received little public circulation. This can be attributed in
part to the whiteness of the media, but partly, too, to the difficulty for African
Americans of reaching any consensus about an appropriate response to the

80   hearings' complex and contradictory mix of race and gender, particularly in front of a white audience.

One widespread Black meaning was that the parade of Black sexuality by and for whites on white media could only damage Black interests: only whites had anything to gain by it. To whites, the imagined large Black penis symbolizes the sexualization of the Black threat to the white social order. The Black male body out of control, whether on the streets of Los Angeles or in the bedrooms of the suburbs, incarnates the white fear of the fragility of the white social order and the racial power it exercises. And as throughout the 1980s Reaganomics widened the gaps between whites and Blacks and depressed African Americans even further, it increased the white fear that this sharpened sense of difference might cause the body of Black America to break out of control and erupt. The power of the Black male body has always figured centrally in the nightmare that forms the dark side of the American dream: it was the product and the target of lynchings, and in late Reaganism this figure loomed even larger—Willie Horton, Rodney King, Mike Tyson, and, as its obverse, Clarence Thomas and Bill Cosby.

The White House put Ken Duberstein in charge of its campaign to secure the confirmation of Clarence Thomas to the Supreme Court.[1] His previous job for Bush had been in the 1988 election, when he masterminded the advertising campaign that included the Willie Horton commercial (see chapter 3 and *Sidebar: Willie Horton*, p. 144). Clarence Thomas's strategic and, in the short run, decisive charge that the hearings had become a "high-tech lynching of an uppity Black man" shows the Duberstein hallmark in its button-pushing appeal to this sexual/racial figure in the white imagination. At the immediate instrumental level, the charge put the white Democrats discursively into the category of the lynch mob and tapped into the anxieties that characterize the post-civil rights United States to disable their criticism by coloring it in advance with overt racism, and thus to discredit it in a society whose racism must be covert. By making overt the figuring of Thomas as the overpotent Black stud, this strategy made that figuring impossible. He was thus turned into the category waiting to receive him with open arms, that of the tamed Black man. This Clarence Thomas offered himself to white America as the seductively reassuring obverse of Willie Horton, Rodney King, and Mike Tyson.

If, in these white Republican politics, Thomas was the reassuringly tamed Black man, then Anita Hill had to be turned into the female equivalent of what Thomas no longer was. The uncontrolled sexuality of the Black woman may not loom as large in white fear as her male counterpart, but it is always there, serving as an alibi for the white male use of the Black woman as his sexual property and, at the same time, as a threat to his sexual competence. Orrin Hatch was no fool when he used the horrific world of *The Exorcist* as the ground wherein to locate this threatening Anita Hill.

Some months later, when women, both Black and white, were demonstrably turning Anita Hill's local defeat into a series of broader victories, David Brock in the *American Spectator* tried to recover lost ground by simultaneously pathologizing and hypersexualizing Anita Hill.[2] He recruited to his strategy male students, presumably white and certainly conservative, at Oral Roberts University (whose law school had been bought by Pat Robertson's right-wing Christian organization): one, Lawrence Shiles, claimed that he had found pubic hairs in an assignment returned to him by Anita Hill (see *Sidebar: Hyperreality Hypersexuality*, p. 77); another, when asked how he knew that the hair was pubic, replied with the cliché, "You just know it when you see it." The cliché, which more commonly serves to turn the conservative reaction to pornography into a definition of it, together with the laughter of these adolescent fundamentalist youths, would seem to locate these pubic hairs in a white imagination every bit as fevered as William Peter Blatty's rather than on a can of Coke or in the pages of an assignment. No one would corroborate the affidavit, so the Republicans were unable to use it in the hearings. David Brock, however, felt no such constraint, and used it imaginatively to demonstrate that the "real" Anita Hill was as "real" as the fictional character in Blatty's horror novel, and thus unwittingly revealed that the Black pubic hair's only "reality" lay in the fearful imagination of white men.

In his lengthy and detailed article (which he later turned into a book), Brock cites evidence that leads him to conclude that Anita Hill's accusations stemmed from a combination of professional ineptitude and sexual frustration. His figuring of her as the pathologically sexual woman reproduces that of Senator John Danforth, who, on the morning after Anita Hill's initial testimony, went before the TV cameras to accuse her of "erotomania," a sexual disorder in which a repressed and unsatisfied desire for a man produces delusions in the woman. This obscure disorder was brought into the debate by Bush's nephew, Jamie. He told the White House of a dinner-table conversation in which a Dr. Satinover, a psychiatrist, had described its symptoms. Within hours, the doctor was in Danforth's offices, and shortly after, Danforth went public with the "erotomania theory." He was, however, not allowed to go unchallenged: Alessandra Stanley in the *New York Times* was quick to charge him with "erotomonomania," or the "male delusion that attractive young women are harboring fantasies about them." And Mary Jo, on *Designing Women*, retaliated that the only delusions were those of aging white male senators "if they think American women are gonna continue to reelect them after they get on TV and say stuff like that."

Apart from Mary Jo's one-word recognition of Danforth's whiteness, race was largely repressed from the surface of this argument, conducted as it was between white women and white men. But repressing it did not erase it, and traces of it were always visible although generally seen less clearly by whites than by Blacks. The threat of the sexually uncontrolled woman is intensified

82   when racialized, and, when racial and sexual politics are simultaneous, the stakes for African Americans are much higher than for Caucasians. In these conditions, the politics of the reclaimed dirty joke becomes much more problematic.

Mary Jo's and Bernice's ability to joke about Long Dong Silver and the importance men give to inequality below the waist does not extend to Black women, certainly not when the penis is Black and the audience is white. In a PBS documentary screened on the anniversary of the hearings, some Black women took the opportunity to express their anxiety in public: as one put it, with horror in her voice, "There was this Black, I mean really Black, dark, dark Black man, and here they're going to put his penis all over the screen!"[3] The history of African Americans tells them unequivocally that any white attention to Black sexuality is likely to result in rape or lynching: Black survival depends upon keeping Black sexuality out of the sight of whites. On the same program, Paula Giddings explained this fear:

> Sexuality is taboo in the Black community, in terms of public revelation, for reasons that are very obvious if you know anything about Black history. Racism has always been based, for our community, upon sexual difference in many ways and in many cases—not just racial difference, not just color difference, but Black people were defined by being sexually different from whites in this society. So anything that seems to confirm that view, especially when revealed in public, gives us a lot of ambivalence, makes us very, very nervous. Historically, in the late nineteenth century, for example, that kind of difference got people lynched, that kind of difference got women raped.

bell hooks has traced in detail how whites have historically constructed Black women as "sexual savages" as a racial-sexual strategy of power.[4] She is sympathetic to Black women such as Tina Turner, who attempt to turn this construction to their own advantage, but her final conclusion is that its politics are so oppressive as to make it unreclaimable. Senators Danforth and Hatch, therefore, had a powerful weapon at hand in their assault on Anita Hill in particular and Black women in general. And in their immediate arena, it was effective: not only was the Judiciary Committee unconvinced by Anita Hill, but polls taken immediately after the hearings showed that the majority of Americans, both white and Black, shared their disbelief. In the wider arena of racism-sexism, their invocation of the Black female sexual savage was also effective. bell hooks gives evidence that the anxieties recognized by Paula Giddings were justified:

> Many black folks can testify that the Thomas hearings seemed to have a profound impact on many white Americans. . . . A number of

black females I know have said they have been the objects of
unprecedented assaults both verbal and physical by white males
since the Thomas hearings. Concurrently, the Thomas hearings
exacerbated overall social bashing of black females, and professional
black females in particular.[5]

It is, therefore, not surprising that many African Americans saw the televising of the hearings in terms of lynching and raping, not so much of Clarence
Thomas and Anita Hill in particular as of African Americans in general. Television and the white senators worked together to continue this sexualization of
white supremacy: Trellie Jeffers, for instance, felt that "black women were
raped on national television, and black men were doused with gasoline in front
of one million viewers."[6] Charles Lawrence saw the hearings as a continuation
of "a history of black men lynched and castrated, of black women raped — with
no fear of consequences."[7] U.S. Representative Charlie Hayes considered that
both Thomas and Hill were lynched by the hearings, and that "if one or both
parties were Caucasian the scenario would have been drastically different,
Americans would not have been privy to such a spectacle."[8] The Rodney King
beating was in one sense a lower-class replay of the hearings. The widely replayed video showed a Black man being beaten by four white cops while between nineteen and twenty-three others looked on.[9] Rodney King's beating
was physical, Anita Hill's and Clarence Thomas's verbal: the batons and boots
of the four cops replayed the words of the Judiciary Committee; the circle of
watching cops stood for the Senate; and the white media made a national spectacle of each event.[10]

Many African Americans saw the hearings as further evidence of their "total
subordination in the political machinations of a tiny calculating elite."[11] They
argued that Anita Hill was used by white Democrats and white feminists to
advance their own agendas, but not that of Black people, in the same way Clarence Thomas was used by white Republicans to advance theirs. A Black
woman told me that she and her friends discussed the similarities between the
hearings and the Marion Barry case: both involved the white use of Black female sexuality to bring down a powerful Black man.[12] There were, of course,
crucial differences: Barry's position of power resulted from Black votes, Thomas's from white patronage. Consequently, different white agendas were advanced in each case, but both were white. It was tragically easy to see the hearings as a contest between a Black man and white feminists,[13] and even
moderate Black women were often critical of the feminist performance, Kimberle Crenshaw for one:

> Content to rest their case on a raceless tale of gender subordination,
> white feminists missed an opportunity to span the chasm between
> feminism and anti-racism. Indeed, feminists actually helped maintain

84   the chasm by endorsing the framing of the event as a race versus a gender issue.[14]

For other Black women, however, putting gender second to race advanced Black patriarchy, for it defined the interests of the race as masculine and thus continued the double oppression of Black women. As Barbara Smith put it: "The Hill-Thomas confrontation reinforced the perception that any Black woman who raises the issue of sexual oppression in the African American community is somehow a traitor to the race, which translates into being a traitor to Black men."[15] Calvin Hernton made the point forcefully when he wrote:

> The ideology of race first and sex second fosters both white supremacy and male supremacy, and it underpins the racial oppression of black women and men. At the same time it underpins the sexual oppression of both black and white women. . . .
> Because it is impossible to separate their sex from their race, and since they are at once sexually and racially oppressed, the primary target of the ideology of race first and sex second are black women. . . . the ideology of race first and sex second verifies and denies that sexual oppression exists, and it prohibits and penalizes anyone who says that sexism and racism are intertwined and that they should be fought as one.[16]

In this light, Anita Hill's decision to break the silence imposed by the ideology of "race first" could be seen as a victory. The hearings allowed a Black woman and her oppression to be heard by millions across the nation, and that, according to Julianne Malveaux, is no small matter:

> But here is the bottom line. Supreme Court Justice Clarence Thomas was confirmed because he invoked the image of a black man hanging. They don't make ropes for black women's lynchings or destroy us with high drama. Instead, it is the grind of daily life that wears us slowly down, the struggle for a dignified survival. Black women work the same endless day white women do, but when we juggle work and family, we also bear the burden of the racism that shapes the composition of our households. We are not lynched, just chipped at by the indignity swallowed, the harassment ignored, the gossamer thread of job security frayed by last hired, first fired. We have been taught silence, and Anita Hill's lifted voice is evidence that she finally found the Sojourner within her.[17]

In 1981, bell hooks had pointed out that "no other group in America has so had their identity socialized out of existence as have black women,"[18] and now, ten years later, Black feminists were still having to make the same point. For Kimberle Crenshaw, for example, Anita Hill showed Americans "the place where African-American women live, a political vacuum of erasure and contradiction . . . existing within the overlapping margins of race and gender discourse and in the empty spaces between, it is a location whose very nature resists telling."[19] But Anita Hill told it, and her story was the spur for Black women to form a grassroots organization called African American Women in Defense of Ourselves. Their manifesto, signed by more than 1,600, was published in a full-page advertisement in the *New York Times*[20] and reprinted widely. These Black women continued the public speech that Anita Hill began. Barbara Smith calls this a "watershed in black feminist organizing." "Never before," she writes, "have so many black women publicly stated their refusal to pit racial oppression against sexual oppression," and she goes on to record the continued outpouring of support and the organizers' intention to create a mechanism for organizing and speaking out.[21]

The importance for African Americans of overcoming their silencing by Caucasian America comes to the surface again in the Los Angeles uprisings. Many used looting and arson as public speech, the only Black speech that whites would listen to (see chapter 3 and *Sidebar: Looting So to Speak*, p. 174). For them, the media attention was their victory over silencing. But, when multiaxial oppression works as fluidly as it does, such victories may not be claimed by all, may not be recognized by all. For some, Anita Hill's public speech was so effective because her quiet steadfastness appeared to disarticulate her and therefore Black women from the category of "the sexual savage." For others, however, her calmness fitted her into the category of the "enduring woman" in a way that undercut the positive aspects of her speaking out. bell hooks identifies the contradictory effects of her way of speaking:

> To many viewers, her calm demeanor was a sign of her integrity,
> that she had chosen the high moral ground. Yet to some of us, it
> was yet another example of black female stoicism in the face of
> sexist/racist abuse. While it may not have changed the outcome of
> the hearings in any way, had Hill been more strategic and
> passionate, and dare I say it, even angry at the assault on her
> character, it would have made the hearings less an assault on the
> psyches of black females watching and on women viewers in
> general.
>
> Contrary to those who wish to claim that the hearings were in
> some way a feminist victory, it was precisely the absence of either a
> feminist analysis on Hill's part or a feminist response that made this
> spectacle more an example of female martyrdom and victimization
> than of a constructive confrontation with patriarchal male
> domination. Black women have always held an honored place in the
> hall of female martyrdom. As Anita Hill's friend Ellen Wells declared
> in a passionate defense of Hill not initiating a case against Thomas
> when the harassment first occurred, "Being a black woman, you

86   know you have to put up with a lot so you grit your teeth and do it." With this comment, Wells evoked a tradition of female martyrdom and masochism.[22]

For *Ebony*, however, Anita Hill's speaking out helped Black women to throw off their cloak of invisibility and silence. Twelve months later, the magazine dubbed 1992 "The Year of the Black Woman": "For this year . . . the power and presence of Black women is being felt in politics, literature, sports, entertainment, science, education and religion."[23] The magazine led its account of Black women's achievements with that of Carol Moseley Braun, the Illinois Democrat and first Black woman to be elected to the Senate. Her success was attributed to the alliance that she forged among inner-city Blacks, women, and other Democrats; the most influential factor in making this alliance possible was Anita Hill. Braun is not alone. Black women challenged for seats in either the House of Representatives or the Senate in at least ten states.[24] Johnetta B. Cole, the first Black woman president of Spelman College, summarizes "The Year of the Black Woman":

> What dynamics have come into play to make this possible? Surely it is a complex of factors, but among them must be: The role of law professor Anita Hill in bringing the issue of sexual harassment before the eyes of millions of Americans: the fact that large numbers of Americans are tired of the antics of so many politicians and are interested in seeing if women can do any better; and the coming of age of Black feminism as a connector between the modern Black Liberation and Women's movements.[25]

Gender Articulations

In the public domain, these Black contestations over the hearings came after the female ones. This may be because white women immediately united around the more straightforward gender politics of the hearings, whereas African America was far more conflicted about their racial ones. It may also be because the white media allowed readier access to white female voices than to Black ones. But whatever the reasons, the women's fight to regain the ground lost by the confirmation was the one that first gained public recognition. This struggle was so successful that nine months later, the *New York Times* could run a front-page story that began,

> Sexual harassment complaints to the Equal Employment Opportunities Commission are up sharply [by over 50%], Congress and the White House have responded to complaints of sexual abuse in the military in ways that would have been unimaginable nine months ago. Employers are scurrying to hire sensitivity trainers to

teach men how to treat women. And men are wondering how they failed to notice the anger of their female colleagues. This change in American attitudes, experts of both sexes and all political persuasions agree, is a direct result of last fall's nationally televised colloquium on sexual harassment, the Anita Hill-Clarence Thomas hearings.[26]

The article could have added that donations to the Women's Campaign Fund have run at double their prehearings rate, that more women than ever before stood for election in 1992, that enrollments in women's studies courses in universities surged, and that for months after the hearings women were wearing lapel buttons proclaiming, "I believe Anita Hill." Anita Hill herself has had a hectic schedule of public lectures in which she used her "defeat" to continue women's struggles against harassment at work, and *60 Minutes* ran a sympathetic portrait of her. *Designing Women* joined in women's reclamation of the defeat, and, in the episode in which its characters watched the hearings on TV, gave a national voice to women's pride in Anita Hill's courage, to their anger at her treatment, to their dismay at the verdict, and to their determination not to take it lying down. The episode climaxed with a passionate outcry by Mary Jo:

> I'm sorry! Your time is up. Listen, I don't mean to be strident and overbearing; I used to be nice, but quite frankly, nice doesn't cut it. We want to be treated equally and with respect. Is that too much to ask? Like a lot of women around this country tonight I'm mad! I'm mad because we're 51 percent of the population and only 2 percent of the United States Senate. I'm mad because 527 men in the House of Representatives have a pool, a sauna, a gym and we have six hair dryers and a Ping-Pong table. I'm mad because in spite of the fact that we scrub America's floors, wash her dishes, commit very little of the crime, and have all of the babies, we still make 58 cents on the dollar. As a matter of fact, I don't know about the rest of the women out there, but I don't give a damn anymore if you call me a feminist or a fruitcake—I just know I am so mad I am going to get in my car and drive to the centermost point of the United States of America and climb to the top of a tower and shout, "Don't get us wrong, we love you, BUT . . . who the hell do you men think you are?"

A graduate student of mine held long telephone conversations with women about this episode.[27] Two of the words used most frequently by those with whom she spoke were "validation" and "vindication"; these were combined with a sense of solidarity among all women, and a sharp sense of how rare it was for women's point of view to gain public circulation. Typical comments included the following: "It was powerful and validating—on prime-time TV! I get so tired of the male media." "You know, the show made me feel vindicated, like I knew I was right. I know she was right, the show reminded me of that."

88   "She made me proud to be who I am. The program was healing for me, I was finally able to laugh about this." "What really sticks out for me was that this was on mainstream TV, and I didn't feel alone." This sense of validation and solidarity could extend into the politics of personal behavior, and women reported they felt emboldened to stand up against harassment at work or to answer back to the jerk at the bus stop.

It is interesting to note that many of these women considered *Designing Women* to act as a corrective not only to masculine power in the workplace, but also to the masculine bias of TV. In this, it joined *Murphy Brown* (which ran immediately before it in the schedule). Despite including Anthony, a nonthreatening Black male, among its characters, *Designing Women* did focus on gender, rather than racial, issues. Indeed, the script for this particular episode contained only four explicit references to race, and of those, only two survived the editing deck to reach the screen. Both these shows appear to me to repress racial discourse. Some of *Designing Women's* viewers, however, disagree with me; they considered that racial differences were not repressed, but transcended by emphasis on gender. One, for instance, a half-Irish, half-Cherokee woman, said of Anita:

> Her color had nothing to do with it—she represented all women and what is happening to all women. I was angry, but also proud to be a woman. . . . We talked about this at work, too. Does it matter if all the women I work with are Black? I don't think it does, we all watch the show and we all watched the hearings. We all work together all day, and we keep bringing up points that piss us off: everybody's got stories on sexual harassment—the color of the man isn't the important thing, though it was funny to hear these women talk about how common it is for Black men to be so arrogant and into their own sexuality. The biggest thing is that no one believes you. They don't take you seriously, you know, you're the one overreacting. Nobody takes you seriously, even some women. We all felt good about this episode, though, and we were all proud of her. We felt bad for her, too, but she did it for all of us. She'll be remembered for what she did, she's a very courageous woman to do that.

We must note, however, that this woman is not Black, and, for her Black coworkers, gender solidarity did not overcome racial difference altogether; they experienced a specifically Black dimension to sexual harassment that whites did not.

On the other side of the gender battlefront, conservatives mobilized to hold the ground the vote had given them. Rush Limbaugh and Phyllis Schlafly, for instance, quickly recognized that the conservative victory in the hearings was temporary at best. Both of them have radio shows, and Schlafly is as tireless as

Anita Hill on the lecture circuit. Limbaugh claims that the liberal media (most of his examples of which are mainstream TV) have combined to show "how far America is being dragged into the cloud-cuckoo-land of feminism,"[28] and that feminists didn't care if Anita Hill was telling the truth, the airing of her charges was what they wanted: "Anita Hill was nothing more than a football to be kicked around to score points for feminism."[29] Interestingly, his charges are almost identical to those made by some Black women, but similar accusations articulated differently in different alliances have quite different politics: Limbaugh's advance dominant conservative male interests, the Black women's those of a minority oppressed by both gender and race.

Phyllis Schlafly, who came to fame as leader of the successful "Stop ERA" campaign in the early 1980s, has never flagged in her campaign against women's rights. She, too, believes that radical feminists used Anita Hill and the hearings to push their views, through the liberal media, upon the American public. The feminists' use of the sexual harassment issue is, Schlafly claims, an example of "trying to have it both ways: they want to be a macho man and they want to be a victim someone will protect."[30] Like Rush Limbaugh, Schlafly sees Hillary Rodham Clinton as promoting the same agenda, and her argument moves back and forth between Anita Hill and Hillary Clinton as easily as does Quayle/Buchanan's between Murphy Brown and Hillary Clinton. She also sets herself against the gains made by women in increasing their political representation in 1992. Despite, or maybe because of, three failed attempts to be elected, she advises most women to stay out of politics because it is just not in their nature: "Women don't like to do what you have to do to get to Congress. Life isn't worth that kind of commitment to the majority of women."[31]

Articulations of Class

If, on the gender front, the victory was uncertain, on a class or populist one, Washington lost. There was a widespread belief that regardless of the outcome, the hearings gave the U.S. public a clear view of how badly politicians could behave. On the front of "them" versus "us," of "Washington" versus "everyday America," television inflicted grievous damage upon the credibility of "the power structure." Not only fictional programs refused to let the verdict be the last word: typical of many responses was that of WXYZ TV in Detroit. An interview of Orrin Hatch by Bill Bonds, one of the station's news anchors, ended with Hatch storming out of the studio in a fury (see *Sidebar: Bonds and Hatch*, p. 90). The antagonism was neither racial nor gendered, but a populist one between the people and Washington. The call for change behind which Clinton rallied his electoral forces included, besides changes in policy, changes in the relationship between politicians and the people. He managed to position his team as part of "us" and Bush's as "them," and in these populist sentiments to activate both class and age politics.

Bonds and Hatch

BILL BONDS: I have to say to you, sir, as an American from the Midwest, that frankly—that was kind of an embarrassing spectacle. Do you regret that that went on?

ORRIN HATCH: It was a tense, difficult process, as it should be. And it was made worse because of one dishonest senator who leaked raw FBI data—

BONDS: Senator, you guys leak all the time.

HATCH: No we don't.

BONDS: Who are you trying to kid? You guys leak stuff all the time.

HATCH: Let me just say something, that's not true.

BONDS: Yes, it is.

HATCH: No, not FBI reports from the Judiciary Committee. I've been here fifteen years. I have not seen leaks of FBI reports, because they contain raw data—

BONDS: Okay, your conduct was great. You guys all looked terrific; 250 million Americans are really proud of Senator Orrin Hatch and all the rest of you guys.

HATCH: I'm not, I'm not—

BONDS: You did a marvelous job. You never made the country look better. Let me ask you something: What are you going to do if you find out six months from now that Clarence Thomas—who you've just about made into a saint—is a porno freak?

HATCH: Don't worry, we won't. But I'll tell you this: If you're going to interview us in the future, you ought to be at least courteous. You're about as discourteous a person as I've ever interviewed with. I don't like it, and I don't like what you're doing. I go through enough crap back here, I don't have to go through it with you. Let me tell you something—

BONDS: No, let me tell you something—

HATCH: No, you tell yourself something. I'm tired of talking to you. [Removes microphone and steps off-camera.]

BONDS: Okay, fine. I'm tired of talking to you. See you later.

(interview transcript in *Washington Journalism Review*, December 1991, and reprinted in *Harper's*, February 1992, 18)

Populism, as a way of inflecting class difference, has uncertain and risky politics. In recent history, the right has generally been more effective than the left in claiming the class resentment that fuels it. Clinton succeeded in tapping into some of it, but there is no fixed relationship between populist sentiments and party affiliation, and Rush Limbaugh consistently gives populist resentment a right-wing accent. His constant attacks on today's women—Murphy Brown, Hillary Rodham Clinton, and Anita Hill—recode class resentment into gender antagonism, a strategy also used by Peggy Noonan, a white speechwriter for Reagan and Bush, who argued that the hearings revealed "class division" between the "chattering classes" who supported Anita Hill and the "normal humans" who believed Thomas. She figured the difference between them by analyzing the character witnesses for each: Susan Hoerchner, one of today's women supporting Anita Hill, was characterized as "professional, movement-y, and intellectualish," with an "unmakeupped face." But Clarence

Thomas was validated by J. C. Alvarez, who was "Maybellined," "straight shooting," and "the voice of the real, as opposed to the abstract, America." Noonan read Anita Hill's professional behavior as a marker of class difference: a "real American" (that is, a blue-collar one), when faced with the harassment Hill suffered, "would kick him in the gajoobies and haul him straight to court."[32] The mobility of class difference is astonishing: lower-class resentment is here mobilized for Clarence Thomas (the boss) against Anita Hill (the subordinate)! Class power, when taken up by currents of masculinism and Republicanism, can be turned and made to flow "upstream," against its normal social topography. Nellie McKay recognized a similar resentment among lower-class Black women of Hill's ineptitude at handling Thomas's dirty remarks: they would have put their hands on their hips and given him a good tongue-lashing, and, if that failed, a well-aimed kick would have followed.[33]

Nancy Fraser gives an insightful class analysis of the currents and countercurrents swirling around the hearings. She cites a *New York Times* article that also reported that blue-collar women (we presume white) were put off by Anita Hill's soft-spokenness and, in their eyes, failure to deal with Thomas on the spot. The article contrasted this "blue-collar" view (in which, incidentally, we can hear an echo of bell hooks's race-gender based strictures) with those of the professional classes who strongly supported and believed Anita Hill. Nancy Fraser's analysis grants this class resentment a degree of validity, but points to its limitations: "Working-class people who felt that Hill should simply have told Thomas off and quit and found another job were not attuned to professional career structures, which require cultivation of one's reputation in the profession via networking and long-term maintenance of relationships."[34]

In the *Frontline* documentary screened by PBS to mark the first anniversary of the hearings, a similar pattern of gendered class difference was given a racial inflection. Most of the Black women that it showed supporting Anita Hill were ones with professional careers; the criticism of her was voiced by women with lower-class jobs, such as hairdressing, and, of course, by some men. Race, gender, and class differences are each structured and experienced in terms of the others, and the multiaxiality of power as it is both exerted and resisted results in a fluidity and multiplicity of positions from which any event may be viewed. Cornel West, for instance, laments that from the point of view of most Black leaders, class seemed to be invisible. With passionate clarity he shows the racism of economic policies:

> For example, both Thomas and Hill would be viewed as two black
> conservative supporters of some of the most vicious policies to
> besiege black working and poor communities since Jim and Jane
> Crow segregation. Both Thomas and Hill supported an
> unprecedented redistribution of wealth from working people to well-
> to-do people in the form of regressive taxation, deregulation policies,

cutbacks and slowdowns in public service programs, take-backs at the negotiation table between workers and management, and military buildups at the Pentagon. Both Thomas and Hill supported the unleashing of unbridled capitalist market forces on a level never witnessed before in this country that have devastated black working and poor communities. These market forces took the form principally of unregulated corporative and financial expansion and intense entrepreneurial activity. This tremendous ferment in big and small businesses—including enormous bonanzas in speculation, leveraged buy-outs and mergers, as well as high levels of corruption and graft—contributed to a new kind of culture of consumption in white and black America.[35]

Here, he prefigures some of the more radical explanations of the "looting" in the L.A. uprisings: that the real looters were the unregulated corporate capitalists of Reaganomics and that those carrying boxes of Pampers and Nikes from the stores of South-Central were minuscule imitations of the corporate model.

When class power and economic inequality are interwoven with race, gender, and age distinctions, no alliances can be relied upon as structurally determined or taken as self-evident: they have to be consciously and laboriously forged and maintained in a social order characterized by the fluidity of alliances, the multiaxiality of power, and the instability of meanings.

Articulations and Alliances

Articulation is the discursive equivalent of forming social alliances, for making meanings and making allies are part of the same process of putting meanings into social circulation, giving them an effectivity and thus a politics.

Anita Hill was articulated so differently because she was pulled into so many different and often contradictory alliances in which gender, race, class, party politics, and a sort of populism were pulled together in multiple and, at times, surprising configurations. The hearings were so significant and controversial partly because their politics were so complex and so contradictory. They could be understood in a number of different ways, according to how the social axes involved were articulated: party political thought articulated them around the axis of Democrat versus Republican, progressive versus conservative, left versus right; in gender politics they showed a lone woman up against ranks of men wielding immense institutional power; in racial politics they showed white against Black; in more populist politics they showed one of "us" against "them," the ordinary person against "Washington"; and in class politics they showed the professional classes fighting over what lower classes often saw as trivial.

Each of these axes of power could be, and in many cases were, articulated with and disarticulated from any or all of the others. Each point where these different axes were brought to intersect was a point of articulation: it was a hinge point from which one could speak and thus identify oneself, one's allies, and one's enemies. The multiaxiality of speech and alliance is a multiaxiality of social identity. Each articulation changes the meanings carried by each power axis. The meanings of femininity, for instance, depend upon their racial articulations and on their class ones: femininity may be an axis of unity among all women, but its intersections with the axes of race and class produce differences that may disrupt that unity. Being a Black woman in the United States is necessarily different from being a white woman because of the different histories that lie behind each social identity or point of intersection, but alliances can be formed across these differences if *both* parties consent to the repression of difference involved. And the intersections of class or age with gender and race bring other points of difference into the picture, so that Murphy Brown (white/ middle-class/mature/feminine) differs multiaxially from the figure of the unmarried Black teenage mother, despite the commonality of single motherhood by which Dan Quayle linked Murphy Brown to the L.A. "riots." Unities and alliances along some axes necessarily repress the differences of others, and, for the alliance to be effective, any repression of difference must be consented to by all, particularly by those for whom the axis of difference is one of subordination. A social identity formed at any one point of intersection can always be shifted to another by reconfiguring the play of similarity and difference that is central to the multiaxial politics of identity. The concept of identity here is not essentialist or individualistic but relational, for it forms the point from which social alliances are entered: the social identity of Anita Hill, who she was or could be made to be, was important because it determined which alliances she could be pulled into and therefore which political ends she could be made to serve. But not all social axes are brought into play in every point of identification or alliance: for instance, I heard little evidence from those speaking as Black/female/lower-class that party politics mattered much at all. For those speaking as white/female/upper-class, however, the Republican-Democrat axis was salient, because it was determinate in the abortion rights issue that mattered so intensely to them.

This multiaxiality of discursive and social alliances means that the identities it produces are as fluid as the process. Because Anita Hill came into Washington as unmarried, Black, female, successful, and quietly self-assured, the Beltway had no pigeonhole to fit her into. Who she *was* appeared an open question, and the politicians rushed to answer it. A year later, Anita Hill gave her perception of this process:

> Not only did the Senate fail to understand or to recognize me,
> because of my lack of attachment to certain institutions, like marriage

and patronage, they failed to relate to my race, my gender, my race
and gender combined, and in combination with my education, my
career choice and my demeanor. . . .

Because I and my reality did not comport with what they accepted
as their reality, I and my reality had to be reconstructed by the
Senate committee members with assistance from the press and
others. In constructing an explanation for my marital status as single,
I became unmarriageable or opposed to marriage, the fantasizing
spinster or the man hater. An explanation of my career success had
to be introduced which fit with their perceptions about the
qualifications of people of color, women and the myth of the double
advantage enjoyed by women of color.

I thus became aloof, ambitious, an incompetent product of
affirmative action and an ingrate who betrayed those who had
worked for my success.[36]

These hearings provided a clear example of the problems facing the analyst
in poststructural politics when the social categories have lost the fixity of their
relations to each other. In them, progressive women who supported Anita Hill
formed a tactical alliance with Senator Edward Kennedy, whose personal sexual politics, like those of most of the Kennedy men, are ones they would vehemently oppose. But the intersection here of the gender politics of the workplace (sexual harassment) with the gender politics of the law (Thomas was
believed to want to overturn *Roe v. Wade*) and with progressive social policies in
general not only allied them *on this issue* with a male chauvinist but against an
African American who was about to maintain the only nonwhite presence on
the Supreme Court (an objective they would normally applaud). For them,
Thomas's conservatism and maleness were articulated more emphatically than
his Blackness; on other issues the articulations may have been reversed. Some
Black women, however, saw the Anita Hill-Democrat-feminist alliance as a
white one that worked against them: at the articulation of the categories of the
"haves" and the "have-nots" with those of gender and race they saw Anita Hill
being swept up into the "haves" by whites, and thus being taken out of the
"have-nots" in which most Black women are firmly positioned. Other African
Americans, both men and women, allied themselves with Clarence Thomas because they saw him as a Black man about to break through the glass ceiling and
the Democrats as whites trying to stop him: his conservatism, in racial as other
matters, was relegated to the margins. Equally contradictorily, white Democrats and feminists formed their alliance around a conservative woman who,
previously, had supported "that man with the notoriously racist and sexist reputation, Judge Robert Bork, in his unsuccessful campaign for a seat on the Supreme Court,"[37] and had taught at the right-wing Christian fundamentalist
Oral Roberts University. (Anita Hill claims to have been misunderstood on her

support for Bork.)[38] Similarly, racist Republican supporters would have had to
ally themselves with Democrats, feminists, and a Black woman to maintain the
glass ceiling and "keep Blacks in their place." So it is not surprising if, on this
issue, some progressive nonsexist Black men gave highest priority to the racial
axis and allied themselves with white Republicans whom normally they would
oppose. Robert Staples gives his account of the tactical and strategic fluidity
and the consequent apparent contradictions of the alliances involved:

> And old alliances meant nothing. The former segregationists, the
> current perpetuators of racial buzzwords (eg, quotas, welfare, crime)
> found themselves supporting a black man, with a white wife. Anita
> Hill's most visible supporters were middle-class white women, who
> identified with the issue—if not with her. Most non-southern white
> Democratic males sided with Hill and Republican white males
> overwhelmingly supported Thomas. Since people claimed it was
> impossible to tell who was telling the truth, they came down on the
> side of their racial, gender or political preferences and interest—at
> least the whites did. Blacks were almost divided down the middle
> over Thomas (about 60% supported him after the hearings).[39]

Politics that are fought on a multiaxial terrain, politics that are fought
around perceived social interests in which gains often have to be paid for with
losses, politics that involve tactical alliances formed for occasions and issues,
are politics of fluidity, contradiction, and uncertainty: difficult though they
may be, they are the politics with which we have to cope in late capitalism. The
struggles that these fluidities make possible and necessary are well illustrated
in the aftermath of the hearings. On its own turf, in front of its own crowd, the
power bloc won, and Clarence Thomas took his seat on the Supreme Court.
But, as the Rodney King case also demonstrated, verdicts in the courtroom or
the Senate do not necessarily carry over into the streets and workplaces of everyday life. A verdict that closes the argument in one setting may stimulate it in
another.

If the Anita Hill case can indeed be made to forge alliances between the
Black liberation and the women's movements and to bridge the gaps that have
sometimes separated them, then this may prove in the long term to be the most
politically significant victory of all. Nellie McKay believes that it can; she is confident in her belief that Anita Hill is the best thing that has happened to the
feminist movement for the past twenty-five years.[40] The electoral success of
Carol Moseley Braun is a welcome indicator that the possibility can be realized.

The struggles to reclaim the verdict of the hearings were as contradictory
and multiaxial as the alliances formed around them. But we must recognize
that this analysis of their multiaxiality comes with the benefit of hindsight and
from outside the battleground: those who engaged in the struggle at the time
did not fight on all axes, but tended to give high priority to one or two, and to

96   minimize others. It would appear that effective engagement requires a focus of
energy that reduces the fronts on which one fights and therefore the alliances
one forms, whereas long-term coalition building requires a much broader grasp
of the contradictions that may, in the short term, make effective action harder
to organize. It is difficult to fight on all fronts at once without dispersing one's
energy, and a tightly focused struggle may, in its immediate effects, appear
more likely to succeed. But if the alliances formed to fight it make other potential allies feel excluded, then the outcome may be hostility where there ought to
be friendship.

The complications of these multiaxial politics, however, produce opportunities as well as difficulties: their multiplicity means that the position of every
social formation will overlap to some extent with that of others, that every
alliance will have social axes along which it can reach out to others. Sexual
harassment, for example, whether in the workplace, on the streets, or in the
home, is a common experience for all women in our society: although the
experience of it will be inflected by racial and class positions—African American women and blue-collar women, for example, will experience it quite differently from Murphy Brown—it retains a gender commonality that may facilitate
interracial and interclass alliances. Black and white women in lower-class
positions, to give another example, held very similar views of Anita Hill's
method of coping with Thomas's harassment, which offered an opportunity,
unfortunately not taken, to form an interracial alliance along the axis of class.

These opportunities for alliance building, or, in Gramsci's terms, bloc formation, are not offered equally to all: our history of dominations has seen to
that. The dominant alliances that characterize the power bloc have a long history of effectiveness. The result of this is that whiteness, masculinity, the upper classes, and older ages can be so effortlessly articulated together that the
alliance appears natural. The history of applied and effective power has
smoothed any rough edges between their different axes with the result that
their mutuality of interests makes them so interwoven that, in effect, their
multiaxiality becomes monoaxiality. But there are more ways of being subordinated than of dominating. As a result, subordinated social formations are
more varied and more numerous than dominant ones. Their histories are more
varied, too, and have developed fewer means of smoothing out the differences
between them. Consequently, alliances between subaltern social formations are harder to form and maintain than are those within the power bloc.
Opportunities to form them, however, do occur, and if the politics of a poststructural world are to be progressive rather than oppressive, we must learn
to develop our skills of alliance building and maintenance. If we do not, the
danger of a one-superpower world will become a national as well as a global
reality.

Black Figures: Clarence Thomas and Bill Cosby

The battles around Anita Hill and Clarence Thomas were as strong as they were because both figured wide and deep conflicts in U.S. culture. Fast-flowing and deep cultural currents, such as those bearing meanings of race, sexuality, and the family, will surface in different places and in different configurations. If the hearings were a maelstrom, *The Cosby Show* appears a calm backwater in comparison. Yet its benign surface is precisely that, for only just below it similar currents and countercurrents muddy its waters.

The Cosby Show is relevant to my analysis for a number of reasons. The conservative strategy in the hearings was, though not explicitly, to join Clarence Thomas with Bill Cosby/Cliff Huxtable to figure the "tamed Black male": its corollary, therefore, was to figure Anita Hill as the sexual savage, the opposite of Clair Huxtable. Figures can always be positive or negative, they can always be written with a plus or a minus. So, if x = the Black male and y = the Black female (in white figuring), then $+x$ = Clarence Thomas and Bill Cosby/Cliff Huxtable, and $-x$ = Willie Horton and Rodney King. Similarly $+y$ = Clair Huxtable, $-y$ = Anita Hill. It was thus an appropriate calculation for Tom Bradley, the Black mayor of Los Angeles ($+x$), to advise people to stay at home and watch the final episode of *The Cosby Show* ($+x$) rather than go out on the streets to participate in the uprisings ($-x$). The fact that the final episode coincided with the uprisings is one of those noncoincidences of history. If, in the realm of family values, *Married . . . with Children* (see below) was known by Fox executives as "not *The Cosby Show*," so, in the realm of race relations, the events on the streets of South-Central Los Angeles could be known nationally as "very definitely not *The Cosby Show*."

The Cosby Show grew and flourished alongside Reaganism: indeed, Henry Louis Gates has called the 1980s "the Cosby decade."[41] First screened in 1984, it headed the ratings from 1985 to 1989, dropped to second place in 1989-90, to fifth in 1990-91, and ended on the second night of the L.A. uprisings in 1992. On the surface it promoted pure Reaganism (and, indeed, Ronald was one of its fans), celebrating as it did the achievement, happiness, and harmony of a professional nuclear family, who happened to be Black. It invited us to watch parents coping cheerfully and successfully with common family problems in raising their kids and adapting traditional gender roles to the changed, if only slightly, conditions of the eighties. Cliff Huxtable/Bill Cosby (the figure merged the fictional and real just as thoroughly as Murphy does) was a gynecologist, Clair a lawyer, and their children, Theo, Sondra, Denise, Vanessa, and Rudi, grew up into and through their teens into young adulthood. Murphy Brown may suffer from the hollowness at the heart of yuppiedom, but for Cliff and Clair the core was solid and satisfying. White conservatives loved what they showed. William Buckley, for instance, thought that "it is simply not correct

98   . . . that race prejudice is increasing in America. How does one know this?
Simply, by the ratings of Bill Cosby's television show and the sales of his books.
A nation simply does not idolize members of a race which that nation de-
spises."[42] The confirmation of Clarence Thomas could, in the same discourse,
be used to prove exactly the same point.

Others have claimed that Bill Cosby is a contemporary Uncle Tom, or Afro-
Saxon, who provides white racism with the alibi that it needs in order to continue working in the post-civil rights United States. But, wherever we stand in
the debate, Bill Cosby was a central figure in the way that Americans struggled
over meanings of race, gender, class, and the family throughout the Reagan
and Bush administrations.

In their book on the show and its audiences, Sut Jhally and Justin Lewis
carefully add up the positives and negatives and calculate that, for whites at
least, Bill Cosby is finally a figure of "enlightened racism."[43] A key calculation
in their analysis, as in one account of Clarence Thomas, is the effectiveness of
"bootstrapping." The concept continues the conservative strategy of laying the
responsibility for failure upon the weak, not the powerful; upon the individual,
not the social order. Everyone, bootstrappers would have us believe, can rise
up through the system by their own efforts, and those who fail have simply not
made the necessary effort. The bootstrap offers the conservative comfort of
knowing that the means of overcoming contemporary racial inequalities lie in
the attitudes and abilities of individual African Americans: white society need
only provide the opportunity and leave the rest to them. The laws of physics
may prove the physical impossibility of lifting oneself up by one's own bootstraps, but the conservative imagination is not hampered by such inconve-
niences as gravity: so in it Clarence and Cosby can easily demonstrate the effectiveness of the bootstrap as an elevator.

Welfare is the opposite of bootstrapping. In conservative discourse, welfare
not only rewards those who have failed to grasp their opportunities but produces in them a dependency mentality that ensures they will never even look
for their bootstraps, let alone tug on them. Clarence Thomas had previously
castigated his sister, Emma Mae Martin, for welfare dependency; at a convention of Black conservatives he told a reporter, "She gets mad when the mail-
man is late with her welfare check, that's how dependent she is. What's worse
is that now her kids feel entitled to the check too. They have no motivation for
doing better or getting out of that situation."[44] (This was his account of her;
others painted a quite different picture—see below. By the time of his nomination, she was supporting her family.) This "welfare mentality" lay, according
to Bush and Quayle, at the heart of L.A.'s problems. Their white imagination
saw it given form in the body of the Black unwed teenage mother, easily recoded as "the welfare mother," whose "poverty of values" was endorsed by
Murphy Brown's fatherless baby. The fear is that welfare will replace the father
with the state (it was, we recall, the "irrelevance of fathers" that worried Rush

Limbaugh so much) and will thus undermine the traditional "family values" to which the Republicans had hitched their campaign wagon. Such beliefs are well rooted in the Republican imagination: in 1986, for example, Gary Bauer opined that "the values taught on *The Cosby Show* would do more to help low-income and minority children than a bevy of new federal programs. [A] lot of research indicates that values are much more important than, say, the level of welfare payments."[45] Views like that cannot have hindered his appointment to head the family planning office within the Education Department. Republicans will always reward those who tax their intelligence rather than their wallets. Bauer later expanded on these views, and underscored the masculinism he shared with both Limbaugh and Quayle, by explaining that what he found most edifying about the show was its depiction of a family where "the children respect the father."[46] Dan Quayle used the same opposition between masculinist family values and welfare in his account of the causes of the L.A. "riots": "A welfare check is not a husband," he explained gravely. "The state is not a father" (see *Sidebar: Dan Quayle*, p. 68). For him, there would have been no riots in South-Central L.A. if it had been populated by bootstrapping, family-centered Clarence Thomases and Bill Cosbys instead of Cripps, Bloods, and welfare mothers.

Much of Clarence Thomas's statement to the Senate Judiciary Committee consisted of his personal story of bootstrapping, in which his individual history was used to authenticate a Republican version of social history. Time and again he returned to his humble origins in Pin Point, Georgia, and his disadvantaged family background (he was raised by his grandparents). This individual history of a man improving his life by struggling up from rural poverty to Yale to the Supreme Court in only forty years was used by him and his conservative supporters to validate not only his own character, but also implicitly their own racial policies, particularly that affirmative action is demonstrably unnecessary. In their critical analysis of the racist effects of *The Cosby Show* within white America, Budd and Steinman cite a 1988 poll showing that 83 percent of whites saw no need for affirmative action, and one in 1991 showing that only 35 percent of whites believed that Congress should do anything to help the position of African Americans.[47]

Many white viewers read the same message in *The Cosby Show*. Typical was one who said while discussing it, "I think there really is room in the United States for minority people to get ahead, without affirmative action,"[48] and Jhally and Lewis's study gives many examples of whites using the show to validate their often passionate belief that affirmative action is unfair to whites. Judge Thomas's opposition to affirmative action policies, like that of some other successful conservative African Americans, speaks indirectly through these readings of Bill Cosby.

However antiracist in intention and origins, affirmative action has all too often been co-opted into white policy, for its implementation remains under the

100   control of white employers, admissions officers, and the courts. Affirmative action was a product of multiracial struggles, and many formations of color still
struggle to claim it as theirs, for it is one of the few institutionalized antiracist
strategies to which they have access. But white power over the ways in which
it is implemented often produces effects that countervene its original intentions. One, which is widely recognized in Black if not in white America, is that
the social formation that has gained most from the policy is that of white
women, particularly professional ones. From this viewpoint, Murphy Brown
and "today's women" appear to have made their progress at the expense of
African Americans. Another, equally distressing, has been the increase in class
differences within African America. In general, the middle-class Blacks who
are least threatening to white society have benefited most from the policy, and
their benefit has widened the gap between them and the blue-collar and underclasses. Michael Eric Dyson identifies another effect of this class divisiveness: "With black track from the inner cities mimicking earlier patterns of white
flight, severe class changes have negatively affected black ghettos. Such class
changes have depleted communities of service establishments, local business
and stores that . . . could provide full-time employment."[49] Black track offers
one partial explanation for the influx of Korean store owners to Black neighborhoods that proved so incendiary in South-Central L.A. (see chapter 3). The
Oprah Winfrey Show on the L.A. uprisings (see *Sidebar: Race and Class*, p. 172)
provided a glimpse of this intraracial conflict between the "haves" and the
"have-nots" in action. Long-term white interests are thus served by the selective and strategic implementations of the policy that contradicts its explicit intention. The solution to the problems that selective affirmative action has
caused within African America lies in taking white power and strategy out of
its implementation. Clarence Thomas, however, used his version of his history
to argue the opposite, that universal opportunity exists and that affirmative action, however implemented, is neither necessary nor beneficial. In opposing
his nomination, the Congressional Black Caucus pointed to the way he himself
had benefited from affirmative action both at Yale and in his subsequent career
in Washington, and thus to the racist effects of his denying that he was selected
as a beneficiary.

     African Americans opposing Clarence Thomas, then, had to rewrite his in-
dividual history to refigure him in the political debate. By figuring in the role of
affirmative action they showed that his rejection of it was also a rejection of the
majority of African Americans whom it was intended to benefit. The NAACP
stated:

> While we appreciate the fact that Judge Thomas came up in the
> school of hard knocks and pulled himself up by his own
> bootstraps — as many other black Americans have — our concern is for
> the millions of blacks who have no access to bootstraps, theirs or

others. It is particularly disturbing that one who has himself so benefitted from affirmative action now denigrates it and would deny those opportunities to other blacks.[50]

In a candidly worded open letter to Clarence Thomas, Justice Leon Higginbotham also reminded him of how much he owed, not only to affirmative action, but to the long Black struggles that produced it.[51] Thomas's criticism of past and present Black leaders in the civil rights movement raised Higginbotham to some of his sternest language, for their work, which Thomas belittled, had made his success possible.

This distance between Thomas and much of African America is authenticated by the rewriting of his individual history. A friend of his family contradicted Thomas's account of the closeness between him and his grandfather, and between him and the Black community of Pin Point (see *Sidebar: Pinpointing Clarence*, p. 102).

Clarence Thomas, too, had to rewrite his family history to turn his sister into the welfare scrounger who was hardly fit to polish his bootstraps. Nell Irvin Painter tells a different story of Emma Mae Martin:

> It turns out that she was only on welfare temporarily and that she
> was usually a two-job-holding, minimum-wage-earning mother of
> four. Unable to afford professional help, she had gone on welfare
> while she nursed the aunt who had suffered a stroke but who
> normally kept her children when Martin was at work.[52]

Thomas had to erase this part of her story because it showed all too clearly that lack of effort and poverty of values were in no way to blame for her "failure," but that the absence of welfare was.

Emma Mae Martin had to be distorted by her brother to fit the stereotype of "the lazy Black welfare scrounger." Her case reveals the degree to which counterevidence has to be repressed for stereotyping to be an effective discursive strategy. The L.A. uprisings gave the inhabitants of South-Central the chance to plead in public for jobs, but Dan Quayle repressed these pleas in order to fit them into his stereotype of "people who are dependent on drugs or the narcotic of welfare" (see *Sidebar: Dan Quayle*, p. 68). This black dependency figures powerfully in the white conservative imagination, but one has to look hard to find it in African America.

As Dan Quayle used the inhabitants of South-Central Los Angeles to advance his agenda, so Clarence Thomas used Emma Mae Martin. The gap between brother and sister is evidence of the divisive effects within African America that the selective implementation of affirmative action may have, particularly when it is turned into bootstrapping. A painful paradox underlies the widely differing attitudes of African Americans to Clarence Thomas: he exemplifies both the good and the bad effects of affirmative action.

Pinpointing Clarence

A scene from the PBS *Frontline* documentary, *Clarence Thomas and Anita Hill: Public Hearing, Private Pain* showing an interview with Tim Williams, a friend and business partner of Thomas's grandfather in Pin Point, Georgia, intercut with shots of Thomas's statement to the Senate Judiciary Committee:

CLARENCE THOMAS: I've always carried in my heart the world, the life, the people, the values of my youth.

TIM WILLIAMS: Down here, all we only had at that time was the NAACP. . . . we had lawyers that we couldn't even pay. And he, er, he had in mind that Clarence could help us out like that, and he went so far as to get him through school, and train him and all, like that. I think that's what he had in

his mind more than anything else—to help us out—the awful things we were in down here.

INTERVIEWER: And Clarence did not?

TIM WILLIAMS: No, he didn't. Even after he got out of school—as a civil rights—under Reagan, there. No, he didn't do anything for us.

CLARENCE THOMAS: I watched as my grandfather was called "boy," I watched as my grandmother suffered the indignity of being denied the use of a bathroom, but through it all they remained fair, decent, good people.

INTERVIEWER: Thomas cried when he talked about his grandfather.

TIM WILLIAMS: I know he did. But I really didn't buy that.

INTERVIEWER: You didn't?

TIM WILLIAMS: No, I didn't, because his grandfather was disappointed in him.

CLARENCE THOMAS: I can still hear my grandfather, "You all going to have more of a chance than me." And he was right.

TIM WILLIAMS: I don't know whether he changed or not, but the only thing he had was a Black skin, Clarence: everything else was as white as a sheet.

On the surface, Bill Cosby/Cliff Huxtable seems a much less contradictory figure than Clarence Thomas. Under the surface, however, currents and countercurrents disturb the waters in much the same way. In particular, the crosscurrents between the figures of the few successful Blacks and the majority firmly held at the bottom of white society make for muddy waters in which no truths can be clearly seen. For many whites, as we have noted, the few successful African Americans act as an index of the decline of white racism, and they therefore extend this into their understanding of the "failure" of the majority. White television shows both the successful Black (Cosby, Oprah, Magic Johnson, Clarence Thomas) and, on the news particularly, the unsuccessful— the criminal, the teenage mother, the drug abuser, the welfare leech, the homeless man.[53] The two are opposite sides of the same figure.

There were Black viewers of Cosby, however, for whom the figure's double-sidedness meant something different. Jhally and Lewis's study showed that Black audiences of Cosby were much more likely to point to the contrasts between the two sides of the figure than were whites. They were so pained by the constantly negative pictures of Blacks on the news that they welcomed any representation of the successful Black, because of both its rarity and its contradiction of the more normal public image of Black failure. Michael Eric Dyson makes a similar point when he claims that Bill Cosby undercut the dominant stereotype of the Black male and that the show "permitted America to view black folk as *human beings.*"[54] John Downing (who is white) also contrasts the news's negative portrayal of African Americans with Cosby's: " *The Cosby Show* may operate as a reinstatement of black dignity and culture in a racist society where television culture has generally failed to communicate these realities and has often flatly negated them."[55] Similar arguments were made about the way the hearings showed dignified Blacks to white America. *New Yorker* magazine, for example, thought that "the nation was treated to a parade of blacks who—for once—weren't crack dealers, athletes, welfare mothers, or any of the other stereotypes, but solid citizens, fine friends and excellent character witnesses for the two principals."[56]

Such representations can have quite different political circulations in white and Black America. Whereas for whites, the Huxtables' success could demonstrate the death of racism, for many African Americans it offered a rare affirmative and inspiring image: precisely those features that enabled whites to deny racism allowed Blacks some hope that they might prosper despite it. Cosby provided a source of hope and energy to counter the far more numerous sources of despair. Similarly, some African Americans were pleased that Cosby showed them to whites in a way that they could be proud of. They understood how racism could be justified and made legitimate to whites by constantly negative representations of Blacks.

Being Black in the United States today necessarily produces a double consciousness of one's identity: Blacks have to be as aware of how they appear to whites as of how they appear to themselves. This dual consciousness is characteristic of subordinated social formations in general, whose very survival can depend upon their ability to see how they and their actions appear to the alliances that dominate them. Dominant formations, however, rarely acquire this duality, for they have little need of it. So women are much more conscious of how they appear to men than vice versa, and workers see more clearly how their behavior looks to bosses than bosses see how theirs may look to their employees; and, of course, whites are not good at looking at their actions through the eyes of Blacks, whereas, from the slave auction onward, Blacks have always had to understand how whites see them. Much of the Black criticism of Anita Hill's allegations was based upon this knowledge of what whites would make of them, not upon their truth, or upon their gender politics within Afri-

104   can America. The knowledge that both Bill Cosby and Clarence Thomas were viewed positively by powerful formations within white America led many African Americans to support them in the absence of any more positive figure of the Black man. If, in current conditions, Cosby and Thomas are the best that is available, then it may appear to make tactical good sense to make the best possible use of them. The problem, of course, is that in the longer term and the larger arena the strategic values of these figures to conservative whites is likely to outweigh their short-term tactical value to Blacks.

This absence of any more positive figure must be contextualized by the looming presence of a much more negative one. When the alternative to Clarence Thomas is Willie Horton (see chapter 3 and *Sidebar: Willie Horton*, p. 144), the positives of Thomas may justly seem to outweigh the negatives. The racial-sexual threat of the untamed Black male in the white imagination has had such devastating effects in the white treatment of Blacks that any contradiction of it can be seen as a step in the right direction. Sadly, this is not the case. The figure of the tamed Black male is at least as likely to serve, in the white imagination, to justify the intensified oppression of his untamed obverse and to provide an alibi against the charge of racism: if we love Bill Cosby and seat Clarence Thomas on the Supreme Court, then we cannot be charged with either racism or injustice in the beating of Rodney King.

Race and "Today's Woman": Clair Huxtable, Anita Hill, and Murphy Brown

The struggle to figure Clarence Thomas with either Bill Cosby or Willie Horton was not a racially balanced one: whites stood to gain from either figuration, Blacks only from the former, and even there, any gain could be achieved only at considerable cost. The conflict between Anita Hill and Clarence Thomas presented whites with clear choices, and generally they made them unequivocally and unhesitatingly; for African Americans, however, the issues were less clear-cut, the choices harder to make, and unequivocality very difficult to achieve.

The struggle over Anita Hill was as difficult to engage in as that over Thomas. White opponents figured her as the female equivalent of Willie Horton and the opposite of Clair Huxtable. White supporters put her alongside Murphy Brown as an example of "today's woman." For her Black supporters she could be another Sojourner Truth; for Black opponents, Delilah or Jezebel, a betrayer of men's strength.

Different meanings of today's woman and of her relations to men and to the family swirl around the figures of Anita Hill, Clair Huxtable, and Murphy Brown. In the Murphy Brown-Anita Hill-Clair Huxtable configuration, racial difference comes into the picture as it does not in the Murphy Brown-Zoë Baird-Hillary Rodham Clinton one. Despite racial difference, however, it is worth noting that all of these women, except Murphy, are lawyers, and that the legal profession has been good to today's women, who have increased their numbers within it from 8 percent to 21 percent during the past twelve years (another of them, incidentally, is Marilyn Quayle, Dan's wife). It was appropriate, then, for the American Bar Association to honor Anita Hill, and for Hillary Rodham Clinton to present the award (see *Sidebar: Today's Legal Women*, p. 30).

But my point here is a different one. This configuration of Anita-Clair-Murphy carries hot issues in the debate around family values, single motherhood, and race: Murphy the white single mother, Anita the hypersexual Black woman or the oppressed raceless one, and Clair the Black opposite of both, the embodiment of every possible family value. The visible currents and countercurrents within this configuration of professional women barely mask the powerful subcurrent into which Clarence tossed Emma Mae Martin—that of the Black welfare mother. Dan Quayle tapped into it, too, in his attack on Murphy Brown: in emphasizing the statistics that demonstrated the disintegration of the Black family, he made the Black single mother into the key figure of this "disintegration." The issue of William Buckley's *National Review* discussing the causes of the L.A. "riots" contains a cartoon that all too neatly brings together the different Black "family values" of the Cosbys and South-Central: it shows a Black man watching a television on which an annoucer is saying, "Tonight, the final episode with the Huxtable family"; beside the viewer on the couch is a newspaper with a headline that reads, in a direct reference to Dan Quayle's speech, "63% of children live with a single parent"; a balloon shows the Black man thinking, "What's a family?"[57]

The statistics do show a dramatic increase in Black single motherhood; they also show that sex, race, and marital status are important elements in poverty—families headed by a single woman, particularly if nonwhite, are more likely to live below the poverty line than those with both parents, particularly if white. But statistics have to be given meaning, they do not come equipped with it: to be made to mean, they have to be articulated with other facts. One articulation is to relate these statistics to economic ones, particularly the sharp decline in the employment of young Black males over the past twenty years, which has paralleled closely the increase in Black single motherhood. When the dominant discourses define fatherhood primarily by the economic ability to be a breadwinner and then economic alliances within the dominant classes export millions of the jobs that used to make this definition achievable, then Quayle and Limbaugh have to work hard to submerge the articulations among an unregulated economy, job loss, and the absence of fathers, and to create new ones that articulate the absent father to absent values.

The interests that produced unregulated economic policies also produced the welfare policies of the 1980s and, in them, as in employment, discourse and economics work together. Like single motherhood, "welfare" does not contain its own prescription of how to understand it. In Dan Quayle's discourse, wel-

106   fare causes the family to disintegrate by producing a dependency mentality and by substituting a government check for a male breadwinner. The policies of his alliance underwrote this meaning: the regulations of AFDC (Aid to Families with Dependent Children) for most of the 1980s were such as to have made it almost impossible for a woman married to an unemployed man to qualify for welfare—she had to be single to receive the check. This was compounded by the economic conditions in which even a fully employed man on the minimum wage, rare though even he be in South-Central L.A., could not lift her and her two children even close to the poverty line, let alone above it. Whether her man was employed or unemployed, the poor woman was economically better off without him. It is not surprising, then, that many African Americans see the undermining of the Black family by unemployment and welfare regulations as part of a white racist strategy that amounts to genocide: racism is recoded, and racial power applied along the axis of economics. In its effects, then, welfare can be similar to affirmative action: both appear to promote the interests of disadvantaged African Americans, but their implementation can all too easily ensure that any Black advantage is controlled and directed by whites.

     Herman Gray criticizes a CBS documentary called *The Vanishing Family: Crisis in Black America* because of its blaming of the victims for their own situation.[58] In telling the stories of "typical" Black families in Newark, New Jersey, it showed image after image of Black men "irresponsibly" hanging out on the streets while women, many of them single, struggled to raise their children. The documentary was screened in January 1985, at the period when *The Cosby Show* was steadily climbing in the ratings. At one point the documentary's host, Bill Moyers, implicitly brought the two programs together:

> There are successful strong black families in America. Families that affirm parental authority and the values of discipline, work and achievement. But you won't find many who live around here.[59]

Although Moyers is publicly seen as a liberal, neither Reagan, Bush, nor Quayle would have been provoked into any liberal bashing by a comment like that. Quayle, too, would have enjoyed the way that Moyers predicted his "Murphy Brown" speech:

> A whole lot of white families are in trouble too. Single parent families are twice as common in America today as they were 20 years ago. But for the majority of white children, family still means a mother and a father. This is not true for most black children. For them, things are getting worse. Today black teenagers have the highest pregnancy rate in the industrialized world, and in the black inner city practically no teenage mother gets married. That's no racist comment. What's happening goes far beyond race.[60]

As a liberal, Moyers does not blame the victims for their own victimization 107 quite as explicitly as does Dan Quayle. But by submerging the links between conservative economic and welfare policies and the "welfare mother" under a current of liberal concern, he hides the knowledge that "welfare mothers" are the inevitable product of the policies that have advantaged those from whose position he speaks, regardless of their party allegiance. The same social forces underlay the emergence of both Clarence Thomas and Emma Mae Martin, and to deny their influence, Thomas had to individualize the difference between him and his sister in order to make his "success" the consequence of his abilities, and her "failure" that of her inadequacies. We should not be surprized, then, to find Clarence Thomas using statistics in the same way as Dan Quayle and Bill Moyers to paint a similarly stereotypical picture: in a speech to students at historically Black Clark College in Atlanta, he pointed out that 48 percent of Black mothers were unmarried and that 40 percent of Black youths were on welfare, and concluded that massive federal involvement has still left African Americans at the bottom of the ladder and that more government intervention is not necessary, for "we control the values that our kids have."[61] Stereotypes, such as that of the "Black welfare mother," are neither reflections of social reality nor merely distortions of it: they are active in producing it. The power interests that control economic and welfare policies also control the discursive policies that produce stereotypes. The stereotype is an application of discursive power that is as material as the application of economic and political power, and the effectiveness of any one power axis is affected by its multiaxial relations to the others.

One multiaxial commonality is the need to recode racial power and thus to deny its operation while exerting it. Bill Moyers has to deny the racism that underlies his commentary and, inevitably, to echo Bush's denial that race played any role in his nomination of Clarence Thomas. Moyers, however, may have been less confident than Bush that his denial would work, for when the program was repeated, three months later, he included in its opening shots one of a Black welfare worker reassuring viewers that the problems of poverty have nothing to do with racism, and that their solution lay within the Black community itself.[62]

Moyers may be a liberal and Quayle a Republican, but that does not prevent the same discursive strategy being used by both of them: as whites, both can recode racism into "family values." *The Cosby Show*'s popularity during this period aided this recoding. As Jhally and Lewis point out, it tended to be seen by whites as the story of a Black *family*; for African Americans, however, its topic was a *Black* family. The shift in emphasis is subtle but important, for it carries a significant redirection of the racial politics of the show.

As I have argued, for both African and European Americans racial anxieties become intensified when sexuality enters the picture. Whether the family be Black or white, one of the key functions of its values is to contain sexuality, and

when the family is a Black one that is highly visible to whites this containment increases in urgency. As Paula Giddings has pointed out, Black sexuality when seen and interpreted by whites has historically resulted in rapes and lynchings. Equally, for Bill Moyers and Dan Quayle it underlay the so-called collapse of the Black family and thus the disintegration of the Black neighborhood and of Black society. Incarnated in the figure of the unwed teenage mother, Black sexuality is used to put the blame for the public problems of African America upon its own private parts.

This frail figure of the pregnant teenaged African American has a lot to bear, and in this context it is not surprising that *The Cosby Show* handles Black sexuality with kid gloves (or, given Cliff's profession, rubber ones). In one episode, for example, Cliff rushes into the house, tells Vanessa to assemble the kids for a family conference, and goes into the kitchen, where Clair is, predictably, preparing supper. Instead of his usual designer sweater, he is wearing his white doctor's coat, a sign that he is bringing his professional persona home with him. The following exchange takes place:

CLIFF: Do you think our children tell us everything?

CLAIR: Who's in trouble?

CLIFF: No one's in trouble. I've just come back from the office: now a young girl comes in scared about what she might have. It turns out all she has is a mild bladder infection which can be cleared up in a couple of weeks . . . a lovely girl, intelligent, beautiful, could have been one of our children . . .

CLAIR: But what's the point?

CLIFF: The point is that she never told her parents and she let it go four weeks. Now the question is do we have the kind of children who never get into any kind of trouble whatsoever, or do we have children who get into trouble—and don't tell us?[63]

The family conference that follows is typical Huxtable domesticity. The kids   109
tease their parents, the parents stumble around an embarrassing subject but
finally succeed in exerting their parental authority in a noncoercive, good-hu-
mored way. The children turn the discussion away from their own "troubles"
to their parents' propensity to get mad when "troubles" are raised. All the
troubles are hypothetical ones, but even so, Cliff and Clair are provoked into
anger. The pedagogical point, however, that good families can solve their
problems by drawing upon their own resources, is strengthened, not weakened, by the comic difficulty of the Huxtables in following their own advice.
The hypothetical trouble that Cliff finds hardest to cope with is that Theo may
have driven his car with neither permission nor a license. Clair's difficulties are
caused by Denise's pretending that, instead of sleeping over with a girlfriend,
she had spent the night at her boyfriend's house when his parents were on
vacation—although "nothing happened." The Theo-Cliff trouble is resolved
through an all-boy pillow fight. The Denise-Clair one remains more open as
Clair leaves to phone the mother of Denise's girlfriend to check that she really
had slept there.

What is not spoken is at least as significant as what is. The almost repressed
figure here, of course, is that of the Black unwed pregnant teenager who is so
firmly centered in Bill Moyers's and Dan Quayle's discourse. The race of Cliff's
patient is never given, though her being just like the Huxtable daughters hints
she is African American. If so, the adjectives Cliff uses to describe her, "beautiful" and "intelligent," recode "Black," and "young" recodes "single." In addition, not only is none of the three Huxtable teenagers nor Cliff's patient pregnant, nor is the word ever spoken, but none of the Huxtables, at least, could
have been, not because of practicing safe sex but because of practicing no sex.
The historically pertinent figure of the Black single mother, so central to white
strategy, is not countered here but marginalized, just as she was in *Murphy
Brown*. Even if the traces are recovered, and the figure pulled back into visibility, her "problem" is restricted to the relationships among the young woman,
her doctor, and her parents. Any viewer who wishes to articulate this Black
young woman's nonpregnancy with the current social conditions of the African
American family and the political uses made of them has to overcome a double
dose of discursive repression. One wonders if many viewers would find the
semiotic labor worthwhile. Indeed, it almost appears as though the topic were
raised in order to repress its social context and thus to contain it safely within
the family values shared by conservatives of all races.

It is also worth speculating here about what white viewers might make of
the choice of gynecology for Cliff's profession. As Foucault has shown us, the
medicalization of sexuality throughout the nineteenth century worked to contain it socially and to pathologize any forms that escaped their container. Orrin
Hatch and his colleagues had to fight as hard as they did to deny the existence
of any loose sexuality in Clarence Thomas because they knew the sanctions it

110   would occasion: Clarence Thomas had to be sexually contained to be acceptable to white America. One wonders if making Cliff into a gynecologist is a way of rendering Black sexuality safe by medicalizing it and thus of defusing its threat to the white imagination. To carry this line of speculation to its extreme, one might also wonder whether Thomas's white wife, constantly glimpsed behind him on our screens, and Cliff Huxtable's possibly white patients, never spoken nor shown, might not serve as guarantors of their safeness, as living proof that Black male sexuality has, in these men at least, been tamed, and is thus containable within family values.

It is common white strategy to make sense of Black single motherhood, unemployment, welfare, and the disintegrating family by linking them, through family values, to morality rather than to economic and social policy. By this means the problem can be laid squarely upon the shoulders of its victims, and any white assistance in reaching its solution must at least begin, and in some cases end, with preaching.

Today's women are readily deployable in this strategy: Murphy Brown can figure single motherhood by choice, not by circumstance; Anita Hill can figure Black hypersexuality or immorality (another white reason for Black single motherhood and the disintegration of Black family values that need not be spoken to be put to work); and Clair Huxtable can be made to demonstrate that family values are both effective and available to all who choose to adopt them, regardless of their race. When Dan Quayle blamed the L.A. uprisings on Murphy's single motherhood and when Tom Bradley urged Los Angelenos to watch Bill Cosby instead of "rioting," they were both tapping into the same currents of meaning as had Bill Moyers some seven years previously.

Clair Huxtable may be the opposite of what white conservatives made Anita Hill into, but from other viewpoints the two could appear to be similar. Both are successful lawyers, and their privilege has caused class resentment among some less-privileged Black women. One audience member in Jhally and Lewis's study commented:

> I can't stand [Clair]. . . . Because she's not a typical black person.
> She walks around dressed up all the time, now come on. We don't
> walk around dressed up all the time. She's a lawyer and we
> understand that. She comes home from work . . . how come her
> hair's not in rollers? How come she can't walk around with her blue
> jeans on? You know what I'm saying? Now come on.[64]

This echoes Nellie McKay's account of why some lower-class Black women did not support Anita Hill: We can recall, too, that Zoë Baird's illegal alien childcare worker provoked anger among women who were excluded from her privileged solution to a problem that they shared. Social identities and thus social alliances always include elements of class, race, and gender, but the proportions of the mix cannot be predicted or generalized.

Other audience members, therefore, allied themselves strongly with Clair's Blackness and overlooked any economic differences. In particular, her way of speaking could be a signal of Black community:

> One reason is that we talk differently. I can close my eyes and tell it is a black show. They still use in the show street language, they are comfortable at home. . . . Clair is a lawyer, you never see her use legal jargon, or whatever; she talks just like a black woman. I was raised by a black man and woman and this is how they talked, so when I close my eyes I can totally tell the difference. Also we have a tone to our language and it comes from our history. It is a singing type, very melodic type of talk, or conversation that is just natural for our people. So if you are watching an all-white show, you will not hear that; you would hear the standard English. You will not hear the melodic sound of the voice as you can when the Huxtables speak.[65]

Significantly this offers a Black pleasure from which whites are excluded: "You can hear like Clair with a little accent to her voice: you know, like an accent that only black people would understand."[66] The way of talking is an embodied language, a way of making direct bodily connections between those who share it. It is therefore uncolonizable. However white the language, however white the television system, Blacks can still accent both to speak to each other.

Anita Hill allowed whites to see what Blacks would prefer them not to; Clair, however, is quite different:

> I like Clair's character per se. She's a strong, black woman, very independent. . . . I like her character per se because it depicts blacks in a different mold than what white America thinks.[67]

It is not easy to negotiate among Clair's Blackness, her privilege, and the positive image she presents to both Blacks and whites.

> You know, it's always that upper middle class, upper class mentality. . . . It's just not real for me. Again, I like the show per se because it does depict blacks in a more positive way than we usually—we're not killing each other. We're not raping people. You know, we're some ordinary people who like the nice things in life like everybody else.[68]

The figure of Willie Horton lurks just below the surface of this woman's discourse as the one commonly used by whites to distance or "other" Blacks: she counters it by emphasizing Blacks' similarity to "everybody else" without losing the awareness that "everybody else" is predominantly white.

Both Downing and Lewis argue that Clair Huxtable demonstrates gently progressive gender politics, insofar as when there is gender conflict between

112   her and Cliff or Theo, she generally wins both the argument and the audience's
sympathy.[69] (We must note here that not all feminists, particularly Black and
"third" world ones, would agree with their sense of the word *progressive*.) But
such progressiveness as there may be is traditionally framed. She plays all the
conservative feminine roles in the economy of the household, and the kitchen
is unequivocally her room: Cliff rarely cooks a family meal, and his occasional
attempts to get himself a sandwich invariably end up with a comic display of
feminine control over food consumption, as Clair monitors his attempted in-
take of unhealthy foods. But in the social economy of the household, that of
ideas and influence, Clair often appears stronger than Cliff. Cliff's attempts to
be masculine are typically subject to gentle mockery, almost never reach their
objective, and frequently cause mild chaos. By contrast, Clair's femininity provides a calm core of common sense that works to solve each episode's family
crisis. The gender progressiveness of the show *is* gentle, it *is* contained within
a conservative value system, but it is demonstrated week after week and both
female and male viewers comment favorably upon it. There were some
women, however, who judged the containment to be stronger than the
progress, but most found pleasure in the way they saw Clair advancing wom-
en's interests.[70] Indeed, many viewers of both sexes applauded the show's del-
icate balance in managing to promote feminine causes without alienating men
and provoking their hostility.

But, having recognized that achievement, we must also note that Clair has a
full-time profession, is raising five children, does all the cooking and household management, all without any hired help or child-care workers, and, to
cap it all, she never has a hair out of place and rarely shows any signs of strain.
Murphy Brown and Zoë Baird found incomplete and unsatisfactory ways of
coping with "today's woman's" problems in negotiating the demands of career
and motherhood: Clair offers no solution because she has no problems. Neither her Black sexuality nor her feminine gender pose a threat to white male
security: Murphy Brown caused Dan Quayle far greater anxiety.

Equally, Clair Huxtable is not the Anita Hill who troubled Orrin Hatch so
deeply, though the words that a Black fan used to describe Clair ("a strong
Black woman, very independent"[71]) could well have been directed toward her.
Both are Black women who speak in public. Clair's speech may not challenge
the power structure as directly as Anita Hill's, but accommodating and un-
threatening though her voice may be, it is still a Black woman's public voice,
and, as we hear in Jhally and Lewis's book, Black women take pleasure in listening to one of their own, a pleasure that public discourse offers all too rarely.

Nancy Fraser has pointed out that much of the gender politics of the hearings was fought around the gendering of the public sphere, and the public-pri-
vate dichotomy that accompanied it.[72] As a man, Clarence Thomas was able to
control which aspects of his life and opinions were suitable for which sphere in
a way that Anita Hill could not. Thomas, for instance, was able to assert, "I am

not here . . . to put my private life on display for prurient interests or other   113
reasons. I will not allow this committee or anyone else to probe into my private
life" or "I will not get into any discussions that I might have had about my personal life or my sex life with any person outside of the work place."[73] The committee accepted his definitions of the private and the public, and his right to
keep the private to himself.

That was not the case with Anita Hill. Despite her struggles to control and
defend her privacy, her "private" characteristics were dragged into the public
arena by men in order to disqualify her public speech. She was called, at various stages in their strategy "a lesbian, a heterosexual erotomaniac, a delu-
sioned schizophrenic, a fantasist, a vengeful spurned woman, a perjurer and a
malleable tool of liberal interest groups."[74] Fraser concludes:

> Given the gender differential in ability to define and protect one's
> privacy, we can understand some of the deeper issues at stake in
> Thomas's insistence on avoiding the "humiliation" of a "public
> probe" into his "privacy." This insistence can be understood in part
> as a defense of his masculinity: to be subject to having one's privacy
> publicly probed is to risk being feminized.[75]

Anita Hill's attempts to control her presence in public have a long history of
masculine power to overcome. From at least the nineteenth century, a woman
in public without a man was all too easily cast as a prostitute: Orrin Hatch had
a deep history to help him hypersexualize Anita Hill. The woman walking (or
talking) in public lays herself open to male abuse because of the masculine
power to define and control the public domain as men's. Faced with this power
and danger, women have seized on what limited public space they can define
as theirs. Rachel Bowlby has argued, for instance, that the department store
and, later, the shopping mall are public places where a woman alone could
move without danger or masculine harassment. They constitute a feminine
public space, albeit one that is physically and discursively contained. Similarly,
one might argue that sitcoms, soap operas, and talk shows can serve as feminine discursive places, where women's discourse can circulate comparatively
free of harassment within the containment of sitcoms, soap operas, and talk
shows. Once Murphy Brown's single motherhood was brought out of this feminine space into the "masculine" one of "real" politics and the "real" public
sphere, she, like Anita Hill, could be constructed as a social-sexual threat.
Quayle's attempts to degrade her were less vicious than the Hatchet job on
Anita Hill, probably because racial guilt could not be mobilized against her and
also because the public arena into which Quayle pulled her, that of the news
media, was less directly under masculine control than the Senate chamber in
which Anita Hill had to speak. Murphy could return to her sitcom to answer
the politician in her terms and on her terrain, and beat him. On television and
in public, Anita Hill had more feminine power than in the Senate, and could

114   turn her defeat in one arena into victories in the others. Clair Huxtable, however, remained safely within her sitcom and never provoked male, public hostility, but, nevertheless, she still managed to say what many Black women
wished to hear.

The public domain is one where white masculinity guards its power most
zealously. The Black women who cringed on hearing issues of Black sexuality
raised in front of a white audience knew all too well that once out in public the
meanings of Black sexuality would be out of their control and would be directed against them. On the television documentary that aired these fears, a
Black woman student at Spelman College lamented that Black gender struggles
had to be fought out on white media.[76] Her complaint that African Americans
do not have a national broadcast medium where they can control and circulate
their own discourse is well founded and not accidental; at the local level, however, radio stations such as WLIB in Harlem and Black Liberation Radio in
Springfield, Illinois (see chapter 5), do fill the lack she identifies.

Not *The Cosby Show*

The Cosby Show, with its clearly conservative meanings of race and family, although contested, however murkily, by quite contradictory ones, came under
attack from 1988 onward by the upstart Fox network and its two "antifamily
values" sitcoms, *Married . . . with Children* and *The Simpsons*.

A brief look at these two shows will enable us to trace how the axes of class
and age can be mobilized alongside those of gender and race within that contested terrain of "family values." It is not surprising that sitcoms should be so
hotly political, for generically, most of them are about, and designed to be
watched by, the family. And the family is the site where the internal politics of
age, gender, class, and race are most immediately put into practice.

In the 1992 campaign, the family was important to the Republicans because
it was the only domestic issue on which they could fight with any confidence—
the Bush presidency had ignored the economy, the inner cities, the public
school system, the public health system, and almost all the other domains of
everyday life in which Washington's actions (or lack of them) become the mun-
danity of lived experience. Citing the restoration of the traditional family as the
solution to all these social problems has long been Republicans' strategy to justify their refusal to address them directly. When Dan Quayle blamed the L.A.
uprisings on the collapse of the Black family he was treading a well-worn path.

Ronald Reagan, too, had made family values as central in his election campaigns of 1980 and 1984 as had Bush in 1988 and 1992. The so-called collapse of
the traditional nuclear family has been a fact of U.S. life for the past fifty years,
so the conservative emphasis on the need to return to it was a reaction to social
conditions that were moving in the opposite direction. The 1980s continued the
development of nontraditional families so far that the ideological norm became

one that only a minority could achieve. When most people live in conditions that differ from such a norm, social anxieties are bound to result. *The Cosby Show*, with its deeply nostalgic vision of a golden age of the family, was one consequence of these anxieties; *Married . . . with Children*, with its skeptical disbelief in that same utopian family, was another; and *The Simpsons* was a third.

Even fans of *The Cosby Show* commented on its lack of "realism," and found the Huxtables just too perfect in both economic and ethical values: the family demonstrated too precisely the glossy opposite of Quayle's "poverty of values." This "unrealisticness" could produce pleasure for the fans only as long as they could believe that the gap between the material conditions of most families and the utopian ones of the Huxtables was bridgeable. This belief became harder to sustain as the Reagan years passed. Murphy Brown's baby was one sign that Cosby's nostalgic utopianism had lost its broad-based credibility; *Married . . . with Children* and *The Simpsons* were earlier signs of the same loss.

The first televisual cracks in *The Cosby Show*'s hegemonic family values were opened around generational differences, though they quickly spread to include ones of class and gender. Since its origin in the 1950s, the category of "the teenager" has always been a source of anxiety for adult America, because within it traditional family values have been most keenly tested and contested. Rupert Murdoch, Fox's owner, decided in the mid-1980s that this highly charged controversial terrain was the best upon which to fight the dominance of the three national networks. He planned to develop his new Fox network by combining the existing networks' wide geographical reach with a new ability to deliver accurately segmented audiences, particularly ones that lay outside the massed middle America over whom the three other networks vied with one another. So he launched his new network on weekends with a schedule aimed at the teenage and young adult nonfamily audience. With programs such as *The Tracey Ullman Show* and *It's Garry Shandling's Show*, Fox quickly won a core audience in its targeted segment, but *Married . . . with Children* and *The Simpsons* were its first shows to achieve general ratings that challenged those of the big three.

But Fox's success was not solely the result of its ability to produce shows whose skepticism could be used to disrupt and interrogate traditional family values. Change in a nation's structure of feeling never occurs on one front alone. There were also significant technological changes during the 1980s. The dominance of network television in home-based entertainment was steadily eroded by new technologies, particularly cable, but also VCRs, video games, and home computers. During the 1980s, network audiences shrank from 91 percent to 67 percent.

New technologies cannot in themselves produce social change, though they can and do facilitate it. These new technologies met the marketing strategies of late capitalism, or post-Fordism, which can be summarized briefly as ones of product differentiation and market segmentation rather than mass production

116   and mass marketing. The networks, however, were irredeemably Fordist—
they had grown and prospered by attracting the largest and least differentiated
audiences possible.

However dominant the market economy is, our society is not determined by
it entirely. Post-Fordism's market segmentation was not just a result of industrial strategy, but was also an economic transformation of changes in the social
order at large. Throughout the 1970s and 1980s people's sense of social differences began to challenge the homogenizing effect of consensual social norms.
The women's movement was one key player as it asserted women's rights to
control not only their economic and domestic relations, but also the sense of
the feminine and thus the meaning of feminine identity. Similar demands were
made by the Black power and gay liberation movements. As Reaganism and
Reaganomics widened the gaps between rich and poor, men and women,
whites and those of color, the sense of social differences sharpened and became conflictual. *The Cosby Show*'s appeal depended largely upon its ability to
paint a consensual gloss over differences of race, class, and gender; and so, by
the end of the Reagan/Bush administrations, it had lost touch with the nation's
changing structure of feeling.

This conjuncture of forces, sociocultural, technological, and economic, was
part of the changing structure of feeling within which *Married . . . with Children*
gained, and *The Cosby Show* lost, popular appeal. This change may be characterized by interpreting *The Cosby Show*'s slide down the ratings as a sign that a
dominant cultural current was changing to a residual one, and *Married . . . with
Children*'s climb up them as an emergent current pushing its way into the mainstream. In 1989 Cosby still topped the ratings, but the Bundy family's loud and
obnoxious voices were becoming widely heard. And many of those who heard
them were deeply offended, mainly because the show was sending the
"wrong" message to teenagers. By publicly inverting the norms of the "good"
family, it offended those whose social interests were inscribed in them and ap-
pealed to those who identified themselves as outside-the-family.

The relationships among the family members conflict across both age and
gender. The language in which they are conducted is scatological and often
emphasizes their bodily and sexual attributes as markers of identity and of social relationships. Indeed, much of the comedy of the show falls in the disciplinary category of "the dirty joke" (see *Sidebar: Dirty Jokes and the Bundys*, p.
117). Clarence Thomas used the dirty joke of claiming to find a pubic hair on
his Coke can as an expression of masculine power. The Bundy males frequently make these traditional dirty jokes, but, in *Married . . . with Children*,
unlike Thomas's EEOC office, they are quickly countered by the Bundy
women, who, like the Designing Women, have developed a subversive genre
of antimale dirty jokes. The politics of turned dirty jokes is contradictory and
risks alienating some women who might applaud its ends but be offended by

Dirty Jokes and the Bundys

The Bundys have just been ejected from a party at their respectable neighbors' house.

AL: But you've got to give me credit, I did try to liven things up.

PEG: You know, Al, I don't think a banker's party is the right place to stand on the buffet and yell, "Let's wet the wives' T-shirts and rate their hooters."
AL: You'd have won.
PEG: Oh, Al.

KELLY (as Buck, the family dog, takes a fur coat from next door's party upstairs): Mom, why can Buck have the coat upstairs and I can't have boys in my room?

PEG: Because the coat can't get pregnant.
BUD: Obviously neither can Kelly!

BUD (after having been caught stealing gas from the guests' cars): Kel, this is it, the last time I'm working for Dad. From now on, I go solo.
KELLY: Much like at Lover's Lane?

FORTUNE TELLER (from the party, as she sits on the couch): Sit down, I feel very strong vibrations here.
AL: Did you leave your toy running under the couch again?
PEG: No, it's in the shop. It's being turbo-charged.

its means. And there were many liberal women who were offended by the show and saw nothing progressive in it.

But their offense was minor compared to that of conservative women. Terry Rakolta, for example, was a wealthy Michigan housewife who gained much publicity for her campaign to persuade advertisers to withdraw from the show on the grounds that the offensive bodies and jokes of the Bundys resembled soft-core pornography, and that the show contained "blatant exploitation of women and sex, and anti-family attitudes."[77] According to a front-page story in the *New York Times*, Procter & Gamble, McDonald's, Tambrands, and Kimberly-Clark all withdrew advertising support or promised to monitor the show's values more carefully in future.[78] Procter & Gamble cited the show's "negative portrayal of American family life"; the chairman of Coca-Cola wrote to Rakolta that he was "corporately, professionally and privately embarrassed" that ads for Coca-Cola had appeared on it; and Gary Lieberman, chairman of

118   Columbia Pictures Television, which produced the show, offered Rakolta "our sincere apology."[79]

    Rakolta's husband was president of a family-owned construction firm worth $400 million (which gives a particular inflection to the term *family values*), so the social positions of those forming this set of right-wing alliances were particularly close, in the upper reaches of corporate America. Although class was not explicitly cited as a feature of the offensiveness of the program, the class difference between the Bundys and their objectors inevitably framed the contestation. Rakolta attempted to broaden the allegiance, but not its intent, by enlisting the support of lobbying groups within conservative "middle America" and the religious right, specifically, Concerned Women of America and the American Family Association (which had started life as the National Federation for Decency, an organization founded by a fundamentalist minister, the Reverend Donald Wildmon). Rakolta's rallying cry, around which this allegiance was forged, was "Free TV is the last bastion for the American family, or anybody who wants decent programming."

    Initially, the press reaction to her campaign was favorable. The *Detroit News* (her local newspaper) was typical in applauding "Mrs. Rakolta's stand for decency."[80] (It is noteworthy how frequently the concept of "decency" is used to disguise class taste and power under the mask of universally agreed-upon standards.) But the press support for the alliance weakened as its narrow social base and repressive strategy became clearer: in the months that followed, the typical line became "If the show offends you, switch it off, don't try and censor it."[81] Ironically, the longer-term result of Rakolta's campaign was to increase the show's ratings and expose an alliance within the power structure to popular rejection.

    Rakolta's campaign against the program did not originate in her own living room only; it was part of a sociocultural context in which "family values" were a crucial political battlefield. Many of my undergraduate students recognized that the difference between *The Cosby Show* and *Married . . . with Children* reproduced the difference between "normal" family values and the material conditions of the majority of U.S. families. Consequently, they considered *Married . . . with Children* to be the most "realistic" show on television (an accolade that was later bestowed on *The Simpsons*) and used its carnivalesque elements as ways of expressing their sense of the differences between their experience of family life and that proposed for them by the dominant social norms.

    A graduate student of mine spent a season watching the show with a typical audience of young people.[82] They were undergraduates, mainly freshmen and sophomores, of both sexes who attended a Catholic university and met every Sunday after evening Mass, which many attended, in one or another of their apartments. Some of the group had known each other through high school, others were more recent members, but this particular social formation was organized around the shared taste for *Married . . . with Children*.

The seven members who attended one particular Sunday met in Mick and John's apartment, the main room of which had once been the living room of the single-family house that was now converted into student apartments. The furniture was an eclectic mix of whatever they had been able to scrounge from their families. The couch, for instance, carried the scars of its history, during which it had moved from living room to family room to kids' basement, to student apartment. Its stains and tears spoke against the domestic order still faintly discernible in the traces of what it used to be. During the show, beer was spilled on it and nobody cared, a half-eaten hamburger on a thin piece of paper was set down on it with no thought of grease or ketchup stains seeping through, and, later on, John and Sarah lay on it in a body-hugging embrace that would have sent their parents into conniptions had the couch still been in the family living room.

The walls were decorated with posters of pop and film stars that may have been tolerated at home, though not in the living room, and with signs advertising beer, which would certainly have been prohibited, particularly as they had clearly been stolen from a bar, not purchased from a store. Nobody in the apartment had reached the legal drinking age, so the signs were doubly illicit.

The theme music of the show, "Love and Marriage," a Frank Sinatra number from their parents' generation, provoked the group into singing along in vacuous parody of both its "older" style and "older" sentiments. A similar parody of their parents' taste (as they saw it) hung on the wall—a somewhat moth-eaten painting of Elvis on black velvet. The "bad taste" of the picture was different from the "bad taste" of the program, for it was their view of teenage culture then as opposed to now. The picture was a site for experiencing the differences between their parents-as-teenagers and themselves, just as the program enabled them to mock the differences between their parents now and themselves.

Watching the program involved a series of interactive comments that took every opportunity offered to draw disrespectful parallels between the show and the families these viewers had so recently left. These comments ranged from delight in representations of a counterknowledge ("My Dad does that"— said of an action that a father would disown as typically his but that a teenager would know differently) to more engaged family politics ("I wish Mom had seen that").

The show enabled these viewers to engage in and reconfigure the age politics of their relations with their absent parents; equally, they used it to engage in gender politics with their present partners. The gender conflicts between the parents and the children consisted of verbal punches and counterpunches in which, generally, the females outpointed the males. This caused few problems for the men in this particular audience, and though both sexes would cheer the punches thrown by their own sides, they also gained great pleasure from the well-aimed riposte. When a girl nudged her boyfriend at a remark on the TV,

120   she was bringing their own interpersonal history to the program just as significantly as the Fox network was bringing the program to them.

This particular audience, or rather group of people who came together to
"audience" the show, did not appear to align themselves with the class identities of the blue-collar Bundys, but confined their observable alignments to
ones of gender and age. The fact that no class alignments were observable does
not necessarily mean that none were made, but it probably indicates that if
made they were made with a fluid sense of class that enabled class disempowerment to stand in for age disempowerment, particularly when experienced as
lack of money. Lack of money is a constant in the Bundy family. Al never earns
enough, and consequently his wife and children are always bemoaning their
inability to become real American consumers. Blue-collar sitcoms, such as *Married . . . with Children* and *Roseanne* provide some of the few televisual sites
where the failure of Reaganomic wealth to trickle down is consistently represented. Class difference is often experienced as shortage of money, and thus,
for most teenagers, it can be readily used as an expression of age difference. In
this sense, age and class were axes of alignment along which to oppose official
family values.

Three ways of valuing the family were at stake here: for Fox it was a market
segment defined by its consumer preferences and buying power; for Rakolta,
as for Dan Quayle, it was where values were inculcated; and for the students it
was a site where they could develop their own sense of their social identities
and social relations. Fox and Rakolta struggled over the concept of "the teenager." For Fox the teenager was a market segment to be differentiated from the
adult; for Rakolta, a child to be kept under adult control within the family. This
prefigured Quayle's argument with "the Hollywood elite," whose liberalism,
in his eyes, pandered to the taste of the wrong market segment and so led the
"real" America away from the great traditions that had shaped it, particularly
the traditional family. Between Rakolta and this particular student audience
was a struggle over the meanings of the family, over the age and gender politics within it, and thus over the social identities of those occupying different
roles within its structure of relationships. And between Fox and the teenage
audience was the struggle between incorporation and excorporation, in which
the industry constantly seeks to incorporate the tastes and practices of subordinate social formations whose members, in their turn, scan the products of the
culture industries looking for elements they can excorporate and use to promote their own sociocultural interests.

This particular student audience is better understood as a social formation
than as a social category, though most of its members belonged to one—that of
white middle-class youth. They formed themselves as a group around this particular program and a set of sociopolitical interests, but they did not experience
all their social relations in this antifamily mode, nor did they necessarily spend
much time together as a social formation with other interests in common. A

social formation, then, unlike a category or class, is formed and dissolved according to the interests activated in its immediate context, and as such is better identified by what its members do than by who they are. And what this audience did was to engage in the practice of culture, to participate in the generation and circulation of meanings. They themselves were not necessarily a representative sample of the total accumulation of audiences of the show (though they did conform closely to the profile of its target audience): their "audiencing" of the program was, however, an instance of culture in practice, just as speaking a sentence is an instance of language in practice.

Even the most trivial objects of everyday life can be used as a cultural practice. When John places his half-eaten hamburger on a sofa that was once in a family living room while watching Peg Bundy "failing" to produce a family meal, he is making the hamburger part of the family values debate. On most Sundays he will have bought it from the nearby McDonald's, but if he feels particularly self-indulgent and wishes to reward himself he will have gone further afield to buy a "better" burger at a small one-off burger joint. Which burger he bought will be connected to whether or not he finished a class paper he had to write, or whether or not he and Sarah had had a minor tiff, or whatever. The couch is where hamburgers, beer, *Married . . . with Children*, and Sarah come together in John's Sunday night, and where he turns them into ways of living that weave antifamily values into the politics of his everyday life. Whether the hamburger was one-off or mass produced by McDonald's connects not only with John's sense of the week or day that has passed, but also with the fact that McDonald's advertises on the show despite Terry Rakolta's campaign to persuade it not to, and that its advertising promotes its restaurants as places for the family, particularly for parents to take children. In doing so, it is attempting to deny the contradictions between fast food and the family dinner table, and thus to defuse any suggestion that it might be implicated in the breakdown of the family. John, of course, is using his hamburger in precisely the antifamily way that McDonald's, though happy to sell it to him, wishes he wouldn't. A hamburger is much more than ground beef; and had he thought to do so, Dan Quayle might have as persuasively attributed L.A.'s problems to McDonald's as to Murphy Brown.

Black Bart

Like his vice president, George Bush also took a swipe at a popular sitcom: "We need a nation closer to *The Waltons* than *The Simpsons*," he said. Bart Simpson was too smart to miss the opportunity: on the night of Bush's acceptance speech at the Republican convention he fired back, "Hey, we're just like the Waltons. Both families spend a lot of time praying for the end of the Depression."[83]

122 Bush had picked the wrong opponent. *The Simpsons* had developed a large and devoted audience of young people and young-thinking leftish adults. The generational gap between the parties that the Democrats stressed and eventually rode to the White House was here invoked by the president, who, in one stroke of naïveté, associated himself and family values with the older generation, the 1930s, and the Great Depression. The media paid little attention to his remark, probably because, unlike Quayle's swipe at Murphy, it was not linked directly with a specific issue such as the L.A. "riots."

The Simpsons are a cartoon family of working-class characters who developed out of weekly segments on Fox's *Tracey Ullman Show* into their own program. They continued the subversion of traditional family values begun by *Married . . . with Children,* and by October 1990, Fox felt confident enough in its youngster's strength to schedule it against *The Cosby Show.* For seven years *The Cosby Show* had been invincible in its time slot, but on the first night of competition between them, *The Simpsons* held it to a tie; 29 percent of the audience watched each.[84] From that moment, *The Cosby Show* began the slide down the ratings that ended in its death as Los Angeles erupted. It may be going too far to claim that Bart sank Bush in the same way, but the change in the family values of *The Cosby Show* to those of *Married . . . with Children, The Simpsons,* and *Murphy Brown* is both a sign and an agent of the change in the structure of feeling that did.

Bart Simpson is the family's troublemaker. He is a cocky preteenager, a failure at school and misunderstood at home, who struggles not always successfully to keep his spirits up in a world that appears to have no place for him. He is street smart, not school smart: his smarts are those of an oral culture, not a literate one, and many of his sayings have been enthusiastically taken into the vernacular cultures of the United States, including those of African America. One of his sayings in particular attracted the anger of authority. Reproduced on a best-selling T-shirt, it proclaimed, "Bart Simpson, underachiever and proud of it." Other "Bartisms" (which in T-shirt form alone had sold more than 15 million by the spring of 1990)[85] included "I'm Bart Simpson, who the hell are you," "Eat my shorts," and "Don't have a cow, man." On *Murphy Brown,* Bart's voice echoed in the headline of one of the fictional papers as it proclaimed "Quayle has a cow."

One of many nonfictional authority figures who also had a cow was Principal Brown of the Cambridge Elementary School in Orange, California, who thundered, "For a child to wear a T-shirt with the word 'hell' on it—that's not exactly the type of behavior we hope elementary schools model. And I don't want kids even thinking that being an underachiever is cool."[86] William Bennett, then U.S. secretary of education, also condemned the show, and Bart T-shirts were banned from schools across the nation. Bart quickly became the mascot of America's disaffected youth, particularly Black youth. Unlicensed "Black Bart" T-shirts were widely sold, one of which depicted him mooning and saying, "Kiss the butt of this." Bart's defiance, his street smarts, his oral skills, together with his rejection, appeared to resonate closely with many African Americans. The Simpsons are a blue-collar family whose class difference from mainstream America is frequently emphasized, and as race is often recoded into class, so class difference can be decoded as racial. Bart's double disempowerment, by class and age, made him readily decodable as socially "Black." The fact that he was actually bright yellow made it easier to blacken him visually, which the illegal T-shirts did, thus appropriating his color along with his sayings. Bart could readily be made to speak, visually and orally, with a Black accent.

Bart was not only scheduled against Bill Cosby, he argued with him (as he did any authority figure). For Bill Cosby and his show, education was of supreme value. In the show's credits Cosby's name carried his Ed.D.; he stressed the value of education in interviews and filled the show with good educational advice. His son on the show, Theo, is a nonsubversive Bart; as Downing points out, he is a muted echo of the alienation of the high school dropout.[87] His scholastic problems, however, unlike Bart's, provide the excuse for constant messages about the value of education. His math teacher is a Latina who in one episode tells Theo of her previous jobs as a waitress and cab driver and concludes, "I didn't mind. I was in America. I knew that if I worked hard I could be whatever I wanted. That's why I make you work so hard. I don't like it when I see children take education for granted."[88] The Huxtables would have agreed with her, despite Theo's problems. Their oldest daughter, Sondra, was at Princeton, the next, Denise, went to college later in the series, and indeed became the star of her own sitcom, *A Different World*, set in and around her dorm. At least three generations of Huxtables were college educated: none of the Simpsons was. Indeed, according to Budd and Steinman, "Cosby has acknowledged that for a time the show became a bit too educational."[89]

Downing sets Cosby's pedagogic earnestness in the context of the debate about Black scholastic underachievement and the arguments about whether the fault for it lies in the white education system or in the Black community. *The Cosby Show* and *The Simpsons* positioned themselves on opposite sides. As more African Americans came to believe that the white education system was the reason for, not the solution to, their "underachievement," so Black Bart voiced their concerns better than Bill Cosby.

Bart Simpson, a rejected ten-year-old with no apparent place in his society's educational or economic systems, who cockily refuses to submit and ingeniously turns to his advantage the few opportunities that come his way, was not surprisingly expropriated by Black youths to figure their own disaffection with the white social order. Equally unsurprisingly, Cliff Huxtable and Theo were not. The race-age-class disaffection that was worn on the Black Bart T-shirts in cities across the nation in 1990 and 1991 erupted violently on the streets of Los Angeles in 1992. Like Bart Simpson, Rodney King refused to submit.

Chapter 3

Los Angeles:
A Tale of Three Videos

Blurred video images of a Black man, Rodney King, being beaten by white officers of the Los Angeles Police Department (the LAPD) still resonate powerfully in the national imagination. They figure, all too vividly, what the mainstream United States likes to know it is not. For those pushed out of the mainstream, however, their figuring was as accurate as it was painful. They ignited an explosive mix of racial disempowerment and pauperization among African Americans and Latinos in South-Central Los Angeles; they shaped the actions and the words of police, politicians, and the militia; and they served the mainstream media as a reference point from which to try to make clear white sense out of the disruptions in L.A., in Atlanta, in Las Vegas, and, most disturbingly, in the white view of its own social order. Historic though these images have proved to be, they are still, in themselves, inadequate. But when they are set alongside images from two other videos—of the beating of Reginald Denny and of the killing of Latasha Harlins—they can provide, in just two minutes of television, hypervisual glimpses of the surging undercurrents that white Americans wish fervently, but vainly, would stay out of sight and out of mind. They won't. The physically violent clashes between Rodney King and Stacey Koon, between Reginald Denny and Damian Williams, and between Latasha Harlins and Soon Ja Du are focal events upon which historical forces of race, class, and gender converged and took material form in courtroom arguments, in street battles, and in media struggles over meaning. Each became a media event whose significance lay in both the broad antagonisms that structured it and its distribution across the nation and the world. Briefly, we may describe each of the videos and its main figures thus:

1. *Rodney King (and Stacey Koon)*: A home video camera owned and used by George Holliday, a blue-collar white man, videoed a Black motorist, Rodney King, being beaten and arrested by white officers of the LAPD, under the command of Sergeant Stacey Koon.

2. *Reginald Denny (and Damian Williams)*: A professional camera owned and used by a Los Angeles TV station videoed a white truck driver,

125

126   Reginald Denny, being beaten by Black youths, one of whom, allegedly, was Damian Williams. (The youths, while awaiting trial, became
known as the Los Angeles Four Plus, or the LA 4 +.)

3. *Latasha Harlins (and Soon Ja Du)*: A security camera in a grocery
store owned by a Korean, Soon Ja Du, videoed a teenage Black
woman, Latasha Harlins, arguing with Du over a bottle of orange
juice, hitting her across the store counter, and being shot by her in
the back of the head.

Each video was a discursive instance in which racial and economic antagonism was both expressed through bodily violence and pushed into hypervisibility. Each video was a major player in a white courtroom, in front of a white
judge and jury. The videos were not just video witnesses, technological exten-
sions of the eyewitness, but became video accusers, video defendants, and
video verdicts. The trials were trials by and of video, of what each did and did
not show, and of what meanings could and could not be made out of what it
showed.

The video made each event and its trial into a media event. A media event is
a composite reality comprising everything from the process of videoing the
original event through to its uncountable viewings and reviewings in Califor-
nian courtrooms and in living rooms around the world. A media event is hypervisual, for besides its condensation of social antagonisms, it is technologically distributed and thus inserted into unpredictably different social contexts.
Its mediation gives it a different social reality from an event that is confined to
the immediate conditions of its occurrence.

Rodney King and Stacey Koon: Power Working

Videolow and Videohigh

The Rodney King videos were the most widely shown, the most widely dis-   127
cussed, and the most acutely experienced of the three. I refer to them in the
plural because there were at least two, and arguably four. First there was the
low-tech video shot by George Holliday (which I call the *videolow*). Then there
was the technologized version of this used by the defense in both trials:[1] computers enhanced it, technology froze its individual frames, slowed or reversed
its motion, and inscribed explanatory arrows and circles upon it. This I call the
videohigh. Extracts of both these videos were also shown on television, and thus
given a new discursive frame, thus giving us if not four videos, at least two
videos each in two frames.

Social power was applied technologically. The videolow was characterized
by its poor and unsteady focus, its unplanned camera position and angle, and
its subservience to "real time" (no editing). This low-technicity meant that it
was low in clarity but high in authenticity. The "lowness" of its technology in-
dexed the "lowness" of the social position from and for which it spoke, and
carried a sense of authenticity that depended upon the videolow's apparently
continuous or metonymic relationship with the experiential truths (or "true"
experiences) of the socially disempowered. It is not unusual in our hierarchical
society to look for the authentic in the low, to see the blue collar in closer proximity to a "real" reality than the white. There is a sense that, because the low or
the weak have only limited power (economic, social, discursive) to manipulate
or control their conditions of existence, they are trapped in an authenticity that
the powerful have the fortune to escape and the misfortune to lose.

This equation of low power with high authenticity has become convention-
alized in film and television by a low-tech mode of representation, first in the
handheld cameras of cinema verité, of naturalistic (as opposed to realistic) documentary, and recently through the miniaturization of video technology in
what is called "reality TV." Minicams travel with cops and rescue squads to
give us shaky, tilted, real-time representations whose low-technicity urges us
to believe them. In sport, these cameras give us driver's-eye views of race
tracks, sky diver's-eye views of the ground below, and soon, we might imagine, the boxer's-eye video of the punch that floors him.

The miniaturization of the technology results not only in extending the cameras' reach (they can go in places where preminiature technology could not—
even into the arteries of your body) but equally in their social dispersal. The
process that miniaturized them multiplied them, made them cheaper and thus
dispersed them socially. Videotechnology extends the panoptic eye of power
into the grocery store, where it watches Latasha Harlins and Soon Ja Du, but it
also enables those who are normally the object of surveillance to turn the lens
and reverse its power. The popularity of the home video camera (as of the still
and moving film camera) lies less in its products (most of which are once
viewed and soon forgotten) than in its access to the power of the visible, with
its ability to give presence to the temporally and spatially absent. TV shows

128   such as *I Witness Video* and *America's Funniest Home Videos* extend this power of the visible from the private into the public domain.

On network news, Rodney King's beating became America's unfunniest home video. Its authenticity was underlined by the contrast between the low-technicity of its images and the high-tech gloss of the rest of the news. Its authenticity appeared uncontestable because the initial conditions of its screening and reception contained no motivations to contest it. Much of white America is fiercely attached to the common sense that the United States is a nonracist society and that the civil rights movement has dismantled the racism of previous generations. As Kimberle Crenshaw and Gary Peller put it, "The videotape exemplified an old-style of racial domination that, today, virtually the entire American culture opposes. The videotape reverberated with the skeletons of American apartheid."[2] They argue that it gave the moderate right an opportunity to oppose overt racism (and President Bush, for one, seized it; see *Sidebar: Bush on L.A.*, p. 188), but that it also allowed them to use this denial of racism to oppose affirmative action. The Clarence Thomas affair was, as we have seen, another site where the denial of racism went hand in hand with rejection of affirmative action. Such denials of overt racism are necessary if nonracist racism is to continue to work effectively, for its power depends upon the degree of its invisibility. The video was racial pornography, for it brought what is properly unseen into hypervisibility, and most of white America was both fascinated and horrified by its view of the genitalia of racism at work. Like videoporn, it showed a close-up truth that was publicly unacceptable, however fascinating in private; it provoked white America to throw up its hands in moral outrage and thus drive its racism back under the surface where it properly belongs.

Its hypervisibility was a consequence of high and low discursive technologies (the home video image uplinked to geostationary satellites and globally distributed), the variety of its discursive conjunctures (we have to imagine the stories it may have been linked with on the TV news in South Africa, in Cuba, in Nicaragua, in Somalia), in the variety of social conjunctures (in the living rooms of whites and Blacks and Latinos, in Native American reservations, in shelters for the homeless, in South-Central L.A. or Harlem, in Orange County, Manhattan, or Simi Valley, in precincts and cop houses): hypervisibility entails an inexhaustible visibility.

This visibility was most highly charged in the Simi Valley courtroom where the police officers were put on trial for using excessive force on Rodney King. In effect, it was the video that stood trial. Of course there were witnesses and statements by the accused, but the video was the verdict—for the jury, for the media and the nation, and for Rodney King's fellow inhabitants of South-Central L.A. Indeed, Rodney King never appeared; his presence, which pervaded the trial in the courtroom and around the nation, was a video presence, a body of electronic dots.

And the defense lawyers set to work on this body just as efficiently as the defendants had worked on its incarnation in muscle and bone. First, they had to detach its low-technicity from its sense of authenticity and the accents of the "low." By retechnologizing it they relocated it socially and deauthenticated it so it could be made into another truth. The transformation from videolow to videohigh was not just technological, but also social and semiotic: its technological effectiveness depended entirely upon the social conditions, for its transformation of Rodney King into an animalized threat to white civilization succeeded, with the jury at least, only because it was a current instance of a long history of similar white constructions of the Black male. However high the tech, technology alone could not account for the power of the videohigh.

But in the social conditions of the courtroom, technology was effective. Computer enhancement made the images of the videolow tell a new high truth of high tech in a panoptic version of what Barthes called "bourgeois clarity." The high-tech vision of the infrared bomb aimer and of the surveillance satellite gives truths that the powerful use for their own power, and the videohigh joined their operations. High tech restructures the field of the visible, redraws the interrelationships of what it sees. The videohigh slowed the motion of the videolow, froze it, and sharpened its blurred outlines to give it a bourgeois clarity and to dislodge its low authenticity. The videolow, however, reproduced in its disadvantaged viewpoints and its insecure images the experience of the socially low, which is why, to them, its blurred images were perfectly clear.

One key moment occurred early in the beating. Encircled by police officers and still in the agony of the 50,000 volts the Taser gun had shot through his body, Rodney King rose and lurched forward in an attempt either to escape or to charge one of the officers. The verdict of most of the nation, watching only the videolow, was the former; the jury, however, saw the videohigh. Its slowed motion stretched the links between action and reaction until they could be broken. Frozen at its maximum velocity, his body became an ever-present threat. In real time, with its low authenticity, King's movements as he rose from the ground were closely linked to the blows of the batons and the jolts of the Taser. In his sworn deposition after the trial, Rodney King put into words what the videolow had already shown—that his body movements were reactions to the agony of 50,000 volts; their direction was *away from*, not *toward*; their intention was avoidance, not confrontation. But in slow motion the links between his body and the Taser were broken and his movements were transformed from reactions into actions, their intentions redirected toward the police instead of away from them.

On television, Rush Limbaugh was as video-smart as the defense lawyers were in the courtroom. He, too, retechnologized these two or three seconds of the videolow, making them into a loop that he played continuously in real time. The loop showed only the moment when, as Limbaugh put it in his voice-over, "Rodney King gets up off the ground and lunges at a cop" (see *Sidebar: Limbaugh on King*, p.

130   131). It does not show, before this moment, Stacey Koon and his Taser, or, after it, Laurence Powell knocking King to the ground with his baton.

The defense lawyers regularly froze the video*high* and wrote upon it. Some two-thirds of the way through the beating, there was a lull in the action that was suddenly broken by Officer Briseno stamping on the back of King's neck and driving his face into the pavement, whereupon the beating started again. Rodney King had been lying face down and slowly moved his hands behind his back as though preparing to be handcuffed. As he did so, his left foot moved, in my judgment, two inches upward and three or four inches to one side. It could well have been an involuntary movement balancing that of his hands. The defense froze the leg at its maximum elevation, drew a circle round it to isolate it from his hands, and argued that it showed King was about to rise and attack the officers once again: his leg was "cocked." Retechnologizing the video*low* enabled King's body to be held indefinitely at the moment of maximum threat, to be remade into a primed bomb, an ignited fuse, a cocked gun.

This retechnologized discourse was materially real in its effects. In the first trial, Officer Briseno testified that he tried to restrain his fellow cops because he considered their beating was excessive: in the second trial he refused to give this testimony, and agreed with his colleagues that the force was reasonable. The reason for his change? His first testimony was based only on his experience of the event; by the time of the second, however, he had seen the computer-enhanced video, and its higher truth.[3] In the second trial, therefore, the defense included a *video*tape of Briseno's original testimony as evidence of what he *really* saw!

Retechnologizing the video*low* involved the verbal as well as the visual: its sound track was even more unclear than its visuals; the throb of the police helicopter dominated it, other shouts, cries, and sounds could be heard only dimly. In the first trial, the prosecution seemingly felt that the video*low*'s au-

Limbaugh on King

The Rodney King trial—first one; the—the—trial of four cops, in most people's minds—and by the way, since this is being tried on TV, it's about time there was a little balance. So we're going to enter the case here on this show tonight. And that's what I want to get to next, and that's the ver—the Rodney King video. You saw over and over again, fifteen seconds of this video, where he was being clubbed and beaten relentlessly. And you were led to believe—I mean, for a year and a half, we all saw this. We were repulsed by it. We were sickened by it. We couldn't believe that this could happen in America. And we demanded a verdict of guilty. There was only fifteen seconds of it.

Well, I've seen the whole video. And I want to show you parts of it—a part of it that you haven't seen—maybe. You may—it's been shown, but not very much. And to replicate the way this video has been shown to the country—the fifteen seconds of horror; we've taken the beginning of this; we've done what's called looping it. We've taken the first—What is it?—two or three seconds of this, and are just going to show it to you over, and over, and over again.

And I want to tell you what you're going to see here. This is the beginning of the whole incident. This is when Rodney King has been got—has been asked to get out of the car. He's on the ground and the cops are surrounding him. I want you to watch this and watch it. Surprised? You seen that before? Maybe a little, but you haven't seen it very much. Watch it again. Watch it some more times. We've got a lot of ground to make up here on this video. Watch this again, folks.

. . .

Rodney King gets up off the ground and lunges at a cop—after being told to stay down. I'm convinced, if he'd have stayed down, nothing would have happened to him at that point; if he would have just submitted and been handcuffed. But he gets up and lunges at the cop. And you haven't see [*sic*] that. They don't show you that. But this show has just shown you that. And what you don't see—if we had time, we'd show you again. He tries to get up again. He doesn't lunge at the cop again, but he tries to get up again.

Now I think it's understandable that the cops, after having Tasered him—that's juice—and I've—any cop will tell you that if you Tas—Taser somebody, and they don't go down, that they're on something. That's what the manual says. You don't have time to ask there. You're dealing with somebody that maybe you can't control, or you don't think. Now why am I telling you this? You think, "My gosh, Rush, you're being unfair." No. If we're going to try this case on TV, folks, then we're going to get in the game here. And we're going to show all the other sides of the evidence that you haven't seen for lo, these many—two years that you've been watching Rodney King get beat. Because it was two years ago that it happened, practically. The trial took a year before it happened.

(March 10, 1993)

132   thenticity meant that it could speak for itself. The defense knew better and saturated it with words. And not just any words, not the oral discourses of the
weak, but the logorational discourse of high power. In calling it logorational, I
use *logos* as a signifier of the power of the word—of God, of the Father, of the
law—and also of *logic*—the rationality that accompanies it—and of *-ology*—the
form of knowledge that it produces. The videolow was wordless, its truth authenticated only by its movement between the material event and the video; its
silence nudged its viewers to fill it with words, the network news verbalized
for and around it, viewers spoke with and against it, articulating their experience with its visibility, and in the courtroom logorationalism saturated it.

The verbal manipulations of the defense lawyers that anchored the technological ones of the videohigh moved Black legal scholar Patricia Williams to angry sarcasm:

> Who could not but tingle with admiration as the police officers
> invoked the goddesses of soft restraint and even sensuality, in their
> description of the "application" of "departmentally approved" baton
> "power strikes" to the upside and downside of Rodney King's head.
> Or the employ of all those terms that turned Rodney King's body
> into a gun: what to those of us who saw only the plain old normal
> version [of the video] looked like King's body helplessly flopping and
> twitching in response to a rain of blows, became in the freeze-framed
> version a "cocked" leg, an arm in "trigger position," a bullet of a
> body always aimed, poised, and about to fire itself into deadly
> action. . . . Who could fail to be touched by the inventive whimsy of
> that police paramedic who described King, hog-tied and admittedly
> choking, as "belligerently spitting" blood.[4]

The defense lawyers put into words the fears of white America: they made the
movements of Rodney King's body on the ground into signs of a Black refusal
to comply with the white social order. In the second trial, however, Rodney
King was allowed to give his meaning to his movements, "I was trying to stay
alive, sir—trying to stay alive, and they never gave me a chance to stay still. I
never had a chance to stay still."[5]

The *logos* of the courtroom may not always, to outsiders at least, appear rational, but its power is beyond dispute. In such a setting, the videolow could
not speak for itself, and the prosecution's apparent belief that it could was both
shortsighted and professionally damning. No truth can speak for itself in a
court of law, it always has to be spoken: legal truth is always a product of discourse. Whose discourses are admittable then becomes a crucial question. In
the first trial, Rodney King, for instance, was not allowed to speak. Houston
Baker puts King's silencing into a historical continuity: in the last century, he
writes, "it was unthinkable for a black person to offer testimony against any
white act whatsoever. African American slaves were, thus, literally 'out-

lawed.' "[6] Slaves were denied any form of public discourse, and *"slave truth*
[was], therefore, not only an oxymoron, but an impossibility."[7] The seeming
authenticity of the videolow (a "slave truth") could not survive its elevation
into the high discourse of the courtroom. A similar fate befell Anita Hill. The
authenticity of her experience (another "slave truth") could not survive in the
Senate. Outside the places of high power, however, "slave truths" were harder
to repress, and millions of Americans believed both the videolow and Anita
Hill. In the streets of South-Central, "looting" became the only public discourse available to those who were, in normal conditions, as silenced as Rodney King and banned as utterly as any nineteenth-century slave from testifying
against white oppression. Patricia Williams points out that the logorationality
of the courtroom is based not upon reason alone, but upon the discursive and
social power that produces its own truth while repressing that of others. "It is
possible to see the King verdict as not merely rational," she writes, "but as the
magnificently artful product of an aesthetic of rationality—even to the extent
that it rationalized and upheld an order of socialized irrationality."[8]

In the second trial the prosecution was as active as the defense in using the
words of experts to make the images mean. The videolow was amateur in its vi-
sualization; verbalizing the videohigh brought it into the domain of expertise,
where truth depends on the credentials of the expert. For the defense, Sergeant
Duke talked the jury through the video, proving that it showed not brutality but
the efficient application of police procedure. Sergeant Costa then, for the prosecution, talked them through it again, proving that it showed a clear violation of police policy. Similarly, medical experts showed video representations of King's
skull: they brought in plastic three-dimensional reproductions of it, which
showed, according to prosecution verbalization, that his injuries resulted from police batons, whereas the defense words proved they were the result of his fall to
the pavement. Each side of the case spent much of its energy arguing the credentials of the expert on the stand, for the credibility of the expert was the foundation
of the power of his or her discourse to produce the truth.

Our age may be that of the visual simulacrum, where what is seen is what
matters, and any distinction between an unseen ("true") event and its (false)
representations no longer seems achievable. Much of the thrust of our cultural
technology is to extend what can be made visible and to technologize a panoptic power that lies in the means of seeing as much as in what it sees. The eye of
the "smart bomb" makes visible the experience of power: we can see why the
United States "won" the Gulf War, and in the seeing experience a videohigh
that is the pleasure of power. But this hypervisuality has not swept logorationality out of the picture—history is never dislodged as simply as that. Rather,
the visual and the verbal enter complex relations with each other as they move
up and down the social and discursive hierarchies, as they oppose or endorse
each other's ways of knowing.

134   Words work through categories, so putting an event into words involves categorizing it. The LAPD had produced a precise system of categories into which its officers placed any event they encountered on the streets. The lawyer defending Stacey Koon showed the jury a man-sized chart on which were drawn boxes representing the seven categories into which events were to be put and the police behavior appropriate to each (see *Sidebar: The LAPD Tool Kit*, p. 135). This table of "escalating force" is an instruction manual for the technological application of power to the body. Its categories enabled the police to "write" their meanings on Rodney King's physical body in the same way as the defense lawyers wrote theirs upon his electronic one in the videohigh. On the street, the police officers translated Rodney King's body movements into a discourse that was not his and so made them mean differently; in the courtroom, the videohigh similarly translated the videolow into another discourse. This translation enabled the lawyers to persuade the jury that the categoric system of the LAPD tool kit was not part of the grammar of police discourse, but was part of reality itself, and therefore, as part of that reality, Rodney King moved his behavior up the table from one category to the next: he was thus in control of his beating. Fortunately for him, the defense argued, the police were able to prevent him reaching the final category, that of "deadly force," in which, presumably, he would have committed suicide.

The argument was successful. The anonymous jury member who explained on television that King *was* in control was thinking logorationally: On CNN *Newsnight*, she said, "The policemen just were not guilty of any abuse in our mind. They did simply what they were trained for, using the tools that were given them; and, based on Rodney King's actions, *he's* the one that was controlling the action all the way through." Her reasoning assumed that King's behavior, the categories it fell into, and the police action that ensued were all part of an objective reality in which the police behavior was the natural effect of King's actions, just as pain is the natural effect of putting one's hand into a fire.

This discursive strategy puts Blacks in control of their own subordination through their control over the degree of their submissiveness, and erases white power and responsibility from the picture. The defense's table of escalating force was therefore made to measure not white power but Black submissiveness. By such means the awkward contradiction between the Blackness of King's refusal to submit and the whiteness of the categories into which it was inserted could be dissolved, and the fact that those categories do not exist in Black understandings of this refusal could be ignored.

The strategy of erasing any difference between white and Black ways of understanding the event was effective with the white jury. The nonsubmissive Black is a troubling figure to whites but an inspiring one to many Blacks. Rodney King was surrounded by at least twenty-one police, four visible cars (more must have been there, but were not shown on the video), and a helicopter. A man refusing to submit in the face of these odds may be categorized as crazed

The LAPD Tool Kit

From the opening statement to the jury of Darryl Mounger, Stacey Koon's attorney:

You will hear testimony that it is the suspect who controls what happens on the streets; that the officer is standing there in his uniform, with his badge, and he tells people what to do by verbalizing, "Get down, get on your face!" When that does not work there is an array of tools that the sergeant has. You will hear basically what the Los Angeles Police Department gives him. You will hear about the escalation of force and the de-escalation of force. This chart will show you the tools that Sergeant Koon had available to him [he shows a vertical chart with seven labeled blocks on it]. He started off with verbalization, and then he goes to the next one, which is called "firm grip"; in essence what it means is that you grab hold of somebody, whether it's by the arm, or you twist a wrist, a wristlock. Then you go to a chemical agent, which might be tear gas or Mace, which officers carry on their belt, but that's only used in certain situations, not here where the suspect might have been on drugs. The next level up is the Taser, which is meant to incapacitate, it shoots 50,000 volts and causes most people's motor nerves, causes them to collapse. The next tool up is the handheld baton; a metal baton is a tool to protect yourself against an attacker. In addition to that, on the same level, the experts will tell you, there are kicks, and officers know how to use those kicks. But when these tools are ineffective, ladies and gentlemen, then you rise to the level of deadly force—restraints that can kill, like the carotid chokehold, or you have firearms—you have instruments of death.

in one discourse, heroic in another. To make his refusal appear crazed, the defense discursively filled his body with drugs and alcohol to produce this white sense of its behavior. In some Black discourses, however, Rodney King's refusal to submit was an index of how African Americans have survived four centuries of slavery, and he spoke for many when, in the second trial, he explained, "I was trying to stay alive, sir—trying to stay alive."[9] Rodney King's behavior was categorically different in white and Black discourse. Discourse is, of course, continuous with social experience, so discursive differences are always social ones. African Americans knew instantly the trouble that Rodney King was in merely by seeing him surrounded by cops; the brutal beating that followed, was, in the light of their experience, the logical and predictable outcome. Many whites, however, with their quite different social experience, were unable to see that situated "logic" and thus had to look to King's behavior for an explanation. The defense lawyers capitalized on this and turned much of the trial into an investigation of what Rodney King did rather than what the police officers did. For them, the beating could be made to make sense only through white categorizations of Rodney King's behavior.

The power to produce a category system and the power to determine which category fits which event is a material power that results from the social institutions that give it its strength. King had no access to those institutions, and

136 their discourse was therefore not his; it was one applied upon him, not one by which he made sense of his experience. His own experience of the event was, therefore, not the "true" one.

This power over the discursive production of truth attempts to extend itself over the technology of its distribution. But as information technology has developed, it has become harder to control. When the book was hand-produced, control over its distribution was total; as printing developed technologically, control over the word was loosened. High-tech print still emanates from power centers underwritten by capital, but very early in printing's history low-tech versions began to contest it. Small radical presses and, today, rebel radio stations have power that may be limited to their own locality (whether defined geographically or politically) but is still the power to produce alternative and contestatory truths. Low tech, verbal or visual, is not the exclusive terrain of the weak, for the weak have no territory that is theirs alone, but it is the terrain upon which they can best contest the strong; high tech is more exclusively the terrain of the powerful, not least because high tech needs high capital.

In the pretech era, as in the nontech domains of our own, the clash between oralcy and literacy replayed similar power struggles. The African American oral tradition puts the world into discourse quite differently from white literacy. Similarly, too, women's gossip is an oral discourse that works outside and often against the literacy that we now widely recognize to be patriarchically inscribed. Rodney King's videolow invites verbalizing quite differently in the oral discourse of African Americans or Latino/as from its logosaturation in the courtroom of Simi Valley. Oralcy is embodied speech, a low-tech speech that reconnects the electronic body of Rodney King to the lived experience of the weak.

Literacy is not only technologized speech via the stylus, the pen, or the word processor, it is also institutionalized speech via the church, the school, and the courtroom. High-tech visibility, too, is both technologized and institutionalized. The video screens of high-tech visibility are clustered in powerful institutions. The war against Iraq was directed on war-room video screens. The conquest of high space is organized on the screens of mission control, and Jupiter is made real as it is made hypervisible on them. On them Jupiter is changed and reconfigured, as was Rodney King, its colors on the screens manipulated so that its geological structure, the physics of its atmosphere reveal their truths in their hypervisibility. In hospitals, too, doctors no longer examine the physical bodies of patients but their electronic bodies on screens, just as the jury examined the electronic body of Rodney King in both its street and its medical forms. Technology applies power and helps direct it, but does not motivate or direct it. Power is social, not just technological, and it is through institutional and economic control that technology is directed. Although technology extends the terrain and the mode of struggle, it does not correct the imbalance of power.

But in extending the terrain, it may offer the weak more opportunities, and as the tactics of the weak are opportunistic, any extension is potentially to their

advantage. The Rodney King videolow was opportunistic; its videohigh version was not, it was strategically deliberate. Malice Green was a Black motorist
in Detroit who, like Rodney King, was pulled over and beaten by cops. He
died. But there was no video of the scene; the incident was made known verbally both through literacy (the media) and oralcy among African Americans,
but the inopportune absence of a camera prevented its hypervisualization. It
could not, therefore, become a media event with its own hyperreality.

The new never replaces the old; it invades its territory, intermingles with it,
pushes it from the center to the margins where it can, and conjoins with it
where it cannot. In the courtroom more than anywhere else the logorational
holds its terrain against the hypervisual; the legal system exemplifies it in its
purest, most uncontradictory form. Legal truth is a product of the way that
people and events are put into words and subjected to reason; legal truth is
that of the "reasonable man" (*sic*). In the institution of the law, the videohigh
conjoined with the high verbal to produce a truth that won. But this truth
never trickled down to the videolow, whose blurred unenhanced authenticity
outside the courtroom stood firm in all its insecurity against the attempts to
revisualize it and make it tell another truth.

The defense lawyers took their videohigh to a new institution—network
television—and attempted to make it work there as it did in the courtroom. But
television is not an Enlightenment institution, and logorationalism has never
been as central or powerful in it. Television had already promoted the videolow
into the hypervisual, and the new videohigh, retechnologized and saturated
with logorationality, could not use TV to transfer its power from the courtroom
to the living room, from Simi Valley to the streets of South-Central. The reasoning of the lawyers that worked so well in the courtroom failed in the living
room: on television the videohigh revealed not the reality of the event but the
power to manipulate it.

As a post-Enlightenment institution, television cannot deal in the singular-
ity of truth; its voices are always multiple, its truths situated and thus provi-
sional. The Rodney King video on TV spoke with the authentic voice of the low
only because that voice was, in this case, the one that most Americans wanted
to hear, if only because it allowed them to disavow a racism whose overtness
made it counterproductive. But its apparent authenticity was no more secure
than the social alliances that were formed around it. Rush Limbaugh understood this well, and he struggled energetically to reclaim its meanings for his
audience (see *Sidebar: Limbaugh on King*, p. 131). He had no doubt about either
the event on the street or the need to manipulate the video and saturate it with
words to ensure that it *really* meant what *really* happened. As his carefully selected extract runs and reruns, he tells his audience that what they have seen
on the "liberal" media is a distortion, but what they are now seeing is the *truth*.
All media commentators present their view of events as the truth, but, unlike
most, Limbaugh explicitly argues that his truth must be fought for in opposi-

138   tion to other truths (which, of course, he calls "lies" or "distortions"). Here, as
in his response to Murphy Brown, he foregrounds the politics of producing
truth and thus encourages his audience to engage actively in the struggle for
meaning. He's clever; I wish he were on my side.

Recoded Racial Power

Racial difference runs through all these struggles over the meaning of the
video, although it is recoded into the difference between cops and suspect, between law-and-order and disorder. The blurred images of the videolow could
not make racial difference visible in skin color, but only in behavior. In the
physical domain of the body, racial difference was stark and imperative: the
impact between baton and flesh, between boot and neck, was a racial impact.

The courtroom, however, needed to keep race central but unspoken, to exploit
its inerasable presence while apparently erasing it. Logorationality has had centuries of experience through which to develop strategies of discursive repression
and marginalization. The form of nonracist racism that works only by denying its
presence can use words to repress the racial from the center while relying on the
visual to carry its traces on the margins, where they can circulate the racism that
cannot be spoken. Contradictorily, however, these traces can also be used to recover what has been repressed, or to recenter what has been marginalized. For
long stretches of the Clarence Thomas hearings race was never spoken but always
visible, and the racial dimension of "family values" could always be glimpsed on
the visual margins of the verbal debate between Murphy Brown and Dan Quayle.
So, too, racial difference was rarely spoken in the trial of the Rodney King video,
or, if it was, was spoken only to be denied, but it was always visible as the all-
white jury, the white defendants, and their lawyers faced off against the Black
prosecutor speaking and standing in for Rodney King.[10]

The nonracist racism that exploits racial difference while denying it was at
work, too, in moving the trial from Los Angeles County, where the incident
occurred, to Ventura County. Lake View Terrace, where the beating took place,
is located in the racially mixed San Fernando Valley. The defense was able to
move the trial to almost all-white Simi Valley in Ventura County by using the
discourse of place to recode that of race. It argued that spatial distance would
guarantee objective distance and thus "truth": distance was articulated with
objectivity or fairness, and proximity with partiality. So the trial could be "fair"
(read "light skinned"?) only by ensuring a distance between the jurors and the
incident. The geographic move from Los Angeles to Simi Valley was in high
discourse a move from partiality to objectivity and in low discourse from Black
to white. Geography is racial as well as spatial. This geographic dislocation of
the trial from the incident is the equivalent of the electronic dislocation of
King's body movements from the Taser darts and the batons, and the racial politics of each dislocation were the same.

Geography's recoding of racial difference went further: Simi Valley is not only   139
almost all white (only 2 percent of its residents are Black), it is also the home of the
Ronald Reagan Presidential Library, and, more significantly in this case, where
approximately 25 percent of the members of the Los Angeles Police Department
have chosen to live. The rest of the inhabitants are happy with this state of affairs,
for, according to Harriet Michel, a Black panelist who appeared on the daytime
talk show *Donahue*: "The function of the police, as far as these people in Ventura
County are concerned, is to keep the Mr. Kings from them. They moved to Ventura County to get away from people just like him."[11] The *New York Times* confirmed her opinion; it opened its account of Simi Valley by pointing out that its
hundred thousand residents had crossed the Ventura County line "to escape the
chaos and discomfort of the city." As one of them explained, "I'm happy to live
away from that kind of atmosphere," citing "gangs, homeless people who don't
work and don't have any money because they don't work."[12] Predictably, he went
on to deny that race had anything to do with it; the key difference was between
those who cared for their neighborhood and those who did not. The Simi Valley
jury pool of more than three hundred, therefore, contained no Blacks and, according to Kevin Uhrich, every one of them had direct social or family links with members of the law enforcement agencies.[13]

The whiteness of this jury must not be understood as specific to this case,
but as part of the whiteness of the legal system in general. Its verdict was as
explosive as it was not because it was a surprise (for, though it may have been
to many whites, it was not to most Blacks), but because it became such a vivid
and painful piece in the jigsaw puzzle of racial injustice. The most often heard
slogan of the uprising, "No Justice, No Peace," pointed not just to this trial, but
to a much broader system of injustice.

In the same month as the uprisings, Judge Reinhardt, a federal appellate judge
in California, told the graduating class at San Francisco's Golden Gate University
how the courts under Reagan and Bush had acted consistently to extend white
power and to reverse whatever gains minority races had made in the wake of the
civil rights movement.[14] He argued that in the 1960s and 1970s the courts had
worked hard to extend human and civil rights to all Americans, particularly Black
ones, when neither the executive nor the legislative branch had had the will or the
courage to do so. But Reaganism brought in a "judicial revolution—one that will
not easily be reversed." One deeply disturbing consequence of this is the belief,
held by 84 percent of African Americans, that they will not receive justice in the
courts. He turned to two points in the justice system for evidence to support his
charge of a judicial revolution and to justify the Black knowledge of its racial injustice. First he considered presidential appointments to the bench: in 1976, when
Carter took office, there were only two Black judges in the appellate courts and
one on the Supreme Court. Of the fifty-nine appointments to the appellate courts
made by Carter, nine (16 percent) were Black; he made no appointments to the
Supreme Court. Reagan, in his eight years in the White House, appointed eighty-

140   three judges to the bench, of whom only one was Black. Bush, in his four years, appointed thirty-two, but the only African American he could find to meet his criteria was Clarence Thomas, so now, after his rapid elevation to the Supreme Court, there are no African American Bush appointees in the appellate courts. Since 1980, therefore, the federal courts of appeal have been presidentially whitened by a ratio of 115:1.

Of course, this pattern of appointments is reproduced in the pattern of rulings handed down—otherwise the Republican presidents would not have made the appointments they did. Reinhardt gave details of a number of recent decisions of which I will give only one, chosen because it is local: In *Los Angeles v. Lyons* the court ruled that a Black victim of the police carotid chokehold could not sue to bar further use of the technique because he could not prove that he himself would be choked again. The ruling deracialized him into a colorless individual and discounted the evidence that the chokehold was used disproportionately against Blacks. The chokehold remained legal and the courts upheld white power yet again. This, and other similar decisions, Judge Reinhardt concluded,

> showed the African American community that the federal judiciary is no longer interested in protecting the rights of minorities, that federal judges are far more concerned with protecting the interests of white males. To minorities—particularly to Black Americans—this was a bitter blow. The age of Earl Warren, William Brennan, and Thurgood Marshall was the golden age of civil rights. Minorities were given the feeling that someone cared, that government cared, that the law was on their side. Understandably, with the Rehnquist Court in full sway, they no longer believe that. Their earlier belief gave them hope. Their current belief leads only to despair—and to disrespect for the law.[15]

Reinhardt then pointed to similar injustices in sentencing. When whites and Blacks are convicted of similar crimes, Blacks receive far harsher sentences, particularly if they are young, male, and unemployed. Alongside this is the drastic difference in sentences for crimes most frequently committed by whites compared with those by Blacks: white-collar fraud involving millions of dollars is often treated more leniently than a Black theft of a wallet.

Just over a year after Reinhardt's speech, *USA Today* printed a report of its analysis of the Reagan-Bush "War on Drugs" that exposed its racism. There were four times as many white users of cocaine as there were Black, for instance, yet more than half those arrested on cocaine-related charges were Black. Nationally, Blacks were four times more likely to be arrested than whites on drug charges—twenty-two times in Minneapolis—despite the fact that whites and Blacks use drugs at approximately the same rate. This distortion within the dominant social understanding of the "drug problem" is institutionalized not only in the courts, but also in police policy, so Black motorists and pedestrians are disproportionately stopped

and searched "on suspicion" merely because they are Black. Among its many sto-   141
ries of racist uses of the "drug war" by police, *USA Today* included an account
from Columbus, Ohio, of the activities of what the police themselves called
"SNAT"—the "Special Nigger Arrest Team." The city turned to the legal system to
guard itself against charges of racism by filing a brief that admitted that SNAT was
"a distasteful slur," but claimed that it did not constitute evidence of a pact among
police to target Blacks.[16]

Recoded, rather than denied, racism was at work in the defense lawyers de-
scriptions of Rodney King's body. Space, time, and the body are interconnected through their physicality: bodies can exist only in space and time;
equally, space becomes a place only when bodies enter it. The success with
which race was silently recoded into place in the geographic dislocation of the
trial was repeated as the defense's verbal discourse referred to every physical
aspect of Rodney King's body except its race. They consistently described him
in terms of his weight, height, strength, and masculinity. Time and again he
was put into discourse as a 250-pound, six-foot-three-inch man with the physical strength to throw off police officers and withstand Taser guns, batons, and
boots. He was repeatedly likened to a bear—a neat analogy in which racism
could be simultaneously denied and exploited. Patricia Williams claims that
this image of a big vicious predator made dangerous by wounding not only resonated in the hunter sensibilities of "those good NRA folks on the jury," but
also, through animalizing King, defended the police behavior against the
charge of racism:

> "He wasn't an animal, was he?" demanded the prosecution in some
> annoyance; "No, Sir," replied the smooth Officer Powell, "He just
> acted like one." So when they got to that stuff about gorillas in the
> mist [see below], it became cast as just another reference to big dark
> furry creatures. Gorillas as racist?! How annoyed the jury was with
> that. Accusations of racism became just as ridiculous as trying to
> make a case of bearism.[17]

The videohigh magnified and isolated this body, slowed and froze its motion, and
made its movements appear the result and evidence of its own size and strength
rather than reactions to the blows of the white bodies ranged around it.

The four cops were accused and defended individually, so each rescreening of
the videohigh articulated the body of King with one individualized white body,
which was often encircled in freeze-frame, visually isolated from its colleagues:
against this one lone cop, King could veritably be made to appear the stronger and
his strength to put him in control of the situation. The collective white body of
twenty-one cops organized around the single Black man was repressed from the
videohigh discourse of the courtroom as it could not be from the videolow.

And this Black body was discursively filled with drugs: time and again its be-
haviors were rationally linked with PCP, and PCP was characterized as the drug

142 that produces superhuman strength. Much, too, was made of the beer that King and his two companions had consumed. This irrational, unnaturally strong body is always, in the white imagination, Black. King's race enabled the white imagination of the jury to discount the scientific evidence that he had not taken PCP, for although no one explicitly argued that beer was equivalent to PCP in producing superhuman strength, it was recruited to the same strategy: the defense made much of the fact that King had consumed more of it than a driver is allowed to. Indeed, in his summing up, Koon's lawyer concluded that Rodney King was "a two hundred and fifty pound man with a belly full of beer."

The Threat of the Black Male: Rodney King and Willie Horton

The hypervisual *saw* Rodney King as the Black victim of white oppression. The logorational *spoke* Rodney King as the Black male body out of control, the threat to white social stability that white law and order has to contain. This figure of the Black male body reaches deep into the white psyche and history: it revives guilt and fear, it recalls lynchings and castrations. In it, the size and strength of this figured body stands in the white imagination for the Black penis and its power to challenge the whiteness of the phallocentric order. The Black male body is not only a social danger but a sexual danger. The masculinity of King's body was necessarily part of its size and strength, but the sexuality of its threat was as repressed from the official discourse as was its race.

Sexuality and race are inseparable in white American history, and each exerts a different form of power. Anxiety is always intensified when powers run counter to each other, as they do with race and sex. The social power of race belongs to whites, but the physical, or even natural, power of sexuality is ascribed to Blacks. The "Cress theory" (see below), offering an Afrocentric explanation of this, argues that whites *are*, through genetics, physically and sexually inferior to Blacks; it reverses the white explanation by locating the difference in nature rather than culture. But whatever the explanation, the socially powerful but physically weak white male does see his threatening obverse in the socially weak but physically powerful Black man. This racial-sexual threat appears to be directed at the white female, whom the white male, in this context, fears that he is unable to protect or, even worse, satisfy. In this power matrix, the role of the Black woman, disempowered both socially and physically, is that of the victim-object of both white social power (rape by the slave owner) and Black sexual power; to fill this double role, and serve as the alibi for the double play of power upon her, she has to be understood, in the white imagination, as hypersexual. Orrin Hatch could tap into deep and powerful anxieties when he cast Anita Hill as the hypersexual Black female; so, too, Clair Huxtable's double containment (racial and sexual) of both "today's woman" and the Black woman within traditional family values was doubly reassuring.

The Black women who, like Paula Giddings, feared that the Clarence Thomas-Anita Hill hearings' display of Black sexuality to a white audience could only harm African Americans had sound historical reasons. The sexualization of racial difference is particularly intense in the relations between whites and Blacks, and is less central in white ways of understanding their difference from other races (although the figure of the white woman captured by American Indians is a product of a similar racial-sexual fear). The unique histories of the white rape of the Black woman on the slave ship and the plantation obviously underlie the intensity with which Black-white racial difference is sexualized.

We might note in passing a point that will be developed more fully later on. Martin Levine, writing on the notorious Tuskegee syphilis experiment conducted on Black men from 1932 to 1972 (see chapter 4), observes that the origins of the experiment lay in this white sexualization of racial difference:

> It was widely believed [among whites] that Black racial inferiority made them a notoriously syphilis-soaked race! Their smaller brains lacked mechanisms for controlling sexual desire, causing them to be highly promiscuous. They matured early and consequently were sexually active; and the Black man's enormous penis with its long foreskin was prone to venereal infections. These physiological differences meant the disease must affect the races differently.[18]

Although today it may be difficult for a white to speak so explicitly of Black sexuality as a definer of racial difference, the loss of explicitness is not a sign of changed thinking. There is still no stronger motivation for white power to rush to the defense of its position than a racial-sexual threat.

The producers of the notorious Willie Horton ad in the 1988 Republican presidential campaign were well aware of this. They selected for their figure a man who was Black, a murderer, and a rapist (see *Sidebar: Willie Horton*, p. 144). This attack ad and its powerful figure of Willie Horton ran for twenty-eight days on cable television across the nation. The ad was widely understood as racist, yet, predictably, its verbal discourse never mentioned race at all: the camera, however, showed Horton's race clearly and had no need to show that of his victims—it could be justifiably confident that the white audience it addressed would align itself with them and supply their missing whiteness. The ad's racism could therefore be denied, and George Bush denied it.

The ad was not produced by the Bush campaign team, but by the National Security Political Action Committee. This was important to the campaign strategists, who could thus disclaim all responsibility for the ad's racism but still benefit from it. Which is what they did. Their trumpeted disavowals in the mainstream media circulated the effects of the ad far beyond those who had actually seen it on cable TV and ensured that Willie Horton was transformed from an individual into a figure.

Willie Horton

"Weekend Passes" is the title of the 30-second advertisement about Willie Horton that was financed by the National Security Political Action Committee.

As side-by-side photographs of Vice President Bush and Governor Michael S. Dukakis flash on the screen, an announcer says, "Bush and Dukakis on crime."

Flash to a picture of Mr. Bush. "Bush supports the death penalty for first-degree murderers."

Then a picture of Mr. Dukakis. "Dukakis not only opposes the death penalty, he allowed first-degree murderers to have weekend passes from prison."

Flash to a police photograph of a glaring Willie Horton.

"One was Willie Horton, who murdered a boy in a robbery, stabbing him nineteen times."

Flash to another blurred black-and-white photograph of the convict, looking as if he is being arrested by a police officer.

"Despite a life sentence, Horton received ten weekend passes from prison," the announcer says.

"Horton fled, kidnapped a young couple, stabbing the man and repeatedly raping his girlfriend." As the announcer gives these details, the words "kidnapping," "stabbing," and "raping" flash on the screen.

The last photo is of Mr. Dukakis. The announcer says: "Weekend prison passes. Dukakis on crime."

("A 30-Second Ad on Crime," *New York Times*, November 3, 1988, B20)

Despite the official distance between them, the NSPAC and the Bush campaign used the same people to make their ads, and Dan Quayle had previously endorsed the NSPAC, calling its ads "a source of real encouragement as well as a great boon to our efforts." During the controversy he disavowed this endorsement, claiming that the letter containing it had been written by an intern and signed not by him, but by an automatic pen. It is hard to conceive of more convincing evidence of postmodernity than an automatic pen, for in destroying the direct relationship between a signature and an individual, it destroys a centuries-old guarantor of the final truth. When a signature is a simulacrum, postmodernity is rampant.

When the relationship between words and events is unstable, the political "spin doctor" becomes a key player in the game of contesting meanings. Words and images may be launched in public, but they have then to be constantly steered in one direction or another, often in two directions at once. So the Republicans could deny giving the NSPAC any approval or encouragement and could emphasize Bush's disapproval of the Willie Horton ad. But, by waiting until the twenty-fifth day of its twenty-eight-day run before doing so, they could ride to victory on it while standing aside and claiming it was out of their control. The founder of NSPAC, Elizabeth Feidiay, knew this as clearly as did the rest of the nation: "Officially," she said, "the campaign has to disavow

themselves from me. Unofficially, I hear they're thrilled about what we're do-   145
ing." Officially, the signature was not Dan Quayle's; unofficially, it was.[19]

The racial-sexual threat to the white imagination is potent, particularly if its
racism can be denied while being exploited. Ken Duberstein knew this as he
oversaw the Republican strategy that included the Willie Horton ad. He knew
this as he oversaw the Republican strategy that turned the verbal discourse of
the Thomas hearings from gender, where Anita Hill was "winning," to race,
where Thomas had to, because white logorationalism can no more handle
overtly the sexual threat of the Black male than the racial.[20] Similarly, in Simi
Valley the defense could not overtly link Rodney King with Willie Horton, but
it had no need to. By recoding racial-sexual threats to white supremacy into the
discourse of law and order, it put Rodney King into the category already occupied by Willie Horton, and that was enough. The Hortonization of Rodney
King is a contemporary instance of a process that has been continuous ever
since Africans were brought to this country: video technology may give the old
process new form, but it does not change the long white tradition of the literary, cinematic, legal, and political reconstruction of inhumane oppression into
rational, defensible behavior.

Though the sexual axis of Rodney King could never be overt in official discourse, triggers to activate it were constantly pulled. There were two white female police officers present at the incident, though not visible or at least identifiable in the videolow. In the courtroom, however, their white femaleness
was clearly visible, as was that of the women in the jury. The jury member
who, in explaining the rationality of the verdict on national TV denied that race
had anything to do with it, spoke this denial in a female voice.

These momentary sightings of race and sexuality are all that the courtroom
needs, or can handle. In everyday life, however, it is a different matter: there
Stacey Koon's language could be as direct as his baton. In the manuscript of his
book on the Rodney King affair, he wrote:

> [King] grabbed his butt with both hands and began to shake and
> gyrate his fanny in a sexually suggestive fashion. As King sexually
> gyrated, a mixture of fear and offense overcame Melanie. The fear
> was of a Mandingo sexual encounter.[21]

Melanie Singer was one of the two traffic cops who originally pulled King over.
Not only did Koon make overt his racial and sexual meanings of the incident,
he spoke with total confidence for both the white woman and the Black man.
Ms. Singer herself never mentioned her fear, sexual or otherwise, of King:
Koon was speaking for, with, and from, white masculinity. The *Los Angeles
Times* commented:

> Koon . . . defended his choice of words saying he was merely trying

146   to draw out the antebellum image of a large black man and a defenseless white woman.

"In society," he said, "there's this sexual prowess of blacks on the old plantations in the South and intercourse between blacks and whites on the plantation. And that's where the fear comes in, because he's black."[22]

Where the normally covert is made overt like this its socially interested power is made visible, and both those who opposed Koon's position and those who, however secretly, supported it joined in the uproar provoked by its publication (his opponents, of course, were opposing racial-sexual power; his covert supporters, its visibility). Whereas white interests may be served by repressing the sexual dimension of racism, Black knowledge is enhanced by bringing it to the surface. So, on Black Liberation Radio, one of Kantako's "war correspondents" explained the white strategy behind both the beating and the verdict: "because they see us armed, armed with our penises, which give us the genetic power to eliminate them" (see *Sidebar: Black Liberation Radio and the Beating*, p. 147).

In its coverage of the case, the media made public much of the normally private discourse within the LAPD: the Christopher Commission listed 703 racial, ethnic, and sexual slurs in radio transmissions between police cars. A few examples will suffice: George Holliday was called "George of the Jungle," an African American family "was right out of Gorillas in the Mist," and, of a Black man he had just shot, Koon said, "You or I, we'd die, but not a Negro. They're too dumb to go into shock." His use of "you or I" to establish a discursive social norm from which to abnormalize, or "other," the "Negro" recalls Daryl Gates's comment when reminded that his cops had killed fifteen Black men with the official restraint called the carotid chokehold: "We may be finding," he said, "that in some blacks when it is applied, the veins or arteries do not open up as fast as they do on *normal* people" (emphasis added).[23] This racist language lends credence to Rodney King's claim, made in the second trial, that he heard one of the cops beating him saying, "We're going to kill you, nigger." It appeared again when Laurence Powell's defense lawyer in the first trial summed up the streets of South-Central as "the jungle out there."

In its own semiprivate domain, such discourse and the power it exerts goes unchecked. When exposed, however, it can be challenged, and even those who benefit from its exertion have to criticize it, distance themselves from it, and try to drive it back under the surface. When Mbanna Kantako broadcasts police radio live over Black Liberation Radio, he knows what he's doing. So, too, did Koon's advisers: his "fear" of a Mandingo encounter was edited out of both his book and his testimony at the trial.

A similar passage, however, remained in the book. Koon describes another arrest:

Black Liberation Radio and the Beating

Mbanna Kantako talks on the phone with a "war correspondent" from Columbus, Ohio:

WAR CORRESPONDENT: . . . these white people, their racism is so deep . . .

MBANNA KANTAKO: So deep, man.

WAR CORRESPONDENT: . . . and their mind is so frayed . . .

MBANNA KANTAKO: Twisted.

WAR CORRESPONDENT: . . . they can stand up there and claim to be rational and say this man was resisting, when we see the brother rolling and crying and screaming in pain. . . .

MBANNA KANTAKO: Right, at a certain point his body was moving involuntarily.

WAR CORRESPONDENT: He was moving from the blows he . . .

MBANNA KANTAKO: Right, right, he couldn't help it . . .

WAR CORRESPONDENT: . . . and each time he would stop, and they still, they stomped him in the back of his head, face down . . .

MBANNA KANTAKO: . . . stomp on the brother's neck . . .

WAR CORRESPONDENT: . . . and then to say that he was the one that controlled the actions, this shows you, as Frances Cress Welsing says, that any Black man killed by a white officer is always gonna be justifiable homicide, any white man that kills a Black is justifiable homicide, because they see us as armed, armed with our penises, which give us the genetic power to eliminate them . . .

MBANNA KANTAKO: That's what it's all about.

WAR CORRESPONDENT: . . . and it's really a matter of survival of the races.

(May 1, 1992)

My boot came from the area of lower California and connected with the suspect's scrotum around lower Missouri. My boot stopped about Ohio, but the suspect's testicles continued into upper Maine. The suspect was literally lifted off the ground. The suspect tried to speak, but it appeared he had something in his throat, probably his balls.[24]

The suspect here was Latino, not African American, but there is no evidence that Koon's boot recognized the difference. Koon did recognize similarities between him and King, however: he "knew" that both suspects were high on PCP. Like the Rodney King beating, this one too was videoed but the video never gained the widespread repeated visibility to transform it into the hypervisual. Quite the opposite, in fact, for it remained visible only to the LAPD, where it was used in training and, in Koon's words, "was to become a legend in its own lifetime."

The racial-sexual significance is kept deep in the social and individual psyche of white America, far below the level of public visibility where official discourse works. A court of law, therefore, finds such racial-sexual motivation extremely difficult to handle, and will work much more smoothly when it can be excluded from its discursive operations. Those states that have introduced

148 the concept of "hate crime" (mainly racial and homophobic) into their courts have found that motivation is difficult to prove through logorational discourse, or, rather, that its presence can be readily discounted by establishing "reasonable doubt." In the second, federal, trial of the police officers in which they were charged with violating Rodney King's civil rights, the judge ruled that the prosecution need not prove a racial motivation. This was welcomed as making the prosecution's case easier to prove, but equally we must recognize that it continues the repression of racism from the legal system: it continues the belief that in dismantling the laws that upheld segregation, the legal system has purged itself of racism.

The figure of Rodney King as the racial-sexual threat to white America could not stay confined within the trial and its meanings of the video: it was also used to make sense of the uprising that followed the verdict. On the first night, it informed Pat Buchanan's discourse as, on CNN, he spoke of "an orgy of rioting, arson, murder, and lynching." What a conservative white man saw in television's images of the streets of South-Central was the black, male, sexual body out of control: The words "orgy" and "lynching" come from the same discourse as Stacey Koon's "Mandingo." As the word "orgy" refers to the sexual body out of control that "lynching" racializes, so the social body out of control is a product of the word "riot." The "orgy of rioting" discursively extends the individual body of Rodney King/Willie Horton into the Black social body. The word "lynching" appears to be unintended, if not unintentional, for it is difficult to identify what it could refer to: but, if it had little connection with what went on in the streets of L.A., it indicated very clearly what went on in the mind of Pat Buchanan. It also echoed the voice of Clarence Thomas. (I would like, as an aside, to draw attention here to the masculinism of the mainstream discourse of the uprising, which was unproblematically seen as a Black male matter in which women had no part, just as the public memory of lynching has made it, too, into a masculine experience and repressed the knowledge of the Black women who were also lynched.)

Orgies and riots are the ultimate moral/social disorder against which "family values" will defend us. Like Dan Quayle, Pat Buchanan used them to make Republican sense of the uprisings. The Korean stores were the target of much of the Black anger, so it is not surprising that Buchanan would draw their owners into the position he occupied alongside Dan Quayle, by referring to them as "the brave people of Koreatown" who "live the family values we treasure." George Bush was not to be outdone by his fellow leading Republicans, and took the family values into his own home: the anguish he felt as he watched the Rodney King video and the events that followed the verdict was the anguish of a family man. "How," he thought, "can I explain this to my grandchildren?" (see *Sidebar: Bush on L.A.*, p. 188). Among the images that stunned him (and Barbara and his kids) was one of the "savagely beaten white truck driver." In

this he was not alone; the media placed this image firmly in the center of the   149
white understanding of the uprisings.

Reginald Denny and Damian Williams: Race at Work

In the violence that surged through South-Central in the first few hours after
the Rodney King verdict, a white driver named Reginald Denny was pulled
from his truck and beaten by Black men, one of whom, allegedly, was Damian
Williams. The incident was videoed from a TV news helicopter and relayed live
across the nation; it was also, it transpired later, taped by a Black bystander.
The mainstream media took up the video as *the* image of the first day of the
uprising. The media were professional (and commercial) in their judgment.
The image was semiotically packed; it was a focal point upon which deeply significant lines of meaning converged. The beating was savage and nearly fatal;
Reginald Denny became comatose, had to undergo lifesaving brain surgery,
and still has plastic under his skin to keep his eyeballs in place. The beating
may have been an expression of Black anger, but it was misdirected and counterproductive, for it played into white hands. The Black men involved stepped
straight into the category of Willie Horton and dragged Rodney King in after
them. They justified the police assault on Rodney King.

One of the white hands it played into was that of the Police Protection
League, who used the video in a commercial opposing Proposition F (a measure to make the LAPD more accountable). Here the voice-over explained that
"on April 29, your police wanted to do the job, but weren't allowed to"[25] and
went on to claim that the failure of the police to come to Denny's aid resulted
from political interference from City Hall, which Proposition F, if passed,
would increase. Local stations refused to run the ad, claiming that it was inflammatory, and the Police Protection League modified it by cutting the Denny
footage because, as the campaign manager for the police union put it, "it is still

150   a dynamite commercial." What kept the dynamite in the ad, presumably, was the way it absolved the LAPD by laying the blame for the riots upon three political leaders, two of whom were Black and the third Jewish. Proposition F was approved by an overwhelming 67 percent of those voting.

Another white man, State Controller Gray Davis, also made use of the video in the Democratic primary for the U.S. Senate seat made vacant by Wilson's midterm election to governor. His campaign ads included it with a voice-over that ran:

> It's not white people's fault there were riots in LA. It's not black people's fault there were riots in LA. A few thousand thugs—black, brown and white—terrorized all law abiding citizens.[26]

For Gray Davis, the structuring difference was not race, but that between "thugs" and "the rest of us," the framing discourse that of law and order. Though racial power may have been erased from the verbal discourse, it was inerasable from the visual: the camera showed no white thugs, only Black ones. But discourse often betrays its strategy as it attempts to hide it: the order of words is never determined by events, but by discursive intentionality. So, when the voice-over emphasizes lack of blame, the word "white" precedes "black," but when its focus moves to thuggery, "black" and "brown" precede "white."

From a Black perspective, the hawkish police ad and the dovish Democrat one are both white redirections of the Denny video because they both dislocate white power from its centrality among the causes of the problem and relocate it as the key to the solution. In the police ad, the word "your" in "your police" constructs a white "us" in opposition to the "them" whose nonwhiteness, again, need not be spoken because it has been shown. Greg LaMotte, on CNN, used a similar discourse as he lamented, "When you see your own police department pushed into a position of helplessness, it makes the person on the street feel helpless as well, helpless and angry at how senseless all of this is" (see *Sidebar: LaMotte on the Spot,* p. 178). For LaMotte, the Latino/a and African American "rioters," because they were not one of "us" were not even, apparently, "persons," though they were all too obviously "on the street."

The Reginald Denny video was tailor-made for white interests. Its clarity appeared to leave little scope for struggle over its meaning. The clarity resulted from its (literally) high technology, for it was shot from a helicopter, which could swoop round and down to provide the "best" view, from a classic establishing shot of the stalled truck at the intersection to a close-up of Denny's body; the helicopter carried a professional cameraperson with a high-tech camera—so very different from the "lowness" of the Rodney King video. This clarity, this obviousness, was of the victim; the convulsion of his body as the back of his head was smashed by a brick sent shudders through the nation— particularly its whites. His assailants darted in and out of the frame, seen only

as they delivered blows or kicks to the prone white body. Their anger, the po-   151
sition they were coming from, was invisible, and consequently it was difficult
for most whites to comprehend a Black response such as the following:

> When I saw white people being beaten in the street on TV, I smiled
> ear to ear and jumped up and down with the glee, because it told
> me I'm not crazy. I hate to say I did that, . . . but I've been
> screaming for a long time and nobody has been listening.[27]

To see the Reginald Denny video as a racially reversed replay of Rodney King's,
in which Black and white men exchanged roles equally, whites had to take
power out of racial difference in order to make Black youths into the equivalent
of the LAPD. Similarly, African Americans had to ignore both Rodney King's
driving offense and Reginald Denny's innocence to make the stopping of the
one equivalent to the other.

Any racial reversals in the two videos have to be made equivalent; they are
not essentially so: the videos were different, and in their differences they continued racial inequality. The high-tech clarity of the one was already both bourgeois and white and needed no technological repositioning; the grim efficiency
of the police beating Rodney King showed an institutionalized brutality that
was different from the opportunistic brutalizing of Reginald Denny: one was
the brutality of the strong, the other of the weak.

There was inequality, too, in what the videos did not show. The Rodney
King one, for instance, did not show (and could not, because the camera was
not there) the car chase, his refusal to stop, and his refusal to lie down when
first ordered out of the car. The Reginald Denny video, on the other hand,
omitted what it could have shown—other Black people rescuing Denny, driving him to the hospital, and saving his life. In his presidential address to the
nation, however, George Bush did tell this story (see *Sidebar: Bush on L.A.*, p.
189), but told it to demonstrate his own ability to spot "decent citizens . . . regardless of race," a strategic move by which he was able to divert any suspicion
that racism may have underlain his condemnation of "the mob." The story of
Rodney King's refusal to stop and the subsequent chase, was, however, widely
told on the mainstream media if it could not be shown, but events preceding
the Denny beating were not. Only a radical pamphlet, however, contained the
information that Damian Williams had, some forty minutes earlier, been involved in an altercation with the police during which a sixteen-year-old neigh-
bor had been beaten and Damian's half brother arrested for inciting a riot when
he went to his aid. Damian Williams's family and neighbors insist that the
Denny beating can be understood only in relation to this one, yet this incident
was not mentioned in any media until two weeks later, when the *Los Angeles
Times* referred to it dismissively in an admiring piece about rank-and-file
cops.[28] My point here is not to offer this as a justification of Williams's alleged

152 beating of Denny, but as an illustration of the way the media isolated this video, but not Rodney King's, from the events that preceded it.

If there were equivalences between the two videos on television, they did not carry over into the courtroom. In the state trial of the police involved in the Rodney King beating the defendants faced maximum sentences of less than eight years, and maximum bail of $30,000. Those charged with beating Reginald Denny faced sentences of life imprisonment and bail of $580,000. The police who beat Rodney King were released on bail immediately; the African Americans who beat Reginald Denny were kept in jail for the fifteen months between their arrests and the trial. The federal charges on which Stacey Koon and Laurence Powell were later convicted carried a maximum prison sentence of ten years and a fine of $250,000 (their actual sentences were two and a half years, and no fine). Of course, these differences in legal treatment must be related to differences in the circumstances of each beating: the police did have a legitimate reason to stop Rodney King and order him out of his car, but there was no legitimate reason, in the legal sense of the word, for the Black men to pull Reginald Denny out of his truck. On the other hand, Rodney King was beaten in normal circumstances, Reginald Denny in exceptionally intensified ones. There are no objective scales on which these differences and equivalences can be weighed against the other; counting some and discounting others is a political choice.

The other communication technology involved in these two videos was that of the car and the truck. A vehicle is a technological extension of the body (both individual and social). The police cruisers against Rodney King's Hyundai were technologically loaded—powerful engines, radios, Taser guns, firearms and batons, flashing lights—they embodied the LAPD as well as the officers inside them and carried both into the territory of South-Central. So, too, Reginald Denny was carried by his truck to the intersection of Florence and Normandy. The TV images of his beating were accompanied by others of cars being stopped and their white drivers beaten. The TV news showed us similar images from L.A., Atlanta, and New York: it showed us images from Madison, Wisconsin, of a police garage where thirty-four cruisers had had their windows smashed, and on *L.A. Law*, Stewart, one of the lawyers, was dragged from his car and beaten by Black youths. I was in the classroom when the Rodney King verdict was made public and the uprisings began; after class I hurried to the nearest bar (in need of a beer and TV equally) and asked one of the patrons clustered in front of the screen what was happening. "They're pulling people out of their cars and beating them," he replied, visibly shaken. That was my first, white, news of the situation. The national panic in the early 1990s over carjacking may well have been connected to the way that these images positioned the car as a local battleground in the more general race and class wars of America.

There is no need to elaborate on the significance of the car to America in   153
general and Los Angeles in particular. Here I just want to point out that a car
extends the individual body, gives it control over place, and links it to the social
body (the type of car is its driver's social position sculpted in metal). By taking
us into the place of the "other," it can give us a sense of control and the
"other" a sense of invasion. The car is also a panoptic device, not only of police
surveillance, but we, too, drive to look.

In both the Denny and the King video events, there was an undercurrent of
meaning to the vehicles that connected the individual body (or bodies) inside
them with the social body in general: both were working vehicles. The difference between the employed and the unemployed, between those doing a job
and those with no job to do, is one of the central strains in the social antagonism that erupted in South-Central.

Throughout the Rodney King trial, the defense argued that the police were
merely doing their job, that their Tasers, boots, and batons were tools of their
trade that were used according to the instruction manual (see *Sidebar: The LAPD
Tool Kit*, p. 135). The jury agreed. By contrast, Rodney King had no job, no
tools, and therefore no justification for doing anything. Similarly, Reginald
Denny was consistently identified as a "truck driver," and his truck, the vehicle that connected him with the social order, loomed large in the images of his
beating. The difference between the employed and the unemployed becomes,
all too easily, that between the socially useful and the useless, the productive
contributor and the noncontributing dependent: employment becomes a
marker of social inclusion or exclusion, of normality and abnormality. The media's repeated references to Reginald Denny in terms of his job invited employed whites to form an alliance of the normal against, by implication, the unemployed Blacks.

From the Black side of this divide, however, employment may appear not as
a sign of normality, but of racial privilege. The job of Reginald Denny was a
sign of what the social order simultaneously offered as a right and systematically denied: it became a sign of Black exclusion, abnormalization, and deprivation. The sign has a material base: between 1982 and 1989, 131 factories
closed in Los Angeles, with the loss of 124,000 jobs. Driving this was the deregulation of Reaganomics, which encouraged capitalists to seek higher gains
and lower labor costs in the "third" world. The jobs that were lost were, of
course, those that disproportionately employed African Americans. And this
flight of capital and employment did not occur from high or stable ground—in
the four years before 1982, South-Central, the traditional industrial core of
L.A., lost 70,000 blue-collar jobs. In Black eyes, this pattern is produced not by
the raceless free market, but by racism recoded into economics: to them the 50
percent Black male unemployment in South-Central does not look like the result of neutral, let alone natural, economic laws. African Americans in South-
Central are hurting badly, but they not suffering alone: Andrew Hacker shows

154 that, come boom or bust, between 1960 and 1980 the national unemployment rate of Blacks was always approximately double that of whites; in the 1980s, however, the gap widened, so that by 1990 it was almost triple.[29] Even for those with jobs, the Reaganomic years produced a national decline in wages at the lower end of the scale and a spectacular rise at the upper. Rush Limbaugh gives voice to the consequent resentment among the blue- and declining white-collar classes (most of whom are white), but in South-Central, as elsewhere among the underclasses, Reaganomic pauperization is racialized. In these conditions Republicans seeking reelection *had* to blame the "riots" on the rioters, on welfare, on the collapse of family values, and on Murphy Brown, for only thus could they keep their own economic policies out of sight.

Black Liberation Radio brings to the surface currents that the Republicans wish to keep submerged: on one program, the (white) sociologist Sidney Wilhelm told listeners that the sphere of employment was where white supremacy was most firmly secured. He gave a broad account of the ebb and flow of racism in postslavery America, providing evidence for his thesis that America is always as racist as it can afford to be: when it needs Black labor, racism falls; when it does not, racism rises. Wilhelm argued that the recent shift to the "third" world of these manufacturing jobs to which the white economy has traditionally confined Black labor, together with the mechanization of agriculture, means that Black unemployment will be permanent and that, as a result, so will a high level of racism. He continued by arguing that the domestic change to an information economy and the consequent centrality of the computer, when linked with the decline of schools in Black neighborhoods, has resulted in the exclusion of African Americans, through educational deprivation, from this information economy. The less-threatening Asian American is white capital's preference for computer labor. Asian American computer operators stand between African Americans and prosperity in the sphere of production just as Korean store owners do in that of consumption (see the next section). Wilhelm argued that racism working through economic and educational deprivation has made the Black underclass into a permanent category of the excluded and unnecessary, the ultimate result of which will be genocide.[30]

In a multiracial society where the races are unequal, there will often be a racial dimension to class differences, for class is an efficient recoder of racism. Under these conditions economic differences can work to structure antagonism between subordinate races so that only the dominant benefits. In the next section I will show how white interests benefit by antagonism between African and Korean Americans in the sphere of consumption; here I wish to make the same argument with regard to African Americans and Latino/as in that of production. Jack Miles, in the *Atlantic*, makes a convincing case that an important aspect of the uprisings was the clash between Blacks and Latino/as, and suggests that the root cause of this particular piece of racial antagonism was employment. He cites an editorial from *La Prensa San Diego*, a Mexican American

newspaper, which declared that the riots involved Blacks attacking not whites,
but Latino/as and Asian Americans (see *Sidebar:* La Prensa, p. 156). "Faced with
nearly a million and a half Latinos taking over the inner city," the editorial concluded, "Blacks revolted, rioted and looted." Miles contextualizes this by citing
a General Accounting Office report showing that janitorial firms serving downtown businesses have almost entirely replaced their Black labor force with
Latino/as and that during the 1980s downtown hotel workers changed from being almost 100 percent Black to 100 percent Latino/a. He supports the statistics
anecdotally: on his own block of twenty houses, no one employs a Black gar-
dener but many employ Latino/a ones; friends who are white social workers
report that the school district has recently laid off a number of monolingual social workers and replaced them with Spanish-speaking ones—a sensible move,
on the face of it, yet most of those fired were Black and those hired were
Latino/a. Miles agrees with many Blacks that if Latino/as were not available for
the low-paying jobs, employers would have to hire Blacks. As it is, white employers tend to prefer Latino/as, not just because they will work for less
money, but because they trust Latino/as more and fear Blacks more. The individual action of Zoë Baird is repeated a thousandfold by the employers of Los
Angeles.

The racialized dimension of the "free" labor market, and its resulting horizontal racism between Latino/as and Blacks, surfaces again in the trial of
Damian Williams, who, besides being charged with the attempted murder of
Reginald Denny, was also accused of spraying black paint on the face and gen-
itals of a Latino who was lying unconscious after a beating. The blackening of
the face and penis appears to be a racial statement, but the charge was assault
with a deadly weapon (a clear demonstration that no object can control the
words that may be used to refer to it).

The immediacy of the economic competition between Blacks and Latino/as
may well mean that the horizontal racial antagonisms were as urgent as the
oppression of a vertical white racism. These horizontal racisms between subordinate races or ethnicities should be categorically differentiated from the top-
down racism of the dominant. Top-down racism has access to powerful institutions to advance its interests—the media, economics, education, political
parties, the legal system, and, more physically, the police and the military. The
horizontal racism of the subordinate has recourse only to words and physical
violence, whose effects may be immediately devastating and dramatic, but
never as long-term as those of white racism. I must make it clear, here, that I
use the term *horizontal* in opposition to *vertical*, and do not mean to imply that
antagonism between subaltern social formations is a tension between equals. It
is not: there is always a power difference, or at least a perception of one, involved. Korean Americans were perceived by Blacks and Latino/as to be privileged, Latino/as were perceived by Blacks to be privileged. Horizontal racism,
then, is "weak racism," because it never has access to institutional power to

La Prensa

Though confronted with catastrophic destruction of the Latino businesses, which were 60% of the businesses destroyed, major looting by Blacks and by the Central Americans living in the immediate area and a substantial number of Hispanics being killed, shot and/or injured, every major television station was riveted to the concept that the unfolding events could only be understood if viewed in the context of the Black and White experiences. They missed the crucial point: The riots were not carried out against Blacks or Whites, they were carried out against the Latino and Asian communities by the Blacks!

What occurred was a major racial confrontation by the Black community, which now sees its numbers and influence waning.

Faced with nearly a million and a half Latinos taking over the inner city, Blacks revolted, rioted and looted. Whatever measure of power and influence they had pried loose from the White power structure, they now see as being in danger of being transferred to the Latino community. Not only are they losing influence, public offices, and control of the major civil rights mechanisms, they now see themselves being replaced in the pecking order by the Asian community, in this case the Koreans.

(quoted in Jack Miles, "Black vs. Brown: The Struggle for the Bottom Rung," *Atlantic*, October 1992, 51)

make it "strong," but it is never precisely horizontal, and is usually, if only slightly, bottom-up.

The economic pressures of South-Central Los Angeles put three subordinate racial groups—Blacks, Latino/as and Koreans—into conflict with one another, and kept whites safely out of the firing line. In these conflicts race and class interests were inseparable, but they were complicated still further by nativism—the clash between native-born African Americans and immigrant Latino/as or Asians. The change in L.A.'s downtown janitorial and hotel labor force, for example, while a racial one from Black to Latino/a, was also one from native to immigrant and from organized labor to nonunion labor, and thus from working-class wages and benefits to underclass pay. Similar nativism was also a source of difference among Latino/as, for the established Chicano community often distanced itself from newer immigrants from South America and opposed their "rioting." In an op-ed piece in the *New York Times*, Edward Luttwak makes a similar argument when he characterizes the events in L.A. as a riot of the underclass against the immigrants.[31] He identifies a two-pronged assault upon traditional underclass jobs: one comes from below, from immigrants, whom, he claims in a now familiar story, employers prefer to Blacks because, "even if they know no English, they are mostly free of an underclass stigma. . . . Some have useful skills, and almost all are deferential, an attitude that is more attractive to employers than the resentment many underclass job-seekers show." The other comes from above: "In Washington even waiters and

waitresses tend to be white high school graduates . . . and all over America
permanently laid off industrial workers have taken such traditional underclass
jobs as janitors and warehousemen." So, when African Americans who have
been here for fifteen generations lose their jobs to Latino/a immigrants or are
charged high prices in stores owned by recently arrived Koreans, resentment is
inevitable, especially when African Americans recall that, in the early years of
this century, employers in the North also preferred new European immigrants
over African Americans migrating from the South.

Racial and economic power is at work on many axes here, but despite its
multiaxiality and despite the many races involved, the polar opposites around
which race relations in this country are structured are still those between European and African Americans, whereas those involving Latino/as and Asian
Americans lie somewhere in between. Those involving American Indians have
been so suppressed as to be invisible in the events covered by this book, and so
remain beyond the scope of my analysis. In saying this I do not wish to grant
African Americans the status of "the privileged minority," or to deny the com-
plexity of race relations when horizontal ones among subordinated races intersect with the vertical ones of domination, but I do wish to acknowledge the
particularly significant role of Black-white relations in U.S. history.

White immigration and Black slavery have given this country a unique history that, according to some African American cultural critics, has produced a
distinctively American form of racism. The novelist-critic Toni Morrison and
the legal scholar Derrick Bell, for instance, both reveal the usefulness, if not the
necessity, of the African American presence in forging a white sense of U.S.
nationhood. When immigrants from Europe were trying to adapt to their new
nation, they quickly discovered that learning to use the word *nigger* was one of
the readiest means by which they could feel "American" and by which other
European Americans could accept them into the club. African Americans,
then, formed an ever-present other without which European Americans would
have been unable to construct a sense of a white "us" that was strong enough
to sweep aside the historical differences among, say, Scandinavian, Italian, and
English immigrants. It was only the commonality of being not-Black that allowed the national differences that in Europe were divisive to be merged to
form a new (white) America. Toni Morrison argues that this "racial bonding"[32]
by whites has proved as useful in overcoming class conflict within the nation as
it was in assimilating new European immigrants into it.[33]

Derrick Bell goes even further, and arguing that Black "otherness" is so necessary to white America's sense of its own nationhood that the racism inherent
in it has become a permanent and ineradicable part of the American way of life.
He begins his book *Faces at the Bottom of the Well* with this epigraph:

Black people are the magical faces at the bottom of society's well.
Even the poorest whites, those who must live their lives only a few

levels above, gain their self-esteem by gazing down on us. Surely, they must know that their deliverance depends on letting down their ropes. Only by working together is escape possible. Over time, many reach out, but most simply watch, mesmerized into maintaining their unspoken commitment to keeping us where we are, at whatever cost to them or us.[34]

Later, he quotes Toni Morrison making a similar point about immigrants of all races: "Every immigrant knew he would not come in at the very bottom. He had to come above at least one group—and that was us."[35] The economic analyses that predict long-term, if not permanent, unemployment for the Black underclass lead to similar conclusions about the value of having Blacks at the bottom of the well, but, in confining themselves to the economic axis of racial power, they underestimate both the depth and the diffusiveness of American racism.

Economic racism does keep squeezing African Americans—through job exports to the "third" world, through Latino/a immigrants and whites' preferring to employ them, through the role of Korean American store owners in the consumer economy of the ghetto (see the next section), and through the macroeconomic change from an industrial economy to an information one. The only beneficiary of all this is capitalism. And today, the globalization of capital means that its economic practices inevitably have a racial dimension. Its multinational corporations have taken Black jobs out of Southern California to Mexico to save on the wage bill. Conversely, entrepreneurial capitalism (or sweatshops) in California has increased rapidly because the same cheap labor, in immigrant form, is available to it. In their account of the political (and racial) economy of the uprisings, Oliver, Johnson, and Farrell conclude:

> Whereas joblessness is the central problem for black males in South Central Los Angeles, concentration in low-paying bad jobs . . . is the main problem for Latino residents of the area. Both groups share a common fate: incomes below the poverty level. Whereas one group is the working poor (Latinos), the other is the jobless poor (blacks).[36]

Although this aspect of interracial conflict may appear to set African Americans against Latino/as or Korean Americans, the underlying conflict of interest is with European America and with multinational capital. On the streets of South-Central, however, the economic conflicts were transformed into physical violence between individual Blacks, yellows, and browns, while the white police force, on the first day at least, stood to one side and watched.

Anthony Brown, an unemployed Black man and one of the "L.A. Four +" in the Denny case, brought many of these elements together in his account of that afternoon of crisis. He watched the announcement of the Rodney King verdict on TV at home with his family and then wandered over to Florence and Normandie, where the crowd was shouting comments such as "Rodney

King," "Fuck the police," "Kill the white people," "Get everyone who [isn't] 159
Black." He joined an attack on a Latino, "I kicked him because he was Mexican
and everyone else was doing it," and then spat on Denny, who was "just white
in the wrong place."[37] If he had gone on to attack a Korean store, all the racial
antagonism underlying the L.A. uprisings would have played out in the actions of this one young man.

Latasha Harlins and Soon Ja Du: Consuming Race

The video of Latasha Harlins's death was given less visibility and had fewer
repercussions in white America than did the King and Denny videos. Yet,
among the African Americans rising up on the streets of South-Central, her
name joined with Rodney King's as a signifier of their oppression. The mainstream media, zooming over the streets in their helicopters or, when at street
level, using their cameras and reporters' questions as the discursive equivalents of the National Guard's M-16s, saw or heard little of this. Mike Davis, listening to the uprisers, however, was often told, "This is for our baby sister.
This is for Latasha."[38] The security camera in Soon Ja Du's grocery store
showed Latasha Harlins approaching the store counter. Witnesses said she had
her money in her hand. Du appeared to shout at Harlins and grabbed her
sweater. Harlins punched Du three times about the head. Du threw a stool at
Harlins. Harlins put the bottle on the counter, turned and began to walk away.
Du pulled a gun from beneath the counter and fired. Latasha Harlins fell, with
a bullet in the back of her head. The defense later argued that the gun had been
modified, without Du's knowledge, to give it a hair trigger.

The Harlins video, like that of Rodney King's beating, was black and white,
silent, and, at the level of its signifiers, uncertain. It too had an authenticity
stemming from its rawness, with no edits to disturb its "real time" or its single
point of view. But it was not a videolow as was King's. It was shot by a security
camera from on high, in the best possible, but not perfect, position, a camera
already directed *against* Latasha Harlins and *for* Soon Ja Du. In court, therefore,
there was less need to retechnologize it to move it up to a videohigh, for it was
partway there already: saturating it in the logorationality of the courtroom was
enough to control its truth. Its homicide was "justifiable," Du was released on
probation, required to perform four hundred hours of community service and
to pay a $500 fine.

Again, in this logorational discourse the unspeakable remained unspoken.
But in the Black America outside the courtroom, race was loudly spoken and
overtly placed at the center of the incident and the trial. The Black skin of
Latasha Harlins and the non-Black skins of Du and of the judge were embodied
realities around which social alliances were formed and oppositional truths
produced. The bullet shattering the back of Latasha Harlins's head and the
Taser darts invading Rodney King's body with 50,000 volts were both points

160 where the macrostructures of racial power entered the material realm of embodied experience.

Blackness (and non-Blackness) is as much a matter of social alliances as it is a visible identifier of racial identity. As a signifier, skin color indicates simultaneously genetic identity, racial history, and political position, and it is this last that gives the first two meaning, and takes them out of nature, the domain of the biologist, and into culture, that of the historian and social analyst. And so the Korean Du was white. This particular agreement between her and a white judge that a Black girl's life was cheap (worth a bottle of orange juice to one and $500 to the other) is a truth produced by white discourse as it is heard by African Americans, and the racial power in its production is repressed from white knowledge but central to Black.

In her remarks at Du's sentencing, Judge Joyce Karlin repeatedly used the categories of "terrorist" and "victim," but, in a discursive move similar to the one that put Rodney King in control, she positioned Soon Ja Du as the victim and Latasha Harlins as the terrorist (see *Sidebar: Judge Karlin*, p. 161). This white discourse justified the killing by putting Latasha Harlins into the same category as the "gang members" who had "victimized and terrorized" the Du family. The only feature of Latasha Harlins that allowed her to be put in this category was her race. Once having made that categorization, Judge Karlin was then able to equate the fists of a fifteen-year-old girl with a gun: "Although Latasha was not armed with a weapon at the time of her death, she had used her fists as weapons just seconds before she was shot." Her first use of the word "weapon" refers to a gun; her second carries this reference over into Latasha Harlins's fists, thus making them into the discursive equivalent of the gun that materially she did not have, but Du did. Fists can be made the equivalent of guns only by putting their possessor into the same category as "terrorist gangs," and the only discourse that could characterize Latasha Harlins in this way was a racist one. I think, as I read Karlin's remarks, that I can hear in them echoes of the white terror of the Black body.

It was not only Korean storekeepers who were threatened by Latasha Harlins and the gangs: in Judge Karlin's discourse "family values," and the whiteness encoded in them, were too. Du was let off without a prison sentence because her act was motivated by family values and her maternal desire to protect her son. No one upholding family values can be a danger to society, and so Karlin could confidently reply in the negative when she asked, "Does society need Mrs. Du to be incarcerated in order to be protected?" Her answer, of course, conveniently excludes Latasha Harlins and gang members (read "the African American underclass") from "society." Dan Quayle joined her in the exclusion when he described the underclass as "disconnected from the rules of American society" (see *Sidebar: Dan Quayle*, p. 68). Karlin, Quayle, and Buchanan all agree that family values are what African Americans both lack and threaten. For both Karlin and Buchanan, then, the Korean store owners' de-

Judge Karlin
(from her remarks on the sentencing of Soon Ja Du)

... Statements by the district attorney, [which] suggest that imposing less than the maximum sentence will send a message that a black child's life is not worthy of protection, [are] dangerous rhetoric, which serves no purpose other than to pour gasoline on a fire.

...

Does society need Mrs. Du to be incarcerated in order to be protected? I think not.

...

[T]he defendant participated in the crime under circumstances of great provocation and duress. ... One of the questions a sentencing court is required to ask ... is "whether the crime was committed because of unusual circumstances such as great provocation." I find that it was....Although Latasha Harlins was not armed with a weapon at the time of her death, she had used her fists as weapons just seconds before she was shot.

...

But for the unusual circumstances in this case, including the Du family's history of being victimized and terrorized by gang members, Mrs. Du would not be here today. ... The district attorney would have this court ignore the very real terror experienced by the Du family before the shooting, and the fear Mrs. Du experienced as she worked by herself the day of the shooting. But there are things I cannot ignore. And I cannot ignore the reason Mrs. Du was working in the store that day. She went to work that Saturday to save her son from having to work. Mrs. Du's son had begged his parents to close the store. He was afraid because he had been the victim of repeated robberies and terrorism in that same store. On the day of the shooting Mrs. Du volunteered to cover for her son to save him one day of fear.

(quoted in *Los Angeles Times*, November 22, 1991, B7)

fense of those values ensured their recruitment as honorary whites. Many Koreans, but not all, as we shall see below, were happy to join this alliance of interests: the pretrial petitions from the Korean community in support of Du consistently characterized her simultaneously as a good mother and a conscientious business owner.[39] The family business manifests family values.

This particular alliance of interest, embodied momentarily by Karlin and Du, was understood by African Americans as an instance of a broader strategic alliance by which Korean store owners are allied with whites and promote white interests in Black communities. From the position of the "have-nots," Korean store owners appear to have been invited by whites into the "haves." One of the things that they "have" that poor Blacks "have-not" is access to economic power and capital, another is a government that cares for them. As Mbanna Kantako put it, "The Korean, you know what, brother, the Korean government issued a demand to the United States government, according to the crackers, of course, to protect the Korean Americans in this devil country. Who issued such a warning to this government to protect the African American? You better start

162   thinking about this."[40] There are Koreans in South-Central who stress their exclusion from white America and claim a commonality of position and therefore
of interest with other racial minorities, but for most African Americans this
commonality between "minorities" is a misperception; to them, Korean Americans' status as a "model minority" allies them with whites, not Blacks. They
are strategically useful to whites because their comparative economic success
(or assimilation) can be used to "prove" that the cause of Black "failure" lies in
African America and not in European America. Like Clarence Thomas, they are
bootstrappers, and, like him, many appear keen to hitch their wagon to white
Republicans: Asian Americans were second in the league table of Bush supporters; they preferred him to Clinton by a ratio of 55:29.[41] We must not read
these figures too precisely into South-Central; Korean Americans are, after all,
only a subset of Asian Americans, but we must note the unlikelihood of their
voting preferences being significantly different.

Certainly, not all Koreans see themselves as honorary whites. Sumi Cho, for
instance, saw how whites left them to suffer "triple scapegoating."[42] One level
of attack upon them was physical, mainly by Blacks and Latino/as, directed at
their businesses. Equally hostile was the refusal of white police to provide any
protection, and to concentrate their resources on the defense of white, wealthier communities. Mike Davis also records Korean bitterness at the way the police and National Guard protected the South-Central shopping malls owned by
Alexander Haagen, a generous contributor to local political coffers, while leav-
ing Koreans to fend for themselves. One commented to him ruefully, "Maybe
this is what we get for uncritically buying into the white middle class's attitude
towards blacks and its faith in the police."[43] When Korean store owners, in the
absence of police protection, undertook the job themselves, the white media
attacked them on the third level with a barrage of images of vigilante Koreans,
armed to the teeth, firing apparently randomly into the crowd. These images,
Cho argues, resonated happily in the white conservative imagination, for they
made the Korean storekeepers into "a surrogate army acting out the white sub-
urban male's American dream—bearing arms against black men."[44]

The white media also turned against the Koreans by depicting them as eco-
nomic exploiters, profiteering from the poverty of African Americans. The *Los
Angeles Times*, for instance, ran a story that described economic racism at work
and implicitly blamed Korean merchants for most of it. At one market in South-
Central, it told readers, a bag of diapers cost $13.99, compared with $10.99 in
wealthy West L.A., and five pounds of sugar was $2.99 as against $1.79.
Higher-ticket items followed the same pattern: a refrigerator that cost $1,300 in
West L.A. cost, in South-Central, $2,040, and, to finance the purchase, the
South-Central resident had to pay interest rates that were higher by at least 2
percent.[45]

Economic racism, however, is not exerted only across the counters of Korean stores: the ratio of stores to residents in South-Central is less than half that

in Los Angeles County, reducing both competition and choice, and, as most of   163
these are small, for few of the big retail chains will operate here, the picture is
even worse than the statistics show.[46] Shopping is restricted by both poverty
and lack of choice. The large chain stores, whose bulk purchasing and rapid
turnover enable them to offer lower prices, prefer to do their business in white
wealthier areas and to shun South-Central. Similarly, there are only fourteen
banks in South-Central; because virtually no bank in L.A. will cash checks except for its own depositors, South-Central residents on welfare have to take
their government checks to check-cashing stores that charge 10 percent of the
check's face value, which is meager enough in the first place.

To those who experience this double-barreled poverty of low income and
high prices, the Korean store is a point of economic exploitation that they cannot avoid. There are no alternatives. A greater distance, however, allows us to
see that the Korean store has been pulled into its position by the workings of a
market system that are racist in effect if not in overt intention. The racism of
Judge Karlin's discourse as she sentenced Soon Ja Du was continued by her
evacuation of white economic forces from the scene and thus her confinement
of responsibility to Koreans and Blacks: whites had nothing to do with it. The
conditions are the same in the stores of South-Central; the interracial antagonisms between subordinate races apparently have nothing to do with whites
yet serve white economic and political interests. The racism of the "free" market (in both labor and commodities) is apparent only in its economic effects.
Although the system of the market may appear neutrally colorless, where its
transactions are interracial the economic exchange between merchant and customer is inevitably racialized. And as the Korean vigilantes acted as white sur-
rogates as they fired upon Black bodies, so the Korean merchants are seen as
troops deployed in the white strategy of weakening the Black communal body
by ensuring that such money as it has flows into pockets other than its own.
Alberto Machon, a South-Central resident, made this clear to the *Los Angeles
Times*:

> And the money that we are giving to the stores, they're taking it to
> their own community, Koreatown. If a black man owned the store,
> the money would stay among us and help build the community up.
> (see *Sidebar: Race and Class*, p. 173)

The position of the Korean store depends upon the position from which it is
seen: its in betweenness is economic, legal, political, and racial. And it is also
geographic. Koreatown's physical position between South-Central and Hollywood literally places the model minority as the middle minority. One of the
first stores to be attacked in the uprising was, not surprisingly, Soon Ja Du's
(though, ironically, it survived). It was a physical point of application of multiaxial power—economic, geographic, legal, and racial—and the attack upon it,
and other stores, must be seen multiaxially and not reduced to a single axis,

164 such as the legal one of "looting," nor must it be fixed in a single set of alliances, whether racial, spatial, or economic. The Korean store's location on all these axes of power made it a strategically opportune target.

For the Black and Latino/a communities, the store is an active agent in the colonizing of the place where they live: it works to prevent economic as well as territorial self-determination. The absence of territorial and economic control disempowers the dispossessed in the broader social arena. Having a place from which to speak is vital: the more displaced a social formation is, the less the voices speaking from it will be heard. Self-determination, the power to control one's own local conditions, has to be as multiaxial as the imperializing power that it contests. It has to be able to work spatially, economically, discursively, legally, politically. The ghetto is a place that is out of the control of its inhabitants. On *Black Liberation Radio*, Sister Adwba from South-Central argues against those who accused the "rioters" of destroying their own community: "We have to understand the definition of a community," she says. "It's not just because you live in it—do you own it, do you control it, do you run it?" (see *Sidebar: Looting Sense*, p. 184). Unwittingly, and much less explicitly, the news anchor who introduced Greg LaMotte's story (see *Sidebar: LaMotte on the Spot*, p. 178) made a similar point: "Unrest that at first affected a predominantly black area in South-Central Los Angeles," he said, "has now spread to communities several miles away." His contrast between "an area" where Black people live and "communities" where whites do is part of the white discourse that gave us the stream of images of South-Central as an area of (burnt and "looted") property and businesses, not a community of people. This discursive evacuation of the residents erased from the white news what Sister Adwba made perfectly clear in hers—that the "alien" ownership of the property and businesses was what prevented the "area" from becoming a "community" for those who lived in it. Alberto Machon, too, saw that it was lack of economic control that prevented the "ghetto" from becoming a "community" (see *Sidebar: Race and Class*, p. 173).

The video of Latasha Harlins's death was significant because, like that of Rodney King, it condensed into a moment of hypervisibility long and complex histories. The transaction across Du's counter—arguments, physical blows, no money, a shot—was a material instance of larger historical and social transactions. In it we can trace multiple movements across this counter: bullets and punches, the gaze of the video camera and of the store owner, money and commodities, interpersonal and interracial behavior.

The bullet of Soon Ja Du carried the histories of many others. The Korean American Grocers and Retailers Organization (KAGRO) in Southern California tried to prevent exacerbating the tension between its members and African Americans, but, while doing so, had to recall the forty-one Korean merchants killed by Blacks between 1975 and 1990, and the twelve Blacks killed by Koreans defending their property.[47] From this viewpoint Du's grocery store was the front line of a racial war, in which the transactions across its counter were skir-

mishes. This history of racial anxiety and antagonism is activated every day.   165
The video gaze that follows the Black customer with unrelenting suspicion is
repeated by the store owner, and Black customers complain bitterly of the humiliation and disrespect embedded in such constant surveillance (see *Sidebar:
Disrespect and Counter Measures*, p. 166). Being watched mistrustfully is the lot
of Los Angeles African Americans, according to Jack Miles, a white journalist,
who writes:

> Black men [*sic*] complain that they cannot shop without being
> shadowed by a suspicious shopkeeper. The same in effect goes for
> the black teenagers who show up unannounced on our block. These
> are kids who skip out of junior high school in the next block, picnic
> on our lawns, steal from our garages and back yards and
> occasionally vandalize parked cars. The retirees living on the block
> watch the kids especially closely. One retiree once managed to
> videotape an attempted garage break-in. The school's officials—not
> always sympathetic (until recently the principal was a black
> woman)—identified the culprits from the tape.[48]

Shadowed, so they have no sense of controlling the space they walk in, under
surveillance as permanent intruders into somebody else's territory, always spoken of in the same sentence as theft and vandalism, African Americans must be
prepared to experience antagonism at any and every moment. Social distrust
and exclusion can be experienced by the senses of the body: on a televised discussion of interracial tension in Crown Heights, New York, a Black woman told
of the daily hurt she felt when Jewish American storeowners dropped her
change into her hand from a height of five inches so that their skins should not
touch.

The suspicious gaze of the camera and the merchant and the refusal of
bodily contact are signs of social exclusion, of being "othered" from one's own
society. At the immediate level of personal and interpersonal experience, this
excluding is experienced as "disrespect" or "diss"—words that in white discourse can be seen as curiously unemphatic, if not trivial. Yet they point to the
way that racial, economic, legal, and social disempowerment can be condensed
into a glance or a tone of voice (see *Sidebar: Disrespect and Counter Measures*, p.
166).

The store is a key site where this multiaxial disempowerment is put into
practice. It is where racial power can be redirected along economic and legal
axes. Du's counter, then, is encumbered with a history within which both she
and Latasha Harlins are held and to which their transaction contributed. Store
counters are the furniture of capitalism, the equivalent in the sphere of consumption of the workbench in that of production. The workshop and the corner shop are where the two key economic relations of capitalism are made ma-

Disrespect and Counter Measures

BLACK WOMAN: They [Koreans] were targeted because they are rude to us in our neighborhoods [applause], they're rude to our kids, Latasha Harlins was just an incident, I'm talking about our everyday living. I walked into the store and I spoke, 50 years old, one woman, by myself, and I spoke—one woman behind the counter, she wouldn't speak to me, in my neighborhood, you hear me!

KOREAN MAN: It's not right to demand our respect, that we've got to give you respect . . .

BLACK MAN 1: I do not demand respect, but I expect it. If I walk into your establishment to make a purchase and I pass by you, and I say, "Hi, how are you?" I expect the same from you. I don't want you to come out from behind your counter and follow me around the store assuming I'm going to steal from you. (*The Oprah Winfrey Show*, May 5, 1992)

BLACK MAN: That shooting [Latasha Harlins's] is just proof of the problem, just another example of their disrespect for Black people. You go in their stores and they think you're going to steal something. They follow you around the store like you're a criminal. They say "Buy something, or get out." (quoted in *Los Angeles Times*, November 3, 1991)

No More to Disrespectful merchants . . . Clean Up or Move Out!!!

In response to the brutal slaying of 15-year-old Latasha Harlins and the past history of disrespectful treatment of African-American residents by certain merchants operating in the minority community, the Brotherhood Crusade Women in Action support group is demanding accountability. BCWIA support group is calling upon other African-Americans to join us in another phase of "Taking Our Community Back" from all forms of oppression including merchants who take our money but step on our character. (press release, BCWIA, in *Los Angeles Sentinel*, April 4, 1991, 8)

terial in interpersonal relationships between supervisor and worker, merchant and customer. And racial difference is at work in both.

For the unemployed—and, as argued above, unemployment has a racial axis—the sphere of consumption contains their only direct economic entry into the social order, for they are excluded from the sphere of production. But when consumption is constrained by poverty, the store is as much a site of exclusion as of entry. The commodities that pack it to the bursting point are material indices of the society that pretends to invite them to join it and to offer its goods as their right, and that simultaneously rejects them by denying them legitimate access (money) to them.

For the deprived, shopping is not, as it is for the wealthy, where success in

the sphere of production is materially rewarded: it is an experience of exclusion
and disempowerment. Shopping is painful. The way a store owner treats a
Black or Latino/a person entering the store is, quite literally, an embodiment
and an emplacement of the way that white capitalism treats the racially unemployed or underpaid.

Under these conditions, disrespect in the stores is loaded with social and
racial significance. In the interpersonal relationships of everyday life, demanding and expecting respect from other individuals, particularly those who embody signs of social privilege, is one of the few ways in which the deprived can
feel accepted into the social order. If the economic, legal, and racial relations of
society have rejected you completely, then "respect" in personal relationships
is all you have left, and it's worth fighting hard to maintain.

Many of the critical battles of the civil rights movement took place in the
sphere of consumption: the store, the restaurant, the public bus, and the rest-
room are sites within it where race relations have historically been experienced
most acutely and contested most bitterly. We should note, too, that when social struggle occurs in the sphere of consumption women are encouraged to
join in, for that sphere is the one in which patriarchy has traditionally allowed
them some power. Rodney King and Reginald Denny, the men, were beaten in
the streets; Latasha Harlins, the woman, was killed in the store. The few images of women's role in the uprising showed them almost exclusively in the
stores.

Lizbeth Cohen traces two main phases of the civil rights movement—the
boycotts and sit-ins of the 1950s and early 1960s, and the ghetto riots of the late
1960s—and posits the centrality of consumerism in both.[49] Arguing that from
the 1950s onward, African Americans associated their sense of citizenship with
free access to consumer goods and services, she emphasizes first the political
motivation provided by the personal experience of indignity or "diss" in the
sphere of consumption and second the political effectiveness of organized boycotts of stores, restaurants, and buses in dismantling the structure of segregation.

Steven Classen finds similar concerns in his study of the struggles over
the license renewal of WLBT, a Jackson, Mississippi, TV station notable for
its racism. The local civil rights movement, in which this struggle played
a significant part, included boycotting Jackson stores. In their letter to Jackson
business owners, the protesters claimed that the boycott was aimed to end
"discrimination against Negro workers and Negro consumers," and demanded

> 1. hiring of personnel on the basis of personal merit without regard
> to race, color or creed; and promotion of such personnel on the ba-
> sis of both merit and seniority without regard to race, color or creed;

2. an end to segregated drinking fountains, an end to segregated
restrooms, and an end to segregated seating;

3. service to all consumers on a first come, first served basis;

4. use of courtesy titles—such as "Miss," "Mrs.," and "Mr."—with
regard to all people.[50]

Three of the four demands are located in the sphere of consumption, and the
last two focus specifically on racial "disrespect." Similar demands lay at the
core of the civil rights movement. Rosa Parks's historic refusal to sit at the back
of that Montgomery bus sparked one of the first uses of a consumer boycott to
demand civil rights. On its first evening, a meeting organized by Martin Luther
King agreed that African Americans would consider that the bus company was
denying them their civil rights until (1) its drivers treated them with the courtesy they accorded whites, (2) its passengers were seated on a first-come, first-
served basis, and (3) it employed Black drivers.[51]

In Los Angeles in 1992 these rights were still being denied. One small example that in this context signifies much is provided by Judge Karlin's remarks
on her sentencing of Soon Ja Du (see *Sidebar: Judge Karlin*, p. 161). On every one
of her eighteen references to Du she gave her the courtesy title of "Mrs." Never
did she refer to Latasha Harlins as "Miss," and once she called her simply
"Latasha." In this she was continuing a long history of domination in which,
from emancipation onward, Black women were systematically denied the titles
of *Miss* and *Mrs.*, were not allowed to try on clothes in stores before buying
them, and were banned from using the same toilets as whites. Gerda Lerner
interprets these denials, particularly when linked to laws against interracial
marriage and taboos against social mixing, as signs of the white myth of the
Black woman's "bad" sexuality.[52] To whites, the use of courtesy titles may
seem a comparatively trivial matter, but in Black discourse their absence is a
clear sign of "diss," a refusal to accord respect, and is thus a practice of social
exclusion. There is nothing trivial about it. When "looting" reversed the normal economic relations of the store, the "looters" changed the social relations
also: as Sister Adwba reported on Black Liberation Radio, whereas whites
could see only a "feeding frenzy," she saw Black "looters" treating each other
with "respect and harmony and cooperation . . . they were helping each other,
saying 'excuse me'—it was beautiful, it was just beautiful." Judge Karlin's failure to grant Latasha Harlins the respect of a courtesy title may not have been
intentional, but the intentionality of the practice has a long and highly charged
history that does not allow us to dismiss her failure as mere carelessness. Al-
locating a courtesy title to the Korean but not to the African American was
practicing racism. It was also an instance of monodiscursivity, that is, of the
failure to recognize that Black discourses differ from white, and of the refusal of
the powerful to make any effort to recognize, let alone learn, subaltern dis-

course; Judge Karlin was guilty of universalizing white meanings into the only
meanings.

The toilet also links the civil rights movement of the 1960s with today's downtown Los Angeles, where the absence of public restrooms and drinking fountains is the result of a city policy to discourage those without the money to use restaurants and stores from occupying its so-called public space.[53] In South-Central, even those who use the stores are subject to the same, very physiological, racism: a *Los Angeles Times* comparison of shops in white and pigmented neighborhoods found as great a disparity in the provision of restrooms as in prices and choices.[54] The racial power that was once applied by the segregation of toilets is now applied by their absence: disrespect is physical, indignity is colored.

"Looting" and the Media

In the second of the peak phases of the civil rights movement Lizbeth Cohen identifies "at least 329 separate significant incidents [riots], in 257 American cities . . . leading to 52,000 people arrested, 8,000 injured and at least 220 killed."[55] She gives a detailed account of how then, as today, the economic system of the inner city disadvantaged the Black consumer through credit restrictions, higher prices, and smaller selections, and concludes that the most prevalent and significant activity of the rioters was looting.

Little has changed. In 1992, TV cameras showed the nation image after image of "looting." With this history and in these conditions, "looting" cannot be understood as simple theft; indeed, it cannot be understood simply at all. It is an engagement in a multifrontal struggle where antagonistic social relations are contested in the domains of law and economics and in the material and psychic conditions of everyday life.

In writing this account, I attempted to avoid using the word *looting*, but failed. Property rights appear to be so deeply ingrained in capitalism's legal, economic, and discursive systems that the only words referring to the transfer of property to the weak from the strong without payment are ones that put this transaction into the discourse of crime. A word such as *confiscation* refers to the noneconomic transfer of property to the strong from the weak, and not vice versa, and, as another disqualification, it lacks any sense of the opportunism that characterizes the tactics of the weak. It is interesting that the struggle over material property in the streets of South-Central has not yet become a discursive struggle, so the discourse has been left in the control of the power bloc. *Looting* was one of the key words by which the media attempted to confine the dominant understanding of the uprising to the discourse of law and order (*arson* and *murder* were others), and in using it, I set it within quotation marks in an attempt to disarticulate it from its normal discursive, and therefore social, relations. The power over discourse is a material power, for the power to call

170   the activity "looting" is not only the power to put those who engage in it into prison but also to know that prison is the solution to the problem. Those few who tried to set the media images of "looting" into another discursive framework were severely hampered by the lack of an alternative word: they had to rely on explanations, and not only do explanations lack the impact of a word, they also invite argument. The words *rebellion*, *uprising*, and *insurrection* challenged the dominant word *riot* with a directness that an explanation lacks.

    Of course, one sense of "looting" must be the dominant legal one: "looters" knowingly break the laws that underpin property rights and organize the economic relations between buyers and sellers. "Looting" does involve grabbing goods illegally, it does involve seizing the opportunities afforded by a breakdown of law and order, and in some cases this may have been all that it involved—there were reports, for instance, of "yuppies in BMWs" joining in[56]—but limiting its meaning to its legal dimension is a strategy of the power structure that represses others. The white media, like the white politicians, consistently put "looting" into the discourse of law and order, but did so in ways that made the "order" invisibly white and the "disorder" very visibly Black and Latino/a. Images of whites engaged in behavior that this discourse made "black" were repressed both from the airwaves and from mainstream common sense. At WITI, the CBS affiliate in Milwaukee, Wisconsin, for example, two reporters were compiling a roundup of the second day's events for the late night news. In an attempt to achieve a degree of balance, they included footage from KTLA, a local Los Angeles station, of a white woman "looting" designer dresses into her Mercedes who explained her behavior with a casual "Because everyone else is doing it." The producer cut the footage. The reporters were Black, the producer white.[57]

    To the disempowered who engaged in it, however, "looting" was multidimensional, and its racial dimension was never far below and usually on the surface: it could be, for example, both a form of public speech and a statement of self-assertion. "Looting" enabled the racially silenced to be heard and the overlooked to be seen. For those who are normally denied an identity and refused a social presence, "looting" could be a way of giving the nation a forceful reminder: "We *are* here. We *are* here" (see *Sidebar: Looting So to Speak*, p. 174). The young Black woman who spoke these words of Frederick Douglass so passionately on *The Oprah Winfrey Show* may remind us of Kimberle Crenshaw's point that Anita Hill managed to break out of "the political vacuum of erasure" to which Black women are normally confined. Indeed, many of the Black "looters" justified their actions to Oprah and to listening whites as a means of getting attention. Without the uprising, Oprah would not have taken her show from Chicago to Los Angeles, and they would not have had the public platform that it afforded them. They seized the opportunity to break out of the silencing that never allowed Rodney King to speak at his own trial and that continued the history of silencing "slave voices" to which Houston Baker refers (see

above). On Black Liberation Radio, Mbanna Kantako makes the point that the
official Black leadership has failed to make white America pay attention to
Black suffering, but, "these young brothers, in the space of three days, have
made it a national, no, an international issue, international."

Commodities are goods that speak as well as goods to use, and unequal access to commodities is part of the same system that makes access to public discourse unequal. "Looting" can temporarily correct both inequalities in one guerrilla action. Baby Saye, a South-Central resident who has spent her life on welfare, understood this clearly as she "looted" eighteen rolls of two-ply Charmin toilet paper. "I know what you're thinking but basically fuck you," she said. "I've been wiping my ass and my children's asses with that scratchy shit all my life because I can't afford the good shit. Now I got Charmin, just like those white jurors. So there!"[58]

Calling looting "theft" and "senseless," as the white media so often did, involved seeing each "looter" as an individual thief. But when "looting" is a form of public speech, it not only makes sense, but that sense may be communal, and "looters" then become not individual criminals but popular spokespeople whose actions give voice to a communal sentiment. One study of the 1965 Watts uprisings emphasized their popular nature by pointing out that some 50,000 to 60,000 people lined the streets cheering on the 22,000 who actually "looted" (much, we might think, as a chorus supports a folk singer).[59] Mike Davis saw the same pattern in South Central, but estimated that the numbers were probably double, though the ratio remained about the same.

But "looting" was not just speech; much of it was occasioned by simple survival needs: with stores closed, power off, and refrigerators not working for an unknowable period, many "looted" as their only means of providing for their families. As a Chicana mother said, "No, this has nothing to do with Rodney King. This is about trying to get something to eat for our kids. Who knows where they're going to get food, now that everything has been destroyed? We have no choice."[60] (See also *Sidebar: Race and Class*, p. 172.) It is worth noting how consistently national television figured "looting" by images of young Black and Brown men taking "nonessential" goods, particularly shoes, and how rarely, if ever, it gave us images of women stocking up on groceries. But even the category of "nonessentials" is problematic: Octavo Sandoral, for example, a seventeen-year-old Latino, "looted" three beds so that he and his brother and sister would no longer have to sleep on the floor. "I felt I was doing something good for my family," he said. Cars complicitly stopped for him as, with two friends, he carried them across the street, and when asked by a reporter if he minded that so many Latinos were "looting" replied, "We're accustomed to being a low minority here, so I thought, let's have fun while we can."[61] For him, as for "Black Youth #4" on *The Oprah Winfrey Show* (see *Sidebar: Race and Class*, p. 172), "looting" made sense only in the intertwining of class and race, and although whites may be tempted to understand his sense of

Race and Class

BLACK YOUTH 2: As far as people being oppressed, I feel like this (points downwards). Brothers and sisters don't have it like the so-called people who go out and work everyday and get in their nice cars and get in their nice houses; we come from the streets, we live in hell, we go through the trials and tribulations of all types of things, and when a situation happens like this, and people want to get theirs, and they work hard and they still can't get groceries, and they see the place burning up, what you gonna do ...

OPRAH: I don't know, but you know what ...

BLACK YOUTH 2: ... what you gonna do? You're going to go out and get the food for your family, because you don't know if that place gonna be standing tomorrow ....

OPRAH: Oh, is that why you were out there, looking for food for your family? Well, you know what, it's interesting, you speak of brothers and sisters, I consider myself to be a sister, okay, but you don't represent all the brothers and sisters, and most of the brothers and sisters were not out there looting.

BLACK YOUTH 2: Well, you can't ... if you weren't there, you can't speak for them.

OPRAH: No, but most of the brothers and sisters, most of the brothers and sisters were not out there looting (applause).

BLACK YOUTH 2: You don't understand, we're not only the minority, we're the majority here.

BLACK YOUTH 3: You had to be there to be caught up in the, in the, in the intensity of what was going on. We had no intention of being involved, we went to see, man, what was happening, I want to see what was happening in my ghetto, I want to see what's happening in my county ...

OPRAH: That's what he's saying, what I'm saying is most of the brothers and sisters are hardworking, struggling, taking care of their children, everyday, working hard, that's what most brothers and sisters are doing (applause).

BLACK YOUTH 3: What I'm trying to say is I work hard everyday, too, but I've seen regular people, just like those out here, taking stuff, and I'm driving down the street and I see a man about to stop me, and I think of the way the Koreans treat me, like this (he gestures), and I'm going, man, they have it, and I'm having some (applause), I'm having some. (*The Oprah Winfrey Show*, May 5, 1992)

KOREAN: I'd just like to say that there's no doubt we understand your anger, we understand it so well, and we're so sorry that we cannot work together on this. It's not the majority of Korean

people who is rude and who is disrespectful, but there are a lot of them, that's exactly the reason we have to try to work together, you know, we have to try to understand each others culture . . . (an off-microphone voice interrupts him)

OPRAH: Why do you say we can't understand, 'cause if we don't understand . . .

KOREAN: . . . why can't we work together on this . . .

OPRAH: . . . if we're not going to understand then we're all going to destroy each other. (she points the microphone at the interrupter)

KOREAN: . . . give us a chance to work together . . .

BLACK YOUTH 4: The Black people got their own problems to work out first of all, the Koreans go to your side and work your problems out, then you come with us . . .

OPRAH: But don't we all live in this world together, don't we all live in this world together?

BLACK YOUTH 4: Miss Oprah, when you leave this show, you go home to a lavish place, lots of us don't go home to lavish things, we go home to empty refrigerators, you know, crying kids, no diapers, no jobs, you know what I'm saying. (she puts her arm around him) Everybody ain't got it like everybody—the people who didn't want to loot didn't want to loot because you

had something to live for, you had a job to go to, lots of people haven't got a job to go to, I had a job, I had a job to go to, that's why I didn't loot. (*The Oprah Winfrey Show*, May 5, 1992)

"The white man ain't been doing us no good, so we didn't do him no good." "The white man got the jobs, and we don't got no jobs." "The white man got everything and we got nothing." "The only way to get the message across is to set this town on fire." (Black voices heard by Robert Neuwirth and published in the *Village Voice* and *Inside the LA Riots*, ed. Institute for Alternative Journalism [New York: Institute for Alternative Journalism, 1992], 76)

We have a corner store which was owned by a black man who leased it to Koreans. So they were selling their products to the neighborhood, and they burnt that down. A couple of blocks down, they burnt the whole ABC grocery market. It was like all around here, it's like every Korean store that was up was burnt down—either looted or burnt down.

When they were taking the stuff . . . when they were looting the store . . . when they were taking the goods or whatever from there, I didn't pay no mind. I was just laughing 'cause I was outside lookin' at 'em. I didn't actually go in there and take something, but I didn't mind. At some point, I felt that they deserved it for the way they was treatin' people.

When there's an opportunity people will take it. There was an opportunity to get a lot of free stuff—especially food—because food around here is like a lot of money. ABC is high priced.

And the money that we are giving to their stores, they're taking it to their community, Koreatown. If a black man owned the store, the money would stay among us and help us build the community up. Just because it's labelled the ghetto doesn't mean it has to be. (Alberto Machon, eighteen-year-old South-Central resident who immigrated from El Salvador ten years previously; quoted in *Los Angeles Times*, May 13, 1992, T10)

Looting So to Speak

BLACK WOMAN: The looting? Okay, I'm not saying that attacking the Koreans solved the problem, but when this Rodney King verdict came down, people were angry, and I'm still angry, I get angrier daily, how are we supposed to get it? We're not allowed to rally, we were going to meet Saturday, but that was canceled—I'm not saying attacking Koreans was the way, but it did get national attention. We *are* here, we *are* here. (*The Oprah Winfrey Show*, May 5, 1992)

WESLEY SNIPES: They confront on a daily basis issues of race relations, exploitation, and oppression and despair that's in this country—the upper echelons of people will never experience many of the things that people are acting out, and crying out, that's what I felt it is. Women with children are out there, protesting and doing other things, these are the people who don't usually have a voice, and usually feel that the powers that be are so great that they'd never win anyway, so why open my mouth about it? But this situation affords them the opportunity to look out and cry out, and basically to take what they feel they deserve, what is constantly being pumped down their throats—I mean out here in Hollywood you're seeing a Mercedes, a fancy car every ten seconds—this is my day to take everything you have been pumping down my throat because it's mine now. (interview on CNN *Showbiz*, May 1, 1992)

MAXINE WATERS: Riot is the voice of the unheard. (*ABC News*, April 30, 1992)

ICE CUBE: Real rap is the only way young Black people have of kicking the real knowledge. . . . We've gotta uncover this mystery of why we are poor and why we're killing each other in the streets. That's got to be uncovered in the music, and if you want rap that's not on the political route, there's so many rappers out there, you can find somebody who's just rockin' beats. But we gotta use our outlets because this is our only outlet that we can use, almost uncensored, so what else can we do? The classroom ain't getting it done for us, the news, the newspapers, the church, none of these are getting the job done. (quoted in *Right On*, March 1992, p. 30)

"fun" as evidence of the meaningless irresponsibility of his behavior, we must recognize that "fun" is the experience of the release from constraint, typically the constraints of work. For the residents of South-Central, however, the constraints whose temporary relaxation enabled "fun" are far more oppressive and comprehensive than those of the workplace. One of the relaxed constraints was that of white law and order, and Octavo Sandoral denied the criminality of his action by explaining that police inactivity had signaled that what he and his fellows were doing was not stealing: that, we might assume, is what made it

"fun." His mother, however, saw it differently, and so, two days later, he re-   175
turned the beds.

The *Los Angeles Times* recognized that "the protest over police abuse had become a poverty riot"[62] and other, more sympathetic, commentators referred to
them as "bread riots." Omi and Winant consider that, for the urban poor of all
races, the riots exhibited class alliances rather than racial ones, but for middle-
class Blacks who identified with the rioters, the racial alliances overcame class
difference.[63] Many of this group made their way to South-Central later in the
uprisings, not only to check on the safety of friends and relatives, but also to
express solidarity. In general, this would seem a convincing account, but it
needs complicating even more: middle-class Blacks whose businesses were attacked tended to align themselves with Koreans and whites, and Oprah Winfrey tried (without complete success) to stop herself joining the same alliance
and thus distancing herself from the economically deprived Blacks of South-
Central. She wobbled on a discursive tightrope as she gave "looters" a rare
chance to put their case on national television, but still equated looting with
stealing and saw no sense in it (see *Sidebar: Looters Speak*, p. 176). The contradictions were clear in one image on her show: a Black man passionately
pointed out the differences in the African American community between the
haves and the have-nots, and as his words put him and Oprah into opposite
class alliances, she put her arm around his shoulder to draw them into the
same racial one (see *Sidebar: Race and Class*, p. 173). In a similar attempt to negotiate the same contradiction, a Black business owner accused those who
looted his store of not understanding how difficult and expensive it is for a
Black business to get insurance. The power of the white economy to deny middle-class African Americans equal access to insurance, mortgages, and venture
capital is the same power that denies underclass African Americans equal access to jobs and commodities: the power is directed to a different class of African Americans, so the place and method of its application is different. Consequently, the fact that it is the same power can remain unseen and unrecognized
by those who experience it differently. In both these cases, however, we must
recognize that the divisiveness of class difference was overlooked by the successful, but loomed large in the eyes of the deprived.

For the mainstream white media, however, the complications of race and
class were largely repressed. For them, "looting" was a matter of criminality
and ethics in which race could be criminalized. ABC's *Nightline*, for example, in
summarizing the first twenty-four hours of the uprisings, used three main image clusters of the "riots" to portray them as "nigger chaos" — one of attacks on
white drivers (including Reginald Denny), one of burning buildings, and one
of looting (see *Sidebar: ABC's Looters*, p. 177). Against these images of disorder,
it showed the order of the National Guard being mobilized and, in between as
ever, the Korean vigilantes. Ted Koppel's introduction conforms to the standard, if simple, journalistic definition of objectivity as paying attention to both

Looters Speak

Watts 1965:

INTERVIEWER (to man carrying a sofa): Brother, brother, do you realize what you're doing?

"LOOTER": Don't bother me now, I've got to hurry back to get the matching chair.

Detroit 1967:

"LOOTER": I was feeling proud, man, at the fact I was a Negro. I felt like I was a first-class citizen. I didn't feel ashamed of my race for what they did.

South-Central 1992:

OPRAH: There are people here today who say they normally don't steal, but who called us and said they were angry, and they looted stores last week. And as I sat home and watched my television, as so many of you did, I asked, too, what does the looting, the television, the shoes, whatever it is you're looting for, have to do with Rodney King? So we wanted some of them to answer that question. Why did you do it?

BLACK YOUTH 1: You have to understand what happened, why we did it. The reason we did it was we needed self-satisfaction, we needed self-satisfaction. We had none. We had no satisfaction in what happened to Rodney King, we had no satisfaction in what happened to Latasha Harlins, we've never had no satisfaction. I've had twenty-five years of being unsatisfied. What am I to do? What am

I to do? I'm looking at the news and they're telling me my life is not worth a nickel, they're telling me they can beat me, they can do to me whatever they feel like, and I'm supposed to accept it and say, "Well, I gotta go and vote and make it all better." It hasn't got better, and we've been voting for years. Every time they get to the vote for me, the president's already been elected.

OPRAH: Are you registered to vote?

BLACK YOUTH 1: Yes, I'm definitely registered to vote.

OPRAH: Okay, so you were out looting. Did you get stuff?

BLACK YOUTH 1: Well, I was out there, I was out there. Yes, I got stuff.

OPRAH: Let me ask you, after the stuff, some of the things you got, did you feel better?

BLACK YOUTH 1: Definitely I felt better.

OPRAH: You did?

BLACK YOUTH 1: I felt better, 100 percent better, I can't even lie about it.

OPRAH: You did? And how was it you felt better?

BLACK YOUTH 1: Because I felt satisfaction, and I think and I believe that every human being that was out there was getting self-satisfaction one way or another.

BLACK MAN (to Oprah): America is a loot. America came over here and genocided the Indians, and looted America, and split Africa, and looted Africa, because she gotta take what she wants. I'm the best businessman in the world, I've learned for four hundred years, you can't want, you gotta have. Let's paint the White House black!

(*The Oprah Winfrey Show*, May 5, 1992)

ABC's Looters

(*Nightline*, April 30, 1992)

TED KOPPEL: It has already begun turning into another dialogue of the deaf. On the one hand those for whom the verdict in the Rodney King case confirmed yet again the insensitivity, the callousness, the downright racism of The System, capital T and capital S. And then, on the other hand, those who view the violence spreading throughout Los Angeles as an expression of sheer lawlessness, unwarranted, unjustified, and unrelated to the King verdict except insofar as it is being used as an excuse. Most tragically of all, the country seems to have run out of honest brokers, anyone genuinely capable of bridging the gap between the two sides. There is a reservoir of hostility on both sides of the line.

. . .

REPORTER IN LOS ANGELES: National Guard troops were deployed in the troubled areas to reinforce the police, but even all that law enforcement didn't stop the looting. Nor did the vigilante attacks stop the looting. These Korean shop owners defended their property with

bullets. More than one hundred Korean businesses have been looted or burned since last night.

KOREAN STORE OWNER: We have a lot of shotguns in here, and a lot of handguns, and we have to use them, we have to defend our lives, defend our property . . .

. . .

REPORTER: Most of the trouble is taking place within a one-hundred-and-five-square-mile area of South-Central L.A., but there are reports now of looting in Hollywood, Beverly Hills, and several locations in the San Fernando Valley. In South-Central the looting has become brazen. There seems little connection to outrage over the King verdict. Most of the looters, like these seen breaking into a Sears store, seemed to be making the most of the chaotic situation to grab some goods. In fact, one looter arrived at this location in a yellow cab.

At a nearby grocery store, a local reporter confronted some of the thieves:

LOCAL REPORTER: Why did you do this?
"LOOTER" (Latino in appearance): I don't know, because it's free.
LOCAL REPORTER: It's free?
"LOOTER:" Yeah.
LOCAL REPORTER: Don't you know it's wrong?
"LOOTER:" No.
LOCAL REPORTER: You don't care.
"LOOTER:" I don't care.

sides of the issue (as though an issue such as this has only two!). But even here the intentionality of his language (it is white journalese) betrays his professional intention: the modifier "yet" before "again," and the tone of "capital T, capital S" are discursive alienators in his account of "their" position for which there are no equivalents in his description of "ours."

LaMotte on the Spot

GREG LAMOTTE (to camera): Now if your picture appears a bit darker than normal, it's because we've been told by the police we cannot turn on our lights. A short time ago a sporting goods store was looted, where ammunition and guns were taken. The police tell us that a light would make us a target, and after having had beer bottles thrown at us today during live shoots and our windshield smashed, if the police say, "No lights," I say, "No problem."

It has been a very sad day today in Los Angeles, very sad. When you see your own police department pushed into a position of helplessness, it makes

the person on the street feel helpless as well, helpless and angry at how senseless all of this is. (*Voice-over, live footage*): The forces of the police and the National Guard com-

bined, anticipating another hellish night in the City of Angels. All in the day, we've seen the worst looting here since the 1965 Watts riots. There have been more deaths; this man was shot in the back and the head while standing in the street. Even the paramedics who showed up to help say they are fortunate to be alive because rioters fired bullets at them while they were trying to save the victims of this violence.

This gesture toward objectivity is as empty as it is professionally necessary; from this point on, the story is told entirely in the language of those who saw the uprisings as "sheer lawlessness, unwarranted, unjustified, and unrelated to the King verdict." Koppel was quite typical in treating the verdict as the only justifiable cause of the "riots," for this allowed the large numbers of whites, including George Bush, who agreed that the verdict was unjust to see it as an abnormal instance when the system didn't work instead of an example of an unjust system working normally. ABC's reporter on the spot followed Ted Koppel's lead in her concern to distinguish "looting" that was merely "grabbing some goods" from "looting" that expressed "outrage over the King verdict." She did not have to use the presumably psychic insight into the motives of the "looters" that this distinction would entail, for all of the "looting" she could see was, as it turned out, of the grabbing goods variety. Her understanding of the cab arriving at a "looting" scene was indelibly white and middle-class: she gave no pause to consider that it may have carried the driver (who was almost

The fact is there are too many looters, too many arsonists, and too few police officers to do anything about it. Police stand helplessly by as hundreds of looters bash their way into stores and take, seemingly, whatever they want. The looting is sporadic, but it is citywide; Hollywood and Beverly Hills are affected. Three major banks have been closed

down out of fear of robbery, most stores have closed in the downtown area but the looters just crashed through the glass and gates with no fear of being caught. In fact, the police, when they do see it, only try to scare them away. Given the level of crime here, only a handful of people have been arrested, because police are too busy trying to contain certain areas, not make arrests. At stores that are looted, it's almost like a feeding frenzy; they pour in, grab what they want, and run out. There is thick black smoke everywhere from the hundreds of fires that have been set. The National Guard is now on the streets, but it seems as each hour passes, the strength of the masses grows — people realize that they canget away with something, so they do, and nobody seems to know when it will end.

(To camera): National Guardsmen are now able to set up perimeters of protection so that the Los Angeles police officers can move into certain sections of the city and arrest looters. In fact, just a short time ago, a couple of dozen looters were brought to this parking lot and taken away. They're also arresting any curfew breakers. Just where we're standing is so different from what it was like earlier today, it's calm now, but earlier today there were fires everywhere, and easy looting. In fact, one looter was seen getting away on a skateboard.

(CNN *Newsnight*, April 30, 1992)

certainly Black or Latino/a) to the scene of the action, but was content with the class- and race-based assumption that cabs carry only their passengers.

CNN's Greg LaMotte walked the same path (see *Sidebar: LaMotte on the Spot*, p. 178). He talked of a "feeding frenzy" and of how "senseless" it all was. He called the people "the masses," Pat Buchanan, like George Bush, called them "the mob" (see *Sidebar: Buchanan*, p. 56); both terms deny the uprisings any purpose. This discourse has to constuct the uprising as "senseless" because to do otherwise would bring whiteness into the picture by situating it, even if only implicitly, as the order that the disorder targeted, and thus to nominate it as the position from which LaMotte-Buchanan spoke.

In his speech to the nation on May 1, 1992, President Bush tried to occupy a more moderate position within whiteness than LaMotte or Buchanan (see *Sidebar: Bush on L.A.*, p. 188). He was "stunned" and "pained" by the video and the verdict, and unconvinced that justice had been served. Consequently, he announced a federal investigation into the possible violation of Rodney King's

180   civil rights. He ended with a call for healing and an end to racism and bigotry. But running alongside this moderate, conciliatory discourse in his speech was one as extreme as Buchanan's, LaMotte's, or the ABC reporter's. Bush used the same words as other Republican politicians and mainstream television to make the same sense of the events in Los Angeles — "random terror," "lawlessness," "senselessness," "brutality of the mob," "murder, arson, theft, and vandalism," "wanton destruction," "mob violence." His characterization of the police as underpaid community peacekeepers echoed LaMotte's telling his viewers that the police were their own. With such words echoing behind his "rallying cry of good and decent people," there is little doubt who has to change so as to "allow our diversity to bring us together" — and it is not Bush, Buchanan, Quayle, Limbaugh, LaMotte, or Koppel.

    The discourse of "mobs" and "masses," or "senselessness" and "lawlessness" absolves white society from any responsibility for the uprisings. By using this as their dominant discourse, the mainstream media were able to submerge both the broader social situation in which their role is so formative and the history of dominations of which they are themselves a product. The mainstream media's refusal to see anything from a point of view other than their own repressed any alternative knowledge that there was an order, a purpose, and a sense to the uprisings. On Black Liberation Radio Mbanna Kantako saw it, as he repeatedly reminded his listeners that the burning and "looting" were systematic, not random. Starting four thousand fires in less than twenty-four hours and confining them to businesses was, for him, clear evidence of organization and purpose.[64] Max Anger saw kids using mobile phones to "coordinate the movements of their gangs with the arrival of the police and fire trucks, warning looters when the police were on their way."[65] He noted, too, that before liquor stores were torched, people got hoses ready to prevent the fires' spreading to nearby homes. The sense of purpose and organization that the white media had to repress to continue putting the events into the discourse of riots, senselessness, and chaos was not confined to L.A.: in Springfield, Illinois, Dia Kantako pointed out on Black Liberation Radio that Springfield's Channel 20 repressed any sense of order by not reporting that the property damage in the rebellion in the John Hay Homes was confined to apartments occupied by the police or the Housing Authority (see *Sidebar: Blackened White TV*, p. 182). In South-Central, too, almost no private residences were burned or "looted"; as one gang leader put it, "We didn't burn our community, just their stores." Sister Adwba, reporting on Black Liberation Radio by phone from L.A., saw order, purpose, and mutual respect or politeness in the "looting" (see *Sidebar: Looting Sense*, p. 184). Even the conservative *National Review* allowed its correspondent Alan Keyes to trace a purpose to the damage:

        It's too easy to assume that the rioters acted irrationally, destroying

the businesses that symbolized what they wanted most. It makes
more sense to assume that what the rioters destroyed, and what
they rioted about, symbolized what they hated most—outside
influences, outside powers, and the fact that outsiders dominate
every aspect of their lives. Because they have power over nothing,
nothing in their environment reflects their own image. Because they
see themselves in nothing, it is not long before they see nothing in
themselves.[66]

A diametrically different account is given by Pat Buchanan's story of the "mob" advancing on a convalescent home to "ransack and loot the apartments of the terrified old men and women inside" (see *Sidebar: Buchanan*, p. 56). For Buchanan the "mob" takes advantage of the weak; for those involved, the exploiters are the target. Buchanan would surely have enjoyed the cover of the *National Review* issue that contained Keyes's story: superimposed on a photograph of a Latino "looting" a case of Coca-Cola was the headline, "How to Get a Week's Groceries Absolutely Free, PLUS $600 Million in Federal Aid."

Although African Americans, Korean Americans, Latino/as, and others may suffer under the white media, they do not always suffer in silence. The Koreans who complained so bitterly and justifiably about their media treatment were not alone: on Black Liberation Radio, Dia Kantako did more than complain—she took apart her local TV station's coverage of the uprising in the John Hay Homes with a media savvy every bit as sharp as Rush Limbaugh's (see *Sidebar: Blackened White TV*, p. 182). She used low-tech radio to counter each discursive attack of high-capital television: she changed the terms of the discourse, turning "arrests" into "kidnappings," a "rampage" into "the defense of our community" and "rioters" into "warriors"; she relocated referents by making "violence" refer to police action instead of Black action; she recovered the repressed, such as the information that the only apartments burned were the ones occupied by the police and the Housing Authority; she rearticulated events, so that hostility to the firefighters was disarticulated from their public service and reconnected to the often fatal tardiness of their response to fires in Black-occupied buildings; she refused the individualizing of events and did not allow her people's anger and unrest to be understood as an isolated incident that could be dealt with and forgotten but insisted on historicizing it within 527 years of anger. She sees clearly that the mainstream media are part of the white assault, and knows how to defend her people against them.

ABC and CNN merit similar deconstruction, for their discourse is the same as Springfield's Channel 20. ABC's journalistic discourse is as media-typical in what it submerges as in what it brings to the surface. The only ethnicity mentioned verbally is that of the Koreans, who, as property owners, are aligned with the National Guard, the police, and the white "us" that is addressed by

Blackened White TV

Dia Kantako replays and comments on her local TV station's coverage of the uprising in the John Hay Homes following the verdicts in the first Rodney King beating trial:

DIA KANTAKO: Let me explain the attack on our community—the part of the attack waged by Channel 20.

MALE ANCHOR: Violence breaks out in the John Hay Homes in Springfield. Police in riot gear seal off the area in an attempt to keep the disorder from spreading.

DIA KANTAKO: As you can tell, the first line contained many lies. Number 1, there has always been violence in John Hay as long as the pigs have been in John Hay. Number 2, if the pigs did seal off the area they were not successful in containing what they call the violence, for they, the pigs, waged violence on the John Hay community long after our warriors were gone, long after all their activity had ceased.

FEMALE ANCHOR: Good evening. It's been a night of anger and unrest in the Hay Homes.

DIA KANTAKO: Now let us take the lies out of the next line. Number 1, it is not a good evening, and we, as human beings, haven't had a good five seconds in this devil country, let alone a good evening. Number 2, the girl went on to say it was an evening of anger and unrest in the John Hay Homes, and that is a bald-faced lie—we have been angry and restless for 527 years in this devil country.

MALE REPORTER: Hundreds of youths went on the rampage there, setting fires, breaking windows, and clashing with firefighters.

DIA KANTAKO: All their estimates of how many were involved were off, and when they characterize our youth as rampaging, that's an attempt to con-

fuse you. The young people rose in defense of our community.

MALE REPORTER: When fifty officers from the city, county, and state were called to the scene shortly after midnight, they said their first goal was to contain the violence to the Hay Homes area.

POLICE OFFICER: When I was coming down Main Street I stopped four or five individuals walking toward the downtown area. They went back across Main Street toward Eleventh Street.

DIA KANTAKO: That didn't indicate whether those he stopped were involved in the defense of our community, all he said was he found them and they ran back toward John Hay. They could have been on their way to work or to home.

MALE REPORTER: Police set up a perimeter by blocking off Eleventh, Madison, and Carpenter Streets around the Homes. Police tried to keep innocent passers-by away from the scene. At one point they stopped a couple at the entry to the Hay Homes, escorted them out of their vehicle and across Eleventh Street.

DIA KANTAKO: Another lie. Those people had driven all the way from the east end of the neighborhood, and I know they were allowed to go. But those in the vehicles behind them were arrested, listen to these peckerwoods:

MALE REPORTER (over confused shouting): Police called a prison transport bus to the scene. Ten people were arrested and charged with mob action. There were no injuries.

DIA KANTAKO: A prison transport bus was brought into the area—needless to say this is another lie. Four Mass Transit buses were brought into the area. And those that were kidnapped were not physically involved in the defense of the community. And as far as the injuries—until you can account for all those they attacked in the John Hay Homes, you can take their word for it, or can you?

FEMALE ANCHOR: *You can see evidence of the fires that burned last night. Seven apartments were damaged.*

DIA KANTAKO: My, isn't she intelligent! Of course if something was burned last night and not cleaned up last night there would be evidence of a fire the following morning. Wasn't that clever how they said seven apartments were damaged, but didn't say all were being used by either the pigs or the Housing Authority.

FEMALE ANCHOR: *The fire department chief described the situation as the worst he'd seen in his nineteen years in Springfield.*

DIA KANTAKO: Either she was lying or he was lying, because nobody died in those fires as opposed to the fire that burned one block from the fire station last summer.

FEMALE ANCHOR: *Firemen say while they were trying to put the fires out they were shot at and pelted with rocks. Police were forced to set up an armed guard situation so the firefighters could do their job. At least one fire engine's windows were shattered. Fire Chief Russ Steel would say very little about last night's events, but hoped for a more peaceful night tomorrow.*

DIA KANTAKO: Those devils know they were not shot at while they were putting out the fire, unless it was the police that did it. Don't they know how many windows were broken on their trucks?

FIRE CHIEF: *There were one or two pieces of equipment that, as you can see, sustained damage to the windshield, and, er, we'll get 'em repaired, and we certainly don't want a situation like this to repeat itself because we are jeopardizing the innocent lives of firefighters who are there serving the public out of their commitment to duty.*

DIA KANTAKO: Did you hear that? Peckerwood! He thinks we don't know all

about those people who have died in fires on this side of town, with them right around the corner. Why didn't they show one of those victims' bodies as quick as they showed a damn truck?

FEMALE ANCHOR: *Chief Steel says the fire department is running a normal schedule today with the same number of firefighters on duty as usual.*

MALE REPORTER: *However, police say they will be beefing up their patrols tonight. One of their squad cars was damaged last night when someone fired a shotgun at the side of the vehicle. Two windows were shattered and the body was dented by pellets.*

DIA KANTAKO: They didn't mention anything about the pig that ran into ... [?] and no shots were fired at any time by those that were defending their community.

MALE REPORTER: *Police will be ready for any trouble tonight.*

POLICE OFFICER: *We've set up some different teams that we will be activating tonight, to take a proarrest policy, and as long as people are peaceful—to be out there—but as soon as they do something to break the law, we're going to go and proarrest and we're going to get those people out.*

DIA KANTAKO: Can you imagine the audacity of the peckerwood! Says that we, the original people on this planet earth, will be allowed the free movement on the earth when we're at least 1.6 million years old!

MALE ANCHOR: *... says he does not believe this violence is related to the Rodney King verdict. He calls it copycat violence based on the looting and violence happening elsewhere.*

DIA KANTAKO: Well, there you have the devil's report by Channel 20, another branch of the Springfield police department. This is Black Liberation Radio, and I'm Dia Kantako.

(Black Liberation Radio, May 2, 1992)

Looting Sense

SISTER ADWBA (on phone from L.A.): . . . and these are the very kids that were so orchestrated and organized that nobody could stop them. And it was so organized—if you could have seen it happen, them moving around, doing businesses and stuff . . .

MBANNA KANTAKO: Just like we saw it, right here, last night.

SISTER ADWBA: It was something, it was really something, because with me, I had a sense of pride in me, I could see the city falling all around me, and some Black people were complaining, and they were saying, "We're destroying our community," and you have to understand the definition of a community, it's not just because you live in it, do you own it, do you control it, and do you run it? And so it wasn't our community that we destroyed, anyway.

MBANNA KANTAKO: Yes, sister, it was strategic. In fact they were more precise than those "smart bombs" that Bush dropped on Baghdad.

SISTER ADWBA: Exactly, but then they said, "Well, our property value's going down," and my response was, "Good, maybe now we'll get a chance to own it." We ought to be glad the property value's going down. So that's right, we ought to turn this around and butt out all the markets and stuff. I was very

pleased, you know, I was really pleased, I was really pleased to my soul, because I told the people, I said, "Now you'll maybe see the Black-owned grocery in our neighborhood. . . . It makes a Black woman like me, I was so proud, these were our children, and we had raised them correctly. The people talk about them looting and whatever, I think that five hundred years of free labor is supposed to be paid for by any means necessary, and they was taking Pampers and stuff, who can blame them for looting for their babies?

MBANNA KANTAKO: Who can blame them for taking food?

SISTER ADWBA: Yes, they were so organized, brother. You've never seen so much respect and harmony and cooperation in a looting situation, half the stuff that people didn't know, they were helping each other, saying "Excuse me"—it was beautiful, it was just beautiful. (Black Liberation Radio, May 2, 1992)

Graffiti in South-Central: "Day one: burn them out. Day two: we rebuild." (in Mike Davis, "Burning All Illusions in LA," in *Inside the LA Riots*, ed. Institute for Alternative Journalism [New York: Insititute for Alternative Journalism, 1992], 99)

the story. The subaltern ethnicities of the uprisers who are cupped in "the one hand" of Ted Koppel's "even"-handed introduction are never made explicit, nor is the dominating whiteness of those in his "other." His discourse thus constructs the differences between the two "sides of the line" as ones of opinion, not ones resulting from a long history of racial and economic power. This same history is kept deeply submerged by the assumption underlying the piece that the only possible (though still inadequate) justification of the looting would be its direct connection to "outrage over the King verdict." This color-power evasion in the public discourse of the white media parallels precisely its use in the private discourse of the white women studied by Ruth Frankenberg (see chapter 1).

LaMotte, too, represses white interests from his story. As noted above, the "certain areas" that police are protecting are white ones, not Black, Latino/a, or Korean. Similarly, the "certain sections of the city" into which the police can now move to make arrests are Black and Latino/a. The word "certain" represses overt racial references that might embarrass white interests (as in "certain areas"), but allows racial meanings to seep back in when white interests are served (as in "certain sections of the city").

Media discourse is not always as clearly white or Black as the contrast between the mainstream TV news and Black Liberation Radio. TV talk shows fall somewhere between the two: though socially devalued (though not as far as Black Liberation Radio), they are nonetheless on network television, though not on prime time. They are in-between. Oprah Winfrey exemplifies this in-betweenness: though she is African American, she is also a national media personality, and her interrogation of Black "looters" often echoed the white discourses of ABC's local reporter and Greg LaMotte (see *Sidebars: Looters Speak*, p. 176, and *Race and Class*, p. 172).

But at least Oprah allowed "looters" to speak at some length on her show. Mainstream TV news was far more monovocal and admitted far fewer discursive positions onto its screens. As the uprisings began on April 29, the networks had to cover them live, on the wing, and, initially, cracks appeared in their discursive control. Representative Maxine Waters, for instance, was able to mount a lengthy argument on CNN that the "insurrection" (her word) was about racism, economic deprivation, social rejection, and political disenfranchisement, and that the verdict was the ignition, not the cause. Rapidly, however, the news industry got itself organized, and began to fit the events into the white discourses of law and order, of ethics, of individual responsibility, and of singular cause and effect.

A pattern began to emerge: the less mainstream the media, the more minority and subaltern voices were likely to be heard. Daytime talk shows and the alternative press brought to the surface discursive currents that were submerged or marginalized by the nightly news and the dailies. Even on a given channel the same pattern could be observed. On CNN's *Newsnight*, for example, Greg LaMotte put the events into a discourse of which even Pat Buchanan would have approved. But on CNN's *Showbiz Tonight*, Black actors such as Wesley Snipes, radical white ones such as Charlie Sheen, and Latino ones such as Jimmy Smits were allowed quite lengthy expressions of sympathy with, and understanding for, the uprisers. An African American friend of mine, a member of the professional classes, told me that the best coverage of the uprisings he could find was on MTV. Mainstream television scrambled to get the pundits that whites wanted to hear, so their analytic commentaries were provided by

186 university professors, politicians, civil rights leaders, and law enforcement officers. On MTV, however, the pundits were rap artists: they spoke from their
own experience of pauperization, of police brutality, of social exclusion, and of
racism, and brought to the nation's screens voices and viewpoints that its mainstream media repressed.[67]

Rappers are the best journalists for Heather Mackey also: "When Chuck D
says that rap music is like CNN for black people, it makes complete sense to
me, because I use rap as a news source. My sources of information are different
from the evening news—they have to be, because I don't watch a lot of TV."[68]
Her friends told her, time and again, how uncannily the events in South-Central mirrored songs in their collections. Ice-T's "Cop Killer" provides one example: its chorus includes "Fuck the police for Daryl Gates, Fuck the police for
Rodney King." Ice Cube's rap "Black Korea" is about Black anger at the way
Korean grocers distrust Black customers and "watch every damn move that I
make"; it ends with the threat, "So pay respect to the Black fist / Or we'll burn
your store right down to a crisp." Ice-T and Ice Cube are both criticized by
whites for inciting violence, and "Cop Killer" was withdrawn from sale after a
campaign by the Police Federation and white supporters. But the rappers explain that they are giving information about Black experience and warnings
about Black anger. Violence is incited not by rap, but by white ignorance of
Black social conditions: "If you weren't prepared for this [the uprising]," Ice-T
told the white liberal journalist Terry Gross on *Fresh Air*, "if you didn't think it
was going to happen, or if you are at all surprised, then it's your fault."[69] During the interview, Terry Gross's questions were all posed from the unmarked
space of whiteness from which Black violence appears antisocial and whiteness
its victim. "What have the cops done to you," she asked in pained bafflement,
"that you see them as the enemy?" Ice-T told her and her listeners in no uncertain terms:

> Put me in jail, kill a couple of my frends, beat me, harass me, look
> me in my eyes because I'm in my car and told me to get over, put
> me on the side of the road, laid me down in the street like a punk.
> All that has to do is to happen to you once and you'll hate them.
> You know, I live it. If you're not from L.A. you don't understand the
> Gestapo force of police that they have in L.A. They're not humans. I
> just think white America, of the upper class, don't even have any
> way of understanding the injustices that go on in the ghetto, and
> until you do it's just a waste of my time explaining it to you.[70]

This Black frustration with white refusal to listen is what whites miss when
they understand the anger in rap as merely incitement to violence. Terry Gross,
for example, described the lyrics in Ice-T's album *Body Count* as "inflammatory," and failed to hear the question that the album was really asking, which
was, as Ice-T explained to her, "What is a brother gotta do to get a message

through?" Ice Cube is equally convinced that rap is the only medium by which
Black knowledge can be circulated in Black voices (see *Sidebar: Looting So to Speak*, p. 174).

Hearing words does not constitute listening: the same words in different discourses may signify quite differently, for the verbal dimension of discourse is always connected with the social. Although whites may be able to hear Black words, they will misunderstand them if they make no effort to understand that Black discourse carries, besides audible words, sociocultural conventions that are clear to native speakers but inaudible to outside eavesdroppers. The "inflammatory" lyrics of rap are a case in point. In his study of cultural differences between Blacks and whites, Thomas Kochman devotes a chapter to "fighting words."[71] His main conclusion is that whites see a continuity between verbal threats or insults ("fighting words") and physical violence, whereas African Americans maintain a clear boundary between them. This means that "angry verbal disputes, even those involving insults and threats, can be maintained by blacks at the verbal level *without* violence necessarily resulting."[72] The purpose of Black verbal aggression, he concludes, "is to gain, without actually having to become violent, the respect and fear from others that is often won through physical combat."[73] In this light, the chorus of Ice-T's controversial rap "Cop Killer," which includes "die, die, die, pig die, Fuck the police," might serve to reduce, rather than inflame, physical violence. I must make clear that I do not know if the verbal violence of rap does work among African Americans in this way, for I have not heard any Black person explain that it does: I put forward the possibility, however, as a caution that whites should not assume that because they know the language they know the discourse; they should not assume that the three English-language words "Fuck the police" mean the same in Black discourse as in white.

There are many voices normally excluded from the mainstream media that are allowed to speak on them in times of crisis. National Public Radio did air Terry Gross's interview with Ice-T during the uprisings, but she would have been unlikely to interview him in more normal times. And that is Ice-T's point—the uprisings were, in part, loud public speech by those whose voices are normally silenced or confined to their own media. The uprisings made the white media make room for the occasional Black voice, and they made white America listen. But the few Black voices that struggled to push Black meanings into public discussion were overwhelmed by white voices and marginalized by the white media. We must recognize, too, that Black voices were heard more often and more clearly than Latino/a ones, and that Korean ones were heard hardly at all. The white media, and the mainstream white imagination, did tend, as we have seen, to simplify the antagonisms that erupted in L.A. down to Black-white ones.

Although the media may carry a wider range of voices than some left-wing critics will allow, they do structure these voices in a hierarchy of legitimation

Bush on L.A.

(extracts from his speech to the nation, May 1, 1992,
"Civil Disorder in Los Angeles: Justice Will Be Served")

. . . Fifteen minutes ago I talked to California's Governor Pete Wilson and Los Angeles Mayor Tom Bradley. They told me that last night was better than the night before; today calmer than yesterday. But there were still incidents of random terror this afternoon.

In the wake of the first night's violence I spoke directly to both Governor Wilson and Mayor Bradley to assess the situation and offer assistance. There are two very different issues at hand: one is the urgent need to restore order. What followed Wednesday's jury verdict in the Rodney King case was a tragic series of events for the city of Los Angeles. Nearly four thousand fires, staggering property damage, hundreds of injuries; and the senseless deaths of over thirty people.
. . .

What we saw last night and the night before in Los Angeles is not about civil rights. It's not about the great cause of equality that all Americans must uphold. It's not a message of protest. It's been the brutality of a mob, pure and simple. And let me assure you: I will use whatever force is necessary to restore order.

What is going on in L.A. must — and will — stop. As your president I guarantee you this violence will end.

And now let's talk about the beating of Rodney King. Because beyond the urgent need to restore order is the second issue, the question of justice; whether Rodney King's federal civil rights were violated. What you saw and what I saw on the TV video was revolting. I felt anger. I felt pain. I thought: How can I explain this to my grandchildren?
. . .

Viewed from outside the trial, it was hard to understand how the verdict could possibly square with the video. Those civil rights leaders with whom I met were stunned. And so was I and so was Barbara and so were my kids.
. . .

In this highly controversial court case, a verdict was handed down by a California jury. To Americans of all races who were shocked by the verdict, let me say this: You must understand that our system of justice provides for the peaceful, orderly means of addressing this frustration. We must respect the process of law whether or not we agree with the outcome. There's a difference between frustration with the law and direct assaults upon our legal system.

In a civilized society, there can be no excuse — no excuse — for the murder, arson, theft and vandalism that have terrorized the law-abiding citizens of Los Angeles. Mayor Bradley, just a few minutes ago, mentioned to me his particular

that is a product of the dominant value system. This hierarchy of legitimation reproduces a hierarchy of taste, particularly on television, so that talk shows are not only seen as lower brow and less "good" than the network news, but their core audience is "lower" in the social hierarchy. And MTV is even "lower" than talk shows. Many of those who criticize the media's coverage of political issues have a structure of taste that leads them to watch the network news rather than talk shows, *Nightline* rather than *Murphy Brown*, and to walk

oppressed, such as those of Mbanna and Dia Kantako, are rarely quoted on their pages, whose space is more likely to be reserved for middle-class white dissidents.

We must recognize that the populism of tabloid TV, of MTV and the talk shows, carries a wide variety of topics and points of view, only some of which would be applauded by progressive critics. But when these same critics dismiss "low" TV or ignore it completely they are participating in the same hierarchy of legitimation as the media they criticize. Our media resources are limited, and will always be so, particularly when they are commercial or reliant on corporate sponsorship, so it is doubly important to take advantage of the range that they do offer. Using them productively and progressively involves grazing around their margins and in their lower reaches: our TV time can be spent more productively than by sitting fuming at the network news while increasing its ratings. The more that the mainstream media lose their audiences to ones in the side streams or backwaters, the more pressure they will feel to diversify the voices they carry and the wider circulation those voices will receive.

And if, while exploring the margins, we whose native territory is the center hear information in accents that are alien, or even alienating, then we may be motivated to extend our discursive repertoire and to gain some sense of how our world appears from positions that are far removed from ours. Although our native discourse will always remain central in our sense making, we must, if we are to live in a multicultural world, learn something of the discourses of others and develop as best we can the ability to handle the differences between ours and theirs; we will never build a multicultural society out of monodiscursive people. Caucasian Americans can hope to live peaceably with Sister Adwba only if we understand that when she talks of the beauty of "looters" saying "excuse me" she is using a discourse in which "respect" means something very different from in ours. Of course, such understanding, although necessary, is not sufficient; it is no more than a first step, but the Greg LaMottes and Pat Buchanans of America are determined not to take it. They can feel secure only by keeping their feet firmly planted on old ground and their heads tucked safely under their right wings.

These right wings shield eyes and ears from discourses that discomfort them. Black Liberation Radio may be one of the most marginalized media of all, and it is unlikely that Greg LaMotte and Pat Buchanan have ever heard of it, let alone listened to it. It carries information about the way whiteness works that would, if they heard it, and even more if they believed it (an unimaginable condition), both disturb their complacency and increase their fear. The next chapter provides an example from Black Liberation Radio of a particular Black knowledge of the evil of whiteness. It is an extreme example, and thus a controversial one, and I must emphasize that although many African Americans accept and try to propagate this knowledge, many, probably more, do not.

concern, among others, regarding the safety of the Korean community. My heart goes out to them and all others who have suffered losses.

. . .

Television has become a medium that often brings us together. But its vivid display of Rodney King's beating shocked us. And the America it has shown us on our screens these last forty-eight hours has appalled us. None of this is what we wish to think of as American. It's as if we were looking in a mirror that distorted our better selves and turned us ugly . . . . We cannot let that happen. We cannot do that to ourselves.

We've seen images in the last 48 hours that we will never forget. Some were horrifying almost beyond belief. But there were other acts — small, but significant acts in all this ugliness that give us hope. I'm one who respects our police. They keep the peace. They face danger every day. They help kids. They don't make a lot of money — but they care about their communities and their country. Thousands of police officers and firefighters are risking their lives right now on the streets of L.A. and they deserve our support.

And then there are the people who have spent each night not in the streets, but in the churches of Los Angeles — praying that man's gentler instincts will be revealed in the hearts of people driven by hate.

And finally, there were the citizens who showed great personal danger, helped the victims of violence — regardless of race.

Among the many stories I've seen and heard about these past few days, one sticks in my mind — the story of one savagely beaten white truck driver — alive tonight because four strangers, four Black strangers, came to his aid. Two were men who had been watching television and saw the beating as it was happening, and came out into the street to help. Another was a woman on her way home from work — and the fourth, a young man whose name we may never know. . . . The injured driver was able to get behind the wheel of his truck and tried to drive away. But his eyes were swollen shut. The woman asked him if he could see. He answered, no. She said, "Well, then I will be your eyes."

Together, those four people braved the mob and drove that truck driver to the hospital. He's alive today — only because they stepped in to help.

. . .

We must understand that no one in Los Angeles or any other city has rendered a verdict on America. If we are to remain the most vibrant and hopeful nation on Earth we must allow our diversity to bring us together, not drive us apart. This must be the rallying cry of good and decent people.

the dog rather than watch MTV. The print media, from the mainstream dailies to the alternative weeklies, do cover a broader spectrum than television, but they still reproduce a similar hierarchy of legitimation. Unlike television, however, the radical or alternative press rarely uses discourse that appeals to the structures of taste of those lower in the social hierarchy: they lack the populist tone of an Oprah Winfrey, and rarely, as do MTV and the music press, allow rappers to speak directly of their material conditions. Communal voices of the

Chapter 4

Blackstream Knowledge: Genocide

The logical conclusion to racism is genocide.
Martin Luther King, cited by Zears Miles on Black Liberation Radio

Genocide is a difficult concept for whites to come to terms with, and consequently the word rarely appears in mainstream media. But out of the mainstream, particularly in Black media, it is used with disturbing frequency. There is, for instance, among some African Americans, a "counterknowledge" that AIDS was intentionally engineered within the government biowarfare research program, and that it has been deliberately introduced into Africa and Black America as a covert form of population control, or genocide.

AIDS is not one of the media events around which this book is organized, but it has been one of the hottest media topics of the 1980s and 1990s. Its direct connection with condoms, sexual practices, and homosexuality ensured that it was never far below the surface of the "family values" debate, and its connection with intravenous drug use brings race into the story by linking it with the drug war. But its mainstream meanings have been circulated largely through the discourses of medicine and sexual morality. Whereas it is often presented in the white media as a "gay disease," it is less commonly characterized as a Black one. Yet that is how many African Americans see it. Black Liberation Radio, for instance, frequently reminds its listeners that, globally, more than 80 percent of those dying with AIDS are Black—and that hardly any of them are homosexual or intravenous drug users.

Polls taken in 1990 showed that approximately one-third of African Americans considered there might be some truth to the belief that AIDS had been deliberately created by white scientists to infect Black people, and that 64 percent believed that it might well be true that the government was deliberately encouraging drug use among their people.[1] Producing such a counterknowledge involves, among other processes, recovering facts, events, and bits of information the dominant knowledge has repressed or dismissed as insignificant. Other bits of information in a counterknowledge may once have been part of official knowledge, but have been disarticulated from it and rearticulated into a counter way of knowing, where their significance is quite different. Black Liberation Radio carries the voices of many of these "knowledge gangsters," who are expert at stealing information from white systems of knowl-   191

192 edge and rearticulating it into a Black one. Counterknowledge must be socially and politically motivated: recovering repressed information, disarticulating and rearticulating events, and producing a comprehensive and coherent counterknowledge involves hard labor, and hard labor always requires strong motivation. In writing this chapter, I have tried to treat this Black counterknowledge in a way that respects its credibility. I have tried to analyze the struggle to produce it, and to provide glimpses of its immediate uses within the particular formation of Black America within which it circulates.

This Black knowledge of AIDS-as-genocide is linked with a wider political discourse that advocates Afrocentricity and separatism as the best, if not the only possible, solution to the all-pervasiveness of white racism. The argument derives from the recognition that white power has been so effectively insidious in colonizing all aspects of African American life, from identity to the economy, that the only hope for a degree of Black self-determination by which African Americans may control the immediate conditions of their lives lies in cutting as many links as possible with white America. This would require not only a self-sufficient Black economy and a self-determined Black identity, but also Black-controlled education and health systems. Such a political program is, of course, highly controversial among African Americans, many of whom believe that the most effective struggles are those directed at deracializing the social order rather than setting up a Black parallel one. For most of the contributors to Black Liberation Radio, however, the existing social order is so deeply white that separation from it appears to be the only route along which African Americans can make some progress toward self-determination. Mbanna Kantako argues that the key to self-determination is the control over knowledge, so he devotes much of his radio time to producing and circulating counterknowledges of the white social order and the way it insinuates its power into Black consciousness, Black bodies, and Black everyday life. But the politics of a counterknowledge are not confined to the immediate social conditions of its production and circulation: when circulated more widely in society, counterknowledge can provide a deconstructive jolt to what Foucault calls "official knowledge," and thus question the means by which that status is maintained.

It is possible that some readers will want to reject the Black counterknowledge that I trace. I would ask those who do to read two texts—that of the counterknowledge and, alongside it, that of their own disbelief. I would ask them, then, to question how much of the difference between these two texts can be traced back to the different histories and social conditions of their producers, and to note the strategies by which their disbelief is validated and the Black counterknowledge is discredited. Later I shall analyze some white media dismissals of this counterknowledge, and a comparison of the two may be instructive. Finally, I would ask such readers not to extend their disbelief in the counterknowledge itself into a refusal to recognize the significance for all of us that a sizable fraction of African Americans do believe that white power is capable of deliberately manufacturing the AIDS virus as an ethnic weapon by which to maintain its supremacy.

I start, then, with a brief sketch of some features of both Black social conditions and a Black counterhistory that together provide both the motivation to produce a counterknowledge and the ground where it is rooted. The three previous chapters have shown some of the wide variety of ways by which African Americans are oppressed and white supremacy maintained. I have traced their workings in the economic and legal systems, in the media, politics, and the police, and finally, or perhaps originally, in the white imagination. Articulating these individual recodings of racism together constitutes the power system of nonracist racism. In some Black knowledges, however, they add up to more than white supremacy: each individual instance of recoded racism can be understood as a more or less effective deployment of the strategy of genocide. There are countless events and facts in the lives of African Americans that can be articulated into a counterknowledge; the report of the 21st Century Commission on African American Males brings together some of them:

> Black males have the lowest life expectancy of any group in the United States. Their unemployment rate is more than twice that of white males; even Black men with college degrees are three times more likely to be unemployed than their white counterparts. About one in four Black men between the ages of twenty and twenty-nine is behind bars. Blacks receive longer prison sentences than whites who have committed the same crimes.
>
> Suicide is the third leading cause of death for young Black males. Since 1960, suicide rates for young Black males have nearly tripled, and doubled for Black females. While suicide among whites increases with age, it is a peculiarly youthful phenomenon among Blacks.
>
> Many Black males die prematurely from twelve major preventable diseases.
>
> Nearly one-third of all Black families in America live below the poverty line. Half of all Black children are born in poverty and will spend all of their youth growing up in poor families.[2]

The report might have extended its account of the economic assault on Blacks to include the following facts. The economic assault on Blacks means that currently Black income is 60 percent that of whites, that the net worth of an African American (i.e., assets less liabilities) is one-tenth that of a white, and that not only is the poverty rate of Blacks three times that of whites but poor Blacks are poorer than poor whites. Nearly half of Black children (45 percent) live below the poverty line, whereas only 16 percent of white children do. The pattern continues even among college-educated Blacks, whose salaries are about three-fourths of those of their white counterparts and only a few dollars

194 above those of whites whose education stopped at high school. In times of both boom and recession, the unemployment rate of Blacks is double that of whites, and, since 1980, the difference has been steadily increasing.[3]

The Black family is being consistently undermined and weakened. AFDC regulations work to keep the Black man out of the family, in order that his wife or partner and children may qualify for welfare. The shortage of jobs, combined with the fact that most of the available ones pay below minimum wage, decreases the number of Black marriages by reducing the number of men who can act as breadwinners. The fact that more than 60 percent of African American children will grow up in single-parent families and will thus be more likely to live in poverty, suffer malnutrition and ill health, and die sooner is the result not of Black immorality but of white economic strategy. In 1991 in Los Angeles, the median household net worth for Anglos was $31,904; for non-Anglos, $1,353.

The pattern continues in the realm of health, upon which the rest of this chapter will focus. The flow of illegal drugs into Black communities not only increases the flow of Black men into white prisons but also weakens the health and earning power of those who remain. What African Americans call "environmental racism" continues the attack on Black health: three out of five African Americans (and Latino/as) live in communities that contain uncontrolled toxic waste sites, and a 1987 study found that the racial composition of the neighborhood was the single most influential factor in locating toxic waste dumps. Five out of the six Manhattan bus depots are in Harlem; these are blamed by residents for the high rate of respiratory ailments and tuberculosis among the local children.[4] Tobacco and alcohol companies flood Black neighborhoods with billboards for their legal drugs, and in South-Central Los Angeles before the uprisings the only stores of which there was no shortage were ones selling liquor.

In isolation, or articulated differently, any one of these facts might not constitute evidence of genocide; articulated together, however, they provide evidence of a systematic assault on the Black body, both the Black individual body and the Black social body. The weaker the body, the sooner it will die. Historical facts, when articulated together in a similarly Black way, also contribute to this Black knowledge.

Black Liberation Radio rewrites white history as assiduously as it deconstructs white media. For Mbanna Kantako, a strong Black knowledge is the necessary basis of freedom, and he dedicates his life to countering the knowledge (which he calls "lies") by which whites keep his people submissive and to recovering Black truths that whites suppress. One such truth is that medical science has consistently destroyed Black bodies to improve the health of whites. Typical bits of information that his "knowledge gangsters" circulate to produce this truth include the following:

Fragment 1:

As the slave ship's cargoes were auctioned off, their damaged goods, too battered or sick for productive work in the plantations, were sold for about a dollar apiece to businessmen who kept them alive until hospitals needed their bodies for research. They were then killed carefully, often by being strapped to a chair and bled to death through a cut in the foot. Their bodies were sold and turned into white profit—economic and scientific.

Fragment 2:

When Nat Turner, the leader of a slave rebellion, was captured he was sick, injured, and dying. His white captors offered him food on condition that he sign away his body to them, to do with it what they would after his death.

Fragment 3:

In 1932 the U.S. Public Health Service recruited 400 Black men suffering from syphilis in Tuskegee, Alabama, charted the course of the disease through their bodies for forty years, and denied them treatment for the whole period. At least 254 died as a result of their infection. None of the men knew they were taking part in an experiment; they were told that they were being given medical treatment.

Fragment 4:

Between 1880 and 1910, a Black man, Sam McKeever, lived in Washington, D.C. He earned his living in the daytime picking up old rags in a pushcart for resale. At night, he caught and killed other Blacks and sold their bodies to local hospitals.

Fragment 5:

The South Carolina Medical College advertised in the *Charleston Mercury* in the 1830s: "Some advantages of a peculiar character are connected with this institution, which it may be proper to point out. No place in the United States offers as great opportunities for the acquisition of anatomical knowledge. Subjects being obtained from among the colored population in sufficient numbers for every purpose, and proper dissections carried on without offending any individuals in the community!"

In one articulation, these bits of information may add up to the simple and probably obvious truth that whites turn Blacks into a body of knowledge as profitably as into a body of labor: the slave was as valuable on the dissecting table as on the plantation. But no truth is ever complete in itself and no mean-

196   ing is ever fixed, so as more facts are entered into the system, the meanings of those already in it are modified, and so is the truth they produce.

Zears Miles is among the most relentless of Mbanna Kantako's knowledge gangsters, and he consistently brings back valuable booty. A favorite target of his raids is U.S. scientific and military policy, particularly where they come together in the Chemical and Biological Warfare Department. Adding these bits of information to the medical ones already in the counterknowledge system changes the whole picture. Zears Miles tells how his interest in germ warfare was aroused when he heard a shortwave radio program broadcast on the Armed Forces Radio and Television Service in November 1970. The program was called *Ethnic Weapons*, and Zears Miles explains to his listeners, "and you have to understand that when white people talk about ethnic weapons they mean diseases which other people can contract but they cannot." He quotes a military scientist speaking on the program:

> One of the basic strategies of war is to destroy members of certain nations or ethnic groups while sparing other populations, so it would be necessary to create chemical or biological agents that limit their efforts to targeted groups. Southeast Asians, for example, have a different genetic composition than do Caucasians. It is therefore possible that these people are susceptible to diseases Westerners are not, and we know that is true. . . .
>
> Blood types that we call A, B, O, and Rh appear in different frequencies among different types of people; for example, blood type B almost never occurs in American Indians but accounts for almost 40 percent of certain populations in Southeast Asia.[5]

In 1970, of course, the Vietnam War was in full swing, and the Korean one still alive in the U.S. memory, so Southeast Asians were an obvious target for ethnic weapons research. Other information gangsters, though, bring the target closer home: Jack Felder, for instance, an African American biochemist who has worked in U.S. germ warfare laboratories, tells of attempts to produce a melanin-sensitive gas that would bind to Black skin but not to white.[6] Another article that is frequently referred to in this Black knowledge appeared in 1970 in *Military Review*, an official journal of the U.S. Army Command General Staff College, at Fort Leavenworth, Kansas. Written by Professor Carl Larson, it, too, is called "Ethnic Weapons" and talks of "the possibility of great innate differences in vulnerability to chemical agents between different populations." The *Christian Science Monitor* considers this article to be one of the few pieces of hard evidence that military strategists are seriously interested in the idea of an ethnic weapon, and it refers unequivocally to military research that has revealed physiological differences between races:

> These genetic differences have not escaped the notice of the

Pentagon. Documents indicate that over the last three decades, the Defense Department has either conducted or funded research on diseases and disorders that occur more frequently among American blacks and American Indians.[7]

As he reads this extract over the air, Zears Miles reminds listeners of the anxiety that the Black Panthers, the Nation of Islam, and the American Indian Movement aroused in white America in the late 1960s. He goes on to string together more bits of information purloined from various government sources:

Fragment 6:

Zears Miles: In 1942 Secretary of State Stimson suggested to President Roosevelt hiding the Germ Warfare Advisory Group in the New Deal Welfare Agency called the Federal Security Agency that oversaw the Public Health Service. . . . Now we all recall the Tuskegee experiment that started in 1932 and went to 1972 under the Public Health Service . . . now you have the Chemical and Biological Warfare Department and the Public Health Service sharing the same budget.

Fragment 7:

Zears Miles (reading from the 1970 *Congressional Record*, House Bill 15090 Part V, p. 129, a record of a meeting on Tuesday, July 1, 1969): Dr. George McArthur of the Chemical and Biological Warfare Department of the Pentagon is recorded as saying, "Within a period of 5-10 years it would be possible to produce a synthetic biological agent, an agent that does not naturally exist and for which no natural immunity could have been acquired. . . . A research program to explore the feasibility of this could be completed in approximately 5 years at a total cost of $10 million."[8]

Fragment 8:

Zears Miles (reading from the World Health Organization *Bulletin* 47 [1972]: 215-438, recommendation 3): "An attempt should be made to ascertain whether viruses can in fact exercise selective effects upon immune functions, that is to say by suppressing 7-S versus 19-S antibodies or by affecting T-cell functions as opposed to B-cell functions." (Later, he calls this "an engineering specification for AIDS.")[9]

Fragment 9:

Zears Miles (summarizing a paper, "OKT-4 Epitome Deficiency in Significant Proportions of the Black Population," *Archive Pathological Laboratory America* 110 [August 1986]): The AIDS virus is basically a T-cell destroyer. . . . Now this is the very thing that they found out in our genetic makeup that is different in us than white people, because our T-cell counts, at least those of us who have a low T-cell count, are ten times lower than those of the average white person.

. . . Another effect of this [genetic difference] is that the tests for the AIDS virus are in fact insensitive to Black people's genetic makeup."[10]

Fragment 10:

Zears Miles (summarizing a paper titled "Surveillance for AIDS in a Central African City, Kinsasha, Zaire," *Journal of the American Medical Association* 255 [January 20, 1985]): Table II gives the possible means of exposure to the AIDS virus of 144 men with AIDS: the highest number of the possible means of exposure is one category, okay, and for 154 women the largest number, 82, was under the same category: the category is "Medical Injection." And the next highest category, the next largest means of contracting the virus, 32 for men, 41 for women is "Hospitalization." . . . In the full list of means of infection, neither homosexuality nor intravenous drug use occur.[11]

Fragment 11:

ZEARS MILES: A front-page article in the London *Times* on May 11, 1987, headlined "Small Pox Vaccine Triggered AIDS Virus," second paragraph "The World Health Organization . . . " is that familiar?

MBANNA KANTAKO: Who?!

ZEARS MILES: The World Health Organization. You will recall I read last time I was on how they had an engineering specification drawn up for the AIDS virus, remember that?

MBANNA KANTAKO: Yes sir!

ZEARS MILES: The paragraph in the London *Times* says the same organization, the World Health Organization, which "masterminded a thirteen-year campaign, is studying new scientific evidence suggesting that immunization with the smallpox vaccine *vaccinia* awakens the unsuspected dormant human immunodefense virus infection, HIV. An adviser to WHO who disclosed the problem told the *Times*, 'I thought it was just coincidence, until we studied the latest findings about the reaction which can be caused by *vaccinia*. Now I believe the smallpox vaccination theory is the explanation of the explosion of AIDS in Africa.' " Now, over in the second column:

"The World Health Organization information indicated that the AIDS league table of Central Africa matches the concentration of vaccinations, the largest spread of HIV infection coincides with the most intense immunization programs, with the number of people immunized being as follows: Zaire — 36,878,000" (that is 100 percent of the population), "Zambia — 19,060,000 injected" (100 percent of the population) . . .

MBANNA KANTAKO: We're talking about all Africa now . . .

ZEARS MILES: Exactly, "Tanzania — 14,972,000" (75 percent of the population) . . .

MBANNA KANTAKO: Brother, brother, is what you're saying to us, according to these devils writing themselves, that if you want to find out where the most number of AIDS cases will be, find out where they've given the most vaccinations?

ZEARS MILES: Exactly . . .

MBANNA KANTAKO: Oh man, oh man.

ZEARS MILES: . . . the smallpox vaccine, the WHO's eradication campaign, and we have mentioned that it was the World Health Organization that submitted to laboratories around this country an engineering specification to make the AIDS virus.

Later in the discussion, Zears Miles quotes again from the *Times* article: "Brazil, the only South American country covered in the eradication campaign, has the highest incidence of AIDS in that region," and reminds Kantako that Brazil and the United States have the largest Black populations of any non-African countries.[12]

These Black suspicions may be confirmed by attitudes like Dr. David Heymann's; he is the head of the WHO's Global Programme on AIDS, and he refused to discuss the possibility that AIDS was introduced into Africa by a vaccine: "The origin of the AIDS virus is of no importance to science today," he told journalist Tom Curtis. "Any speculation on how it arose is of no importance."[13]

Fragment 12:

On another program, Bryan Harris provides another piece of the puzzle. He asks rhetorically, "How did the AIDS organism previously regarded by scientists to be weak, slow, and vulnerable begin to behave like a type capable of creating a plague?" In answer, he reads from *Science News*, June 15, 1985, the headline of an article: "A Vaccine for All Seasons: Genetic Engineering Is Remodeling the

Smallpox Vaccine." From the article he quotes, *"Vaccinia* is a large and rather complex virus: it has an impressive capacity for carrying excess baggage," and comments, "which means that this virus cannot only carry its own—which you can inject into people, but this virus can hold other viruses, and can carry other diseases which you can inject whatever else they put in it, like AIDS, you know. . . . A reason why they use this *vaccinia*, they say *vaccinia* can be kept alive as a freeze-dried preparation that can be shipped to all parts of the world in the absence of refrigeration. So they don't even have to refrigerate it, send it all over the world, you know, and not worry about it dying or going bad or anything."[14]

Fragment 13:

ZEARS MILES: In another report the World Health Organization has estimated that there will be 75 million Africans dead of AIDS because of these vaccines by the year 1995.

MBANNA KANTAKO: Eighty-seven percent of people on the planet that have AIDS are Black.

ZEARS MILES: Exactly.

MBANNA KANTAKO: When they show you the TV programs they're always showing these white people, you know . . .

ZEARS MILES: Exactly.

MBANNA KANTAKO: . . . because that's part of their game . . .

ZEARS MILES: . . . that's part of the image they're trying to paint . . .

MBANNA KANTAKO: They're reversing, just like the crack thing, when they want to talk about cocaine they show young black men, yet 80 percent of those addicted, according to the Senate Foreign Relations Committee Report, April 1989, 80 percent are white that are addicted . . .

ZEARS MILES: Exactly.

MBANNA KANTAKO: So they just flip it around.

. . .

MBANNA KANTAKO: Let me just interrupt you for a moment, brother, for the brothers and sisters here it's 9:25 on Monday evening, if you notice a high concentration of pigs in the neighborhood, they're apparently going to create a disturbance, so that you'll stop listening to Brother Zears, they're alleging that someone was trying to shoot at them so they're crawling all over the neighborhood as an attempt to create a diversion.

Fragment 14:

ZEARS MILES: The base constituents of the AIDS virus are largely that of the visno virus of sheep, a pathogenic lymptovirus, and basic leucemia virus of cattle.

MBANNA KANTAKO: Break it down here, what you're saying brother is that it is actually nothing but a cow and sheep disease brought off in us.

ZEARS MILES: Yes, and actually to get these cow and sheep diseases which do not normally cross species to human beings they took them, spliced them together through a recombinant DNA or gene-splicing technology and then grew them in a human cell culture called the "HeLa-cell," which is short for Henrietta Lack, who was a Black woman who died of cervical cancer in 1953 out of Chicago, kept her tumor alive and now it's the standard medium for virus and bacteriological development in laboratories. So the AIDS virus itself was actually grown in a Black woman's cell culture being kept alive since 1953.

MBANNA KANTAKO: And you know who they made it for.

ZEARS MILES: That's who they made it for.

I may have overemphasized the fragmentedness of each bit of purloined information: on Black Liberation Radio these are explicitly articulated together in the knowledge that AIDS is genocidal. The word is not easily applied by whites to their own actions in regard to the Black people of the world, though there is a reluctant and limited acceptance among whites that the history of white relations with American Indians has been genocidal. But the word is widely used among a significant proportion of African Americans; it appears frequently on Black Liberation Radio, on WLIB in Harlem, and in the Black press. An article in *Essence* titled "AIDS: Is It Genocide?" is only one further example of many.[15]

In his book *AIDS: United States Germ Warfare at Its Best* and on Black Liberation Radio, Jack Felder identifies Fort Detrick, in Frederick, Maryland, as the place where AIDS was made. In 1971, under orders from President Nixon, the U.S. Army Biological and Chemical Warfare Unit, the National Cancer Institute, and the army's DNA and genetic engineering programs were all coordinated and placed at Fort Detrick. The NCI laboratories specialize in retroviral research and are credited with both discovering the way to keep T-cells alive long enough for infecting viruses to be cultured within them and isolating the AIDS virus. Jack

202   Felder has no doubt that it was these laboratories that manufactured the AIDS virus for the U.S. army germ warfare program. Bryan Harris, in his detailed account of the origins of AIDS (which was presented over three ninety-minute programs on Black Liberation Radio)[16] also concludes that all the signs point back to Fort Detrick as the place where AIDS was manufactured.

Such information fits well with the bits purloined by Zears Miles. Thrown all together, they look something like this:

1. The Biological and Chemical Warfare Department has a research program for an "ethnic weapon."

2. Blacks tend to have lower T-cell counts than whites.

3. The AIDS virus is not natural, but was developed in a laboratory, relies on T-cell deficiency, and can be carried by vaccines.

4. The government laboratories in Fort Detrick have worked on T-cells and AIDS; they are housed with the Biological and Chemical Warfare Department.

5. The WHO is associated with both the development of the virus and its dissemination throughout Africa.

6. The WHO, like the PHS in the Tuskegee experiment, is a white medical organization operating in the nonwhite world.

The knowledge at work here is an oppositional knowledge, partly because it recovers the genocide that white knowledge represses, and also because writing and disseminating it counters the process by which this genocide is repressed from white knowledge. The process of gathering it is an antagonistic one; Zears Miles constantly recounts the difficulty he has in getting this information, and will often gloss on his victories with such comments as "the ancestors must have been working because . . ." Conversely, when the "raid" is an easy one, he will comment on the ineptitude of whites, who appear not to realize the strategic values of the information he obtained so readily. Mbanna Kantako often reads this phenomenon somewhat differently: for him whites are so arrogant in their power that they see little need to hide its oppression under benignity and have little fear that it can be turned against them. "In your face, man," is a common expression of his when he meets naked power that one would expect to be decently covered up.

The normality is that whites guard knowledge that is strategically useful and prevent it getting into the wrong hands and being turned against them. So when Mbanna Kantako calls the police incursion into the John Hay Homes an attempt to stop Zears Miles's information reaching the residents, he is fitting it neatly into the normal pattern of white power. Dr. Barbara Justice gives another example.[17] She is a Black physician who works with AIDS victims in New York and broadcasts regularly on WLIB in Harlem and occasionally on Black Liberation Radio. She tells of how the white conservative medical professional does everything it can to silence her argument that the treatment of AIDS must recognize its racial dimension, must recognize that statistically it is an African disease above all else: both worldwide and in Harlem it is the number-one killer of Blacks. She argues that the accepted (white) treatments using AZT and interferon produce side effects that are as damaging as the disease; she also gives details of an African treatment developed in Kenya, called Kemron, and claims that the few Black patients she has been able to send over there have responded far better than to white treatment, so much better indeed that no one who was treated while the virus was in its asymptomatic stage has yet developed full-blown AIDS. Not surprisingly, African American media actively promote information about Kemron. The *New York Amsterdam News* devoted a front-page story to it, and Gary Byrd on radio WLIB in Harlem spent six hours discussing it.[18] But, Barbara Justice tells Mbanna Kantako, the white medical establishment constantly attempts to suppress the knowledge of this African treatment. She calls herself a "warrior queen" who is fighting for her people, and tells how vulnerable and lonely she felt until the Nation of Islam came to her support. This sense of vulnerability was not a product of her imagination: her house has been broken into and her records rifled. As a scientist, she has to use official medical discourse, but she still concludes that AIDS is genocidal, if not in origin then certainly in the way it is handled.

In his book, and on the radio, Jack Felder tells of the odd events surrounding Dr. Robert Strecker, a scientist who concluded that the AIDS virus could not be a freak of nature, but had to have been manufactured for a specific purpose. Two people who were helping him disseminate this information died under unexplained circumstances — his brother, Ted, an attorney, was shot, and State Representative Douglas Huff, of Chicago, was found dead in his home. Felder concludes, "It seems like there are some forces out there that don't want the message to get out that AIDS was man made."[19] Felder is convinced that the 75 million Africans predicted to die of AIDS before 1995 are evidence of a deliberate policy to depopulate Africa and the U.S. ghettos. He fears that the immunization clinics in Black neighborhoods are working in the United States in exactly the same way as the WHO did in Africa, and argues that their absence from white neighborhoods is part of the same pattern.

Another part of this pattern is the introduction of AIDS into the gay population. Indeed, both Jack Felder and Zears Miles consider that the infection of gay men in Manhattan and San Francisco was part of the same biowarfare research program that introduced AIDS into the worldwide African community. Felder follows Dr. Alan Cantwell, a white gay biochemist, in identifying Dr. Wolf Szmuness, a professor of epidemiology at Columbia Medical School,

204 as the central player in the scheme.[20] With the support of the U.S. Centers for Disease Control and the National Institutes of Health, Szmuness began a trial of the hepatitis B vaccine on homosexual men in Manhattan in November 1978. The men had to be young, healthy, and promiscuous. After screening the blood of 10,000, he selected 1,083 for the trial. By the spring of 1979 the first cases of AIDS in the world were reported—all in this sample. Felder claims that every one of these men has now died from AIDS. Cantwell points out that we do not know the actual death rate, because the National Institutes of Health will not release the information. He agrees, however, that the death rate is high, and that any who may still be alive are doomed. The second field trial of the vaccine was held in March 1980 in San Francisco, Los Angeles, Denver, St. Louis, and Chicago. The first case of AIDS in San Francisco was diagnosed in the fall of 1980, and within the next six months, AIDS was officially recognized as an epidemic. Szmuness also died in what Felder calls "funny circumstances" soon after the gay men in the first trial group began to die of AIDS.[21]

Felder is convinced that the vaccine was laced with the AIDS virus, and that Dr. Szmuness was an unwitting pawn:

> The vials containing the experimental hepatitis vaccine were
> produced and sealed in a US government supervised laboratory. The
> vaccine experiment was a dangerous game, and this one particularly
> so. The men in the experiment who would receive the three
> injections were from a segment of society that was the most hated
> and despised group in America.[22]

Vaccines keep entering the story. On another program on Black Liberation Radio, Bryan Harris tells of a Black worker in a vaccine laboratory in California who inadvertently transposed the addresses on two parcels of the "same" vaccine: the one that had been designated for a Black clinic was sent to a white one, and vice versa.[23] His account of the laboratory's desperate scramble to retrieve the parcels and readdress them becomes yet another "telling fragment" in his Black knowledge. This sort of oppositional knowledge depends upon a proliferation of "telling" details whose interconnections are not traced because the tellingness of each detail reverberates with the others and finally tells what is already known—in this case, genocide. These telling details are where more abstract knowledge is given flesh and blood and made part of lived experience. Keith Brown, a Harlem resident (see below), came to believe that AIDS was genocide because the details that his brother died of it and another relative had been part of the Tuskegee experiment "told" him the truth. It is through such telling details that the individual body is linked to the social body, for in them Black knowledge is, literally, embodied.

This Black knowledge is used in self-defense. It warns African Americans to be very wary of the white medical system. Dr. Barbara Justice, for instance, ad-

vises Black patients to seek out doctors who understand them both as individuals and as Black; Mbanna Kantako warns Black mothers to take afterbirths
home to prevent their being used in research hostile to Blacks and to prevent
their genetic makeup being stored as identifying information about their children; and Dr. Jack Felder argues that African Americans will be safe only when
they have developed their own health system. If some whites, with their widespread belief in the benevolence of medicine, should be tempted to dismiss this
Black mistrust as the product of a paranoid conspiracy theory, they might listen
to Dr. John Heller, the director of the Department of Venereal Diseases at the
Public Health Service from 1943 to 1948. Of the men in the Tuskegee study, he
said, "The men's status did not warrant ethical debate. They were subjects, not
patients: clinical material, not sick people."[24]

This Black knowledge of white genocidal strategy is not confined to the details of its application but also encompasses its motivation. Black Liberation Radio reminds its listeners frequently that whites are the global minority, only 7
percent of its population, yet they control the majority of its wealth and its resources. One U.S. government document frequently referred to in this context
is *Global 2000*, a report prepared by the Carter administration on the world's
population, resources, and environment. In most articulations the attempt to
balance population with resources appears benign and responsible, particularly when nations suffering from the imbalance adopt it as their own policy.
But when population control is shown to be part of a white policy directed at
nonwhite nations whose natural resources are needed by the West, it can appear very differently:

> MBANNA KANTAKO: Brothers and sisters, in *Global 2000* what the
> Devil said is, look, for us to continue to get the resources of
> the earth the way we get them—no charge, we take
> them—we need to make sure there aren't enough people to
> pose any opposition by the year 2000. Now, they were saying
> that by the year 2000 there would be something like 6.3 billion
> people on earth and what they said was, in order for us to stay
> in control we might need to kill 2.4 billion of them. But there is
> something more that we need to add to this whole thing here,
> now they're saying that there might be 10.2 billion people on
> earth by the year 2000, and if they stick with the percentage,
> you know, they're talking about wiping off almost 5 billion
> people.

> JACK FELDER: Possibly . . . these people are serious, man.

> MBANNA KANTAKO: Another thing about it, what they might have to
> do to do it—wipe out about 2 million different species of
> plants and animals, which will cause, you know, the temper-
> ature of the planet to rise which will cause flooding, it might

wipe out the planet, but they were that bent on wiping billions out that they didn't care.[25]

Kantako and Jack Felder have just spoken of the 75 million Africans expected to die of AIDS before the year 2000, and continue by reminding listeners of the almost successful genocide of American Indians and Australian Aboriginals and the total genocide of native Tasmanians.

Global 2000 has become a cardinal document in this Black knowledge of genocide. Zears Miles calls it "the death sentence for Black people on this planet."[26] and, in support brings back other stolen fragments of knowledge to Black Liberation Radio:

Fragment 15:

ZEARS MILES (reading from *Policy Planning Study* 23, February 1948, labeled "Top Secret" and written by George Kinnon, a State Department planner): "We have about 50 percent of the world's wealth but only 6.3 percent of its population. In this situation we cannot fail to be the object of envy and resentment. Our real task in the coming period is to devise a pattern of relationships which will permit us to maintain this position of disparity. To do so we will have to dispense with all sentimentality and daydreaming, and our attention will have to be concentrated everywhere on our immediate national objectives. We need not deceive ourselves that we can afford today the luxury of altruism and world benefaction. We should cease to talk about vague and unreal objectives such as"— now, pick up on this—"human rights, the raising of the living standard, and democratization. The day is not far off when we are going to have to deal in straight power concepts, and the less we are hampered by idealistic slogans, the better."

MBANNA KANTAKO : Oh man, they don't care about no stuff like human rights, no sir.[27]

Fragment 16:

ZEARS MILES (reading from National Security Memorandum 200, October 1974, written by Henry Kissinger and titled "De-Population of Third World States"): "Reduction of the population in those states"—that is, the third world and the so-called developing countries—"is a matter of vital U.S. national security. The U.S. economy will require large and increasing amounts of material from abroad, especially from less developed countries. That fact gives the U.S. enhanced interest in the political, economic, and social stability of the supplying countries. Whenever a lessening of population can increase the prospects of such stability, population policy becomes relevant to the resources, supplies, and economic interests of the U.S."

MBANNA KANTAKO: In plain simple language he's saying that in order for us to take the minerals from these people we've got to ensure that there aren't never enough of them to fight us back.

ZEARS MILES: Exactly.[28]

These information guerrillas raid national as well as international policy documents. *Global 2000* is frequently associated on Black Liberation Radio with the "King Alfred Plan." According to Zears Miles, the King Alfred Plan was developed during the Johnson administration in 1960-64 by the National Security Council. In response to the signs of increasing Black unrest and militancy in the civil rights movement, it proposed, in Zears Miles's words, "to exterminate every Black man, woman, and child in the U.S. during a national emergency which the government would call." He quotes a National Security Council memorandum:

"It is expected, therefore, that when these objectives are denied the minority"—that's us, the Black people—"racial war must be considered inevitable. When that emergency comes we must expect the total involvement of all 22 million members of the minority, men, women, and children. Once the project is launched, its goal is to terminate" [Zears Miles repeats the word, slowly rolling it off his tongue] "to terminate once and for all, the minority threat to the whole of American society, and indeed, the free world."[29]

He catches further glimpses of this necessarily well-hidden plan as it surfaces later, one of which takes the form of a list drawn up in 1969 of the military bases to which African Americans would be taken. The nation had been divided into eleven regions, each with bases converted into concentration camps. He reads a long sample of the list over the air. The information on each base includes its area in square miles, its latitude and longitude, its distance from the nearest major metropolitan area, and the recommended road route to it. The list is "ratified by the Provost Marshall of the 5th Army, who is in charge of the 300th Air Police POW Command, provided by Executive Order 11490, October 19, 1969."[30] His Springfield listeners are, he tells them, in the Great Lakes Region, and their local concentration camp is at Fort McCoy in Wisconsin.

The next time the plan surfaces is 1982. In that year, Zears Miles tells his listeners, Lieutenant Colonel Oliver North amended it to include Latinos within its provisions, and to add the provision to fund, arm, and train "survivalist" groups to aid the military in its execution. "Survivalist groups," Zears Miles explains, are the neo-Nazi, Klan-type groups that are particularly com-

208 mon in Tennessee, Texas, Missouri, and California. The amendments were signed into law by Reagan in 1984, and became known as Rex 84. The government document to which he refers is National Security Executive Directive 52, April 6, 1984, under FEMA (the Federal Emergency Management Agency).

Zears Miles refers to an article in the *Miami Herald* of July 5, 1987, headlined "Reagan Advisors Ran Secret Government," which claims that Lieutenant Colonel North, before his involvement in Irangate and the Contra arms sales, helped draw up a plan to suspend the Constitution in the event of a national crisis such as "nuclear war, violent and widespread internal dissent, or national opposition to a U.S. military invasion abroad."[31] From 1982 to 1984 North was a member of the NSC assigned to FEMA to assist it in revising its plans for dealing with nuclear war or insurrection. What interests Zears Miles is the "Brinkerhoff memo." John Brinkerhoff was responsible for FEMA's national preparedness programs, and the *Miami Herald* summarizes his memo:

> The scenario outlined in the Brinkerhoff memo resembled somewhat a paper Guiffrida [the head of FEMA] had written in 1970 at the Army War College in Carlisle, Pa., in which he advocated martial law in case of a national uprising by black militants. The paper also advocated the roundup and transfer to "assembly centers or relocation camps" of at least 21 million "American Negroes."[32]

With information like this ringing in his ears, Mbanna Kantako warns his listeners of the empty buses the police brought to the John Hay Homes during the rebellion after the verdicts in the trial of the police accused of beating Rodney King, and shares his suspicion that the 12,000 arrests of Blacks and Latinos in L.A. might be a training exercise to prepare police, troops, and the National Guard for "the real thing."

The years around 1970 are frequently identified as the time when these totalitarian policies were formulated. The totalitarian tendency that is always present on the right wing of the United States (see below) is exacerbated by fear, and at that time the U.S. power bloc was deeply frightened. Zears Miles reminds Black Liberation Radio's listeners that the U.S. government felt threatened from a number of directions—the Vietnam War was not going well, white youths were rebelling against their parents' generation, and Black power, the Black Panthers, and the American Indian Movement were threatening racial war. Alan Cantwell also points to this period: the Stonewall riots in 1968, in which New York gays protested homophobic police brutality, were a dramatic sign of the rise of the gay pride and gay liberation movements that continued throughout the 1970s and culminated in the election of Harvey Milk to the San Francisco Board of Supervisors in 1977, the first man to win major public office on a gay ticket. Of course, this provoked a homophobic backlash, which Pat Buchanan is continuing into the 1990s, that in 1978 resulted in Milk's assassination by another member of the board. Cantwell reminds us that 1978 was also the year of the Manhattan hepatitis B trials, and by 1980 AIDS was epidemic in the gay population. The anxiety of the U.S. power bloc around 1970 provides one reason at least why that should be the period when references to its ethnic weapon research program appear, and when the King Alfred Plan was kept in full readiness.

The King Alfred Plan applies the thinking behind *Global 2000* to a national context; in the "Cress Theory," Dr. Frances Cress Welsing raises her sights higher even than *Global 2000* and offers Black people the most overarching, and very Afrocentric, explanation of all for the relentlessness of the Caucasian drive toward supremacy.[33] In it she argues that human life began in Africa and so the original humans were Black. By a process similar to albinism, however, some were born with a melanin deficiency, so they had to migrate northward to avoid the heat of the African sun. The melanin-deficient, or white, people are both in the minority and genetically inferior, for their abnormal whiteness is carried by a recessive gene. Consequently, the white minority can survive only by promoting genetic purity through prohibiting interracial breeding, particularly by its females. If it did not, the laws of genetics would mean that its distinctive whiteness would disappear and the race would become extinct. In albinism, pigment deficiency goes along with a reduction of sexual performance and muscular development of the male. The male albino, therefore, is a "feminized" male, and, by extension, the white is a feminized Black.

According to the Cress theory, the global white supremacist movement is driven by these three interrelated factors: white genetic inferiority, the reduced masculinity of white males, and white status as a global minority. The drive to dominate other races originates in the need to overcompensate for these deficiencies. Cress Welsing uses her theory to explain, for instance, why the gun is a white invention that not only has enabled whites to conquer numerically and physically superior races but is also a phallic symbol—it compensates for numerical and sexual inferiority simultaneously. Her theory explains, too, why white power has historically focused upon Black men, for the male carrying a dominant gene is a greater genetic threat than the female. Cress Welsing would find it all too predictable that Stacey Koon should have feared a "Mandingo" encounter between Rodney King and Melanie Singer, and Kantako's "war correspondent" applies her theory well when he explains that whites are frightened when they see us "armed with our penises" (see *Sidebar: Black Liberation Radio and the Beating*, p. 147).

This Black counterknowledge is explicitly political. It knows that the truth that it seeks is not merely lying overlooked and unnoticed by whites, but that it has been deliberately hidden and that hiding it is another application of the same racial power that grew the AIDS virus in a Black woman's body and hid it in the smallpox vaccine. Understanding any fact involves articulating it with others. The fact that white hospitals use Black bodies for their research may, for example, be articulated into medical science, in which case the Blackness of the

210   bodies does not mean anything; on the other hand, it may be articulated with the Chemical and Biological Warfare Department's search for an "ethnic weapon," in which case it means everything. Similarly, one of the "facts" of the Tuskegee experiment was the observation that Blacks appeared to be more susceptible than whites to syphilis, and white medicine was interested in discovering if this was the case and, if so, why. Articulated with and in the humane discourse of medicine this would mean that such a physiological difference could be used to devise treatments for Blacks and thus minimize the health difference between them and whites. But this fact means something very different when it is articulated with the facts that health differences between whites and Blacks are increasing, not decreasing (the differential spread of AIDS is joined, for example, by differences in life expectancy, infant mortality, and hypertension). If this articulation is then linked to the Chemical and Biological Warfare Department's long-standing efforts to produce an ethnic weapon, it fits neatly into the counterknowledge of AIDS-as-genocide.

When different social formations (such as African and European Americans, or different class formations within African America) believe in different truths, the main reason for the difference is less likely to lie in the evidence that is "out there" in the social world than in the differences of social experience, the different telling details that make up the texture of everyday life. These details tell the truths we have to live with. Keith Brown, the Harlem resident mentioned above whose family has suffered from both AIDS and Tuskegee, explained to the *New York Times* that these experiences told him the truth that he had to live with:

> Because of who's being devastated the most, and growing up in the
> US and knowing the history of slavery and racism in this country,
> you can't be black and not feel that AIDS is some kind of plot to hit
> undesirable minority populations. I hope I don't sound too radical,
> because I'm not. I don't want to believe that AIDS is some kind of
> Government plot. But I guess I do. I do believe it.[34]

The article carrying Keith Brown's words was occasioned by a telephone poll in New York City showing that about one-third of African Americans believed that the genocide theory of AIDS was, or might possibly be, true; nine out of ten whites, however, disbelieved it. The writer, Jason deParle, interviewed more than fifty Black public officials, doctors and health workers, professors and students, and "average citizens" who all confirmed that "serious discussion of racial plots is now common, springing from an American soil rich in racial distrust."

One of those interviewed was Dr. Alvin Poussaint, the Harvard psychiatrist who was a consultant for *The Cosby Show*, who said, "The theory that AIDS and drugs are part of a white conspiracy to commit genocide or to damage the black community—that's popping up in questions more and more. . . . I've heard it

discussed among middle class Blacks who would not in any sense be considered militant. It's spinning around out there."

One of the middle-class Blacks who, presumably, would not in any sense be considered militant is Bill Cosby himself. On CNN's *Showbiz Today* he said, "AIDS was started by human beings to get after certain people they didn't like."[35] He later told the *National Enquirer*, "I believe AIDS was man-made. The people who created AIDS didn't realize the holocaust they would cause."[36] Grace Jones also agrees that "AIDS was something planted—germ warfare that got out of hand."[37] Benetton, a clothing company using the advertising theme "the United Colors of Benetton," took an eight-page advertising supplement in the twenty-fifth anniversary edition of *Rolling Stone*; in it, in exchange for a donation of $50,000 to the United Negro College Fund Malcolm X Scholarship, Spike Lee wrote an opinion piece that included his belief:

> A lot of people will have to do a lot of explaining on AIDS one day. All of a sudden a disease appears out of nowhere that nobody has a cure for, and it's specifically targeted at gays and minorities (Hispanics and blacks). The mystery disease, yeah, about as mysterious as *genocide*.
>
> I'm convinced AIDS is a government engineered disease. They got one thing wrong. They never realized it couldn't just be contained to the groups it was intended to wipe out.[38]

If so many Black Americans from all walks of life acknowledge at least the possibility of a genocidal strategy, why do so few whites? Partly, for straight whites at least, the answer may lie in their lack of immediately "telling details" such as those that led Keith Brown to believe; another part of the answer may be traced to the media and the way they are used by Blacks and whites. None of the nationally famous African Americans who believe in AIDS-as-genocide was quoted in the *New York Times* or other "serious" news media, but were confined to entertainment or tabloid news; their opinions were marginalized by their media placement. The one *New York Times* article (cited above) that does pay serious attention to the Black belief in AIDS-as-genocide is quite untypical of the mainstream media. But even here its taken-for-granted basic assumption is that the belief is mistaken: never once does it consider the possibility that it might be true. Its discursive techniques constantly invite its white readers to distance themselves from this belief and from those who hold it. It achieves its version of "balance," for example, by quoting prestigious Blacks who reject the belief and only "average citizens" who hold it. Keith Brown is joined, for instance, by Mark Russell, 24, who says, following the economic reasoning of Sidney Wilhelm on Black Liberation Radio,

> I think it's a conspiracy because it's very strange that all the sudden this disease popped up out of nowhere and it hits populations that

the government considers undesirable. There's no more need for
black labor. . . . So, you know, this is one way of getting rid of us.

Mark Russell is discredited once by his youth and again by being labeled a
student of Professor Leonard Jeffries, who, to most whites, is an extremist, an
anti-Semite, and a reverse racist. If we substitute antiwoman for anti-Semite,
the same could be said for the white view of most rap artists, so one of them,
Kool Moe Dee, is allowed to say that AIDS is part of a clean up America campaign intended to hit target markets of homosexuals and racial minorities.
Identifying the source of a belief as Dr. Jeffries or a rap artist is a clear invitation
to most whites to oppose it.

The article invites whites, however, to agree with the arguments of the Black
university professors, Alvin Poussaint (Harvard) and Shelby Steele (California), that not only is AIDS-as-genocide a false knowledge, but that Blacks who
hold it damage themselves and their people; the counterknowledge, much to
the comfort of the (white and Black) dominant alliances, is thus doubly discredited. As if this were not enough, when the genocide theory is put in the journalist's own words it is colored with skeptical references to "conspiracy theory": "Talk of white conspiracy against blacks can take almost limitless forms"
or "In the case of AIDS, the talk of conspiracy has been fueled by the nature of
the disease itself: its mysterious origins and the eerie way it has seemed capable of singling out populations." Most straight whites do not have the social
experience of a Keith Brown to motivate them to read this sort of media skepticism skeptically.

The respected white media carry very little information about ethnic weapons or genocide. The London *Times* story on the rapid surge of AIDS through
Africa in the wake of the WHO's smallpox vaccination campaign is a rare exception in that it not only contained the information, but treated it as credible.
For the more radical and thus less respected *LA Weekly*, Jon Rappoport inves-
tigated why no major U.S. news organization had picked up the story: he
found that none of the major news agencies of AP, UPI, and Reuters in Washington, New York, and Boston would admit even to having heard of it.[39] The
Christian Science Monitor did publish a long and detailed supplement on the
U.S. biowarfare program, including the fact that part of it involved research
into ethnic weapons, but nowhere did it suggest that AIDS might be a product
of that program.[40] *Time* magazine, in a brief article, did, but it called the theory
"bizarre" and "far-fetched," and traced its origin to Soviet disinformation, as
clinching evidence of which it reproduced a *Pravda* cartoon showing a scientist
handing a vial of the AIDS virus to a grinning U.S. soldier.[41] Black paranoia,
rather than Soviet disinformation, was the favored explanation of a *New York
Times* editorial headlined "The AIDS 'Plot' against Blacks."[42] The quotation
marks around "plot" invited whites to disbelieve it, and to recognize it as an
alien, Black discourse almost as foreign as that of *Pravda*. The *New York Post*,

hardly one of the country's most respected organs, doubly discredited Bill Cosby's belief that AIDS was intentionally manufactured, once by dismissing it as yet another product of conspiracy theory, and again by calling it "inflammatory," a word that promotes white interests more explicitly and antagonistically even than usual.[43]

This is typical of the white media; on the rare occasions when they refer to the idea of genocide they put it, whether literally or metaphorically, into quotation marks. Identifying the foreignness of the discourse containing the concept not only is an invitation to disbelieve it, but implies that the problem for whites is the Black *belief* in genocide, not the possibility that the strategy might really exist. Jason deParle's article in the *New York Times* does contain some evidence that this Black belief is grounded—he cites, for instance, two statistical nuggets that are fairly widely known among whites, probably because they are often expressed so resonantly—that there are more Black men in prison than in college, and that the mortality rate in Harlem is higher than in Bangladesh. But he gives none of the telling details that encourage or motivate belief —just the reverse.

Drugs, particularly crack, are more widely understood as evidence of a government conspiracy against African Americans than AIDS: some 70 percent of African Americans believe that this is, or possibly could be, true. Again, the majority of whites, in this case 75 percent, disbelieve it. If AIDS and drugs are weapons in a genocidal strategy they are well-chosen ones, for white conservatives can readily argue that the damage they cause to minority populations (Blacks or gays) is self-inflicted; they can then locate the source of the problem in the behavior of the minority, with the consequence that its solution will absolve straight white conservatives from doing anything more than prescribing a good dose of "family values."

Like the knowledge gangsters of Black Liberation Radio, Dr. Alan Cantwell is convinced that AIDS was deliberately made at Fort Detrick for genocidal purposes. In his two books *AIDS and the Doctors of Death* and *Queer Blood* he gives a research scientist's account of how the virus could have been manufactured, and concludes that everything that science has discovered about it points to its unnatural origin.[44] As a physician, he can pick out further evidence that points to the Manhattan hepatitis B trials as the introduction of AIDS into human beings. One study that praises these trials concludes, "In those who received all three injections, 96% developed antibodies against the [hepatitis] virus. . . . These findings are of an order of magnitude that has never been equaled in any vaccine trial, either before or since."[45] The triumphant "success" of the trials is actually, Cantwell points out, an admission of their guilt: other studies have shown that the hepatitis B vaccine is not effective in immunodepressed people (i.e., those with AIDS). So, for the trials to have been as successful as they were, none of the men could have had AIDS *before* the experiment, and thus their infection must have been caused *by* it.

214   Though the focus of his books is on gay men as the primary genocidal target, Cantwell recognizes that their fate and that of Blacks are inextricable. He, too, is persuaded that the WHO vaccination campaign did for Africa what the hepatitis B vaccine did for gay America. One of the studies to which he refers was conducted in Uganda in 1986; it revealed not a single case of AIDS among fifty-three elderly people who had not been sexually active for five years, whereas the infection rate in the country as a whole was 15 percent. The researchers conclude, "The results presented here do not support previous suggestions that the virus might have originated in Uganda: on the contrary, if interpreted correctly, they indicate it arrived in the country only recently."[46] Cantwell uses this finding to argue against the theory that AIDS began in animals in Africa, probably in green monkeys, and then jumped species to humans. The "green monkey theory" was proposed in the early 1990s by a number of scientists, some of whom worked at Fort Detrick, and may well be a piece of disinformation as clever as anything the Soviets ever produced. It was immensely offensive to African Americans because it assumed sexual contact between Africans and monkeys; usually this assumption was implicit, but this was not always the case: some scientists proposed what Tom Curtis calls "the kinky-African-sex-theory" of a "bizarre sexual practice in which, to heighten sexual arousal, male and female members of tribes bordering the large lakes of Central Africa introduce monkey blood into their pubic areas, thighs and backs."[47] Even the more oblique versions of the theory would have had their effectiveness enhanced by their resonance with the white animalization and hypersexualization of Black people; they kept alive a history stretching back at least to 1781 and Thomas Jefferson's *Notes on the State of Virginia*. Here, one of the founding fathers described a hierarchy of beauty and sexual desire in which the lust of the Black man for the white woman was as natural as that which the Black woman aroused in the orangutan. Cantwell's research, however, argues too, that the theory that AIDS spread from Africa to the United States, instead of vice versa, cannot explain why a Black heterosexual disease in Africa (almost none of the millions of whites living there have contracted it) could have become a white homosexual disease in the United States. The disease, he concludes, can only have had dual, and almost simultaneous, origins, each aimed at a different population.

There are many Blacks and gays who recognize their mutual status as target, one defined by race and one by sexual orientation, much as Jews and gays were covictims of the Nazi extermination campaigns. But Cantwell is worried that too many U.S. gays are living in a state of denial, refusing to see the evidence in front of them. He fears they may be repeating the state of mind of German Jews in the early stages of the Holocaust, the possibility of which horrified them so much that they were unable to recognize it, and thus contributed to the ease with which the Nazis were able to operate. He sees evidence, too, that

the U.S. public in general, like that of the German Third Reich, is looking everywhere except the right place to find the cause of AIDS:

> The scientists blamed the green monkeys and African blacks; the
> public blamed the homosexual lifestyle; the gays blamed themselves;
> and the US government did as little as possible to stem the rising toll
> of gay AIDS deaths. During his first term of office as president,
> Ronald Reagan never once mentioned the word AIDS in public.[48]

We will never know "objectively" whether or not AIDS is part of a genocidal
strategy, for any evidence that might establish such a truth will be "lost," or,
should it survive, be strenuously denied. This case is extreme only in the de-
liberateness with which the means to one truth will have been repressed and
those to another promoted. Apart from this it differs little from normality, for
in the social world there are no facts that cannot be argued against or be contradicted by others. Absolute truth is unattainable, so we are constantly faced
with the need to decide what to treat as true. This requires a complex process
involving the selection of bits of evidence from "out there" and the articulation
of these bits with others into a mutually endorsing relationship without which
the truth can never be believable. The resulting knowledge of the "out there"
can be treated as true only if it meets the needs of the social position from which
the process is undertaken and that provides the motivation to engage in it. When
all these things come together, we treat evidence as factual—that is, we believe it.
The better that bits of evidence from "out there" fit together in a system of articulation that meets the needs of the "in here"—that is, the social formation
that produces it—the more likely it becomes that those bits will be moved along
the continuum from the possible through the probable to the true. There is a
point along this continuum of credibility at which knowledge becomes true in
its effects; that is, it can be made to work as though it were true.

When, however, it is difficult to fit the bits of evidence "out there" into an
articulation system "in here," it becomes simpler to disbelieve the evidence, or
to put it into an articulatory set of relations with which we are already comfortable. In the absence of motivation to do otherwise, we avoid discomfort and
effort, and most white heterosexuals have little motivation to make new, dis-
quieting, and difficult articulations among vaccination programs in Africa and
Manhattan, AIDS, and secret government research programs. A similar absence of motivation might lead some liberals, white and Black, gay and
straight, to articulate the bits of medical information and the ethnic weapons
program together, but to disarticulate them from the Tuskegee experiment,
Global 2000, the Kissinger memo, the ethnic weapons research program, and
the WHO's "engineering specification for AIDS"; their conclusion, then, might
be that AIDS was intentionally manufactured but unintentionally released.
These disarticulations might make the consequent knowledge of AIDS less dis-
ruptive to mainstream common sense, and that possibility alone raises the

216   question of whether the motivation to make those disarticulations might not
originate precisely in the common sense that they preserve. Radicals, however,
might construct a quite differently articulated knowledge, and might link to it
their suspicions that segments within the CIA and the Pentagon are constantly
formulating and executing covert policies such as Irangate without the knowledge of the U.S. people, the Congress, and possibly even the president. These
suspicions might motivate them to believe that AIDS may well be part of a covert genocidal strategy.

As I weighed the different bits of evidence in this chapter, I found myself
pondering which of two possible "wrong" beliefs would have the worse
effects—not to believe AIDS-as-genocide if it were true or to believe it if it were
not. And I wondered, too, if the answer might not be different for Blacks and
whites, for hetero- and homosexuals, for conservatives and progressives. How
do I, as a member of the safest group of all (monogamous, white, straight, non-
IV-drug-using, and living in a small midwestern town) weigh the Black conservative argument that the belief in AIDS-as-genocide increases African Americans' sense of themselves as victims and thus their helplessness against the
Black radical one that the knowledge arms Blacks in their fight against white
supremacy and that what makes them helpless is not knowing the weapons
deployed against them? When some Black doctors argue that their counterknowledge will warn African Americans against a white medical system that
history has shown to exploit rather than cure them, and others argue that it
weakens Black people's health by keeping them away from immunization programs and prevents their gaining from the few benefits that white society does
offer them, how should I make up my mind, and when I make it up, should I
confine my opinion to my fellow whites, or enter the debate in African America? But among all the uncertainties, one surety stands out: if AIDS is a genocidal strategy, widespread disbelief that this is so is necessary for its success.
That alone should motivate us to ask the question seriously. Whether or not we
ourselves believe it is not the point at issue: what matters is that many Americans do believe it, and that this counterknowledge is one way they have of
defending themselves against the racism and homophobia of the society whose
majority, for a wide variety of reasons, disbelieves it.[49]

≡ Chapter 5

Technostruggles

I n a country as diverse as the contemporary United States and as well
equipped with multiple forms of media, counterknowledges can never be
repressed entirely. They may be marginalized, submerged, and diverted,
but there are always traces that the motivated can find and recover. The problem lies in the motivation, or lack of it. It is comfortable and effortless to live in
a homogenized social formation from which all contradictions and abrasive
edges have been smoothed out. There are many reasons, none of them admi-
rable, for not enlarging our world of experience to include knowledges, possibly discomforting and disrupting, that come from the experiences of other social formations. This, of course, is a temptation for the dominant only;
subordinated ways of living and knowing must always carry the traces of domination, so the luxury of comfortable, uncontradictory complacency can never
be theirs. The complacency that flourishes in a self-protective comfort zone will
never motivate us to ask awkward questions about how power operates, and
the resulting silence is, of course, precisely what power requires.

The previous chapters have traced some of the main ways by which various
social formations have engaged in discursive struggles as we enter the final decade of the century. Discourse is now mediated and its struggles must therefore engage with the technology of mediation. But communication and information technology does not merely circulate discourse and make it available for
analysis, it also produces knowledge and applies power. In this final chapter, I
focus on communication technologies both as ways of engaging in discursive
struggles and, through their surveillance capability, as ways of producing a
particular form of social knowledge, and thus of exerting power. The power to
see while remaining unseen, the power to put others into discourse while remaining unspoken, is a particularly effective form of power. Struggles over
meaning have to be extended into struggles over seeing, for the power to
speak, the power to know, and the power to see are politically and technologically interconnected. Mediated discourse and technologized surveillance will
always be interrelated, not only because they share similar technologies, but,   217

218 more important, because unequal access to those technologies ensures their use in promoting similar power-bloc interests.

Discursive power has always been politically crucial, and media technologies have enhanced it, but not categorically changed it. The power to surveil, however, may be different; Foucault has shown how modern states have increasingly relied on surveillance to maintain themselves, and there is a case to be made here that new technologies have so far enhanced this power as to have changed it. The three videos upon which chapter 3 focuses were not only technologized into media events but were also where surveillance was exerted and contested. Because I believe that surveillance is rapidly becoming the most efficient form of power, the most totalitarian and the hardest to resist, I end this book by focusing on it.

Videotech

The Rodney King video was significant not just because its eighty-one seconds of electronic reality condensed four hundred years of racial history into the nation's experience of contemporary race relations, but also because, technologically, it operated at a crucial turning point in the flow of knowledge and visibility.

We live in a monitored society. In Liverpool, England, two youths abducted a two-year-old from a shopping mall. Video cameras in the mall watched and recorded their every move (as of every other shopper) and outside in the street more cameras recorded them (and all the other pedestrians). The videotapes played a vital role in helping police identify and catch the criminals. Thousands of other actions, interactions, and identities were also recorded by those cameras, a plethora of potential knowledge of people who did not know they were known. In Minneapolis, USA, the Mall of America uses 109 cameras to monitor its customers and staff: each of them can zoom in on an object as small as an ID card. David Guterson described in *Harper's* the giddy power he felt as he watched the bank of monitors in its security room.[1] Suddenly, a security guard noticed something of interest occurring in one of the parking lots, and zoomed in on a couple making love in their car: although their passion may have been all-consuming, they were not, so a guard was dispatched to put an end to such inappropriate behavior. Earlier, Guterson had himself been monitored, and had been chided by the mall's public relations officer, who had seen him talking to a garbage cleaner on one of the concourses. Not to be outdone by its famous mall, the city of Minneapolis plans to cover all its downtown streets with video monitoring to improve its traffic management. The cameras will see more than traffic jams.

Outside the Ronald Reagan Office Building in downtown Los Angeles, Mike Davis asked a homeless African American why he never went into the shopping mall that occupied the building's lower floors. The answer was predictable: he knew that cameras would instantly identify him as an inappropriate person in that precisely monitored place, and that security guards would rapidly escort him outside.[2] Gated and guarded neighborhoods throughout L.A.'s suburbs have video cameras at their entries. An African American professor told me how monitored he feels as he passes them, knowing that they see his Blackness and accord it special attention.

Information technology is highly political, but its politics are not directed by its technological features alone. It is, for instance, a technical feature of the surveillance camera that enables it to identify a person's race more clearly than his or her class or religion, but it is a racist society that transforms that information into knowledge. The video camera directs its gaze impartially on Black and white, the criminal and the law-abiding, the welcome and the unwelcome. But African Americans entering a Korean grocery store or an exclusive housing development know that the impartiality stops at the moment when the electronic signal is turned into knowledge; they know that they are seen differently from whites. Social differences that are embodied, such as those of race and gender, are the ones that are most efficiently monitored; because in today's public life racial difference is seen to pose a greater threat to the dominant order than gender difference, video works particularly effectively in the monitoring of race relations.

The video camera is efficient in the information-gathering phases of surveillance, but in storage and retrieval the computer is king. As its sophistication increases, so does our power to know each individual and to track his or her movements through the places and times of ordinary life. The economics of everyday life are where this power is most efficiently applied. Our social security numbers document how much money we earn, and where and how we earn it; they record our loans, mortgages, and pension plans. In the sphere of consumption, our credit card numbers are routinely used to track our purchases of goods and services, and how we move around the neighborhood and the country as we make them; the last four numbers of our zip codes document where we live and the demographics of our neighbors. All this knowledge is combined to produce a "consumer profile" that serves, in the domain of economics, as a social identity. If this surveillance is confined to the economic, its effects are unlikely to be worse than annoying (soliciting phone calls or junk mail) and may be helpful (catalogs matched to our tastes do save us trips to the mall).

A consumer profile, however, is only part of an individual's social identity; the same information technologies could readily supplement it with a "political profile," should one be needed. The magazines we subscribe to, the causes we donate to, the university courses we register for, the books we purchase and the ones we borrow from the library are all recorded, and recorded information is always potentially available. A Korean studying in the United States told me that agents of his government's secret police had warned him that his work

220   was becoming too radical; one of the means by which they had identified him as worthy of special monitoring was through his library loans. Such a profile of what goes on inside our heads can be enhanced by knowledge of where our bodies move. Many parking garages record the license plate numbers of every car that enters; some traffic lights are equipped with cameras to record those who run red lights; the City of London is planning to video-record every car entering it to improve its security against terrorists. In the United States, hydroponic gardening stores have been video-monitored by the DEA, and repeat customers have had their homes searched for marijuana plants. Any of our movements that the monitoring agency might consider abnormal could be fed into a political profile.

Norms are crucial to any surveillance system, for without them it cannot identify the abnormal. Norms are what enable it to decide what information should be turned into knowledge and what individuals need to be monitored. The massed information that is recorded about the majority may never be known in all its details, but it is still used to produce the norms that are necessary to identify the dissident and the dangerous. The power to produce and apply norms, as Foucault tells us, is a crucial social power. It is not hard to imagine circumstances in which political profiles of those who, by some standards, would be judged "not normal" could be as useful to government agencies as consumer profiles are to commercial ones.

The monitoring of the conforming white middle classes may not bear too heavily upon us, for it is our behavior that provides the norms against which others are evaluated. But the equivalent video tracking of African Americans or Latino/as oppresses them every time they enter a store or shopping mall, or visit a gated neighborhood. Such monitoring does not need to be technological: Joe Soto, for instance, has filed a civil rights lawsuit against the Utah Highway Patrol, claiming that he has been stopped repeatedly solely because he is a Latino driving a Cadillac. In Tinicum, Pennsylvania, just outside Philadelphia, Black motorists have filed a similar class action suit against the local police department,[3] and all Black motorists know the odds of their being pulled over increase if they drive through white suburbs (it is worth recalling here that the Rodney King incident began with a traffic stop). Ice-T's anger (see chapter 3) at being pulled out of his car and made to kiss the pavement because he is Black is not just individual, but communal; not just personal, but political. To be seen to be Black or Brown, in all but a few places in the United States, is to be seen to be out of place, beyond the norm that someone else has set, and thus to be subject to white power. In these conditions being seen is, in itself, oppressive.

In no suburb is whiteness more thoroughly normalized than in Simi Valley. As its mayor has said, "There is no question, in this community, that somebody out of the ordinary sticks out quickly. And people are very quick to report anything suspicious, very quick to call the police, and expect them to be there."[4] He has no need to specify that being "out of the ordinary" includes

being Black when his constituents are as effective deniers and recoders of racism as the Arkins:

> "We like living in a place with educated people, people who believe
> as we do," said Brian Arkin, " . . . but I don't believe skin color is a
> criteria [*sic*] . . . There's a black person up our street and we say 'Hi'
> like he's a normal person," Mr. Arkin continued. "This isn't about
> race, it's about whether you let your property run down." "Or
> whether you sell drugs out of your house," his wife, Valerie
> interjected.[5]

We can now enlarge on William Buckley's comment (see chapter 2): this cannot
be a racist society if we love Bill Cosby, appoint Clarence Thomas, and say
"Hi" to a Black man as though he were a normal person.

Video technology may not be essential—Simi Valley residents can spot
somebody out of the ordinary with their naked eyes—but it is efficient. It is
particularly effective in racial surveillance, because racial difference from the
white norm is so visible. Surveillance technology enhances the construction of
whiteness as the space from which the other is viewed, and its development is
so significant because it technologizes and thus extends a power application
that is already widespread. A new technology does not, of itself, determine
that it *will* be used or *how* it will. Similarly, technology may limit what can or
cannot be seen but it does not dictate the way it is watched. Technology may
determine what is shown, but society determines what is seen. The camera always shows racial difference, for instance; who sees it, however, is a function
of social factors. Fewer European than African Americans saw the race of Anita
Hill and of Bill Cosby, but all whites saw the Blackness of Willie Horton. A general principle emerges here. When social difference advances the interests of
the powerful it will be recognized by them; when, however, their interests are
promoted by alliances that cross the social difference at issue, it will be overlooked by them. When it serves the interests of power to "other" those whom
it monitors, the social differences between the seer and the seen will loom
large; when, however, the other is to be enrolled in a temporary alliance with
"us," the differences shrink into insignificance.

Part of the reason for the rapid extension of surveillance technology is the
perfect match between technology's ability to see racial difference and the need
of whiteness to monitor it. Whiteness always needs to see its difference from
the other, even when it suits its purposes to overlook or deny it, for, paradox-
ically, "color blindness" can be strategically effective only if it sees what it pretends not to. While denying that Clarence Thomas's race had anything to do
with his nomination, Bush used his "color blindness" to advance his reactionary white strategy. Less intentionally, liberal white viewers of *The Cosby Show*
and of the Thomas-Hill hearings could also be "blind" to racial difference when
it was in their interests to be so. Members of disempowered races, however,

222   cannot afford the luxury of color blindness, for their social survival depends upon racial awareness. They need to see racial difference constantly in order to defend themselves against the power inscibed in it, and consequently they are at times able to make tactical uses of the technology whose strategy is normally hostile to them. Black viewers of both *The Cosby Show* and the hearings, therefore, were constantly aware of the Blackness of the figures on the screen, and of their difference from the whiteness of most television. Similarly, in the Murphy Brown-Dan Quayle debate, video technology showed racial difference to everyone in the audience, but who was "blind" to it and who saw it was determined by social factors. Although the powerful have privileged access to technology, their access is not exclusive; although they exert powerful control over its social uses, their control is not total. Indeed, video technology often carries traces of the marginalized that verbal discourse represses more efficiently. Putting an event into any discourse always involves centering some elements and marginalizing or repressing others: because verbal language obeys no laws other than those that society has produced to organize it, putting an event into verbal discourse is a *purely* social process.

The camera, however, obeys the laws of optics and electronics as well as those of discourse. I do not wish to suggest that the laws of optics and electronics are objective and exist in nature only, for they are products of a particular scientific way of knowing: they have been "discovered" and elaborated in order to enhance our ability to increase our control over nature and to understand those of its resources that we can turn to our own advantage. The power of scientific knowledge and its instrumental technologies is inextricably part of the domination of the world's physical and social resources by European-derived nations. No knowledge system is nonpolitical. But because the laws of optics or of physics have a grounding in nature, their politics are less immediate than those of discourse, and work rather on the level of the macropolitics of global capitalism as a system than on the more immediate level of the political struggles within it.

The laws of discourse, however, are more immediately political than those of optics and electronics. The saying "The camera cannot lie" is inaccurate and out of date but not stupid, for it does point to key differences between words and photography in terms of the immediacy and totality of the social control that can be exerted over them. The fact that the optical camera is, in part, subject to the laws of nature does not mean that it inevitably tells the objective truth, but it does lend a sense of objectivity that carries an injunction to believe what it shows. The camera always tells us more than it needs to; a photograph always carries more information than is necessary to make its point. These bits of unnecessary information function to substantiate the "truth injunction" of the photograph, but they also, simultaneously, undercut it: they can remind us that the event being photographed, like any other, can always be put into discourse differently. They are the traces through which the repressed alternatives can be recovered, and their inevitability makes the camera much less efficient than verbal discourse in repressing the stories it does not wish us to know. The camera finds it much harder than verbal discourse to keep the traces of these discursive alternatives on its unregarded margins.

Electronic photography may appear even more "objective" than optical photography. When Roland Barthes wrote of the "photographic paradox" by which the camera appeared to produce "a message without a code," he was writing of optical photography.[6] In his account, the truth injunction of photography results from the laws of optics appearing to overpower those of semiotics or discourse, which, until the invention of the camera, were in total control of every message. The camera, however, limited the semiotic control over encoding the message to two points of human intervention in the process—the choice of angle, framing, focus, or film stock when the photograph is taken, and the darkroom processes as it is developed and printed. In low-tech electronic photography even these choices appear to be reduced, for the darkroom is eliminated, and the choices at the moment of shooting are reduced to those of framing, angle, and distance (in most home video cameras, at least, everything else is taken care of automatically).

But even processes as technological as those of video never operate outside of social determinants. The credibility of video depends upon the social domain of its use. In the domain of the low (low capital, low technology, low power), video has an authenticity that results from its user's lack of resources to intervene in its technology. When capital, technology, and power are high, however, the ability to intervene, technologically and socially, is enhanced. The videohigh of Rodney King was a product of capital, technology, and social power that lay beyond the reach of the videolow. Because technology requires capital, it is never equally distributed or apolitical. George Holliday owned a camera, but not a computer enhancer; he could produce and replay an electronic image, but could not slow it, reverse it, freeze it, or write upon it, and his videolow appeared so authentic to so many precisely because he could not. The enhanced clarity of the videohigh lost the authenticity of the low but gained the power to tell its own truth in its own domain of the courtroom and the jury room. And that domain was, in this case, the limit of its victory.

The time gap between the writing and the reading of the previous paragraph may well have made it out of date. The video "toaster" has already brought electronic manipulation of the image within the price range of many amateurs. And electronic manipulation leaves no trace of its operation. This has the legal profession worried, and many legal scholars would agree with Christine Guilshan when she writes, "Today . . . the veracity of photographic evidence is being radically challenged. Computer imaging techniques are rapidly emerging which call into question the belief that photographs are neutral records of reality."[7] When hooked up to a computer, the video camera provides not a photograph, but bits of visual information that can be undetectably enhanced, deleted, or rearranged—just like words. Guilshan's anxieties are those of the power bloc, not of the people: she is not concerned that powerful institutions such as the FBI or the media can manipulate images, for she has faith that their guidelines will prevent the ability being misused; what worries her is what might happen when the "average citizen" has this capability.

It remains to be seen whether technological development will reduce the sense of authenticity that low-tech video still carries. We might hope that it does not, for this authenticity of the videolow allows the weak one of their few opportunities to intervene effectively in the power of surveillance, and to reverse its flow. George Holliday was not alone in grasping it. In Saint Paul, a Hmong teenager, Billy Her, was arrested for assaulting the police. Two days later, a videotape anonymously mailed to the police department resulted in the arresting officer's suspension from duty, because it showed him striking Billy Her repeatedly but gave no evidence of Billy Her attacking the police.[8] On her national talk show, Oprah Winfrey screened an amateur videotape showing Texas police punching Chon Soto as he was trying to attend his hometown city council meeting, where he was signed up to speak.[9] His friends told Oprah that they had expected the city council meeting to be heated, that they had had problems at previous meetings, and so they had asked Raoul Vasquez to bring his video camera to this one. Viewers never learned what was so heatedly disputed, or why only nineteen members of the public were to be allowed to attend the meeting. The camera showed, however, that the police were white and the citizens were Latino, and its microphone caught Latino-accented voices raised in protest. The police claimed that Chon Soto was trying to force his way into the meeting; the camera showed that the only force involved was applied by the police. Chon Soto was hospitalized, and, after the video was played on local TV stations, the chief of police was suspended.

Video plays such an important role in our culture because in its low- and high-tech forms it spreads far up and down our social hierarchy. But videolow does not always oppose videohigh; indeed, often the two work complicitly. Network television has developed a whole genre of programs to incorporate videolow into its high-capital, high-tech system. Shows such as *I Witness Video* and *America's Funniest Home Videos* extend the reach of the high into the domain of the low, to turn it to a profit and to use its stories as they think best. Many of the *I Witness Videos* reproduce the forms of official news—people with video cameras are often present when disasters occur, whereas news crews typically arrive afterward. But like the Rodney King video, their lower-quality images, poor but closely involved vantage points, moments of loss of technical control (blurred focus, too-rapid pans, tilted or dropped cameras), and their reduced editing all serve to reveal the discursive control that official news exerts over the events it reports. Videolow shows that events can always be put into discourse differently from videohigh, and this enhances its sense of authenticity. Local news stations now solicit videolow from their viewers; they use their

viewers' ubiquity to extend their monitoring reach and intensify our system of
surveillance, to capture the immediate and the authentic, and to pull their
viewers into an alliance with the station. Some are also experimenting with reducing the official "news crew" to a single reporter with a camcorder to cut
costs, increase flexibility, and, they hope, gain a sense of authenticity.

Videolow is not only incorporable into the interests of the dominant, it often
intentionally serves them and extends their surveillance. The day *The Oprah
Winfrey Show* screened the videolow of the police roughing up Chon Soto it also
screened others that were shot in order to assist in the policing of our society.
A doctor who has mounted a video camera on his dashboard patrols the late-
night roads of Chicago looking for drunk drivers. We watched him find one,
follow it, videotaping all the time, and then call the police on his CB radio and
offer them his video as evidence. The *New York Times* tells of a civilian video
patrol in Methuen, Massachusetts, that tapes prostitutes and their clients as a
community effort to clean up their neighborhood.[10] The report on their activities claims that everywhere individuals are using video cameras to document
car thefts, drug deals, prostitution, and other unwelcome or illegal street activity. Gerald Arenberg, the director of the National Association of Chiefs of Police, told the reporter, "Ever since the Rodney King incident, anyone who has
a camcorder is using them." Matt Reskin, director of a national organization
that promotes community policing programs, agrees with police officers that
video is a useful amateur policing tool. *The Oprah Winfrey Show* gave further
examples, among them a video of a student party that got out of hand and van-
dalized a car, and, more to our point here, one showing the beating of Reginald
Denny from ground level as the news helicopter videoed it from on high. The
police used this videolow to help identify and arrest the suspects, and the cam-
eraman, who was Black, had to go into hiding because, as he said, "Threats
started to come through the neighborhood, and gang members showed up
looking for me." Although the politics of technology itself may be distant,
those of its uses are immediate.

The uses of videolow to extend disciplinary surveillance can be countered,
as we have seen, by those who turn the cameras back upon the surveillers.
Across the nation, "videoactivists" or "videoguerrillas" are using the technology, particularly in conjunction with local-access cable channels, for explicit social criticism. The police are central agents in the surveillance system, so they
are often the target of videoactivism. In Berkeley, California, for example, an
organization called Copwatch uses video cameras and human eyes to monitor
the police, particularly in their dealings with homeless people and African
Americans, in the belief that watching police behavior is the best way to prevent police brutality. The mainstream media can be as active surveillers as the
police, and in Rochester, New York, a video collective followed local TV news
crews, videoed them videoing events, talked to people they interviewed and to
those they chose not to, and, on the local-access channel, showed not only that

226 events could look very different but that the differences between high and low discourses were obviously political. The cops in Berkeley and the news crews in Rochester did all they could to prevent their actions being videoed.

A step higher up the technical, social, and institutional hierarchy is Paper Tiger Television, a video collective dedicated to criticizing the mainstream media, to providing alternate information, and to increasing popular skepticism about officially mediated knowledge. Longtime video activist Dee Dee Halleck describes the deliberately low-tech, low-budget style of Paper Tiger as it

> proudly flaunts the "cheap art" of its graphics and its production "values." Paper Tiger uses hand-painted backdrops for sets, hastily scribbled felt-tip credits, and transitions that make no attempt to disguise the technology. On-air dialogue with the control room is amplified. "Cue Herb, Daniel!" gets mixed into the overall sound track. The Paper Tiger aesthetic expanded from crayons and paints to include crude but inspired chroma key effects, such as Joan Braderman sliding down the Carrington banister in "Joan Does Dynasty" and John Walden's hugging of Ted Koppel in "From Woodstock to Tiennanmen Square." Many Paper Tiger programs that critique TV use simple TV effects in ways that expose mystified constructions in both television form and ideological content.[11]

Deep Dish Television has grown out of Paper Tiger; it brings satellite distribution to local video activists so that their work need not be limited to their local public-access channels. Of course, high-tech satellite time is high cost, and Deep Dish can afford only two hours a week, which means that much low-tech communication by mail and telephone is needed to supplement it, to ensure that local stations are ready to receive and tape its offerings. Perhaps the biggest success of Deep Dish occurred during the Gulf War, when the official media were harnessed so closely to the White House and the Pentagon that echoes of dissenting voices and views were almost entirely eliminated from the nation's screens. Deep Dish called for other video coverage and received hundreds of tapes from all over the country. It organized them into four half-hour programs and uplinked them to the satellite nine days before the war began. It is impossible to know the full extent of the program's reach, because Deep Dish has no full record of who receives its programs and encourages people to dub them and show them whenever and wherever they wish. But it is known that many public access and public television stations screened the programs, often repeatedly; more than a thousand copies were mailed out in less than a month. In Britain, Channel 4 edited the programs into a one-hour special, which it aired in prime time; in Japan, the programs served as a focal point for antiwar activism.

The better access one has to capital and to the institutional power that goes with it, the better use one can make of video technology. But video has low-tech and high-tech forms and thus contradictory uses. It can be used both to bring us knowledge and to know us, to give us access to one system of power-knowledge while subjecting us to another. It is an instrument of both communication and surveillance. It can be used by the power bloc to monitor the comings and goings of the people, but equally its cameras can be turned 180 social degrees, to show the doings of the power bloc to the people.

Video monitoring and video knowledge are directed upon the body, for it is there that power is made visible. The strategizing of social alliances, the intentions and internal lives of people, and the abstract lines of social power all lie beyond video's capabilities. Video knowledge is that of the application of power to the body; its terrain is that in which broad social interests appear in their embodied form. Policing the social body is a paradigmatic example, for the physical contact between police officer and the individual suspect-citizen-disorderly body is an event that is both significant and videoknowable. The police use video surveillance for their purposes, from identifying bank robbers to monitoring Mayor Marion Barry receiving drugs and sex in their setup; they used it to identify the suspects in the Reginald Denny beating, and then, in the initial court hearing, they covertly videotaped a suspect's friends who attended in order to identify yet more potential suspect criminals (they knew, evidently, that friends of suspects were also suspect, particularly if Black).

Armies of law enforcement agencies and security services use millions of video cameras to monitor the places and the people they are hired to protect. But video technology still allows, on occasion, those who are normally monitored to monitor the monitors. This technological engagement in the social struggle never takes place on equal terms. Opportunistic tactics are set against strategically deployed power; the handheld home video camera has a mobility that makes it a good guerrilla weapon, whereas carefully located surveillance cameras are typical of a powerful strategy that is well planned and highly efficient, but cumbersome.

Audiotech

Video is not the only technology that the weak can use in their daily struggles: voices must be heard as well as bodies seen. The audio technology of radio and telephone and the writing technology of fax, computer network, and photocopier all allow the socially weak access to systems of knowledge and its distribution that can be used to challenge the domains of the powerful and to defend those of the weak.

Black Liberation Radio reaches three or four square miles of Springfield, Illinois. Mbanna Kantako began it in the living room of his family's apartment in the John Hay Homes in 1986. That year was a year of personal and political reappraisal for Dwayne Readus (as Kantako was then called); he had been blinded by a police beating, and adjusting to life in the dark made him change

Mbanna Kantako. Photo by Ken Burnette, Springfield, Illinois.

his lifestyle from one centered on the pleasures of the body to one focused on the power of knowledge. His station is one of the low: low capital and low tech. Its equipment cost less than $600 and came from mall electronic stores and discount catalogs; its signal of one watt can travel two miles on a good day, a mile and a half on a normal one. Operating it requires technological know-how not much greater than that needed to run a home stereo system. The lowness of its capital and its technology limit its reach to the socially "low": because Springfield is so ghettoized, 75 percent of its African American citizens can receive Black Liberation Radio in their homes.

Typically, economic power carries racial discrimination. To qualify for an FCC license a radio station must move up the economic, technical, and social hierarchy: it must have a minimum wattage of 100, and, according to Sakolsky, start-up costs of such a station would be at least $50,000.[12] As a result, Black Liberation Radio remains illegal and low.

It is not just FCC regulations on the use of technology that work to restrict its use to the higher levels of the social order; federal law prohibits the sale of broadcast transmitters in this country. Mike Townsend, talking on the radio with Kantako, explains:

TOWNSEND: I don't know if people know that it's illegal here in the United
States to order the little equipment that you have to run the radio station with it assembled—it has to be sent to you in pieces so that you have to find some kind of an electrical whiz that can put it together for you, but the same company, here in the United States, can sell that same transmitter completely put together in any other country, but not to our own people in this country. Now what does that tell you?
KANTAKO: It's confusing . . . I mean . . .

TOWNSEND: They don't want the people here to be able to communicate with
one another.

KANTAKO: But you can buy an Uzi assembled!

TOWNSEND: Yeah.

Townsend's argument is valid, but he does overestimate the technical wizardry needed to operate a low-wattage radio station: Kantako has made a videotape showing how simple it is to wire the equipment together and to use it. The video has been widely distributed both nationally and internationally, much to his pleasure.

In 1989, the Springfield police reported Black Liberation Radio to the FCC (whom Kantako calls "the Thought Police"). Soon afterward, an FCC official and five police officers arrived at his door to close the station down. Kantako's case was heard first in the U.S. marshall's office and then in the local court; at neither hearing was he allowed a public attorney. He was fined $750, which he refused to pay (out of both principal and necessity), and he decided to go back on the air.

At the news conference on the reopening of Black Liberation Radio, Kantako explained:

It's a question of our rights to the airwaves. When the
communication laws were designed we were still sitting in the back
of the bus. We weren't privy to the initiation of those laws, the
writing of those laws, but we are the victims of the enforcement of
those laws, and this is our challenge today, to our right to have
access to the airwaves, to conduct our communications with our
people in the manner that we see fit.

When he finished speaking he drove to the U.S. marshall's office to be arrested, but his surrender was rejected (incidentally, the officials were more concerned with blacking out the video camera he brought to record the event than they were with arresting him). His aim was to make the repression of Black speech more widely known. He points out that only 2 percent of the licensed radio stations in the United States are owned by nonwhites, and of the four thousand unlicensed ones, most are used for commercial purposes. Black Liberation Radio was singled out for closure because it dared to give voice to the Black experience of the police and because, in Kantako's words, "we are showing people that they do have some control over their own lives, and that nothing is hopeless." He stresses the community base of the station and that he is not an individual star but a voice of his community:

I love to brag about the community I live in. This is a group of
people that society has no need for and instead of laying down and
dying, they've said "Let's arm ourselves with the necessary

knowledge and we'll make a place for ourselves." If those in charge
of the money won't include us, then we'll include ourselves![14]

Kantako sees clearly that the power of money and the power of knowledge
are intertwined and that both oppress his people. He argues forcefully that
white capitalism stays in control by "purposely making the people ignorant."
So on the radio he mixes interviews with Black intellectual activists with readings from Black history, culture, and freedom struggles. As in any Black community, music plays a central role here, but not just any Black music; he plays
only that whose words contribute to Black liberation. As Kantako says, "Our
music format is designed to resurrect the mind, not keep the mind asleep."[15]
For Kantako, knowledge is a weapon and low-tech radio arms his people.

The local police had reported Kantako to the FCC because in 1989 he began
to challenge directly their operations against his people. He acquired a scanner
so that he could listen to police radio instructions and conversations between
the dispatchers at headquarters and the cars on the road. (Hostile though he is
to the Springfield police, he gives no indication that their conversations are as
routinely racist as those of the LAPD analyzed by the Christopher Commission.) Sometimes he broadcasts police radio live; at other times he warns his
listeners when they are planning to enter the projects. When they enter his territory to make an arrest, raid a suspected drug house, or quell a disturbance, he
is often there with his tape recorder, monitoring events as they happen so that
he can broadcast them on his return home.

Black Liberation Radio played a key role in what Kantako calls "the rebellion" in the John Hay Homes after the verdicts were returned in the first Rodney King beating trial. Not only did it relay live telephone conversations with
Black brothers and sisters in cities all around the country, but Kantako also
kept his listeners informed of the police movements being planned against
them. The station's newsletter claims that, as a result,

> some observers have called the "micro-rebellion" at Springfield the
> most sophisticated in the nation. Scores of young people outflanked
> the cops in two nights of skirmishes and destroyed the police
> substation and the housing security office. Amazingly, no one was
> injured and no apartments were attacked.[16]

Besides monitoring police radio and behavior, Mbanna Kantako also encourages local residents to tell their own experiences of police brutality on the
air. An incident in 1990 demonstrates the effectiveness of both forms of monitoring. Two reporters from Chicago (one was Latino, the race of the other un-
recorded) held an on-air discussion of police brutality. When they left Kantako's apartment, they found police officers waiting for them. They were ordered
to spread their legs and place their hands against the wall. For twenty minutes
the police tried to provoke them into "doing something stupid." But then, quietly, neighborhood residents began to appear on the streets; they gathered

around and just *looked*. This inverted "neighborhood watch," which saw the police as the threatening intruder, was effective; the police stopped their harassment and allowed the reporters to leave. The "watch" had been produced by the radio. Kantako had broadcast an account of the incident as it was relayed to him by his wife from her vantage point on their porch.[17] If Simi Valley residents can watch somebody "out of the ordinary," so can those of the John Hay Homes, even if they have to invert the norms of the ordinary to do so.

There are other Black rebel radio stations around the country, and Kantako does whatever he can to increase their numbers, for he is convinced that his race's survival depends upon its being able to produce and disseminate its own knowledge of what it means to be Black in a white-dominated nation and world. He has coined the term "the micro radio movement" to describe what he hopes will eventuate: a nationwide network of community stations like Black Liberation Radio that determinedly remain low-tech and low-cost because that is the only way for impoverished, deprived, unwanted communities to retain control over the communication of their own culture and knowledge. It may well prove that such networks of disobedience are the most effective forms of resistance in a social order whose discipline is as dependent upon knowledge and power as is ours.

Despite Kantako's fears that any upward move in cost or technology will result in the mainstreaming of Black radio and the loss of its communal links, larger African American communities, such as those in New York and Washington, D.C., can and do support licensed, legal radio stations that show no signs of having sold out. The communities have enough Black businesses to provide advertising support, and the radio stations are important instruments in the attempt to build a Black economy that is as independent as possible of white capitalism.[18] Gary Byrd, for example, who broadcasts daily from Harlem on WLIB, circulates voices that are as radical as any heard on Black Liberation Radio.

Kantako uses the telephone to bring Black intellectual activists from all over the country to his listeners in Springfield. Most of these speakers also broadcast frequently on the larger licensed Black stations, and many use photocopiers and desk-top publishing to produce information packages and books that they mail to listeners who want written as well as oral information. Jack Felder's self-published book on AIDS, for example, is a low-tech bricolage of typescript and print that includes photocopied pages from biochemistry books, often with his handwritten annotations on them. The use of comparatively cheap and thus relatively widely available information technology is enabling Black activists around the nation to develop a communication system, and thus a knowledge system, that is under their control and largely unnoticed by whites.

There is a powerful undercurrent of defensive separatism in this knowledge system. White media are seen to operate against African American interests al-

232   most all of the time, and attempts to find space within them for more, and less mediated, Black voices have met with limited success. Consequently, many believe that a separate Black communication system is as necessary as a separate Black economic system.

We whites have much to learn from this Black knowledge, not least because it gives us significantly different understandings of ourselves and our actions. It also shows us that the knowledge that is most easily and widely available to us is not the only one, and it may motivate us to make the effort to scan the information repertoire more widely. If, to return to our river metaphor, we need to pay attention to deep undercurrents that surface only rarely, we must also remember that there are other rivers that never join the mainstream at all, but that carry water in different directions. They may be harder to get to, but the effort is usually worthwhile. Flows that are outside the mainstream are still a vital part of the cultural environment.

This Black communication system also illustrates the principle that what is most visibly and widely disseminated is not always the most significant: the less visible, lower-tech communication by radio, telephone, fax, and conversation is a culture of process, not one of products. It leaves its traces in people's understanding and memories, not in texts—it is thus harder for the cultural analyst to study, but in the local conditions where it operates, it may have greater influence than the mass-mediated, high-tech, high-capital media, whose high visibility may lead us to overestimate their effectivity.

A media and lobbying consultant (cited below) claims that the right wing has easy access to 1,200 radio stations across the country, and that, consequently, conservative voices can be widely heard. Rush Limbaugh's widely syndicated talk show is but one example. In this context, the importance of Black talk radio and the very few progressive local community stations cannot be overemphasized. But we must also question why commercial radio, with its comparatively cheap technology, does not better reflect the diversity of U.S. society. Part of the reason, of course, is economic. The local chambers of commerce whose members advertise on commercial radio are preponderantly white and conservative. Radio's audiences may be more diverse than its advertisers, but in negotiating between the two, station programmers are drawn to push the point of contact rightward. Other radio stations are funded by Christian groups who have a long tradition of raising money by moral imperative and promises of paradise to come. More progressive or radical interests, however, are unlikely to benefit from either of these revenue sources, so they require noncommercial and non-Christian-funded media if they are to be heard publicly.

This leaves them with National Public Radio and its state-by-state equivalents, and this public radio does admit progressive voices to its airwaves in a way that commercial radio rarely does. But, and this is a big but, to gain access these voices have, in general, to speak in middle-class, educated accents. There are no left-wing Limbaughs on NPR. NPR relies upon both public funding and corporate and individual sponsorship. Individuals with the money and inclination to sponsor their local public radio stations will come disproportionately from the middle and upper-middle classes, and a relatively high-brow tone is required if corporate or commercial sponsorship is to pay off in image building. The United States can cope comfortably with progressive or even radical ideas when they are circulated in well-modulated voices around the higher levels of its social order, but becomes anxious when they reach its deprived and oppressed. The communication and cultural needs of the upper echelons are relatively well satisfied, and the likes of Rush Limbaugh meet the needs of the lower right. But in the lower-left-wing corner there is a huge hole. The same gap appears in print media: there are plenty of radical and progressive publications for the well educated, but few with popular appeal. White liberals and democrats have much to learn from the radical populism of Black Liberation Radio and WLIB.

Lower down the technological scale from radio, the telephone has also played an influential role in the currents of meaning and countermeanings that this book is attempting to chart. Many of the contributors to *Court of Appeal* tell how they used the telephone in circulating the meanings of the Clarence Thomas-Anita Hill hearings. Both Black and white women, and some men, spent hours on the phone with friends, weighing the contradictory evidence, working out their responses, and connecting with others to join in producing their communal culture. Rosemary Bray was typical:

> That week in October, my phone rang nonstop. Friends called to talk about their stories of sexual harassment, their memories of vengeful, jealous women who lie, their theories of self-loathing black men who act out their hostility toward black women while lusting after white women. My sister, Linda, called from Chicago the night before the vote, then used her conference call feature to add her good friend to the line, with whom she had been arguing for an hour already. "I already know you believe her," Linda announced to me. "I just want to hear you tell me why."
>
> The buses and trains and elevators were filled with debates and theories of conspiracy. Hill set up Thomas to bring a black man down. Thomas was a man; what man didn't talk about his prowess? In a Harlem restaurant where I sat with a cup of tea and the papers that Saturday, the entire kitchen staff was in an uproar. The cook, an African woman, wanted to know why Hill waited ten years to bring it up. The waitress, an African-American woman, said she couldn't tell what to think.[19]

Like the phoning fans of *Designing Women*, all the contributors to *Court of Appeal* who wrote of telephone culture were women. It was women, too, who

234 swamped Arlen Specter's office with thousands of phone calls protesting his treatment of Anita Hill: he had to employ forty additional staff to deal with them, and at their peak they so overloaded the telephone system that it collapsed.[20]

On television, the breaks between the sessions of the hearings were filled with TV pundits engaging in similar discursive activity, but most of them were "experts," or they would not have been granted TV access; most were white, professional, and from the upper classes. Their attempts to help viewers and to speak for them were limited by their social experience; actual viewers were far more diversified and we must assume, with some supporting evidence, that their discussions took account of more divergent social interests and thus brought more voices into the dialogue. Telephones were not only used to recirculate the hearings as they continued—a week later the *Designing Women* episode generated even more calls.

I have no evidence that the Murphy Brown-Dan Quayle debate produced the number or intensity of telephone conversations that the hearings did. Equally, I have no evidence that it did not. But, as we saw in chapter 1, the Zoë Baird affair was an occasion in which telephones were vital in redirecting one of the currents in that debate and turning it into a counterflow or eddy: 471,641 people, mainly women, telephoned Congress to complain of her actions, and uncounted thousands more called radio talk shows.[21]

There is an irony here, for the Democrat victory grew to a considerable extent from the sense of distance and distrust between the people and politicians. The Clinton campaign promised to change not only policy, but also the relationship between politicians, particularly the president, and the people. Bill Clinton was to be the accessible president, in sharp contrast to Bush's perceived aloofness from those Americans who think of themselves as ordinary. In the campaign, information technology was put forward as a means of overcoming this distance. Ross Perot promised "electronic town meetings" in which television and the telephone would combine to involve the people in the political process. Jerry Brown, one of the Democratic primary candidates, opened a 1-800 number for people to telephone their ideas and anxieties directly to his campaign office. When Clinton moved into the White House, he quickly equipped its switchboard with a voice mail system that invited callers to press appropriate buttons to support or oppose his economic program, his deficit reduction plan, his government spending cuts, and the fairness of the tax burden on upper-income taxpayers. In each case the options ranged from "about right" to "not far enough" to "too far." If they survived this electronic "conversation" and its easily computable results, callers were then given the opportunity to talk with a live operator. On each day of the first month of his presidency, some 64,000 Americans called the service and another 700 used their computers to send him their opinions by electronic mail. The low-tech telephone was intended to build popular alliances for the Democrats between the low and the high, and to signal a political difference between them and the Republicans. This low-tech populism then turned and, in the Zoë Baird affair, delivered the new Clinton administration its first public defeat. The lower the tech, the less control the power bloc has over its uses.

Of course, in a town like Washington, the voices of the people will not be allowed to speak freely without attempts to incorporate them. Though most commentators agree that the calls about Zoë Baird were spontaneous, the ones generated by the "gays in the military" issue were not. Similarly, during the Clarence Thomas hearings, Pat Robertson's staff organized telephone banks to generate thousands of calls to senators urging his confirmation. Popular practices are always subject to incorporation, and telephone calls are no exception. Throughout Washington now there are lobbying or consulting groups that organize and stimulate such "spontaneous" and "authentic" call-ins for large profits. One organization (called, coincidentally, the Clinton Group) uses computer data banks to identify people with specific leanings. They are then phoned by another computer that switches them, if they answer, to a live operator who explains the issue being lobbied and offers to transfer the call, for no charge, to the White House or local member of Congress. This technique can generate a wave of sincere, unscripted, and apparently spontaneous calls. Nancy Clack, the company's vice president, explains that most of its work is for Democratic causes: "Progressive groups have got to do this," she argues. "The right wing doesn't. They've got the Christian Broadcasting Network, The 700 Club and about 1200 radio outlets. All they do is print a press release and read it on the air."[22]

Bonner and Associates is a company that offers similar services to commercial clients. When working for the automobile industry's campaign against national fuel economy standards, for example, it organized waves of calls from handicapped people to their local politicians protesting that the smaller cars the standards would require would be harder for them to get into. Mr. Bonner, the company's owner, is explicit that this new populism is directly related to the change of administration in Washington: "The golden age of grass roots has arrived," he trumpeted to the *New York Times*. "In the past a lot of businesses wouldn't go to the grass roots because they thought they could contain their problems in DC, either by lobbying or by George Bush vetoing anti-business legislation. Well, that veto isn't there anymore."[23] Bonner was once a political aide to a Republican senator, but any political anxieties this "golden age" of grassroots populism may occasion him personally are presumably sweetened by fees like the $3 million a trade association paid him for one month's work. For some, the age is golden indeed.

Hierarchies and Multiplicities

I am using a hierarchical model of inequalities to explore the social distribution of economic, technological, and discursive resources, and to point to the inevitability that culture within such a society is a culture of contestation and struggle. Even within the high-tech, high-capital domain of network television, the social hierarchy is reproduced in miniature. Talk shows such as Oprah Winfrey's afford some opportunity for voices from the lower echelons to be heard in public, but these shows are not prime time. Highly profitable though they are, they are relegated to the whims of syndication and the vagaries of local markets. Similar voices will, in times of crisis, be heard on network news, but in briefer sound bites and in a more tightly controlled discursive framework. One of the pleasures of talk shows is that discursive control of the emcee is always in danger of being lost. The shows typically balance on the fine line between the normal and the abnormal or deviant. Setting norms and defining their boundaries is one of the key disciplinary operations of social power: a norm, as Foucault tells us, is not a description of what does exist but a prescription of what ought to.

The voice of the emcee typically tilts the balance of the talk show toward the normal; some of the guests, studio audience, and callers-in may tug in the same direction, but others pull outward toward the margins, trying to stretch the boundary of the normal or at least extend the tolerance of those within it for those who are not. Daytime talk shows do give access to people who otherwise would rarely be able to speak publicly, and on them female, African American, Latino/a, and other televisually repressed voices can be routinely heard, often in vehement disagreement about what the socially normal should and should not include. The boundaries of normality in network news are more narrowly drawn and vigilantly patrolled. In television's hierarchy of taste, the news is far above the talk show and its audience is similarly higher in the socioeconomic order. Hierarchies of taste, social privilege, and money reproduce each other. And all of them work to hierarchize technology in some way.

Some talk shows have a style, content, and audience that approximates those of the news. CNN's *Larry King Live* and *Crossfire* are two examples, both of which played central roles in the 1992 presidential election campaign. All the presidential candidates appeared on *Larry King Live*, and Ross Perot used the show for much of his electioneering. Pat Buchanan, before hitting the campaign trail, was a regular panelist on *Crossfire* and has since returned to it. These higher-status, evening talk shows mixed pundit and presidential talk with telephone call-ins to address specific campaign issues directly. Most of the lower-status shows did not. Their issues, many of which were relevant to the campaign, were not put into the discourse of party politics, but were recounted as the personal experiences of their guests and audiences. Nonetheless, the connections between everyday life and the campaign were there to be made as the shows discussed, often with high sensationalism, changes in traditional family structures, in gender roles and sexuality, in racial and class differences. It is impossible to assess whether their immediate politics veered to the Democrats or Republicans; equally, one cannot be sure whether their constant display of the abnormal served to reinforce the power of the norm or to interrogate its boundaries. Their political effects are likely to span the spectrum, for their format is based upon contestation, difference, and nonresolution. Consequently, they are risky ground for politicians, where few dare tread.

The Democrats did, however, take part in talk shows on MTV, a channel whose status and audience are both lower than CNN's. MTV's audiences are organized around age rather than class or race, and the Clinton campaign often turned to age politics to attack the Republicans. Clinton used his generational difference from Bush to hitch his agenda for change to youthfulness and the future, and to cast the Republicans as old and of the past. He also sent the same message to a similar audience, though less directly, by playing his saxophone to them on *The Arsenio Hall Show*. Al Gore's appearances on MTV were a direct and probably successful appeal to a young constituency. Worried that the Democrats were reaching people that he wasn't, a desperate George Bush, a few days before the election, also appeared on MTV, scrambling vainly for what he had previously disparaged as "the teenybopper vote." More indirectly, similar shifts in the generational politics of the structure of feeling can be traced in the way that *The Simpsons* and *Married . . . with Children* generated, and thrived upon, adult disapproval while the older, thoroughly approved, *Cosby Show* sank in the ratings.

The 1992 presidential campaign was characterized by the way its politics leaked over the boundaries of the cultural categories that traditionally organized and controlled them: it spread across the whole media spectrum. Entertainment television—sitcoms, talk shows, and MTV—was as active a terrain of political contest as information television. Postmodernism often points to our technological saturation with images as both a cause and a symptom of this liquefying of structural categories: images are so promiscuous as to defy any attempt to control and organize them. The mediated world is not only the world that we in the West live in, it is a world that has overtaken one in which an unmediated experience seemed possible. It never was, of course, but the rapid growth of our technological media does make a world of oral language, print, live performances, and nonreproduced visuals appear unmediated by comparison.

This technological growth is, if anything, accelerating, particularly with the development of computing. Our appetite for new media appears insatiable—we rarely discard the old to make room for new, but add the new to our existing media aggregate. Radio did not replace books, television did not smother the cinema, and recorded music killed neither the concert nor the radio. Electronic mail and bulletin boards will not replace the telephone, and probably even the old postal distribution of pieces of paper carrying handwritten messages will survive. New media technologies may modify the content, function, and use earlier ones, but they rarely replace them altogether, unless, of course,

238   they can perform the same function more efficiently. So the CD has (almost) replaced the LP, and the camcorder the 8mm home movie camera. But in general, the history of media technology is one of aggregation rather than replacement.

In such a world, cultural and political participation will inevitably involve technology. This introduces an economic dimension to the struggle to make oneself heard, but otherwise does not change discursive inequality. In premodern Europe, for example, everyone had a larynx, but few were able to speak in public and political life. Reference books, libraries, and archives are, to come closer to our own times, storage technologies, but not everything is stored in them. Boyd's *Directory of the District of Columbia*, for instance, provides documentary evidence that a man named Samuel McKeever (see chapter 4) lived in D.C. from at least 1883 to 1907. It records his daytime occupation variously as laborer, rag picker, junk buyer, and, in his later years, elevator operator. His nighttime occupation of vendor of Black bodies to hospitals is, of course, undocumented, but it is stored, nontechnologically, in oral history. Gladys-Marie Fry has collected a number of Black oral histories about him, perhaps the most vivid of which is the story of his unwittingly killing his own wife, whom he failed to recognize in the dark street. This knowledge, like that of his nighttime business, is nowhere officially archived, but it is vital to Black knowledge.

Equally alert to the politics of officially stored knowledge, Mbanna Kantako has started the Malcolm X Children's Library for books and information that he knows the John Hay children will find in no school or public library. And when the police raided the Homes during the uprising after the Rodney King verdict, one of their first targets was the library: uncontrolled knowledge can lead to uncontrolled people. Like the information stored in the Malcolm X Children's Library, the oral knowledge of Sam McKeever is functional; it warns African Americans never to lower their guard in white America. Equally, the story of McKeever killing and selling his wife warns that Black people who collaborate with whites for selfish ends will harm their race: Clarence Thomas, similarly "selling" his sister Emma Mae Martin to the antiwelfare lobby, may be understood as a modern McKeever.

A hierarchical society will always attempt to control the documentation and distribution of knowledge; the need to contest these attempts becomes more urgent as the diversity of the society increases. We can make our society one that is rich in diverse knowledges, but only if people strive to produce and circulate them. Technology will always be involved, and, if its potential is exploited, its proliferation may make the control over knowledge less, not more, efficient. The telephone, the radio, and the fax machine evaded government censors and kept the rest of the world informed of events in Beijing's Tiananmen Square and in Moscow's attempted coup of August 1992. Black women used telephones to spread their knowledge of the real issues in the Anita Hill case, and Mbanna Kantako uses illegal radio to tell African American truths

about genocide. Knowledge struggles always involve the struggle over access
to technology. Technology is proliferating, but not equally: its low-tech and high-tech forms still reproduce older hierarchies, and although it may extend the terrain of struggle and introduce new weapons into it, it changes neither the lineup of forces nor the imbalance in the resources they can command.

Postmodern culture is often characterized as one of extreme multiplicity—a multiplicity of commodities, of images, of knowledges, and of information technologies. Multiplicity is also a characteristic of another feature of late capitalism—multiculturalism. We live, we might say, in a society of many commodities, many knowledges, and many cultures. Multiplicity is to be applauded only when it brings diversity, and the two are not necessarily the same, though they are closely related. Multiplicity is a prerequisite of diversity, but it does not necessarily entail it—more can all too often be more of the same. Equally, diversity thrives on multiplicity, but does not necessarily produce it.

The concept of postmodernism is often linked with that of post-Fordism in attempts to explain the multiplicities of late capitalism: what postmodernism is to culture, post-Fordism is to economics. Post-Fordism describes capitalism's move away from mass production and mass marketing toward batch production, niche marketing, and market segmentation. Under Fordism, capitalism tried to maximize its profits by making one commodity appeal to as many people as possible. Its profits derived from what people shared, so it used its advertising and marketing skill to increase areas of commonality, and thus worked as a homogenizing social force. But not all people in all historical periods consider their similarities with others to be most salient in forming their social identities and social relations; for many, in fact, what mattered most to them was where they differed from others. And as capitalism increased its efficiency and distributed its products ever more widely and rapidly, across the globe as well as across the nation, so it gave the contradictory tendency toward diversity something to fight against. But, true to its nature, capitalism spotted a market in what appeared to oppose it, and post-Fordism rapidly diversified its products and their marketing in order to incorporate this tendency.

Post-Fordism, then, is a capitalism of multiple and diverse products and multiple and diverse markets. But there is a big difference between a diversity that is produced by social formations (particularly subordinated ones) that wish to maintain or reestablish their difference from others (particularly dominant ones) and a so-called diversity that is produced by and for capitalist industries. The first *is* diversity, for it includes differences that may be abrasive and unincorporable; the second is mere multiplicity, for its differences exist only because they are incorporable—this should not surprise us, for they are the products of the system that incorporates them. A social formation, however, is not a market segment, though capitalism will constantly try to turn it into one by matching its products and advertising as closely as possible to people's own sense of their social identities and social relations. If it is success-

240 ful in this it will then begin to contain the production of identity within the production of commodities, and the commodification of people will then be well under way. This may well be the core strategy of late capitalism, but we must not confuse a strategy with its achievement: commodification and incorporation are not achieved states, but terrains of struggle.

The multiplication of communication and information technologies extends the terrains of struggle, modifies the forms struggle may take, and makes it even more imperative that people grasp the opportunities for struggle that the multiplying of technologies offers. Without struggle, multiplicity will not produce diversity but will simply multiply the axes along which power will be exerted, and will thus extend its reach even further into the minutiae of daily life. Without these struggles, multiplicity can all too easily serve the countervailing tendency of greater homogenization and control.

The Scanscape of Fear

If we fail to make the effort to maintain a social diversity and the will to develop ways of living peacefully and respectfully with those who are different from us, there is a real and imminent danger that we will develop, without necessarily realizing what we are doing, a totalitarian state. Anthony Giddens argues that increases in violence and in surveillance have made totalitarianism into a permanent possibility in late capitalist nations.[24] *Totalitarian*, he argues, is an adjective that should be applied not to states themselves, but to their tendential properties that lead to a type of rule within them. He lists four elements of totalitarian rule, of which we can find worryingly clear traces in the United States today:

> 1. *Focusing of surveillance* as (a) information coding, documentation of activities of the population; (b) supervision of activities, intensified policing.
>
> 2. *Moral totalism*: fate of the political community as embedded in the historicity of the people.
>
> 3. *Terror*: maximizing of police power, allied to disposal of the means of waging industrialized war and sequestration.
>
> 4. *Prominence of leader figure*: appropriation of power by leader depending not upon a professionalized military role, but the generation of mass support.[25]

The first condition, that of surveillance, is the most completely developed and most rapidly developing of the four. It may be the hardest to oppose partly because, as Giddens points out, we don't know how to, for traditional sources of resistance such as class dynamics or the extension of democracy cannot be mobilized against surveillance, which is a technique rather than a policy, and partly because so many of its operations, particularly in information storage and retrieval, are invisible, and its more visible ones have clearly benign uses, from counterterrorism to traffic management. But all surveillance is totalitarian, for it allows its victims no say in the way it operates, and we must not allow the general benignity of its uses to mask the fact. Surveillance shifts the relations between the state and its citizens toward the totalitarian while allowing the visible structures of democracy to remain apparently untouched.

"Moral totalism" is an apt description of the politics of Buchanan-Quayle-Limbaugh; their attempt to embed authoritarian values in the authentic history of the American people is an attempt to misrepresent them as traditional, not political, values. Giddens says that the effectiveness of moral totalism depends both upon the restriction of public discourse and its use to couple the history it has produced to a hostile attitude toward "out-groups." The Republican discourse, such as that of Buchanan or LaMotte, seems designed expressly to achieve this effectiveness.

Terror and the maximizing of police power are experienced totally by certain segments of our population, and from others, loud voices are calling for their intensification. The King Alfred Plan, the Brinkerhoff memo, and the provost marshal's list of concentration camps provide listeners of Black Liberation Radio, at least, with evidence of the government's preparedness to resort to sequestration on a massive scale in times of crisis, and gays may feel, too, that proposals to "quarantine" those infected with AIDS are moves in the same direction.

Finally, we must recognize the readiness of the U.S. government to use the military and the National Guard not only against foreign threats, but also against its own citizens when it considers their behavior to exceed the norms of citizenship: student protests, blue-collar strikes, and Black insurgence can all be judged outside these norms when it is strategic to do so. The one condition missing is that of the charismatic leader, and, fortunately, the skepticism of the U.S. media (except in times of crisis), coupled with that of most of its people, makes mass support for a national charismatic leader unlikely. Within certain social formations, however, particularly among the religious right, there are clear signs of such populist, charismatic leadership, but far fewer indications that it will spread more widely. The Republicans misjudged the electorate when they allowed such figures so much centrality in their campaign.

In times of crisis, however, skepticism disappears, and another condition of totalitarianism, which is already widespread, intensifies: that condition is fear. Fear, oddly, is missing from Giddens's list. Fear is a persistent feature of life in the contemporary United States, and, although it is experienced by people in all walks of life, what really matters is the power-bloc fear, a fear that it has created a society that really is dangerous, and that the danger is increasing, not decreasing. Laurence Powell testified that he struck Rodney King so hard and

242   so often because he was frightened. In this he was not alone; Charles Murray speaks for many conservatives when he writes in the *National Review* that "the Rodney King verdict was an expression of white fear of black crime, and this fear is grounded in reality."[26] The Simi Valley that gave us the verdict is an enticingly safe place for frightened people (see below). Murray continues:

> However queasy they may be about what they saw on the videotape,
> large segments of white America sympathize with the implicit
> message of the King jury: A thin blue line of police is out there on
> the perimeter, holding back some very scary people. We rely on
> them, and we will back them up in just about anything they think
> they need to do to protect us.[27]

More moderately, in the same issue of the journal, Alan Keyes also cites fear as the main issue in the "riots": "Fear turned the accused policemen from professionals into thugs. It prejudiced the judgment of the jurors. It brought LA's neighborhoods to the brink of open war."[28] Fear pushes a society toward realizing the totalitarian tendency that Giddens has identified. Fear intensifies surveillance, mobilizes the police and the military, and drives the ruling classes to build enclaves to protect themselves from the danger they have created.

The United States is rapidly turning into an enclave society. In *City of Quartz*, Mike Davis shows how in Los Angeles white neighborhood after white neighborhood is enclosing itself by erecting gates and hiring security guards to keep out those who are identifiably not residents or guests.[29] In Minneapolis, a city with one of the lower fear levels in the nation, a gated, high-security development called Bear Path was announced in 1993, and almost immediately sixty-five people paid $10,000 each to join the priority list for its three hundred lots.[30] The enclave's single entrance will be guarded around the clock, and there are plans to install a central security system that will monitor individual houses and scan all open spaces with security cameras. For those who cannot afford the high real estate prices of such electronically surveilled developments, Neighborhood Watch programs provide a low-tech alternative. In many cities police help organize residents into squads, each with a territory and a "block captain" to spot and report anyone "suspicious," or, in the words of Simi Valley's mayor, "out of the ordinary." Indeed, part of the reason Simi Valley feels so safe to its residents is that it is almost an enclave without having been designed as one: "The geographic configuration of the 12-mile long valley, and its carefully planned street grid, makes a safe place safer. Just as each sub-division in Simi Valley is a web of self-contained cul-de-sacs, so the whole city can, in effect, be cordoned off simply by blocking four highway exits."[31]

In Los Angeles, of course, Minneapolis's future is the present. Not only are gated neighborhoods becoming the norm, but at least one downtown area closely adjacent to South-Central, coincidentally called Bunker Hill, has been

turned into a fortress. Mike Davis tells how the uprisings vindicated the fore-
sight of its designers:

> By flicking a few switches on their command consoles, the security
> staffs of the great bank towers were able to cut off all access to their
> expensive real estate. Bullet-proof steel doors rolled down over
> street-level entrances, escalators instantly stopped and electronic
> locks sealed off pedestrian passageways. As the Los Angeles
> Business Journal recently pointed out in a special report, the riot-
> tested success of corporate Downtown's defenses has only stimulated
> demand for new and higher levels of physical security.[32]

Inside this enclave, intelligent skyscrapers monitor what goes on inside them
with sensory systems that already include

> panoptic vision, smell, sensitivity to temperature and humidity,
> motion detection, and, in some cases, hearing. Some architects now
> predict the day when the building's own AI security computer will
> be able to automatically screen and identify its human population,
> and, even perhaps, respond to their emotional states (fear, panic,
> etc.). Without dispatching security personnel, the building itself will
> manage crises both minor (like ordering street people out of the
> building or preventing them from using toilets) and major (like
> trapping burglars in an elevator).[33]

Inside its gated subdivision, the home can be turned into a similar intelligent, self-monitoring citadel. Intruder alarms, video monitoring of the porch
and yard, panic buttons in the kitchen and living room are all built into the
electronic systems that comfortably monitor heat and humidity and enable the
householder to switch on the oven from the office or the TV from the car. Honeywell manufactures Total Home, an elaborate surveillance system, and urges,
"Wrap yourself in the affordable luxury of total comfort and security" (in 1993,
the luxury was affordable to those with $4,000). A ring at the doorbell or the
interruption of a beam across the front boundary automatically displays the
visitor-intruder on the TV screen, and if he or she is unwanted a quick press of
the "panic button" will ensure that help is on the way. Total Home not only
monitors the threat from outside, but also "the enemy within." Activities in
any room of the house can be surveilled and recorded, and, in Bear Path at
least, this internal surveillance system can be linked to the enclave's central
one, so that parents or security guards will be able to monitor sleeping babies
and the baby-sitter, and they will be able to check whether their teenage
daughter is sharing drugs or bodily fluids with her boyfriend.[34] Catalogs delivered to my house as I was writing this chapter offered me a video camera
disguised as a basket of dried flowers or, if I preferred, one the size of a one-
and-a-half-inch thick credit card, both of which can transmit words and pic-

244   tures to my TV from any room in the house. Both were advertised as suitable
for home or office use. This extension of surveillance into domestic space is not
just a technological possibility, it is, for some, desirable: the moral totalism
of right-wing "family values" will be enhanced by it, and the policy, during
Reagan's "Just Say No" antidrug campaign, of encouraging children to report
any drug use by their parents is further evidence of the desire to extend the
reach of power into space previously regarded as private and within the control
of those who live in it.

The enclave is built for the safety of those who inhabit it. Its corollary, then,
is to confine the "others" (those it needs to protect itself against) to the ghetto,
the barrio, or skid row: enclaving entails ghettoizing. And many cities are doing precisely this, sometimes with an explicit city policy, sometimes by the
practices of policing by which street people or Black people, for instance, learn
that they will be moved on from some areas but not others. Los Angeles, to
give one example, has an official policy of "containing" its homeless within the
skid row area of Central City East, and the LAPD herds any strays back into the
corral with ruthless efficiency. A variant of this policy was used in the Watts
riots of 1965, when the LAPD cordoned off the riot zone and left it to be burned
and looted; their only concern was to contain the destruction. In 1992, there are
strong suspicions that the same policy was deployed. Greg LaMotte's report
carries hints of it, the Korean grocers were sure of it, and many L.A. cops
thought that their superiors deliberately stopped them going in to quell the uprisings in the early stages, while they still might have been halted.[35] Chief
Daryl Gates has been widely criticized for not using the LAPD early and decisively enough. The suspicion that the delay was deliberate is fueled by the
knowledge that the police inspector who permitted the contained mayhem of
the Watts riots was none other than Daryl Gates himself. A similar conservative
use of enclaving-ghettoizing is advocated by Charles Murray when he promotes a policy that would encourage the respectable poor in the inner cities to
form law-abiding enclaves for themselves and thus confine the drug dealers
and the killers to the ghetto, where, one assumes, they will destroy themselves
in that no-go land in which nobody cares what happens as long as it is contained. "If," Murray concludes with Republican insouciance, "the result of im-
plementing these policies is to concentrate the bad apples into a few, hyper-
violent, anti-social neighborhoods, so be it."[36]

The separation of neighborhood from neighborhood, of enclave from
ghetto, is producing in Los Angeles and in many other cities a social and geographic structure whose fragmentation appears to be the dark side of postmodernity. The Chicano political scientist Raymond Rocco paints an ambivalent
picture of the diversity of inner L.A.:

> Los Angeles is now a city that is characterized by a sense of social
> fragmentation, a lack of center, multiple communities with little or

no sense of identification with each other, extremes of affluence and poverty, ambition and despair. In particular, in the area immediately surrounding the urban core, there are now dozens of immigrant Third World communities. To the west, centered around the corners of Western Avenue and Olympic Boulevard is a virtually self-contained Korean community. Again to the west, only a few blocks from the financial district, the Pico Union area has been completely transformed into a Central American environment. Further to the south, around Figueroa and Martin Luther King Boulevards, neighborhoods that were until six or seven years ago almost completely Afro-American, now have entire blocks populated by Mexican and Central American families. To the southeast are the cities of Huntington Park and South Gate, which went from being 4 per cent Latino in 1960 to 90 per cent in 1990. And of course to the east is the oldest and largest barrio of East Los Angeles, and to the northeast the Lincoln Heights and Highland Park areas are over 70 per cent Latino. Colombian communities have been established in neighborhoods around the corners of Third Street and Vermont Avenue, as well as in South Gate, Long Beach, Huntington Park, Glendale. Cubans, Puerto Ricans, and Colombians have established a sizeable presence in the Echo Park and Silver Lake area, as well as immediately adjacent to the Pico-Union area around Eighth Street and Vermont. Dominican communities are to be found in Long Beach, South Gate, and in the area around Sunset and Vermont.[37]

Such a description reveals the ethnic diversity that is concealed within the blanket term *Latino*, but, more pertinent to my argument here, it describes a set of precarious conditions whose politics are difficult to evaluate. Through one lens we can see disempowered social formations trying to achieve a degree of territorial and social self-determination that provides a secure place from which to enter social relations with other communities. Without this located security (both social and geographic), intercommunal relations are likely to be suspicious and competitive, especially when economic, cultural, and political resources are severely limited. Through another lens, however, we can see a fragmented society in which intercommunal and interethnic relations are minimized and the opportunities for social alliances reduced. A brief exchange among Oprah Winfrey, a young male African American, and a Korean American encapsulates the dilemma (see *Sidebar: Race and Class*, p. 173):

KOREAN: Give us a chance to work together. . . .

BLACK YOUTH 4: The Black people got their own problems to work out first of all, the Koreans go to your side and work your problems out, then you come with us . . .

246 OPRAH: But don't we all live in the world together, don't we all live in the
world together?[38]

It is worth noting here that the most deprived, the African American, is the
one calling for a temporary separatism, whereas the economically advantaged
Korean store owner is ready for alliance building and Oprah Winfrey, the most
privileged of all, calls for a wider consensual unity. I agree with the young African American, for I do not believe that effective social relations can be entered
until social positions and identities have been secured. Identities cannot be
formed entirely from within, for they are finally social and require socially provided resources. These may be material—a place to live, a job to go to, and a
week's food in the fridge—and some are cultural, for they include the power-
laden question of which senses and whose senses of identity can be made to
predominate: identities for and from self must always struggle against identities for and from others, particularly dominant others.

Social identities are one of the terrains of struggle where imperializing, top-
down power tries to insinuate itself even further into the minutiae of everyday
life, and localizing, bottom-up powers try to construct locales, or interior, social
and spatial territories within which people can control the immediate conditions of the social lives and where a greater self-determination of identity becomes achievable.[39] It is in this area that privacy counts so much, not as a bourgeois luxury, though it always is that, but as a basic personal and communal
space from which the uninvited and unwanted can be excluded.

At this basic level, surveillance invades privacy. Poverty denies privacy too:
to qualify for welfare, single mothers have to open up their private lives, even
their sexual ones, to surveillance, documentaion, and evaluation against the
norm. Surveillance of neighborhoods, streets, parks, and malls may enhance
security as surveillance in welfare discourages fraud (as well as those entitled
to it), but the price is the reduction of privacy, both at home and in public. Public space consists of places where private people may go about their business
and pleasure in the presence of others. In the workplace, surveillance (called
"supervision") has always been part of its defining conditions, for entering employment involves ceding a degree of self-determination and privacy (though
how much is quite properly a matter of acute argument). Public places, however, provided that one is not breaking the law or encroaching on the privacy
or other rights of other people, have traditionally been places of what we might
call "communal privacy." The rapid extension of surveillance to monitor all the
domains of our lives—the economic domain of production and consumption,
the public domain of streets, parks, and neighborhoods, and the private domain of our domestic lives—is changing the nature of our social order and
what it feels like to live in it. But these changes are not felt equally, for surveillance is not democratic and applied equally to all. Surveillance is a way of imposing norms (which are often disguised as "values"), and those whose norms

are imposed are, therefore, for practical purposes, free from surveillance, whereas those who have been othered into the "abnormal" have it focused more intensely upon them.

Legal scholars are beginning to question whether the surveillance of public space might not be unconstitutional or even illegal. Jennifer Granholm, for instance, considers that video surveillance of public places may violate at least three constitutional rights: it may infringe upon First Amendment rights because of its chilling and restrictive effects upon the freedoms of expression and of association—a group of young Black men on a street corner, for instance, may well be dispersed by cops alerted to their presence by a surveillance system, or, more seriously, may not meet at all because they know they will be seen and subsequently moved on; it may infringe upon Fourth Amendment rights by constituting unreasonable search—the camera's zoom lens may see objects or actions that would not be in "plain view" to a police officer on the beat and whose discovery would properly require a search warrant; and it may infringe upon the more general right of privacy found within the "penumbra" of the Constitution.[40] Granholm's concerns remind us of the extent to which we depend upon a widely agreed-upon boundary between the public and the private that organizes much of our social life, both in its everyday routines and in the institutions, such as the legal and medical systems, that underpin them. In this light, she argues, it is fundamentally unconstitutional to monitor people who have done nothing to trigger justifiable suspicion, and she concludes that "television surveillance will destroy the atmosphere and spontaneity of a free and relaxed citizenry."[41]

Between the enclave and the ghetto, the public places necessary for such free and relaxed citizenship are being eroded by fear. It is fear that allows us to accept the right of security guards to exclude those whom they define as undesirable from our shopping malls. It is fear that enables our elected representatives to denude downtowns of drinking fountains and public restrooms, to design barrel-topped seats so that respectable people can rest their butts against them but the homeless cannot sleep on them, and it is fear that produces "gang-free" (read "white") parks. Eroding the public dimension of "public" space confines the danger to the ghetto, where the underclasses may be left to do what they will. A clear indication of this ghettoization of danger and enclaving of the safe and the consequent squeezing of public space is the privatization of policing: in 1990, private security guards outnumbered public police officers by two to one; by 1993 there were 1.5 million security guards, compared with 600,000 cops.[42] Private guards, of course, are concerned only about protecting the security of those who hire them, and those who do not must look after themselves. The tension that often prevails between police and the socially deprived is a result of the *style* of policing, not the lawlessness of the policed: indeed, one of the most common demands of the less privileged is for more efficient and more humane policing of their neighborhoods. If the enclaves look after themselves and the ghettos can be left to themselves, then public policing and public places can both be reduced.

This contraction of physical public space continues discursively in the contraction of the meaning of the word *public* until it encompasses only "those like us." Without this cultural enclaving, physical ghettoization cannot be made to work, so the Reagan and Bush administrations confined the meaning of "the public" whose art should be publicly supported to an enclave definition that excluded the non-heterosexual, the non-Christian, and the nonerotophobic. As a result, public galleries and performance places were reduced in their content as the populations of downtowns are reduced in their diversity. By such means the power bloc can build mental enclaves from which it can exclude all those threatening others.

Surveillance is likely to provoke defensive measures to limit its reach, some of which may well involve establishing exclusionary territories within which a degree of privacy can be maintained and self-determination protected. The ethnic communities in and around South-Central L.A. that Raymond Rocco has described in such detail may become the poor equivalent of the gated, guarded neighborhoods of the wealthy and the walled mansions of the superrich. There is a clear potential for each to become a separated community that is neither enclave nor ghetto, but that has components of both. The prospect of a social order consisting of fragmented and fractious social formations in distinct territories is hardly an attractive one, but it is one of our possible futures, and it is the one toward which the totalitarian tendency and the extension of surveillance is steering us. A separatism that is self-selected for the time being in order to establish a base from which to engage more effectively in relations with the larger social order is quite different from a separatism resulting from the need to defend oneself against central and defining features of that social order.

Enclaves already exist in people's minds as the mental equivalent of the gated neighborhood. Simi Valley's mayor looked out of one as he identified someone "out of the ordinary." Giddens's account of the elements of totalitarian rule are drawn from his analysis of Nazi Germany, Leninist Russia, and Mussolini's Italy, which leads him to overemphasize the coercive role of the state and to underestimate the extent to which the elements of totalitarian rule can flourish uncoerced when the privileged are frightened. Enclaving and ghettoization are noncoercive forms of sequestration; the private security guard and the private surveillance system are products not of the state but of some people's desire for intensified policing, and for them moral totalism is not an imposition but a blanket into which they can snuggle. If the elements of totalitarian rule existed only in the ambitions of a Pat Buchanan, then an electoral defeat might extinguish them. But they don't: Buchanan was a major player in the campaign because he voiced fears and desires already widely experienced on the right wing of our society.

Surveillance, whether technological or human, is the base requirement for the other three elements of totalitarian rule. Technology may not determine the uses

to which it will be put, or even whether it will be used at all, but when it promises
to enhance what people are already doing without it, it *will* be used, and quickly.
Mental enclaving, for instance, is evidence of a social desire that can be met technologically by retinal scanning cameras that can identify each one of us through
the patterns of the blood vessels on our retinas. These are as unique as our finger-
prints, but much easier to scan. A camera using low-intensity, near infrared light
enters the retinal image into a computer, which can search a database of seven
million images for a match in three seconds. Solutions to the problem of compiling
the database have already been proposed, the most comprehensive of which is
that the retinal patterns of all drivers should be photographed, stored centrally,
and printed on drivers' licenses. The benign justification for this plan is that it
would prevent truck drivers who have lost their licenses in particular states from
being issued new ones in others.[43]

According to one report, much of the 1988 federal HUD grant to Chicago's
Housing Authority was earmarked not for repairs, but for security measures,
such as metal detectors and retinal scanners.[44] The Authority's desire for the
technology has already been demonstrated: Cabrini Green, for example, its notorious project on the edge of the business district, is already subject to periodic
"lockdowns," when all its residents are searched and identified, as a means of
controlling squatters, drug dealers, and gang members. For the residents,
these lockdowns turn their homes into prisons; as one, a young man, said,
"This is like the old slavery to me. This lockdown shit, this lockdown shit is for
the birds. I just did time in the penitentiary so I know how it feels to be caged
in. You can't come in and you can't come out of your own free will." Another,
a middle-aged woman, said, "I'm not being bothered by gangs, I'm being bothered by *them*. I can't talk on my phone in my house, I can't walk out of my
house to empty my garbage. I'm being strip searched on the ramp and can't get
back in the house where my baby is."[45] The lockdown is a low-tech process
that the retinal scan camera can perform more efficiently.

Cameras could, if we were frightened enough, cover streets leading out of
designated "containment districts" such as South-Central L.A. or the John Hay
Homes and alert the police if those who "ought" to be contained within them
tried to leave. In those circumstances, Mbanna Kantako and Zears Miles need
have no fears about being transported to the concentration camps listed in the
King Alfred Plan: electronic technology would bring the camp to them.

Surveillance requires categories to organize the information it produces and
turn it into knowledge. The bits of information that could produce a person's
"political profile" will not be pulled together until there is a category of, say,
"the dissident" to which they can be matched. So, too, the "gang-free parks"
in L.A., San Fernando, and Pomona require a decision about which bits of observable information define "gang membership." This decision has, of course,
already been made, for it was used by Judge Joyce Karlin when she categorized
Latasha Harlins with gang members and terrorists (see *Sidebar: Judge Karlin*, p.

250   161): had Latasha Harlins lived, she would have been barred from her city's gang-free parks. This is criminalization by social category, by which individuals are treated according to the category into which they have been put, not by their actions. It is this that enables police to stop motorists because they are Latino/a, storekeepers to follow customers because they are Black, and Nazis to kill people because they are Jews. Categories direct power upon those who may not even know that they exist, let alone what they are, as Rodney King discovered as "his" actions moved up through the escalating categories of the LAPD (see *Sidebar: The LAPD Tool Kit*, p. 135).

The computer requires categories to link its separate bits of information together and turn them into knowledge. But categories are social, not technological, so constructing them is where the power of the computer is politicized. The DEA, for instance, has a category, or social profile, of "likely drug courier," in which bits of information, which are in themselves of no particular significance, are joined with others, also not particularly significant, to produce a highly significant category that results in those who fit its parameters being stopped and searched at airports and bus stations and on the highways. *Mother Jones* has reconstructed from recent trials a list of these bits of information:

wearing gold chains

wearing a black jumpsuit

carrying a gym bag

carrying new luggage

carrying old luggage

paying for a ticket with cash

taking an "evasive and erratic" path through the airport

driving a rental car

driving a car containing an air freshener

traveling to or from a "source city" such as L.A., Miami, or Detriot, or in a car bearing license plates from a state containing source cities, though New York will do

being a member of "ethnic groups associated with the drug trade"

appearing overly nervous

appearing overly calm[46]

The list also includes stupidities such as "traveling alone; traveling with a companion," and "buying one-way tickets; buying round-trip tickets." But the point is that those who fit into the category outnumber by many times those it was designed to catch, but the surveillance system that applies it cannot tell the difference. A similar point is made by a member of the ACLU about psychological testing for job applicants:

> We have some ability to identify people who are potential thieves by a written psychological test. If you were to test 100 potential employees, you could probably catch 8 of the 10 thieves. But the only way you could do it is by rejecting 50 out of the 100 people. So to catch 8 guilty people you're denying a job to 42 innocent ones.[47]

When Zears Miles reads the *Mother Jones* list on Black Liberation Radio, he points out that it works to punish Black expressiveness (in a way that Jennifer Granholm might recognize as a violation of the right to freedom of expression; see above) and that in order to avoid being searched at airports Black travelers must, as far as possible, deny their Black culture and identity, and look and behave like whites. Surveillance identifies and discourages the cultural expression and behavior of social formations that differ from those of the dominant, and thus discourages any public display of difference: it is totalitarian. It does inhibit a free and relaxed citizenry.

Michael Eric Dyson underscores this point with a searing story of attempting to draw some cash on his credit card in a bank.[48] He is a Black man, and was wearing a black running suit. He is also an academic and a Baptist preacher, but these characteristics were not visible; his Blackness, his maleness, and his running suit, however, were. The teller refused to advance him any money. Dyson's request to see the bank manager started an apparently irreversible sequence of events that culminated in the manager slicing Dyson's credit card in two with a pair of scissors. When Dyson protested, the manager called the police. All this occurred in front of both an interested crowd and Dyson's son, who presumably learned some unforgettable lessons about whiteness. Patricia Williams, a professor of law, tells a similar story of being refused entry into, ironically, a United Colors of Benetton store because she is Black, and of the editorial censorship she encountered when writing up the incident for a white legal journal.[49] Racism is, of course, an extension of the process of criminalization by category, and what is significant in these incidents is the clarity with which they reveal the power of whiteness to categorize the other, and to act upon that categorization and thus exert white power over the other. The categorization that enables the DEA to identify drug runners, the bank to identify fraudulent credit card users, and the store to identify shoplifters is a process without which surveillance cannot work, whiteness cannot work, and totalitarianism cannot work. At the core of this process is, of course, the way that whiteness excludes itself both from categorizing and from being categorizable and thus ensures its invisibility—an invisibility that extends into the widespread white ignorance of such incidents. We whites, whose norms are used to abnormalize, categorize, and identify the others who are not us, cannot experience directly the oppressive application of those norms, for they are applied *from* our position, not *upon* it. Indeed, we often do not know that such incidents occur, let alone how routine they are. We need these stories to be told, and we need to listen to them.

Frightened whites build enclaves from which they can exclude any account of the experience of those they have othered: when Greg LaMotte talks of a "feeding frenzy" and Buchanan of "the mob," they are building a discursive wall within which they and their like-minded can feel secure and from which they can look out at those others whose meanings of social experience they exclude from their imaginations as totally as their bodies from their sidewalks. Such enclaving discourse results from fear, but it also produces and strengthens it. In this it resembles the gated neighborhood whose residents are likely to overestimate the terrors of the world from which they have isolated themselves.[50] In this light, Buchanan's speech to the Republican convention (see *Sidebar: Buchanan*, p. 56) reveals a white male terror suffering from multiple fears—homophobia, gynophobia, negrophobia, latinophobia—all combined into an overarching alliophobia, or fear of the generalized other. An enclaving discourse is a ghettoizing discourse for those whom it excludes. When Dia Kantako deconstructs Channel 20, she is countering its ghettoizing effect and preventing her people's knowledge from being confined by it (see *Sidebar: Blackened White TV*, p. 182).

The "family values" campaign, too, is fearful and enclaving. It works to drive people's imaginations back into the family and out of social consciousness, just as fear keeps them behind their own doors and the gates of their subdivision. It thus turns the family that it values into a citadel from which to fend off the values of the dangerous other. Honeywell's Total Home constructs an appropriate house for the "moral totalism" of the Buchanan-Quayle family.

There is a sense, too, in which the market segmentation of post-Fordism can strengthen enclaves, particularly in the cultural sphere. Murphy Brown and "today's woman" are members of a social formation whose wide endorsement results, in part, from the neatness of its fit with a market segment; many of its needs, both material and cultural, can be well met by the marketplace, and, if some within that formation appear reluctant to build social alliances that extend beyond it, part of the reason may be because, to coin an ugly word for an ugly process, they have been too effectively "post-Fordized." Post-Fordism needs only those connections between its market segments that it can turn into profit, so it works, whether intentionally or not, to discourage other alliances. Post-Fordism tempts us to settle comfortably into the media environment designed to match our consumer profile. Upper-class, white, conservative men, for example, will feel relaxed and comfortable inside Greg LaMotte's discursive subdivision, but discomforted and out of place should they happen to stray into Oprah Winfrey's. Consequently, their inclination is to leave it as quickly as possible, without stopping to wonder what the world looks like to its residents, let alone if they might have something in common with them. Back in their own enclave they can then scorn it and dismiss its discourses as trivial or irrelevant. I wonder, too, if the reluctance of most whites to accept genocide as a valid interpretation of at least the effects of current race relations might not be a retreat into an enclave.

Where the cultural diversity of this country takes advantage of the opportunities offered by its plurality of information technologies, genuinely different knowledges can be circulated. But the responsibility to use the plurality of media to produce a diversity, and not just a multiplicity, of knowledges must be shared by all. We readers, listeners, and viewers need to scan the full range of the media repertoire to find voices to listen to that are genuinely different and are not just ventriloquizing our own in slightly different tones. A degree of cultural diversity is available to us if we have the will to look for it, and the more often we find it, and the more often we take advantage of it, then the more we will help it to secure its place. Similarly, by using the mainstream media less exclusively and less often, we will pressure them to diversify the voices they admit onto their airwaves and into their columns: they are market driven, and they do need readers, viewers, and listeners.

Diversifying our own experience of our society is, I believe, vital if we are to break the enclaving tendency and reduce the fear that drives it. If we middle-class whites listen only to Greg LaMotte and Pat Buchanan, we will fear the "looters" of L.A., but if we listen to the residents of South-Central we might learn that they want respect and dignity, they want the chance to be heard, they want jobs, they want some control over their lives, and they want to feel a viable and valued part of the society they have been born into. None of that is so frightening. Black anger is quite properly a cause of white fear: if we essentialize it as Black we will be driven toward building enclaves, but if we recognize it as a product of white domination we can begin to do something about it, and thus reduce our fear.

Reducing fear will also slow, if not reverse, any move toward the totalitarian. The elements that Giddens has identified are most obvious on the right wing of our society, and they moved toward its center during the long years of Reagan and Bush. The change in the structure of feeling of which Clinton's election victory was a part may well indicate that enough social formations within the electorate sensed the danger and wished to halt or reverse the movement. But those forces are regrouping, and the threat has not gone away. The technology needed for them to establish the total surveillance upon which to base their moral totalism is already available. Fear will increase the likelihood of that technology's use and the probability of right-wing forces being in power to use it. It is, therefore, in their interests to confine as many of us as they can to our cultural and geographic enclaves. Is this what we want?

Notes

Introduction

1. *Life*, January 1993, 5.
2. *Time*, September 21, 1992, 44.
3. Ibid.
4. Neither in the United States nor in this book is there any consistency in the use of the terms *Black* and *African American*. I do, however, follow the practice of capitalizing the word *Black* to distinguish its enhanced value (the result of hard struggle) from the denigratory *black*. The word *white* is not capitalized, for it has never needed a struggle to enhance it, though one may now be taking place to devalue it. I also use quotation marks around words from discourses from which I wish to distance myself, such as *riots*, *looters*, *third* world. I have fallen for the convenience of the term *Latino/a* and regret its homogenization of the ethnic differences within it.
5. I use the term *social formation* to refer to what are often called *groups*, *classes*, or *categories*. The word *formation* usefully suggests both a constant process rather than a stable category, and that those within it can exert some agency in forming it: a social formation may be relatively fluid as people enter and leave it; it may disappear as conditions change and it may enter alliances with other social formations to form new, larger ones. I do not use the term to refer to the whole society, for which, in general, I prefer the term *social order*, despite its tendency to stabilize what is also in constant process.
6. Raymond Williams, *Marxism and Literature* (Oxford: Oxford University Press, 1977).
7. These figures are taken from the *New York Times*, November 4, 1992, B1, B4; and November 5, 1992, B5.
8. I am heavily indebted to two main sources for information on events listed in this chronology—that of the hearings compiled by Camille Spencer for the *Black Scholar*'s book *Court of Appeal: The Black Community Speaks Out on the Racial and Sexual Politics of Thomas vs Hill* (New York: Ballantine, 1992), 3-6; and that of the Rodney King saga in the *New York Times*, April 18, 1993, A18.

1. Murphy Brown, Dan Quayle, and the Family Row of the Year

1. Throughout, I used *sic* to identify the misuse of language in quotations; the error may be in spelling, syntax, or sexism.
2. *New York Times*, May 20, 1992, A1, A2.
3. Rush Limbaugh is a self- and loudly proclaimed conservative talk-show host whose radio show is heard on 600 stations with 15 million listeners, and whose TV show is carried by 224 local stations. *USA Today*, May 4, 1993, 1A.
4. Quoted in *Capitol Times*, January 25, 1993, 5D.

255

256   **5.** Susan Faludi, in *Backlash: The Undeclared War on American Women* (Garden City, N.Y.: Doubleday Anchor, 1991), summarizes the economic decline of middle- to lower-income men from the late 1970s to the mid-1980s, when the gender-class resentment became most vocal. Her evidence includes a 22 percent drop in household income where men were the sole breadwinners; the average man under thirty years of age earned 25-30 percent less than his 1970s counterpart, and if he had only a high school education he was hit even harder, earning only $18,000, half of what his counterpart made a decade earlier (p. 65).

6. Ibid., 67.

7. Ibid., 66.

8. *New York Times*, November 5, 1992, B5.

9. Paul D. Colford, *The Rush Limbaugh Story: Talent on Loan from God: An Unauthorized Biography* (New York: St. Martin's, 1993).

10. Rush Limbaugh, "Turn the Voters Loose," *National Review*, October 5, 1992, 40.

11. Hilary de Vries, "Laughing Off the Recession: Diane English Rewrites the Future of Women in Television, Onscreen and Off," *New York Times Magazine*, January 3, 1993, 19-26.

12. Robert Alley and Irby Brown, *Murphy Brown: The Anatomy of a Sitcom* (New York: Delta, 1990).

13. De Vries, "Laughing Off the Recession."

14. *Minneapolis Star Tribune*, January 21, 1993, 19A.

15. A labor and immigration expert at the Carnegie Endowment "said he has known a number of people in Washington, DC, who simply preferred hiring undocumented workers over American black workers." *Minneapolis Star Tribune*, January 21, 1993, 19A.

16. Stuart Hall, "The Whites of Their Eyes: Racist Ideologies and the Media," in *The Media Reader*, ed. Manual Alvarado and John Thompson (London: British Film Institute, 1990), 8-23.

17. Herman Gray, "The Endless Slide of Difference: Critical Television Studies, Television and the Question of Race," *Critical Studies in Mass Communication* 10 (June 1993): 190-97.

18. Mimi White, "What's the Difference? *Frank's Place* in Television," *Wide Angle* 13, nos. 3/4 (1991): 82-96.

19. Gray, "The Endless Slide," 195.

20. George Lipsitz, "The Possessive Investment in Whiteness: Racialized Social Democracy in America" (paper presented at the annual meeting of the American Studies Association, Boston, November 1993).

21. Edward Said, *Orientalism* (New York: Vintage, 1979), 3.

22. Ibid., 20.

23. Ibid., 7.

24. Toni Morrison, *Playing in the Dark: Whiteness and the Literary Imagination* (New York: Vintage, 1993), 39.

25. Ibid., 38.

26. Ibid., 52.

27. Michael Omi and Howard Winant, "The LA Race Riot and US Politics," in *Reading Rodney King Reading Urban Uprising*, ed. Robert Gooding-Williams (New York: Routledge, 1993), 105-6.

28. John Dower, *War without Mercy: Race and Power in the Pacific War* (New York: Pantheon, 1986), 189.

29. The argument that the term "post-civil rights" covers in the United States the period and the phenomenon that "postcoloniality" does in Britain is made by Ruth Frankenberg and Lata Mani, "Cross Currents, Cross Talk: Race, 'Postcoloniality' and the Politics of Location," *Cultural Studies* 7, no. 2 (1993): 292-310.

30. Michel Foucault, *Discipline and Punish: The Birth of the Prison* (New York: Vintage, 1979).

31. Joyce King, "Rethinking the Black/White Duality of Our Time" (paper presented at the Wisconsin Center for Educational Research, January 27, 1994).

32. Ruth Frankenberg, *White Women, Race Matters: The Social Construction of Whiteness* (Minneapolis: University of Minnesota Press, 1993).

33. Justin Lewis, *The Ideological Octopus: An Exploration of Television and Its Audience* (New York: Routledge, 1991), 174.

34. Michael Eric Dyson, *Reflecting Black: African American Cultural Criticism* (Minneapolis: University of Minnesota Press, 1993), 71.

35. Frankenberg, *White Women*, 147.

36. Ibid., 188.

37. bell hooks, "Representing Whiteness," in *Cultural Studies*, ed. Lawrence Grossberg, Cary Nelson, and Paula Treichler (New York: Routledge, 1991), 345; also in bell hooks, *Black Looks, Race and Representation* (Boston: South End, 1992).

38. Lipsitz, "The Possessive Investment in Whiteness."

39. Ibid., 5.

40. Toni Morrison, "On the Backs of Blacks," *Time*, special issue, Fall 1993, 57.

41. *American Demographics*, October 1991, 29.

42. *Time*, special issue, Fall 1993, 15.

43. The 1990 U.S. Census recorded the Los Angeles population as 40 percent Latino, 37 percent Anglo, and 23 percent Black and Asian. Some 49.9 percent of L.A. citizens speak a language other than English at home. *Newsweek*, May 18, 1992, 46.

44. *Time*, special issue, Fall 1993, 5.

45. Julie D'Acci, *Defining Women: Television and the Case of Cagney and Lacey* (Chapel Hill: University of North Carolina Press, 1994).

46. *New York Times*, November 4, 1992, B1, B4.

47. Ice-T, interviewed by Terry Gross on "Fresh Air," National Public Radio, May 1, 1992, reprinted in Institute for Alternative Journalism, ed., *Inside the LA Riots* (New York: Institute for Alternative Journalism, 1992), 126.

48. Quoted in Institute for Alternative Journalism, *Inside the LA Riots*, 39.

49. Quoted in ibid.

50. *New York Times*, March 17, 1993, A11.

51. *CBS News*, March 16, 1993.

52. *USA Today*, April 21, 1993, 13A.

53. Ibid.

54. *Washington Post*, January 29, 1993, A11.

55. Faludi, *Backlash*, 401-2.

56. *New York Times*, November 5, 1992, B5.

57. Faludi, *Backlash*, 409.

58. Story syndicated in the *Minneapolis Star Tribune*, April 26, 1993, 10A.

59. *Minneapolis Star Tribune*, April 26, 1993, 6A.

60. Michel de Certeau, *The Practice of Everyday Life* (Berkeley: University of California Press, 1984).

2. Hearing Anita Hill (and Viewing Bill Cosby)

1. *U.S. News & World Report*, October 21, 1991, 35.

2. David Brock, "The Real Anita Hill," *American Spectator*, March 1992, 18-30.

3. *Frontline, Clarence Thomas and Anita Hill: Public Hearing, Private Pain*, directed and produced by Ofrah Bikel, Ofrah Bikel Production Corp., aired October 13, 1992.

4. bell hooks, *Ain't I a Woman: Black Women and Feminism* (Boston: South End, 1981); bell hooks, *Talking Back: Thinking Feminist, Thinking Black* (Boston: South End, 1989); bell hooks, *Black Looks, Race and Representation* (Boston: South End, 1992).

5. hooks, *Black Looks*, 85.

6. Trellie L. Jeffers, "We Have Heard, We Have Seen, Do We Believe? The Clarence Thomas-Anita Hill Hearing," *Black Scholar* 22, nos. 1/2 (1992): 56; also in *Court of Appeal: The Black Community Speaks Out on the Racial and Sexual Politics of Thomas vs Hill*, ed. Black Scholar (New York: Ballantine, 1992), 119.

7. Charles R. Lawrence III, "Cringing at Myths of Black Sexuality," *Black Scholar* 22, nos. 1/2 (1992): 65; also in *Court of Appeal: The Black Community Speaks Out on the Racial and Sexual Politics of Thomas vs Hill*, ed. Black Scholar (New York: Ballantine, 1992), 136.

8. *Chicago Defender*, October 19, 1991, 16.

9. The *New York Times* counted nineteen; the *Los Angeles Times*, twenty-three. *New York Times*, April 18, 1993; Staff of the Los Angeles Times, *Understanding the Riots* (Los Angeles: Los Angeles Times, 1992), 33.

10. I am grateful to Rose Byrd for this analogy.

11. David Lionel Smith, "The Thomas Spectacle: Power, Impotence and Melodrama," *Black Scholar* 22, nos. 1/2 (1992): 95; also in *Court of Appeal: The Black Community Speaks Out on the Racial and Sexual Politics of Thomas vs Hill*, ed. Black Scholar (New York: Ballantine, 1992), 193.

12. Marion Barry was the mayor of Washington, D.C., who was videotaped receiving drugs and sex from an ex-girlfriend in an FBI setup. He was imprisoned as a result.

13. Margaret A. Burnham, "The Supreme Court Appointment Process and the Politics of Race and Sex," in *Race-ing Justice, En-gendering Power*, ed. Toni Morrison (New York: Pantheon, 1992), 311.

14. Kimberle Crenshaw, "Whose Story Is It, Anyway: Feminist and Anti-racist Appropriations of Anita Hill," in *Race-ing Justice, En-gendering Power*, ed. Toni Morrison, (New York: Pantheon, 1992), 415.

15. Barbara Smith, "Ain't Gonna Let Nobody Turn Me Around," *Black Scholar* 22, nos. 1/2 (1992): 91; also in *Court of Appeal: The Black Community Speaks Out on the Racial and Sexual Politics of Thomas vs Hill*, ed. Black Scholar (New York: Ballantine, 1992), 186.

16. Calvin Hernton, "Breaking Silences," *Black Scholar* 22, nos. 1/2 (1992): 42; also in *Court of Appeal: The Black Community Speaks Out on the Racial and Sexual Politics of Thomas vs Hill*, ed. Black Scholar (New York: Ballantine, 1992), 56-57.

17. Julianne Malveaux, "No Peace in a Sisterly Space," *Black Scholar* 22, nos. 1/2 (1992): 71; also in *Court of Appeal: The Black Community Speaks Out on the Racial and Sexual Politics of Thomas vs Hill*, ed. Black Scholar (New York: Ballantine, 1992), 147.

18. hooks, *Ain't I a Woman*, 7.

19. Crenshaw "Whose Story Is It, Anyway," 403.

20. *New York Times*, November 17, 1991; reprinted in Black Scholar, ed., *Court of Appeal: The Black Community Speaks Out on the Racial and Sexual Politics of Thomas vs Hill* (New York: Ballantine, 1992), 291-92.

21. Smith, "Ain't Gonna Let Nobody," 91.

22. hooks, *Black Looks*, 82-83.

23. "The Year of the Black Woman," *Ebony*, October 1992, 112.

24. Other achievements in the political sphere include the emergence from the L.A. uprisings of "a new political star, Rep. Maxine Waters, who has emerged as the central advocate for urban renewal" and numerous candidates for office at state and local levels. In the arts, three Black women had their novels simultaneously on the *New York Times* best-seller lists, and others won major awards in music, cinema, and television. In sport, Black women won thirty-two medals, including eight gold, in the Olympics, and, professionally they were "presiding in corporate boardrooms, leading national professional organizations and leading major colleges and universities more than ever before." Ibid., 118.

25. Ibid.

26. Jane Gross, "Suffering in Silence No More: Fighting Sexual Harassment," *New York Times,* July 13, 1992, A1, D10.

27. Elizabeth McLemore, University of Minnesota.

28. Rush Limbaugh, *The Way Things Ought to Be* (New York: Pocket Books, 1992), 126.

29. Ibid., 124.

30. Phyllis Schlafly, lecture at the University of Wisconsin—Madison, March 2, 1993.

31. Phyllis Schlafly, remarks made at a press conference preceding the lecture in Madison, Wisconsin; reported in the *Capitol Times,* March 3, 1993, 3A, 4A.

32. Quoted in *New York Times,* October 15, 1991, A15.

33. Cited in Nancy Fraser, "Sex, Lies and the Public Sphere: Some Reflections on the Confirmation of Clarence Thomas," *Cultural Inquiry* 18 (Spring 1992): 595-612.

34. Ibid., 609.

35. Cornel West, "Black Leadership and the Pitfalls of Racial Reasoning," in *Race-ing Justice, En-gendering Power,* ed. Toni Morrison (New York: Pantheon, 1992), 398; and Cornel West, *Race Matters* (Boston: Beacon, 1993), 21-32.

36. *New York Times,* October 17, 1992, 6L.

37. Sarah E. Wright, "The Anti-Black Agenda," *Black Scholar* 22, nos. 1/2 (1992): 109; also in *Court of Appeal: The Black Community Speaks Out on the Racial and Sexual Politics of Thomas vs Hill,* ed. Black Scholar (New York: Ballantine, 1992), 225.

38. Jill Nelson, "Anita Hill: No Regrets," interview with Anita Hill, *Essence,* March 1992, 116.

39. Robert Staples, "Hand Me the Rope—I Will Hang Myself: Observations on the Clarence Thomas Hearings," *Black Scholar* 22, nos. 1/2 (1992): 96; also in *Court of Appeal: The Black Community Speaks Out on the Racial and Sexual Politics of Thomas vs Hill,* ed. Black Scholar (New York: Ballantine, 1992), 196-97.

40. Nellie McKay, talk and reading given at Borders Bookstore, Madison, Wisconsin, December 1, 1992, to promote Toni Morrison, ed., *Race-ing Justice, En-gendering Power* (New York: Pantheon, 1992).

41. Henry Louis Gates, "TVs Black World Turns—But Stays Unreal," *New York Times,* November 12, 1989, sec. 2, p. 1.

42. Quoted in Herman Gray, "Television, Black Americans, and the American Dream," *Critical Studies in Mass Communication* 6 (1989): 376-86.

43. Sut Jhally and Justin Lewis, *Enlightened Racism: The Bill Cosby Show, Audiences, and the Myth of the American Dream* (Boulder, Colo.: Westview, 1992).

44. Quoted in Timothy Phelps and Helen Winternitz, *Capitol Games: The Inside Story of Clarence Thomas, Anita Hill and a Supreme Court Nomination* (New York: HarperCollins, 1993), 85.

45. *U.S. News & World Report,* September 1, 1986.

46. Quoted in Susan Faludi, *Backlash: The Undeclared War on American Women* (Garden City, N.Y.: Doubleday Anchor, 1991), 263.

47. Mike Budd and Clay Steinman, "White Racism and the Cosby Show," *JumpCut* 37 (July 1992): 5-14.

48. Jhally and Lewis, *Enlightened Racism,* 88.

49. Michael Eric Dyson, *Reflecting Black: African American Cultural Criticism* (Minneapolis: University of Minnesota Press, 1993), 188.

50. "Questions and Answers on the NAACP's Position on Judge Clarence Thomas," August 21, 1992; cited in Black Scholar, ed. *Court of Appeal,* 276.

51. A. Leon Higginbotham, Jr., "An Open Letter to Justice Clarence Thomas from a Federal Judicial Colleague," in *Race-ing Justice, En-gendering Power*, ed. Toni Morrison (New York: Pantheon, 1992), 3-28.

52. Nell Irvin Painter, "Hill, Thomas and the Use of Racial Stereotype," in *Race-ing Justice, En-gendering Power*, ed. Toni Morrison (New York: Pantheon, 1992), 201-2. The same point is made by West, "Black Leadership," 394-95.

53. Robert Entman, "Modern Racism and the Images of Blacks in Local TV News," *Critical Studies in Mass Communication* 7 (1990): 332-45.

54. Dyson, *Reflecting Black*, 82.

55. John Downing, " 'The Cosby Show' and American Racial Discourse," in *Discourse and Discrimination*, ed. G. Smitherman-Donaldson and T. van Dijk (Detroit: Wayne State University Press, 1988), 46-73.

56. Cited in hooks, *Black Looks*, 83, 85.

57. *National Review*, June 8, 1992, 31.

58. Gray, "Television, Black Americans."

59. Quoted in ibid., 381.

60. Quoted in ibid., 380.

61. Quoted in Phelps and Winternitz, *Capitol Games*, 88.

62. See Downing, " 'The Cosby Show,' " 50.

63. *The Cosby Show*, August 7, 1986.

64. Quoted in Jhally and Lewis, *Enlightened Racism*, 30.

65. Quoted in ibid., 55.

66. Quoted in ibid., 54.

67. Quoted in ibid., 123.

68. Quoted in ibid.

69. Downing, " 'The Cosby Show' "; Justin Lewis, *The Ideological Octopus: An Exploration of Television and Its Audience* (New York: Routledge, 1991).

70. Lewis, *The Ideological Octopus*.

71. Quoted in Jhally and Lewis, *Enlightened Racism*, 123.

72. Fraser, "Sex, Lies and the Public Sphere."

73. Both cited in ibid., 599, 600.

74. Ibid., 601-2.

75. Ibid., 601.

76. *Frontline, Clarence Thomas and Anita Hill*.

77. Chad Dell, "Secondary Circulations" (paper presented at the annual meeting of the Popular Culture Association, Toronto, 1990).

78. *New York Times*, March 2, 1989, A1, D20.

79. *Los Angeles Times*, March 4, 1989, sec. V, pp. 1, 8.

80. *Detroit News*, March 3, 1989, 8A, 1B, 4B.

81. See, for example, the *Denver Post*, *Detroit News*, and *Wall Street Journal*, all cited in Dell, "Secondary Circulations."

82. David Brean, "Viewers and Viewing: An Ethnographic Study" (paper presented at the annual meeting of the Popular Culture Association, Toronto, 1990).

83. *Time*, September 21, 1992, 44.

84. Budd and Steinman, "White Racism."

85. *People Weekly*, May 21, 1990, 130; cited in Kevin Glynn, " 'I'm Bart Simpson, Who the Hell Are You': Social Identity, Cultural Loser, and Critical Ethnography" (paper presented at the annual meeting of the International Communication Association, Miami, May 1992).

86. Ibid.

87. Downing, " 'The Cosby Show,' " 52.

88. Quoted in ibid., 53.
89. Budd and Steinman, "White Racism," 8.

3. Los Angeles: A Tale of Three Videos

1. The first trial was the state one, in which the officers were charged with using excessive force and acquitted. The second was the federal trial, in which they were charged with violating Rodney King's civil rights and in which two of the officers, Stacey Koon and Laurence Powell, were found guilty. The verdict in the first trial sparked the uprisings; that of the second caused few ripples.

2. Kimberle Crenshaw and Gary Peller, "Reel Time/Real Justice," in *Reading Rodney King Reading Urban Uprising*, ed. Robert Gooding-Williams (New York: Routledge, 1993), 62.

3. *Los Angeles Times*, April 4, 1993, B3.

4. Patricia Williams, "The Rules of the Game," in *Reading Rodney King Reading Urban Uprising*, ed. Robert Gooding-Williams (New York: Routledge, 1993) , 52-53.

5. Quoted in *Newsweek*, March 22, 1993, 64.

6. Houston Baker, "Scene . . . Not Heard," in *Reading Rodney King Reading Urban Uprising*, ed. Robert Gooding-Williams (New York: Routledge, 1993), 39.

7. Ibid.

8. Williams, "The Rules of the Game," 54.

9. Quoted in *Newsweek*, March 22, 1993, 64.

10. The jury contained two nonwhites (an Asian American and a Latina), but in this set of power alliances, by being non-Black they functioned as white, particularly as the axes of conflict in the uprising included ones of Blacks versus Koreans and Blacks versus Latino/as.

11. *Donahue*, May 1, 1992.

12. *New York Times*, May 4, 1992 p. B7.

13. Kevin Uhrich, "Policeville: Why People Who Know West Ventura County Weren't Surprised by the Verdict," in *Inside the LA Riots*, ed. Institute for Alternative Journalism (New York: Institute for Alternative Journalism, 1992), 58.

14. Stephen Reinhardt, "Riots, Racism and the Courts," address published, in part, in "The Trickle Down of Judicial Racism," *Harper's*, August 1992, 15-17.

15. Ibid., 16.

16. *USA Today*, July 23-25, 1A, 6A.

17. Williams, "The Rules of the Game," 53.

18. Martin Levine, "Bad Blood," *New York Native*, February 16, 1987, 7.

19. *New York Times*, November 3, 1988, A1, B20.

20. It is interesting to note further links between the Willie Horton ad and the Republican support for Clarence Thomas as Willie Horton's obverse: an ad attacking the Democrats who opposed Thomas was made by the same team, under Floyd Brown, that made the Horton one. Like its predecessor, it was disowned by the White House, but only after it had been shown. Brown claims that the White House knew of the ad all along, which seems likely in view of the fact that it was produced at the facilities of the National Republican Congressional Committee. See Timothy Phelps and Helen Winternitz, *Capitol Games: The Inside Story of Clarence Thomas, Anita Hill and a Supreme Court Nomination* (New York: HarperCollins, 1993).

21. *Los Angeles Times*, May 16, 1992, B2.

22. Ibid.

23. *Los Angeles Times*, March 28, 1988; cited in Mike Davis, *City of Quartz* (London: Verso, 1990), 272.

24. Quoted in Ibid.

25. Quoted in *Los Angeles Times*, May 21, 1992, B4.

26. Quoted in *St. Paul Pioneer Press*, May 23, 1992.

27. David Weir, "Nobody Listens," *Mother Jones*, July/August 1992; also in *Inside the LA Riots*, ed. Institue for Alternative Journalism (New York: Institute for Alternative Journalism, 1992), 103.

28. Mike Davis, *LA Was Just the Beginning* (Westfield, NJ: Open Magazine Pamphlet Series, 1992), 17-18.

29. Andrew Hacker, *Two Nations: Black and White, Separate, Hostile, Unequal* (New York: Charles Scribner's Sons, 1992), 103.

30. See also Sidney Wilhelm, *Who Needs the Negro?* (Cambridge, Mass.: Schenkman, 1970).

31. Edward Luttwak, "The Riots: Underclass vs. Immigrants," *New York Times*, May 15, 1992, A29.

32. The term is bell hooks's, and is used in her *Feminist Theory from Margin to Center* (Boston: South End, 1984), 54.

33. Toni Morrison, "The Pain of Being Black," *Time*, May 22, 1989, 120.

34. Derrick Bell, *Faces at the Bottom of the Well: The Permanence of Racism* (New York: Basic Books, 1992).

35. Morrison, "The Pain of Being Black."

36. Melvin Oliver, James Johnson, and Walter Farrell, "Anatomy of a Rebellion: A Political-Economic Analysis," in *Reading Rodney King Reading Urban Uprising*, ed. Robert Gooding-Williams (New York: Routledge, 1993), 123-124.

37. Quoted in *Los Angeles Times*, June 25, 1992, B3-4.

38. Mike Davis, "Burning All Illusions in LA," in *Inside the LA Riots*, ed. Institute for Alternative Journalism (New York: Institute for Alternative Journalism, 1992), 99.

39. Gyu Chen Jeon, "The Korean-Black Conflicts in the Postmodern World of Discourse" (Ph.D. diss., University of Wisconsin—Madison, 1993).

40. Black Liberation Radio, May 2, 1992.

41. *New York Times*, November 5, 1992, B5.

42. Sumi Cho, "Korean Americans vs African Americans: Conflict and Construction," in *Reading Rodney King Reading Urban Uprising*, ed. Robert Gooding-Williams (New York: Routledge, 1993), 197.

43. Davis, *LA Was Just the Beginning*, 7-8.

44. Cho, "Korean Americans," 203.

45. *Los Angeles Times*, November 24, 1991, A39.

46. *Los Angeles Times*, November 5, 1991, A38.

47. Yang Il Kim, "What Have We Done, and What Should We Do in the Future?" *KAGRO Newsletter*, May 1991, 14; cited by Jeon, "The Korean-Black Conflicts," 128-29.

48. Jack Miles, "Black vs. Browns: The Struggle for the Bottom Rung," *Atlantic*, October 1992, 55.

49. Lizbeth Cohen, "Consumption and Civil Rights" (paper presented at the annual meeting of the American Studies Association, Costa Mesa, Calif., November 8, 1992).

50. Steven Classen, "Standing on Unstable Grounds: A Re-examination of the WLBT-TV Case," *Critical Studies in Mass Communication*, 11, no. 1 (1994): 5-6.

51. Martin Luther King, *Stride towards Freedom: The Montgomery Story* (New York: Harper & Row, 1958), 47.

52. Gerda Lerner, *Black Women in White America* (New York: Vintage, 1973), cited in bell hooks, *Ain't I a Woman: Black Women and Feminism* (Boston: South End, 1981).

53. Rush Limbaugh, too, brought echoes of the early phase of the civil rights movement into today's Los Angeles by engaging the racial struggle in a restaurant. On the day after Damian Williams was acquitted of the attempted murder of Reginald Denny,

Limbaugh aired a spoof commercial for Denny's restaurants: "If you want to start your day off with a bang, bring your hungry mob to Denny's, Reginald Denny's, that is, for one of our super-duper, head-slam breakfast items, like the all-new Damian Williams omelet. We pick out a few eggs at random, rip them out of their shells, and beat them for you. . . . And if you're concerned about cholesterol, at Reginald Denny's we get rid of all the egg yolks and beat only the whites.

54. *Los Angeles Times*, November 24, 1991, A38.
55. Cohen, "Consumption and Civil Rights."
56. Mike Davis, "Uprising and Repression in LA," in *Reading Rodney King Reading Urban Uprising*, ed. Robert Gooding-Williams (New York: Routledge, 1993), 144.
57. Personal interview with one of the reporters.
58. Excerpted from *LA Weekly*; reprinted in "Riot Chronology," in Institute for Alternative Journalism, ed., *Inside the LA Riots* (New York: Institute for Alternative Journalism, 1992), 36.
59. Cited in Davis, "Uprising and Repression," 144.
60. Reuben Martinez, "Riot Scenes," in *Inside the LA Riots*, ed. Institute for Alternative Journalism (New York: Institute for Alternative Journalism, 1992), 32.
61. Quoted in Staff of the Los Angeles Times, *Understanding the Riots* (Los Angeles: Los Angeles Times, 1992), 68.
62. Ibid., 59.
63. Michael Omi and Howard Winant, "The LA Race Riot and US Politics," in *Reading Rodney King Reading Urban Uprising*, ed. Robert Gooding-Williams (New York: Routledge, 1993), 105-6.
64. Black Liberation Radio, May 2, 1992.
65. Max Anger, "From Gulf War to Class War: We All Hate the Cops," *Anarchy: A Journal of Desire Armed* 34 (1992): 44. I thank David Noon, University of Minnesota, for this reference.
66. Alan Keyes, "Restoring Community," *National Review*, June 8, 1992, 38.
67. Howie Pinderhughes, in personal correspondence.
68. Heather Mackey, "I Told You So," in *Inside the LA Riots*, ed. Institute for Alternative Journalism (New York: Institute for Alternative Journalism, 1992), 128.
69. Ice-T, interview on *Fresh Air*, National Public Radio, May 1, 1992.
70. Ibid.
71. Thomas Kochman, *Black and White Styles in Conflict* (Chicago: University of Chicago Press, 1981).
72. Ibid., 48.
73. Ibid., 49.

4. Blackstream Knowledge: Genocide

1. A *New York Times* poll found that 32 percent of African Americans held this belief; *New York Times*, October 29, 1990, B7. Another survey, conducted by the Southern Christian Leadership Conference, a civil rights organization founded by Dr. Martin Luther King, Jr., found that 35 percent believed that AIDS was a form of genocide; cited in Stephen Thomas and Sandra Quinn, "The Tuskegee Syphilis Study, 1932 to 1972: Implications for HIV Education and AIDS Risk Education Programs in the Black Community," *American Journal of Public Health* 81 (November 1991): 1499.
2. Quoted in Studs Terkel, *Race: How Blacks and Whites Think and Feel about the American Obsession* (New York: New Press, 1992), v.
3. These figures come from Andrew Hacker, *Two Nations: Black and White, Separate, Hostile, Unequal* (New York: Charles Scribner's Sons, 1992), chaps. 6-7; and the Population Reference Bureau's report, *African Americans in the 1990s*.

264   **4.** These figures come from John Fiske, *Power Plays Power Works* (London: Verso, 1993), chap. 11.

5. Black Liberation Radio, March 30, 1992.

6. Black Liberation Radio, April 3, 1992.

7. Gary Thatcher, "Genetic Weapon: Is It on the Horizon?" *Christian Science Monitor*, December 15, 1988, B11-12; quoted by Zears Miles, on Black Liberation Radio, March 30, 1992; Jack Felder, March 4, 1992; Bryan Harris, March 11, 1992.

8. Both fragments 6 and 7 are from Black Liberation Radio, March 30, 1992. Jack Felder quotes more fully from the report cited in fragment 7 (Dr. MacArthur was deputy director of the Department of Defense):

> DR. MACARTHUR: There are two things about the biological agent field I would like to mention. One is the possibility of technological surprise. Molecular biology is a field that is advancing very rapidly and eminent biologists believe that within a period of 5 to 10 years it would be possible to produce a synthetic biological agent, an agent that does not naturally exist and for which no natural immunity could have been acquired.
>
> MR. SIKES: Are we doing any work in that field?
>
> DR. MACARTHUR: We are not.
>
> MR. SIKES: Why not? Lack of money or lack of interest?
>
> DR. MACARTHUR: Certainly not lack of interest.
>
> MR. SIKES: Would you provide for our records information on what would be required, what the advantages of such a program would be, the time and cost involved?
>
> DR. MACARTHUR: We will be very happy to.

[The information follows:]

The dramatic progress being made in the field of molecular biology led us to investigate the relevance of this field of science to biological warfare. A small group of experts considered this matter and provided the following observations:

1. All biological agents up to the present time are representatives of naturally occurring disease, and are thus known by scientists throughout the world. They are easily available to qualified scientists for research, either for offensive or defensive purposes.

2. Within the next 5 to 10 years it would probably be possible to make a new infective microorganism which could differ in certain important aspects from any known disease-causing organisms. Most important of these is that it might be refractory to the immunological and therapeutic processes upon which we depend to maintain our relative freedom from infectious disease.

3. A research program to explore the feasibility of this could be completed in approximately 5 years at a total cost of $10 million.

4. It would be very difficult to establish such a program. Molecular biology is a relatively new science. There are not many highly competent scientists in the field, almost all are in university laboratories, and they are generally adequately supported from sources other than the Department of Defense. However, it was considered possible to initiate an adequate program through the National Academy of Sciences-National Research Council (NAS-NRC). The matter was discussed with the NAS-NRC, and tentative plans were made to initiate the program. However, decreasing funds in chemical/biological (CB) research, growing criticism of the CB program, and our

reluctance to involve the NAS-NRC in such a controversial endeavor have led
us to postpone it for the last two years. . . .

It is a highly controversial issue and there are many who believe such
research should not be undertaken lest it lead to yet another method of
massive killings of large populations, On the other hand, without the sure
knowledge that such a weapon is possible, and an understanding of the ways
it could be done, there is little that can be done to devise defensive measures.
Should an enemy develop it, there is little doubt that this is an important area
of potential military technological inferiority in which there is no adequate
research program.

Testimony delivered before a subcommittee of the Committee on Appropriations for
1970, on July 1, 1969; cited in Jack Felder, *AIDS: United States Germ Warfare at Its Best, with
Documents and Proof* (n.p., 1989), unnumbered page (available from Jack Felder, P.O. Box
13-203 Springfield Gardens, New York 11413); and in Alan Cantwell, *Queer Blood: The Secret
AIDS Genocide Plot* (San Francisco: Aries Rising, 1993), 33-34.

9. Black Liberation Radio, March 30, 1992.

10. Black Liberation Radio, April 13, 1992.

11. Ibid.

12. Ibid.

13. Tom Curtis, "The Origin of AIDS," *Rolling Stone*, March 19, 1992, 106. The vaccine
that Curtis was investigating was for polio, not smallpox.

14. Black Liberation Radio, March 11, 1992.

15. K. Bates, "AIDS: Is It Genocide?" *Essence*, September 1990, 77, 116. Thomas and Quinn
list many more examples, ranging from literature distributed by the Nation of Islam to the PBS
show *Tony Brown's Journal*. Thomas and Quinn, "The Tuskegee Syphilis Study," 1498-1505.

16. Black Liberation Radio, March 11 and 18, October 7, 1992.

17. Black Liberation Radio, November 25, 1991.

18. *New York Amsterdam News*, July 28, 1990, 1.

19. Felder, *AIDS*, 42.

20. Alan Cantwell, *AIDS and the Doctors of Death: An Inquiry into the Origin of the AIDS
Epidemic* (San Francisco: Aries Rising, 1988).

21. Felder, *AIDS*, 1.

22. Ibid., 50.

23. Black Liberation Radio, March 18, 1992.

24. Quoted in John Jones, *Bad Blood: The Tuskegee Syphilis Experiment—A Tragedy of Race
and Medicine* (New York: Free Press, 1984), 79; and cited in Thomas and Quinn, "Public
Health," 1501.

25. Black Liberation Radio, April 3, 1992.

26. Black Liberation Radio, March 30, 1992.

27. Black Liberation Radio, April 13, 1992.

28. Black Liberation Radio, March 30, 1992. This memo is also reprinted in Saundra
Sharp, *Black Women for Beginners* (New York: Writers and Readers, 1993), 178.

29. Black Liberation Radio, March 30, 1992.

30. Ibid.

31. *Miami Herald*, July 5, 1987, 1A.

32. Ibid.

33. Frances Cress Welsing, *The Isis Papers* (Chicago: Third World, 1991).

34. Jason deParle, "Talk of Government Being Out to Get Blacks Falls on More
Attentive Ears," *New York Times*, October 29, 1990, B7.

35. *Showbiz Today*, CNN, November 21, 1991; cited in Cantwell, *Queer Blood*, 118.

36. Quoted in the *National Enquirer*, December 24, 1991; cited in Cantwell, *Queer Blood*, 118.

37. Quoted in the *Advocate*, September 10, 1991; cited in Cantwell, *Queer Blood*, 118.

38. *Rolling Stone*, November 12, 1992, unnumbered pages.

39. *LA Weekly*, June 5, 1987; cited in Cantwell, *Queer Blood*, 52.

40. *Christian Science Monitor*, December 15, 1988, p. B.

41. *Time*, November 17, 1986, 64.

42. *New York Times*, May 12, 1992, A22.

43. Editorial, *New York Post*, December 4, 1991; cited in Cantwell, *Queer Blood*, 118-19.

44. Cantwell, *AIDS and the Doctors*; Cantwell, *Queer Blood*.

45. June Goodfield, *Quest for the Killers* (Cambridge, Mass.: Birkhauser Boston, 1985); cited in Cantwell, *Queer Blood*, 128.

46. J. W. Carswell et al., "How Long Has the AIDS Virus Been in Uganda?" *The Lancet* (May 24, 1986); cited in Cantwell, *AIDS and the Doctors*, 123.

47. Curtis, "The Origin of AIDS," 56.

48. Cantwell, *Queer Blood*, 10.

49. Since writing this chapter I have read Patricia Turner's detailed study of rumor in Black America, which confirms that many African Americans do believe that AIDS is an ethnic weapon. In her analysis of the rumor, Turner cites two official refutations, one contained in a 1988 report to Congress by the U.S. Information Agency, and the other in a letter to her from a CIA spokesperson. Both claim that the only source of the rumor is the Soviet propaganda machine, but both stop short of denying the existence of an ethnic weapons research program. Turner considers that the refutations are as significant for what they do not say as for what they do. Patricia Turner, *I Heard It through the Grapevine: Rumor in African-American Culture* (Berkeley: University of California Press, 1993), chap. 5.

5. Technostruggles

1. David Guterson, "Enclosed, Encyclopedic, Endured," *Harper's*, August 1993, 55.

2. Mike Davis, *Junkyard of Dreams*, video for Channel 4, London, undated.

3. *USA Today*, July 23, 1993, 6A.

4. Quoted in *New York Times*, May 4, 1992, A15; cited in Thomas Dunn, "The New Enclosures: Racism in the Normalized Community," in *Reading Rodney King Reading Urban Uprising*, ed. Robert Gooding-Williams (New York: Routledge, 1993), 189.

5. Ibid.

6. Roland Barthes, "The Photographic Paradox," in *Image-Music-Text* (London: Fontana, 1977), 15-32.

7. Christine Guilshan, "A Picture Is Worth a Thousand Lies: Electronic Imaging and the Future of the Admissability of Photographs into Evidence," *Rutgers Computer and Technology Law Journal* 18, no. 1 (1992): 366. I thank Lisa Parks for referring me to this article.

8. *St. Paul Pioneer Press*, December 20, 1992, C1.

9. *The Oprah Winfrey Show*, February 26, 1993.

10. *New York Times*, March 21, 1993, 15A.

11. Dee Dee Halleck, paper in *Leonardo: Journal of the International Society for the Arts, Sciences and Technology* (forthcoming).

12. Ron Sakolsky, "Zoom Black Magic Liberation Radio: The Birth of the Micro-Radio Movement in the USA," in *A Passion for Radio*, ed. Bruce Girard (Montreal: Black Rose, 1992), 106-13.

13. *Radio Free Detroit*.

14. Quoted in Sakolsky "Zoom Black Magic," 111.

15. Ibid., 112.

16. *Black Liberation Radio Newsletter*, Winter 1992, 4.

17. Luis Rodriguez, "Rebel Radio, Rappin' in the 'Hood," *The Nation*, August 12/19, 1992.

18. I have given a fuller account of these attempts in *Power Plays Power Works* (London: Verso, 1993).

19. Rosemary Bray, "Taking Sides against Ourselves," in *Court of Appeal: The Black Community Speaks Out on the Racial and Sexual Politics of Thomas vs Hill,* ed. Black Scholar (New York: Ballantine, 1992), 53-54.

20. Timothy Phelps and Helen Winternitz, *Capitol Games: The Inside Story of Clarence Thomas, Anita Hill and a Supreme Court Nomination* (New York: HarperCollins, 1993), 346.

21. *New York Times,* March 17, 1993, A11.

22. Ibid.

23. Ibid.

24. Anthony Giddens, *The Nation-State and Violence* (Cambridge: Polity, 1987), 303-4.

25. Ibid.

26. Charles Murray, "After LA: Causes, Root Causes and Cures," *National Review,* June 8, 1992, 30.

27. Ibid., 31.

28. Alan Keyes, "Restoring Continuity," *National Review,* June 8, 1992, 38.

29. Mike Davis, *City of Quartz: Excavating the Future in Los Angeles* (London: Verso, 1990).

30. Julie Canaglia, "Security Blanket," *Minneapolis City Pages,* May 19, 1993, 9-15.

31. *New York Times,* May 4, 1992, A15.

32. Davis, *Beyond Blade Runner: Urban Control, the Ecology of Fear* (Westfield, N.J.: Open Magazine Pamphlet Series, 1992), 4.

33. Ibid., 5.

34. Canaglia, "Security Blanket."

35. Eugene Methvin, "How to Hold a Riot," *National Review,* June 8, 1992, 31-35.

36. Charles Murray, "How to Win the War on Drugs," *New Republic,* May 21, 1990, 25.

37. Raymond Rocco, "The Theoretical Construction of the 'Other' in Postmodernist Thought: Latinos in the New Urban Political Economy, *Cultural Studies* 4, no. 3 (1990): 324-25.

38. *The Oprah Winfrey Show,* May 5, 1992.

39. For a further account of this theory, see my *Power Plays Power Works,* ch 1.

40. Jennifer Granholm, "Video Surveillance on Public Streets: The Constitutionality of Invisible Citizen Searches," *University of Detroit Law Review,* 64 (1987): 687-713. I thank Lisa Parks for this reference.

41. Ibid., 708.

42. Canaglia, "Security Blanket."

43. *Forbes,* April 2, 1990, 160. The retinal scanning systems are produced by a company called Eyedentify Inc.

44. *Revolutionary Worker,* December 13, 1992, 14.

45. Ibid., 7, 14.

46. Barbara Ehrenreich, "The Usual Suspects," *Mother Jones,* September/October 1990, 7.

47. *Time* November 11, 1991, 39.

48. Michael Eric Dyson, *Reflecting Black: African American Cultural Criticism* (Minneapolis: University of Minnesota Press, 1993), 191-93.

49. Patricia Williams, *The Alchemy of Race and Rights* (Cambridge: Harvard University Press, 1991), 44-51.

50. Canaglia cites a number of studies that show that people's fear of crime has increased dramatically in the early 1990s, but that it is often unrelated to any increase in crimes reported. This gap between the level of fear and the likelihood of being a victim of crime is greatest in the safest, whitest, suburbs. Canaglia, "Security Blanket."

Selected Bibliography

Alley, Robert and Brown, Irby. *Murphy Brown: The Anatomy of a Sitcom*. New York: Delta, 1990.

Alvarado, Manuel, and Thompson, John (eds.). *The Media Reader*. London: British Film Institute, 1990.

Anger, Max. "From Gulf War to Class War: We All Hate the Cops." *Anarchy: A Journal of Desire Armed* 34 (1992): 44.

Baker, Houston. "Scene . . . not heard." In *Reading Rodney King Reading Urban Uprising*, ed. Robert Gooding-Williams, 38-48. New York: Routledge, 1993.

Barthes, Roland. "The Photographic Paradox." In *Image-Music-Text*, 15-32. London: Fontana, 1977.

Bell, Derrick. *Faces at the Bottom of the Well: The Permanence of Racism*. New York: Basic Books, 1992.

Black Scholar (ed.). *Court of Appeal: The Black Community Speaks Out on the Racial and Sexual Politics of Thomas vs Hill*. New York: Ballantine, 1992.

Bray, Rosemary. "Taking Sides against Ourselves." In *Court of Appeal: The Black Community Speaks Out on the Racial and Sexual Politics of Thomas vs Hill*, ed. Black Scholar, 47-55. New York: Ballantine, 1992.

Brean, David. "Viewers and Viewing: An Ethnographic Study." Paper presented at the annual meeting of the Popular Culture Association, Toronto, 1990.

Budd, Mike, and Steinman, Clay. "White Racism and the Cosby Show." *JumpCut* 37 (July 1992): 5-14.

Burnham, Margaret. "The Supreme Court Appointment Process and the Politics of Race and Sex." In *Race-ing Justice, En-gendering Power*, ed. Toni Morrison, 290-322. New York: Pantheon, 1992.

Cantwell, Alan. *AIDS and the Doctors of Death: An Inquiry into the Origin of the AIDS Epidemic*. San Francisco: Aries Rising, 1988.

_____. *Queer Blood: The Secret AIDS Genocide Plot*. San Francisco: Aries Rising, 1993.

J. W. Carswell et al. "How Long Has the AIDS Virus Been in Uganda?" *Lancet* (May 24, 1986).

Cho, Sumi. "Korean Americans vs African Americans: Conflict and Construction." In *Reading Rodney King Reading Urban Uprising*, ed. Robert Gooding-Williams, 196-211. New York: Routledge, 1993.

Classen, Steven. "Standing on Unstable Grounds: A Re-examination of the WLBT-TV Case, Consumerism and Legal Standing." *Critical Studies in Mass Communication* 11, no. 1 (1994): 5-6.

Cohen, Lizbeth. "Consumption and Civil Rights." Paper presented at the annual meeting of the American Studies Association, Costa Mesa, Calif., November 8, 1992.

Crenshaw, Kimberle. "Whose Story Is It, Anyway: Feminist and Anti-racist Appropriations of

269

Anita Hill." In *Race-ing Justice, En-gendering Power*, ed. Toni Morrison, 402-40. New York: Pantheon, 1992.

Crenshaw, Kimberle, and Peller, Gary. "Reel Time/Real Justice." In *Reading Rodney King Reading Urban Uprising*, ed. Robert Gooding-Williams, 56-70. New York: Routledge, 1993.

D'Acci, Julie. *Defining Women: Television and the Case of Cagney and Lacey*. Chapel Hill: University of North Carolina Press, 1994.

Davis, Mike. *City of Quartz: Excavating the Future in Los Angeles*. London: Verso, 1990.

_____. *Beyond Blade Runner: Urban Control, the Ecology of Fear*. Westfield, N.J.: Open Magazine Pamphlet Series, 1992.

_____. "Burning All Illusions in LA." In *Inside the LA Riots*, ed. Institute for Alternative Journalism, 96-100. New York: Institute for Alternative Journalism, 1992.

_____. *LA Was Just the Beginning*. Westfield, N.J.: Open Magazine Pamphlet Series, 1992.

_____. "Uprising and Repression in LA." In *Reading Rodney King Reading Urban Uprising*, ed. Robert Gooding-Williams, 142-54. New York: Routledge, 1993.

de Certeau, Michel. *The Practice of Everyday Life*. Berkeley: University of California Press, 1984.

Dell, Chad. "Secondary Circulations." Paper presented at the annual meeting of the Popular Culture Association, Toronto, 1990.

Dower, John. *War without Mercy: Race and Power in the Pacific War*. New York: Pantheon, 1986.

Downing, John. " 'The Cosby Show' and American Racial Discourse." In *Discourse and Discrimination*, ed. Geneva Smitherman-Donaldson and Teun van Dijk, 46-73. Detroit: Wayne State University Press, 1988.

Dunn, Thomas. "The New Enclosures: Racism in the Normalized Community." In *Reading Rodney King Reading Urban Uprising*, ed. Robert Gooding-Williams, 178-95. New York: Routledge, 1993.

Dyson, Michael Eric. *Reflecting Black: African American Cultural Criticism*. Minneapolis: University of Minnesota Press, 1993.

Entman, Robert. "Modern Racism and the Images of Blacks in Local TV News." *Critical Studies in Mass Communication* 7 (1990): 332-45.

Faludi, Susan. *Backlash: The Undeclared War on American Women*. Garden City, N.Y.: Doubleday Anchor, 1991.

Fiske, John. *Power Plays Power Works*. London: Verso, 1993.

Foucault, Michel. *Discipline and Punish: The Birth of the Prison*. New York: Vintage, 1979.

Frankenberg, Ruth. *White Women, Race Matters: The Social Construction of Whiteness*. Minneapolis: University of Minnesota Press, 1993.

Frankenberg, Ruth, and Mani, Lata. "Cross Currents, Cross Talk: Race, 'Postcoloniality' and the Politics of Location." *Cultural Studies*, 7 no. 2 (1993): 292-310.

Fraser, Nancy. "Sex, Lies and the Public Sphere: Some Reflections on the Confirmation of Clarence Thomas." *Cultural Inquiry* 18 (Spring 1992): 595-612.

Giddens, Anthony. *The Nation-State and Violence*. Cambridge: Polity, 1987.

Girard, Bruce (ed.). *A Passion for Radio*. Montreal: Black Rose, 1992.

Glynn, Kevin. " 'I'm Bart Simpson, Who the Hell are You?': Social Identity, Cultural Loser, and Critical Ethnography." Paper presented at the annual meeting of the International Communication Association, Miami, May 1992.

Goodfield, June. *Quest for the Killers*. Cambridge, Mass.: Birkhauser Boston, 1985.

Gooding-Williams, Robert (ed.). *Reading Rodney King Reading Urban Uprising*. New York: Routledge, 1993.

Granholm, Jennifer. "Video Surveillance on Public Streets: The Constitutionality of Invisible Citizen Searches." *University of Detroit Law Review* 64 (1987): 687-713.

Gray, Herman. "Television, Black Americans, and the American Dream." *Critical Studies in Mass Communication* 6 (1989): 376-86.

_____. "The Endless Slide of Difference: Critical Television Studies, Television and the Question of Race." *Critical Studies in Mass Communication*, 10 (1993): 190-197.

Grossberg, Lawrence, Nelson, Cary, and Treichler, Paula (eds.). *Cultural Studies*. New York: Routledge, 1991.

Guilshan, Christine. "A Picture Is Worth a Thousand Lies: Electronic Imaging and the Future of the Admissability of Photographs into Evidence." *Rutgers Computer and Technology Law Journal* 18, no. 1 (1992).

Hacker, Andrew. *Two Nations: Black and White, Separate, Hostile, Unequal*. New York: Charles Scribner's Sons, 1992.

Hall, Stuart. "The Whites of Their Eyes: Racist Ideologies and the Media." In *The Media Reader*, ed. Manuel Alvarado and John Thompson, 8-23. London: British Film Institute, 1990.

Hernton, Calvin. "Breaking Silences." *Black Scholar*, 22, nos. 1-2, (1992): 42-45. (Reprinted in *Court of Appeal: The Black Community Speaks Out on the Racial and Sexual Politics of Thomas vs Hill*, ed. Black Scholar, 86-91. New York: Ballantine, 1992.

Higginbotham, A. Leon, Jr. "An Open Letter to Justice Clarence Thomas from a Federal Judicial Colleague." In *Race-ing Justice, En-gendering Power*, ed. Toni Morrison, 3-28. New York: Pantheon, 1992.

hooks, bell. *Ain't I a Woman: Black Women and Feminism*. Boston: South End, 1981.

_____. *Feminist Theory from Margin to Center*. Boston: South End, 1984.

_____. *Talking Back: Thinking Feminist, Thinking Black*. Boston: South End, 1989.

_____. "Representing Whiteness." In *Cultural Studies*, ed. Lawrence Grossberg, Cary Nelson, and Paula Treichler, 338-46. New York: Routledge, 1991. (Reprinted in hooks, bell, *Black Looks, Race and Representation*, 165-78. Boston: South End, 1992.)

_____. *Black Looks, Race and Representation*. Boston: South End, 1992.

Institute for Alternative Journalism (ed.). *Inside the LA Riots*. New York: Institute for Alternative Journalism, 1992.

Jeffers, Trellie L. "We Have Heard, We Have Seen, Do We Believe? The Clarence Thomas-Anita Hill Hearing." *Black Scholar* 22, no. 1-2 (1992): 54-56. (Reprinted in *Court of Appeal: The Black Community Speaks Out on the Racial and Sexual Politics of Thomas vs Hill*, ed. Black Scholar, 116-19. New York: Ballantine, 1992.)

Jhally, Sut, and Lewis, Justin. *Enlightened Racism: The Bill Cosby Show, Audiences, and the Myth of the American Dream*. Boulder, Colo.: Westview, 1992.

Jones, John. *Bad Blood: The Tuskegee Syphilis Experiment—A Tragedy of Race and Medicine*. New York: Free Press, 1984.

King, Martin Luther. *Stride Towards Freedom: The Montgomery Story*. New York: Harper & Row, 1958.

Kochman, Thomas. *Black and White Styles in Conflict*. Chicago: University of Chicago Press, 1981.

Lawrence, Charles, R., III. "Cringing at Myths of Black Sexuality." *Black Scholar* 22, nos. 1-2 (1992): 65-66. (Reprinted in *Court of Appeal: The Black Community Speaks Out on the Racial and Sexual Politics of Thomas vs Hill*, ed. Black Scholar, 136-38. New York: Ballantine, 1992.)

Lerner, Gerda. *Black Women in White America*. New York: Vintage, 1973.

Lewis, Justin. *The Ideological Octopus: An Exploration of Television and Its Audience*. New York: Routledge, 1991.

Limbaugh, Rush. *The Way Things Ought to Be*. New York: Pocket Books, 1992.

Lipsitz, George. "The Possessive Investment in Whiteness: Racialized Social Democracy in America" (paper presented at the annual meeting of the American Studies Association, Boston, November 1993).

Mackey, Heather. "I Told You So." In *Inside the LA Riots*, ed. Institute for Alternative Journalism. New York: Institute for Alternative Journalism, 1992.

272 Malveaux, Julianne. "No Peace in a Sisterly Space." *Black Scholar* 22 nos. 1-2 (1992): 68-71. (Reprinted in *Court of Appeal: The Black Community Speaks Out on the Racial and Sexual Politics of Thomas vs Hill*, ed. Black Scholar, 143-47. New York: Ballantine, 1992.)

Morrison, Toni. "The Pain of Being Black." *Time*, May 22, 1989, 120.

———. (ed.). *Race-ing Justice, En-gendering Power*. New York: Pantheon, 1992.

———. *Playing in the Dark: Whiteness and the Literary Imagination*. New York: Vintage, 1993.

Oliver, Melvin, Johnson, James, and Farrell, Walter. "Anatomy of a Rebellion: A Political-Economic Analysis." In *Reading Rodney King Reading Urban Uprising*, ed. Robert Gooding-Williams, 117-41. New York: Routledge, 1993.

Omi, Michael, and Winant, Howard. "The LA Race Riot and US Politics." In *Reading Rodney King Reading Urban Uprising*, ed. Robert Gooding-Williams, 97-114. New York: Routledge, 1993.

Painter, Nell Irvin. "Hill, Thomas and the Use of Racial Stereotype." In *Rac-ing Justice, En-gendering Power*, ed. Toni Morrison, 200-214. New York: Pantheon, 1992.

Phelps, Timothy, and Winternitz, Helen. *Capitol Games: The Inside Story of Clarence Thomas, Anita Hill and a Supreme Court Nomination*. New York: HarperCollins, 1993.

Rocco, Raymond. "The Theoretical Construction of the 'Other' in Postmodernist Thought: Latinos in the New Urban Political Economy." *Cultural Studies* 4, no. 3 (1990): 321-30.

Said, Edward. *Orientalism*. New York: Vintage, 1979.

Sakolsky, Ron. "Zoom Black Magic Liberation Radio: The Birth of the Micro-Radio Movement in the USA." In *A Passion for Radio*, ed. Bruce Girard, 106-13. Montreal: Black Rose, 1992.

Sharp, Saundra. *Black Women for Beginners*. New York: Writers and Readers, 1993.

Smith, Barbara. "Ain't Gonna Let Nobody Turn Me Around." *Black Scholar*, 22, nos. 1-2 (1992): 90-93. (Reprinted in *Court of Appeal: The Black Community Speaks Out on the Racial and Sexual Politics of Thomas vs Hill*, ed. Black Scholar, 185-89. New York: Ballantine, 1992.)

Smith, David Lionel. "The Thomas Spectacle: Power, Impotence and Melodrama." *Black Scholar* 22, nos. 1-2 (1992): 93-95. (Reprinted in *Court of Appeal: The Black Community Speaks Out on the Racial and Sexual Politics of Thomas vs Hill*, ed. Black Scholar, 190-93. New York: Ballantine, 1992.)

Smitherman-Donaldson, Geneva, and van Dijk, Teun (eds.). *Discourse and Discrimination*. Detroit: Wayne State University Press, 1988.

Staff of the Los Angeles Times. *Understanding the Riots*. Los Angeles: Los Angeles Times, 1992.

Staples, Robert. "Hand Me the Rope—I Will Hang Myself: Observations on the Clarence Thomas Hearings." *Black Scholar* 22, nos. 1-2 (1992): 95-99. (Reprinted in *Court of Appeal: The Black Community Speaks Out on the Racial and Sexual Politics of Thomas vs Hill*, ed. Black Scholar, 194-200. New York: Ballantine, 1992.)

Terkel, Studs. *Race: How Blacks and Whites Think and Feel about the American Obsession*. New York: New Press, 1992.

Thomas, Stephen, and Quinn, Sandra. "The Tuskegee Syphilis Study, 1932 to 1972: Implications for HIV Education and AIDS Risk Education Programs in the Black Community." *American Journal of Public Health* 81, (November 1991): 1498-1505.

Turner, Patricia. *I Heard It through the Grapevine: Rumor in African-American Culture*. Berkeley: University of California Press, 1993.

Uhrich, Kevin. "Policeville: Why People Who Know West Ventura County Weren't Surprised by the Verdict." In *Inside the LA Riots*, ed. Institute for Alternative Journalism, 57-58. New York: Institute for Alternative Journalism, 1992.

Welsing, Frances Cress. *The Isis Papers*. Chicago: Third World, 1991.

West, Cornel. "Black Leadership and the Pitfalls of Racial Reasoning." In *Race-ing Justice, En-gendering Power*, ed. Toni Morrison, 390-402. (Reprinted in West, Cornell, *Race Matters*, 21-32. Boston: Beacon, 1993.)

———. *Race Matters*. Boston: Beacon, 1993.

White, Mimi. "What's the Difference? *Frank's Place* in television." *Wide Angle* 13, nos. 3-4 (1991): 82-96.

Wilhelm, Sidney. *Who Needs the Negro?* Cambridge, Mass.: Schenkman, 1970.

Williams, Patricia. *The Alchemy of Race and Rights*. Cambridge: Harvard University Press, 1991.

———. "The Rules of the Game." In *Reading Rodney King Reading Urban Uprising*, ed. Robert Gooding-Williams, 51-55. New York: Routledge, 1993.

Williams, Raymond. *Marxism and Literature*. Oxford: Oxford University Press, 1977.

Wright, Sarah E. "The Anti-Black Agenda." *Black Scholar* 22, nos. 1-2 (1992): 109-11. (Reprinted in *Court of Appeal: The Black Community Speaks Out on the Racial and Sexual Politics of Thomas vs Hill*, ed. Black Scholar, 225-28. New York: Ballantine, 1992.)

Index

275

John Fiske gained his B.A. and M.A. at Cambridge University, England. He has taught communication and cultural studies in the United Kingdom, Australia, and the United States, and is currently professor of communication arts at the University of Wisconsin—Madison. He has authored numerous articles and book chapters, as well as several books: *Reading Television* (with John Hartley), *Introduction to Communication Studies*, *Key Concepts in Communication* (with Tim O'Sullivan et al.), *Myths of Oz* (with Graeme Turner and Bob Hodge), *Television Cuture*, *Understanding Popular Culture*, *Reading the Popular*, and *Power Plays Power Works*. He is editor of Routledge's book series Studies in Communication and Culture, and was founding editor of the journal *Cultural Studies*.